D1715131

Poets and Prophets of
the Resistance

Poets and Prophets of the Resistance

Intellectuals and the Origins of El Salvador's Civil War

JOAQUÍN M. CHÁVEZ

OXFORD
UNIVERSITY PRESS

Oxford University Press is a department of the University of Oxford. It furthers
the University's objective of excellence in research, scholarship, and education
by publishing worldwide. Oxford is a registered trade mark of Oxford University
Press in the UK and certain other countries.

Published in the United States of America by Oxford University Press
198 Madison Avenue, New York, NY 10016, United States of America.

© Oxford University Press 2017

All rights reserved. No part of this publication may be reproduced, stored in
a retrieval system, or transmitted, in any form or by any means, without the
prior permission in writing of Oxford University Press, or as expressly permitted
by law, by license, or under terms agreed with the appropriate reproduction
rights organization. Inquiries concerning reproduction outside the scope of the
above should be sent to the Rights Department, Oxford University Press, at the
address above.

You must not circulate this work in any other form
and you must impose this same condition on any acquirer.

Library of Congress Cataloging-in-Publication Data
Names: Chávez, Joaquín Mauricio, author.
Title: Poets and prophets of the Resistance : intellectuals and the origins
of El Salvador's civil war / Joaquín M. Chávez.
Description: New York, NY : Oxford University Press, 2017. | Includes
bibliographical references and index.
Identifiers: LCCN 2016035611 (print) | LCCN 2016055644 (ebook) |
ISBN 9780199315512 (hardcover : acid-free paper) | ISBN 9780199315529 (Updf) |
ISBN 9780190661090 (Epub)
Subjects: LCSH: El Salvador—History—1979–1992. | El Salvador—History—1944–1979. |
Civil war—El Salvador—History—20th century. | Government,
Resistance to—El Salvador—History—20th century. |
Intellectuals—Political activity—El Salvador—History—20th century. |
Peasants—Political activity—El Salvador—History—20th century. | Social
movements—El Salvador—History—20th century. | Education—Political
aspects—El Salvador—History—20th century. | Chalatenango (El Salvador :
Department)—Intellectual life—20th century. | Chalatenango (El Salvador :
Department)—Politics and government—20th century. | BISAC: HISTORY /
Latin America / Central America. | HISTORY / Caribbean & West Indies / General.
Classification: LCC F1488.3 .C45 2017 (print) | LCC F1488.3 (ebook) |
DDC 972.8405/2—dc23
LC record available at https://lccn.loc.gov/2016035611

1 3 5 7 9 8 6 4 2
Printed by Sheridan Books, Inc., United States of America

Chapter 2 originally published as "Catholic Action, the Second Vatican Council,
and the Emergence of the New Left in El Salvador (1950–1975),"
by Joaquín M. Chávez, The Americas, Special Issue: Latin America in the
Global Sixties 70, no. 3 (January 2014): 459–487. Reproduced with
permission of The Americas.

To El Salvador

CONTENTS

ACKNOWLEDGMENTS

During the past decade, many persons and institutions in El Salvador, the United States, Spain, and several other countries have generously contributed to the completion of this book. I am deeply grateful to them all.

This book relies on original interviews with men and women who took part in Salvadoran politics and cultural life in the 1950s, 1960s, and 1970s. The following persons offered insights and information that constitute, along with archival sources, the bases of this book: anonymous informants, Sonia Aguiñada Carranza, Ernesto A. Álvarez, Manlio Argueta, Ester Arteaga, Rafael Benavides, Mario Efraín Callejas, Jesús Cartagena, José Roberto Cea, Héctor Dada, Alberto Enríquez, Eduardo Espinoza, Evaristo, Oscar Fernández, Emiliano Androski Flamenco, Gerardo, Facundo Guardado, Ever Hernández, Miguel Huezo Mixco, Francisco Jovel, Juan-Juan, Carlos López, Paolo Luers, José Romeo Maeda, José Santos Martínez, Héctor Martínez, Ana Sonia Medina, Guadalupe Mejía, Hilda Mejía, Ismael Merlos, Luisfelipe Minhero, Oscar Miranda, Atilio Montalvo, Rafael Moreno, Trinidad de Jesús Nieto, Ignacio Paniagua, Lorena Peña Mendoza, Victoria Ramírez, Julio Reyes, Abraham Rodríguez, Rutilio Sánchez, Salvador Sánchez Cerén, Eduardo Sancho, Domingo Santacruz, Irma Serrano, María Serrano, Manuel Sorto, Luisa Tolentino, Ricardo Urioste, Juan Ramón Vega, Rafael Velásquez, Gumercinda "Chinda" Zamora, and Rubén Zamora. I am thankful to these persons for their vital contributions to this project.

I received a great deal of assistance from directors and archivists at public and private archives and documentation centers in El Salvador and the United States. Verónica Guerrero, the Director of the Centro de Documentación e Información of the Central American University; Margarita Silva Prada, the Director of the Archivo Histórico de la Universidad de El Salvador; Rafael Flores and Rubén Ortiz from the Archivo Histórico de la Arquidiócesis de San Salvador; Carlos Henríquez Consalvi, the Director of the Museo de la Palabra y la Imagen; and archivists and librarians at Archivo del Museo Nacional de

Antropología David J. Guzmán in San Salvador, the National Security Archives at George Washington University, the US National Archives and Records Administration at College Park, Maryland, and Bobst Library of New York University enabled my access to key archival sources that feature prominently in this study. Professor Stephen Wiberley, bibliographer for Social Sciences at Richard J. Daley Library at the University of Illinois at Chicago, offered valuable insights about recent scholarship on the Salvadoran conflict. Ricardo Roque Baldovinos, Carlos Cortez, Florencia Figueroa, Liz Hernández, Miguel Huezo Mixco, Carlos Gregorio López, Israel Martínez, Patricia Morales, Pati Mulato, Jorge Palencia, Alfredo Ramírez, Claudia Rosas, Erica Ruiz, Hari Sharma, Maria Tenorio, Isabel Villalta, Antonio Zúniga, and Toni de Zúñiga also contributed in several ways to the completion of this research.

Greg Grandin, Sinclair Thomson, Marilyn Young, Ada Ferrer, Barbara Weinstein, Aldo Lauria-Santiago, and Jeffrey L. Gould made important contributions to my dissertation, "The Pedagogy of Revolution: Popular Intellectuals and the Origins of the Salvadoran Insurgency, 1960–1980" (New York University, Graduate School of Arts and Science, 2010), which was the basis for this book.

Marilyn Young offered insightful commentaries on several drafts of the manuscript, which allowed me to substantially improve the book's content and readability. Aldo Lauria-Santiago also offered key observations on the manuscript, particularly on chapter 4, "La Masacuata's War." Eric Zolov edited the initial version of chapter 2 published in *The Americas* and offered observations on chapter 4.

At the International Studies Program at Trinity College in Hartford, Connecticut, Vijay Prashad, Dario Euraque, Zayde Antrim, Seth Markle, Gustavo Remedi, Janet L. Bauer, and other colleagues enthusiastically supported my research during my appointment as the Patricia C. and Charles H. McGill III Visiting Assistant Professor in 2011–2012. The courses on global radicalisms and on the history of the Cold War in the Global South I taught at Trinity College informed my analysis of key facets of the Cold War in Central America I discuss in this book.

My colleagues in the Department of History at the University of Illinois at Chicago generously contributed to the completion of this book. Chris Boyer offered insights on the entire manuscript. Jonathan Daly suggested a historiography on Soviet and Cuban foreign policies in Latin America that helped me to rethink the impact of Cold War politics in El Salvador. Robert Johnston offered thoughtful commentaries on the book's introduction. Jennifer Brier, Laura Hostetler, Susan Levine, Mark Liechty, Rama Mantena, Malgorzata Fidelis, Elif Akcetin, Marina Mogilner, Junaid Quadri, Leon Fink, Ralph Keen, Richard S. Levy, Zinon Papakonstantinou, Kevin Schultz, Keely Stauter-Halstead, Kirk A. Hoppe, Jeffrey Sklansky, Javier Villa Flores, and other colleagues offered commentaries and questions on sections of the manuscript I presented at several workshops at the Department of History at UIC. Susan Levine, Linda Vavra, and other colleagues contributed to my research during my one-year tenure as faculty fellow at the Institute for the Humanities at UIC.

Members of the Chicago Area Latin American Seminar and the Midwest Latin America History Conference also discussed earlier drafts of chapter 6. Valeria Coronel organized a panel at the Latin American Studies Association 2015 Congress, in San Juan, Puerto Rico, where I also presented a succinct version of that same chapter. Claudia Rueda organized a panel at the sixty-second annual meeting of the Rocky Mountain Council for Latin American Studies in Tucson, Arizona, in April 2015, where I presented an earlier version of chapter 4.

Susan Ferber, Executive Editor for American and World History, and Alexandra Dauler, Editor for World History, at Oxford University Press offered crucial editorial contributions that enabled me to transform a specialized manuscript into a readable work. Two anonymous reviewers provided insightful feedback on the original manuscript, which inspired me to consider new facets of the history I examine in this book. Julie Mullins, Editorial Assistant at Oxford University Press, prepared the book for production. Maya Bringe, production editor at Newgen, and Susan Ecklund, copyeditor at that same institution, worked in the completion of this book. I am very grateful to all of them.

Pantxika Cazaux, Carlos Henríquez Consalvi, Jesús Delgado, José Aníbal Meza Quezada, S.J., Luisfelipe Minhero, Jacqueline Morales, Roberto Salomón, Manuel Sorto, and Carlos Alberto Velásquez authorized the reproduction of the images included in this book; Jorge Vargas Méndez authorized the reproduction of an excerpt of *Literatura Salvadoreña 1960–2000: Homenaje*; Alfonso Velis Tovar authorized the reproduction of an excerpt of a poem by Alfonso Hernández entitled "Por el ojo de mi ventana vi pasar mi infancia"; Emiliano Androski Flamenco authorized the reproduction of excerpts of his poems "Loco no soy" and "Anastasio amigo"; and Sajid Herrera authorized the reproduction of an excerpt of the article "En la línea de la muerte: Manifestación del 22 de Enero de 1980" by Francisco Andrés Escobar.

An earlier version of chapter 2, "University Apostles," was published in Special Issue: Latin America in the Global Sixties, *The Americas* 70, no. 3 (January 2014): 459–487, under the title "Catholic Action, the Second Vatican Council, and the Emergence of the New Left in El Salvador (1950–1975)." It is reproduced in this book with permission of *The Americas*. An earlier version of chapter 1 was published under the title "Dreaming of Reform: University Intellectuals during the Lemus Regime and the Civic-Military Junta in El Salvador (1960–1961)," in Diálogos, Revista Electrónica Semestral de Historia, Número Especial 2008 Dedicado al IX Congreso Centroamericano de Historia, Universidad de Costa Rica.

The following awards allowed me to complete the writing of this book: a Faculty Fellowship, 2014–2015, at the Institute for the Humanities at UIC; a one-semester sabbatical granted by the Department of History at UIC; and the Patricia C. and Charles H. McGill III Visiting Assistant Professorship, 2011–2012, at the International Studies Program at Trinity College in Hartford, Connecticut. At New York University, I received the following awards that enabled me to complete the dissertation that preceded this book: Henry McCracken Fellowship, 2003–2009; Dean Fellowship, 2003–2009; Torch Fellowship, Graduate School of Arts and Science, 2006–2007; Research Award, Department of History, 2007; and Tinker Field Research Grant, Center for Latin American and Caribbean Studies, 2005.

I am grateful to Salvador Cortez, Ellen DeBremond, Oscar Chacón, Mayra Chacón, Guillermo Chacón, Jacob Fahrer, Christopher Shannon, Roberto Lovato, Natalia Reyes Vales, and Luís Fernández García for the support they offered me during the writing of this book and for their friendship.

During the past decade, Sabela, Nicola, Icía, and Clelia offered crucial intellectual and artistic contributions to this book. I am deeply thankful to them. This book is a way to honor the history that joins our lives to El Salvador.

Poets and Prophets of
the Resistance

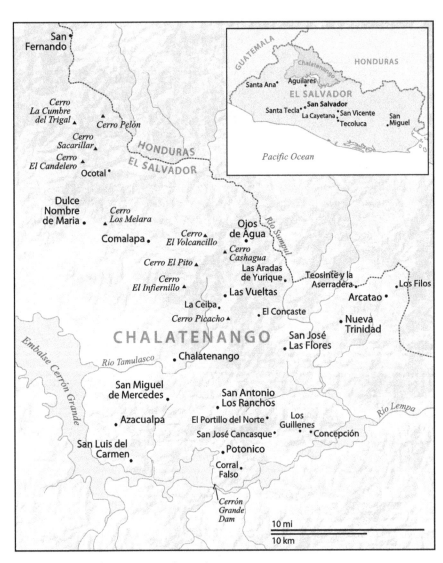

Northeastern Chalatenango. Map by Beehive Mapping.

Introduction

Intellectuals of the Resistance

The French-Argentinian writer Julio Cortázar witnessed a lively conversation between the Salvadoran poet Roque Dalton and the Cuban leader Fidel Castro in Havana circa 1968. Both men casually discussed the uses of an unidentified weapon during a lengthy exchange between Castro and intellectuals associated with the Cuban cultural institution Casa de Las Américas. Cortázar recalled that he felt "an infinite joy" observing the interactions between "the corpulent Fidel and the puny and agile Roque" while the two men exchanged an "invisible machine gun" (i.e., an imaginary weapon) as the dialogue progressed.[1]

This peculiar conversation between Castro and Dalton evokes the intricate roles that intellectuals played in revolutionary politics at the height of the Cold War in Latin America. Countless university students, scholars, journalists, teachers, and writers across the region joined insurgent movements in the aftermath of the Cuban Revolution. Cuba supported radicalized intellectuals like Dalton who formed guerrilla movements in El Salvador, Guatemala, and Nicaragua in the 1970s.[2]

At the time of his encounter with Castro, Dalton wrote extensively about the prospects of the continental revolution announced by Ernesto "Che" Guevara in his "Message to the Tricontinental," a transnational revolutionary forum created in Havana in 1966. In that message Guevara advocated the formation of "two, three, or many Vietnams" to undermine US power in the Americas, Asia, and Africa.[3] According to Dalton, insurgencies in South and Central America clearly responded to Guevara's appeal for the "creation of Latin American Vietnams." In contrast, he deemed most communist parties in the region as obstacles to the "anti-imperialist struggle of the peoples of the continent" due to the conservative, reformist, and "right wing opportunistic" tendencies he attributed to them.[4] Following this logic, Dalton resigned his affiliation with the Communist Party of El Salvador sometime around 1967 and eventually joined the armed resistance against the authoritarian regime in El Salvador.

1

The celebrated Dalton spent roughly a decade in Cuba and other socialist countries, writing about and preparing for revolution in El Salvador. But his participation in the Salvadoran insurgency turned out to be fleeting and tragic. Dalton's problematic integration into the People's Revolutionary Army (ERP) in December 1973 and his assassination on May 10, 1975, at the hands of the militaristic faction that led the organization are testimony to a distinct anti-intellectualism in the Salvadoran left. Militants with middle-class backgrounds accused Dalton of being a "petit bourgeois intellectual" who threatened the organization's security and summarily executed him.[5] Commenting on Dalton's legacy, Miguel Huezo Mixco, a poet who joined the insurgency in the mid-1970s and spent the civil war in Chalatenango, a northern department in El Salvador, caustically observed that Dalton was an exceptional case among his peers insofar as they preached rebellion but never took up arms against the state. "While Dalton was not the archetypical soldier, he went further than all the poets of his generation, who sang to revolution with the invisible machine gun well-stored in their closets," wrote Huezo Mixco.[6]

Posthumously, Dalton became a cultural icon in the Americas. For many, he still remains the quintessential rebel poet, a figure deeply ingrained in the imaginaries of twentieth-century Latin American revolutions. He was indeed an extraordinary individual among members of his literary generation, who joined left parties and movements but never took up arms against the state. His political trajectory parallels that of other post–World War II Central American intellectuals who challenged authoritarian rule through electoral politics and social mobilizations, only to eventually form armed revolutionary movements. In 1960, Dalton joined a protest movement that deposed President José María Lemus, who had ordered a major crackdown against the university community with the purported objective of containing Cuban-sponsored subversion in El Salvador. At that time, Lemus illegally imprisoned him along with other university intellectuals. In 1964, state agents kidnapped Dalton for the second time. After his escape from a clandestine jail in Cojutepeque, near San Salvador, he fled to Cuba.[7] He settled in Havana and became a ubiquitous figure in the city's cultural life. Along with other Latin American and Caribbean writers, he conducted a famous debate in 1969 on the roles that intellectuals played in Latin American revolutions.[8] Dalton has gained a prominent reputation as a major Latin American poet and a precursor of the Salvadoran insurgency. However, he was far from alone; several cohorts of virtually unknown students, peasant leaders, teachers, poets, and workers orchestrated the revolutionary mobilizations that heralded the civil war.

Dalton's tragic experience in the insurgency demonstrates crucial themes that are the focus of this book, particularly the rise of new cohorts of intellectuals who challenged the traditional leadership that communist intellectuals had played in popular politics. Unlike their communist predecessors who had been active in electoral and reformist politics for several decades, these emerging intellectuals rejected reformism and instead created guerrilla organizations and revolutionary social movements to fight the authoritarian regime that had prevailed in the country since 1932. These intellectuals incarnated cultures of resistance that drew on memories of indigenous peasant uprisings and civic mobilizations in El Salvador, revolutionary and anticolonial movements from across the globe, and a variety of intellectual, political, and religious traditions. University students and faculty, Catholic intellectuals, teachers, peasant leaders, and poets were crucial components of this emerging New Left.

This book examines the evolving alliance between urban and peasant intellectuals during the two decades that preceded the civil war in El Salvador (1980–1992). The term "intellectuals" in this context designates individuals— academically trained or not—who articulated the ideology and politics of social and revolutionary movements.[9] In the 1980s, the war between the government of El Salvador and the insurgent Farabundo Martí National Liberation Front (FMLN) became one of the most consequential modern conflicts in Latin America. It claimed the lives of seventy-five thousand civilians and tens of thousands of soldiers and insurgents in a country with a population of five million.[10] Nearly one million people were displaced in El Salvador or became refugees in Central America, Mexico, the United States, and elsewhere.[11] The civil war devastated the country's infrastructure, dominated international headlines, and became the focus of US political, military, and diplomatic efforts for more than a decade. Only in 1992 did a United Nations–brokered negotiation between the government of President Alfredo Cristiani and the FMLN put an end to the conflict, creating the basis for the only sustained democratic period in Salvadoran history.

For all its importance, the history of insurgency and counterinsurgency in El Salvador has received little scholarly attention. *Poets and Prophets of the Resistance* provides a ground-up history of the polarization and mobilization that brought El Salvador to the eve of civil war. Combining social analysis with close attention to political consciousness, it examines the evolution of political and religious mentalities and ideas about historical change among both urban intellectuals and peasant leaders.[12] It studies trans-class political and cultural interactions between city and countryside—particularly secular and religious pedagogy—that drove the revolutionary mobilizations that anticipated the civil war.

The endemic confrontations between the university community and the oligarchic-military regime during the Cold War that prevailed in the 1960s led to the politicization of university students and, to a lesser degree, faculty. Literary groups and other countercultural movements formed in San Salvador, San Vicente, and other provincial cities also became increasingly radicalized.

These groups later played central roles in the formation of the insurgent movement in the 1970s, as chronic repression and widespread ideological and institutional changes within the Catholic Church and at the University of El Salvador
contributed to the radicalization of Catholic intellectuals who first joined the
insurgency.

Peasant leaders, especially in Chalatenango, were particularly influential in
the formation of the insurgency. The alliances between urban activists and peasant leaders were largely formed through popular, institutional, and religious pedagogy, that is, rural cooperative training, literacy programs, and workshops on
Catholic social doctrine. Throughout the decade, the content of this pedagogy
became more radical in response to the structural limitations of Salvadoran politics, political economy, and society, all of which were characterized by authoritarianism, repression, endemic electoral frauds, obsolete agrarian capitalism, and
oligarchic intransigence with regard to the demands of urban and rural workers. In turn, this emerging "pedagogy of revolution" strained and challenged
those structures and politics. The state's coercive reaction to the growing social
mobilizations in the 1970s was accompanied by widely distributed state propaganda that depicted leading intellectuals as the "internal enemy." This propaganda legitimized repression against priests, students, teachers, and peasant
leaders and motivated many of them to support the insurgency, thus becoming
a direct cause of the civil war. Informed by Catholic, Social Christian, Marxist,
Leninist, and Maoist traditions and the insurgent spirit of the sixties, university
students and poets formed urban insurgent groups and rose up against the authoritarian regime in the early 1970s. Peasant intellectuals played central roles in
the transformation of the relatively small urban uprising into the massive rural
insurgencies of 1973 to 1980. The escalation of state terror against peasant communities in Aguilares, Chalatenango, San Vicente, Usulután, Morazán, and other
rural areas further drove this process. Polarization and violent confrontations
between peasants integrated into the state paramilitary structures and those affiliated with the revolutionary movement also grew significantly as the national
political crisis intensified in the late 1970s.

In 1980, military forces conducted scorched-earth campaigns in towns and
hamlets in northeast Chalatenango that resulted in the widespread destruction
of peasant communities. Most members of these communities fled to Honduras,
Belize, Nicaragua, and other regions in El Salvador. Peasants who joined state
paramilitary structures resettled near major army garrisons in Chalatenango. At
that time, peasant intellectuals and urban insurgents created a guerrilla army that
fought a twelve-year revolutionary war against the military and its peasant allies.
The dialectics between the mounting state terror and the urban and rural insurgency in the 1970s turned into a protracted armed conflict between the state and
the FMLN, devastating the country between January 1981 and January 1992.

This book traces the origins of that conflict in Chalatenango, particularly the educational initiatives that predated the creation of the peasant movement and the interactions between peasant leaders and urban militants who formed the insurgency.

Northeast Chalatenango, the regional focus of this book, is a mountainous territory intersected by several rivers that borders Honduras.[13] In the 1970s, this area remained at the fringes of the country's agro-export economy owing to the poor quality of its soils, rugged terrain, and relative isolation from major urban centers. The Lempa, the longest river in El Salvador, traverses Chalatenango and several departments before reaching the Pacific Ocean. Two hydroelectric dams, 5 de Noviembre and El Cerrón Grande, relics of modernization projects in the 1950s and 1970s, form large reservoirs in the Lempa River system. The Sumpul River cuts across northeast Chalatenango, creating a natural border between El Salvador and Honduras.[14] The Tamulasco River flows north to south into El Cerrón Grande reservoir. In the early 1970s, minifundistas (small landholders) and rural workers from Las Vueltas, San Antonio Los Ranchos, El Portillo del Norte, San José Cancasque, Corral Falso, Potonico, Arcatao, and other towns and hamlets in this region created one of the most powerful peasant movements in the recent history of Latin America. These small landholders cultivated sub-sistence crops and endured precarious living conditions as seasonal workers at coffee farms and sugar haciendas in other regions in El Salvador or migrated to the Atlantic coast of Honduras.[15] At the end of that decade, they formed the backbone of the insurgency in the central region of El Salvador.

Peasant leaders in Chalatenango, such as small landholders who founded rural cooperatives, performed autonomous leadership and pedagogical functions among peasant communities in the early 1970s and organized a political movement that seriously undermined oligarchic-military rule. At that time, they joined a regional cooperative training center and served as popular educators in a literacy program sponsored by the Catholic Church called the *escuelas radiofónicas* (radio schools). This program combined daily radio broadcasts of primary school lessons with the formation of local study groups in rural areas. In the mid-1970s, peasant leaders in Chalatenango articulated a counterhegemonic discourse that combined Catholic notions of justice and class-based politics. They also created a potent peasant organization called the Union of Rural Workers (UTC), which played a major role in the period's mobilizations. Eventually some peasant leaders joined revolutionary organizations and became insurgent leaders during the civil war.

Peasant intellectuals were in fact the main catalysts of the peasant mobilizations in Chalatenango, where they set the ideological and organizational foundations for the emergence of the UTC in their roles as teachers of the radio schools, and as cooperative leaders, lay preachers, paramilitaries, political activists, and *rezadores* and *rezadoras* (experts in Catholic prayers and rituals). They organized the massive expansion of the peasant movement into rural areas in Chalatenango with relatively weak state control. This was not the typical case of "unblocking of the peasants' consciousness" promoted by urban intellectuals, for arguably the peasant leaders who founded the UTC in Chalatenango were already "politicized" by the time diocesan priests influenced by liberation theology and urban insurgents arrived in the region in the early 1970s.[16] Instead, the process represented a dialogue between urban and peasant intellectuals that emerged thorough political discussions and the formulation and execution of a common revolutionary strategy. The militant mobilization of peasants occurred gradually, in part as result of their growing hostility toward official repression. Although the urban insurgents played a role in this process, the peasants' decision to fight the state forces emerged from within their own communities and leadership.

The intellectuals in this book used terms such as "politico-military organizations," "revolutionary left," or "popular revolutionary organizations" to designate their movements. They clearly considered themselves an integral part of the "Latin American left," that is, the revolutionary movements that emerged in the region in the aftermath of the Cuban Revolution of 1959 and played major roles in the mobilizations of the 1960s and 1970s, some of which led to the founding of insurgent organizations.[17] University students, Catholic intellectuals, teachers, and poets, as well as communist and Christian Democrat dissidents, became key figures of the New Left. They were a different group from the generation of militants, academics, politicians, and working-class intellectuals associated with the Communist Party of El Salvador (PCS), founded in 1930.

The PCS was a clandestine political organization for most of its history. In 1932, it was nearly exterminated by government forces. In the subsequent four decades, the party actively participated in electoral, university, and trade union politics.[18] Communists embraced electoral politics until 1977 and joined the revolutionary war in 1979, roughly nine years after the insurgencies had initiated hostilities against the state.

The New Left consisted of eclectic movements that blended multiple and often conflicting intellectual and political traditions. This innovative radicalism drew on collective memories of long-standing revolutionary mobilizations in El Salvador. Activists celebrated Anastasio Aquino, an indigenous worker at an indigo plantation who led an uprising against the oligarchic government in 1832; Agustín Farabundo Martí, a communist militant who fought the US Marines in Nicaragua alongside the rebel General Augusto César Sandino in the late 1920s; and other leading figures of the 1932 indigenous peasant uprising in western El Salvador, who were killed en masse by the military in the aftermath of that rebellion. This catastrophic event in early twentieth-century Salvadoran history in particular became a vital component of the imaginaries of the New Left.

The social Catholic thought formulated by the Second Vatican Council (1962–1965) shaped the ethos of some of the most charismatic New Left figures. Founders of these movements thoroughly studied the council's documents to redefine their personal and collective engagements as student activists and revolutionaries. Many of them rejected the legacies of Stalinism (i.e., "the cult of personality" and authoritarianism) present in the old Salvadoran left and were skeptical about the relevance of Soviet socialism in Latin America.[19] The Cuban Revolution, on the other hand, strongly influenced their politics and ideology. Strategically, the Cuban revolutionary experience validated armed struggle as the main path to defeat the oligarchic-military regime in El Salvador. Historically, Castro's revolution made the construction of socialism in Latin America thinkable. New Left intellectuals admired Cuban socialism but were not blind to its challenges. Some of them openly considered the Havana model unsuitable for El Salvador due to the substantial historical, cultural, and geopolitical differences between the two countries. Che Guevara was a source of ethical and intellectual inspiration for most of them, but they rejected his strategy as militaristic and impolitic. Guevara's "foco theory" held that small guerrilla detachments (i.e., guerrilla vanguards) fighting in isolated mountainous areas could ignite revolutionary mobilizations across Latin America. New Left intellectuals were to some extent *guevaristas* but not *foquistas* in that they considered the formation of multiple alliances with social movements a fundamental element of their revolutionary strategies. They also borrowed from insurgent movements in Guatemala and the Southern Cone, Maoism, Vietnamese Marxism, and multiple other sources from across the globe. Social theories developed in the 1960s and 1970s, particularly structuralism as articulated by Louis Althusser and dependency theory, a neo-Marxist interpretation of underdevelopment formulated by Latin American sociologists and economists, informed their readings of Salvadoran society and political economy. They privileged class analyses to explicate oppression in El Salvador but were, in turn, hesitant to use the lenses of cultural, feminist, and race theories. These intellectuals sought to dismantle the authoritarian regime in El Salvador, create a popular revolutionary government, and conduct a transition to socialism. They bore little resemblance to the US or the European New Left proper, though students and intellectuals who identified with "Marxist humanism" played central roles in the articulation of all of these movements.[20] Like New Left activists in the United States and Western Europe, they were quintessential internationalists.[21] They admired Ho Chi Minh, Vo Nguyen Giap, and other Vietnamese revolutionaries, as well as other figures of anticolonial and revolutionary movements in Asia, Africa, and Latin America.[22] New Left activists in the United States and West Germany created small armed groups made up of middle-class and upper-middle-class white youths, which lacked connections with working-class movements and other mainstream sectors of society.[23] In contrast, New Left intellectuals in El Salvador formed enduring alliances with peasant, worker, student, and teacher organizations, constituting an unprecedented revolutionary movement in the country. Transnational processes taking place in this period, such as the expansion of student enrollment at public universities, countercultural movements, advances in mass communications, the musical culture of rock, and foreign travel also had an impact on the emergence of the New Left in El Salvador.[24]

The cryptic tale of the rise of guerrilla movements in El Salvador encompasses the saga of union activists, university and high school students, teachers, scholars, priests, artists, and other intellectuals who created no fewer than five distinct armed left organizations between 1968 and 1974.[25] Radicalized teachers founded a little-known group named the Salvadoran Revolutionary Action (ARS), which had a brief existence in 1968.[26] The poet Eduardo Sancho (aka Fermán Cienfuegos), a cofounder of the literary group La Masacuata, and the Social Christian activists Lil Milagro Ramírez, "Melesia," Julia Rodríguez, Carlos Menjívar, Ricardo Sol, Salvador Montoya, and Alejandro Rivas Mira formed El Grupo in December 1969.[27] Neo-Marxist and Social Christian activists and poets made up El Grupo.[28] Salvador Cayetano Carpio, a union leader and former secretary general of the PCS and other communist dissidents created a guerrilla cell in April 1970, which became the Popular Liberation Forces – FPL–Farabundo Martí in 1972.[29] Former Catholic Action activists and secular university students also played major roles in the foundation of the FPL.[30] The survivors of El Grupo led by Rivas Mira along with university students formerly affiliated with Catholic Action and dissidents of the Communist Youth founded the ERP (the organization Roque Dalton belonged to) in 1972.[31] Fabio Castillo Figueroa, the former rector of the University of El Salvador and the left's presidential candidate in 1967, and university students led by Francisco Jovel founded the Organization of Revolutionary Workers (ORT) in 1973.[32]

Of this first cycle of insurgencies, only the FPL and the ERP became lasting revolutionary forces. The ORT split in 1975, and most of its members founded the Central American Workers' Revolutionary Party (PRTC) in January 1976.[33] After the assassination of Roque Dalton in May 1975, the ERP also split, and a new organization, the National Resistance (RN), emerged that same year. The RN was a merger of survivors of El Grupo such as Ramírez and Sancho, dissidents of the ERP, and to a lesser extent, former members of the ORT.[34]

In sum, by the end of the 1970s, four distinctive armed left movements that self-identified as "politico-military organizations" existed in El Salvador, namely, the FPL, the ERP, the RN, and the PRTC. Each had its own political identity, leadership, theoretical foundation, and revolutionary strategies and tactics. However, they all deemed the PCS "revisionist," that is, a party that had deviated from its original Marxist-Leninist doctrine, advocated reformist and electoral politics, and rejected armed revolutionary struggle. In turn, the PCS considered the politico-military organizations as little more than armed bands led by middle-class adventurers who lacked a solid understanding of Marxism-Leninism or even as agents provocateurs sponsored by the Salvadoran regime or the US government. This virulent schism between the insurgent and the communist intellectuals remained a salient feature of the Salvadoran left throughout the 1970s.

Revolution and counterrevolution in El Salvador encompassed a violent confrontation between forces and ideas seeking a radical transformation of society and politics and those deeply entrenched in old social structures and ideas. This confrontation permeated virtually every sphere of society, politics, and religion. Political parties, universities, rural and urban communities, churches, social movements, and other civil society institutions became increasingly polarized during the 1960s and 1970s Cold War as the conflict between the Salvadoran state and democratic and revolutionary forces intensified.[35]

The emergence of the Salvadoran guerrillas was intertwined with the history of vast social movements led by hundreds of intellectuals, which metamorphosed into potent urban and rural insurgencies largely in response to the country's socioeconomic and political crisis and mounting repression in the 1970s. Elucidations of the origins of the Salvadoran insurgency that unilaterally emphasize the roles that a few urban intellectuals played in this process reinforce the notion that the popular mobilizations were fundamentally elite-led processes.[36] Such an argument, however, profoundly misconstrues the actual historical process. While secular university intellectuals and dissidents of existing political parties were central actors in the emergence of the urban guerrillas, they were far from the exclusive participants in this process.[37] Catholic intellectuals, poets, and teachers were cofounders of these movements. Peasant intellectuals led the transformation of the emerging urban guerrillas in early 1970s into massive rural insurgencies, particularly in San Vicente and Chalatenango. Oral testimonies suggest that a similar process took place in the Morazán region as well.[38]

New Left intellectuals drew on Marxism-Leninism, Catholic social thought, and other traditions to interpret Salvadoran history and society, to articulate the grievances and demands of rural and urban movements, and to formulate revolutionary strategies and programs. However, insurgency as a form of social consciousness and mass phenomenon emerged organically from the radicalization of popular politics provoked by state terror, not from romantic ideas about armed struggle articulated by middle-class intellectuals.[39] The events discussed in this book show that the closing of political spaces, successive electoral frauds, and repression were major factors in the radicalization of social movements and the formation of the insurgencies in the 1970s. Neither the "will" nor a master plan articulated by dissident urban intellectuals satisfactorily accounts for the transformation of vast social movements (especially the peasant movement) into massive urban and rural insurgencies.[40] Peasant leaders became insurgents as they articulated multiple self-defense strategies in response to the intensification of state terror against their communities. University intellectuals played central roles in the foundation of the Salvadoran insurgency, but its rapid mutation into a massive social phenomenon was largely the feat of peasant intellectuals.[41] However, repression was not the sole element that provoked the rapid expansion of the insurgency. Political and religious ideas and countercultural inclinations also played a substantial role in the mobilization of university students and dissidents of political parties. Clearly, the New Left intellectuals advocated class war, popular democratic revolution, and socialism. They were ready to fight, kill, and die for revolution.

The Cuban Revolution had important reverberations in El Salvador, but the Cuban state did not create or control the insurgency.[42] Roque Dalton and a few other Salvadoran revolutionaries in fact received political and military training in Cuba in the early 1970s.[43] However, the radicalization of the vast majority of intellectuals in El Salvador in the 1960s and 1970s had little or nothing to do with the Cuban state's efforts to promote a continental revolution. This political evolution instead involved a process informed by long-standing nationalist and revolutionary currents with origins in the participation of Salvadoran militants in the Sandinista guerrillas who fought the US Marines in Nicaragua between 1927 and 1933, the foundation of the PCS in 1930, the 1932 uprising in western El Salvador, and the civic-military mobilizations against the dictator Maximiliano Hernández Martínez in 1944. The reorganization of worker and student movements during the 1950s Cold War and the participation of Salvadoran activists and intellectuals in the Guatemalan Revolution (1944–1954) were part of this process. The Catholic Church's theological renewal in the 1960s also had important ramifications for the politicization of university students, diocesan priests, and peasant leaders, all of whom eagerly embraced the Church's increasingly progressive social doctrine during that decade. The recurrent electoral frauds and the escalation of state terror in the early 1970s motivated intellectuals to move away from institutional and electoral politics and to either join or support the emerging insurgent groups. The intellectuals who made up the critical mass of the first insurgent movements in El Salvador, namely, dissident communists and Christian Democrats, university students, teachers, poets, and peasant leaders, formulated distinct notions of democracy, social citizenship, and revolution informed by political, intellectual, and religious traditions that preceded and often differed from the ideology and the politics of the relentlessly secular Cuban Revolution.

Intellectuals affiliated with the Salvadoran University Catholic Action (ACUS), a student organization at the University of El Salvador, cofounded the New Left insurgencies.[44] These Catholic intellectuals incarnated the socially committed theology of the Second Vatican Council, breaking with the ritualistic and conservative Catholicism that prevailed in El Salvador during the 1960s.[45] Catholic Action intellectuals were part of a prophetic tradition that emerged in El Salvador at that time. Peasant activists, students, diocesan priests, Jesuits, seminarians, nuns, laypeople, and bishops who frontally challenged the authoritarian regime became prophets and prophetesses of the Salvadoran resistance.

The countercultural sensibilities of the 1960s also informed the emergence of the New Left in El Salvador, as poets, artists, performers, and musicians who embraced social activism or avant-garde aesthetics joined this movement. A cultural boom that involved literary groups, theater companies, and folk bands at the University of El Salvador and other venues in provincial cities matched the rise of the insurgencies. Literary vanguards had a particularly strong resonance in the formation of the New Left. La Masacuata, a literary movement and semiclandestine revolutionary group founded by Alfonso Hernández, Roberto Monterrosa, Eduardo Sancho, Emiliano Androsky Flamenco, Carlos E. Rico Mira, Luis Felipe Minhero, and other poets in San Vicente circa 1967, constituted a critical mass for the foundation of the National Resistance, one of the first insurgent groups in the 1970s.[46] This book therefore examines the porous boundaries between social Catholicism, student movements, literary groups, peasant politics, and insurgencies during the 1960s and 1970s.

The ubiquitous tale of the "fourteen families" that ostensibly ruled the country during most of the twentieth century obscures the intricate character of Salvadoran authoritarianism in the decades that preceded the civil war. Such a narrative serves to mystify the trajectories of economic elites, politicians, bureaucrats, and high-ranking military officers who constituted the Party of National Conciliation (PCN), the new official party founded in 1961.[47] The PCN regime was not merely a repressive and quasi-monolithic bloc that simply echoed US Cold War anti-communism. Like their predecessors in the 1950s, military, technocratic, and economic elites associated with the PCN incarnated a modernizing ethos with deep roots in the country's liberal tradition, which ultraconservative elites and media actively opposed. Drawing on modernization and development theories in vogue in the 1960s, PCN governments conducted a major educational reform that provoked forceful rejection among sectors of the left. Teachers affiliated with the National Association of Salvadoran Educators–June 21 (ANDES), the country's main teacher union, as well as student and peasant movements plainly challenged the initiative.[48] ANDES deemed the values and methods implicit in the educational reform to reflect aspects of a US strategy intended to consolidate dependent capitalism and a fascist-like regime in El Salvador—a transformation that unionized teachers adamantly opposed. In their view, the new pedagogies introduced by the education reform—especially televised education—undermined their own efforts to promote a revolutionary pedagogy among urban and rural communities. ANDES organized national strikes in 1968 and 1971 to resist the education reform. The 1971 state crackdown against the striking teachers and their supporters was a watershed in the radicalization of popular politics during that decade.

Cold War politics exacerbated the growing conflict that set forces advocating democracy and revolution against those attempting to preserve authoritarian rule in El Salvador. The failure of the Alliance for Progress (ALPRO) program to alter oligarchic power and foster democratic rule in the 1960s made revolution thinkable in El Salvador.[49] The PCN governments of Presidents Julio A. Rivera (1962–1967) and Fidel Sánchez Hernández (1967–1972) implemented ALPRO to transform the country's highly polarized socioeconomic structure and to conduct democratic reforms.[50] The country received more ALPRO funds than any of its Central American neighbors. In 1964, the CIA labeled it "one of the hemisphere's most stable, progressive republics."[51] President Rivera's tenure marked the moment when the United States first became a dominant actor in Salvadoran politics by means of the ALPRO program, which above all sought to contain the influence of the Cuban Revolution in Central America. ALPRO promised modernization and a limited political liberalization but came to focus instead on counterinsurgency. More to the point, ALPRO in El Salvador encompassed an economic restructuring that featured industrialization as well as labor and education reforms. Politically, this "soft" US intervention aimed at the creation of an alternative "third way" between Marxist revolution and right-wing dictatorship, which required the legalization of opposition parties like the Christian Democrat Party (PDC) and the introduction of proportional representation in the National Assembly. ALPRO's potentially liberalizing influence was, however, matched by the expansion of the state security apparatus through the formation of the Nationalist Democratic Organization (ORDEN), a vast paramilitary network, and the Salvadoran National Security Agency (ANSESAL), a centralized intelligence agency.[52]

During the 1960s, El Salvador experienced rapid industrialization and high rates of economic growth and became a major actor in the Central American Common Market (CACM) created under the auspices of ALPRO. But the power of the landed oligarchy that had traditionally dominated the Salvadoran economy and politics remained intact at the end of that decade.[53] While the landed elites accumulated massive wealth during the ALPRO epoch, hunger grew in the countryside as oligarchs displaced small landholders and other rural workers to access new lands in their efforts to expand the booming sugar production of the 1960s. By the end of the decade, nearly three hundred thousand

Salvadorans had abandoned the countryside and resettled in Honduras to earn a living.[54] The political liberalization implemented by President Rivera from 1962 onward came to an end during the repressive government of President Arturo A. Molina (1972–1977) as the country sunk into a deep socioeconomic and political crisis after the brief but devastating war with Honduras in July 1969 (i.e., the "Soccer War"), which created nearly one hundred thousand Salvadoran refugees and caused the collapse of the CACM.[55] The most enduring legacy of the ALPRO era was the formation of a counterinsurgent state that comprised ANSESAL, the army, the security forces, ORDEN, and armed illegal groups ("death squads") like La Mano Blanca (the White Hand), which callously repressed the rising social movements and opposition parties throughout the 1960s and 1970s. ALPRO thus ultimately failed to alter the extremely polarized Salvadoran society or to promote democratic reforms.[56] Such a dramatic failure anticipated the upcoming revolutionary upheaval in El Salvador.[57]

Like the Cuban Revolution twenty years earlier, the 1979 Sandinista Revolution that ousted the dictator Anastasio Somoza Debayle in Nicaragua had important reverberations in the Americas. The Nicaraguan Revolution prompted a US military buildup and a revision of Soviet foreign policy in Central America.[58] In El Salvador, it accelerated the ongoing political crisis and elevated the fighting morale of the left. For one thing, members of La Columna Farabundista (the Farabundista Column), as a group of Salvadoran militants who joined the Sandinistas in southern Nicaragua called themselves, were among the first combatants to make their way into Somoza's "bunker," the dictator's notorious Managua garrison that doubled as a torture center.[59]

The foundation of the FMLN in 1980, a crucial moment in the history of El Salvador, took place in this international context.[60] It marked the start of an intricate convergence between the New Left and the PCS, articulating the grievances and demands of vast urban and rural sectors. Between 1979 and 1981, the FMLN consolidated a strategic alliance with Cuba and the Sandinistas as the United States escalated its military buildup in Central America. The Carter administration initially sent mixed signals to the Sandinistas but supported without equivocation the repressive Christian Democrat–military junta formed in El Salvador in March 1980.[61] Starting in January 1981, President Ronald Reagan promoted the further militarization of the Central American conflicts. Reagan's "rollback" policy sought to defeat what he regarded as a Soviet aggression in Central America.[62] In practice, Reagan's policy was an effort to exterminate the FMLN and its social base and to depose the Sandinista government. The FMLN unsurprisingly viewed the civil war in El Salvador as part of a regional conflict given the magnitude of the US military efforts to crush the insurgency.

Throughout the 1980s, the United States provided massive military and economic aid to the Christian Democrat–military junta and subsequent governments, which tried to annihilate the FMLN and its civilian supporters in urban and rural areas of the country. It is well worth pondering the origins and the characteristics of the alliance between Cuba, the Sandinistas, and the FMLN in the context of the Central American conflicts of the 1980s, and quite another to argue that the Salvadoran rebels were simply Soviet-Cuban-Sandinista surrogates lacking any autonomous political and military agency.[63] Such views profoundly misinterpret the origins of the civil war in El Salvador and the history of the insurgent FMLN. They simply overlook the sinuous social, cultural, and political processes that transformed New Left intellectuals in the 1960s and 1970s into leaders of the revolutionary war in El Salvador and major actors of the Central American crisis. They also ignore the pernicious impacts of US counterinsurgency in El Salvador. After all, US administrations in the 1960s and 1970s abetted the authoritarian governments that drove the country into the civil war through a combination of electoral frauds, repression, and political ineptitude, in the name of democracy and anti-communism.

This book suggests that the trajectories of intellectuals and revolutionary movements, even in geographically small countries like El Salvador, can reshape the history of the Cold War in Latin America. This continental conflict involved a massive mobilization of secular and religious intellectuals as leaders of social movements and insurgencies, as well as deliberate efforts by the United States to influence or neutralize them. Intellectuals were key actors in the global conflict insofar as they incarnated socialist ideals or, conversely, capitalist modernity. They promoted such ideologies among large segments of rural and urban populations. In this vein, one can think of the Cold War in Latin America as a conflict that pitted US and regional elites against revolutionary intellectuals: one that involved multiple cultural, ideological, political, and military battlegrounds. It is no coincidence that prior to and during the civil war the forces of repression in El Salvador methodically persecuted university students, scholars, teachers, poets, and peasant leaders, the intellectuals who articulated the ideology and politics of social and revolutionary movements.

Undeniably the conjunction between US anti-communism and counterinsurgency, and authoritarian regimes in Latin America during the Cold War produced a social catastrophe. El Salvador is a prime example, along with Guatemala, Chile, Uruguay, Argentina, Brazil, and Colombia. This catastrophe produced hundreds of thousands of civilian victims across the region and institutionalized surveillance, summary executions, massacres, torture, and disappearances in several countries. It militarized and further polarized societies and politics, and generated a culture of institutional impunity and fear. To date not a single high-ranking military officer or civilian involved in systematic human rights violations committed before and during the conflict in El Salvador has been convicted. US support for government forces that committed those crimes overlooked these violations, even when credible studies indicated the magnitude of the atrocities.[64]

New Left intellectuals rebelled against Cold War terror, militarism, and electoral frauds in El Salvador. Such terror generated thousands of civilian casualties in that country before the initiation of the civil war and became a major but largely unacknowledged cause of that conflict. In the 1950s, public security forces brutally repressed unions, students, and public intellectuals who advocated democratic reforms. Hundreds of activists were tortured, sent into exile, and in some cases murdered by policemen. In the next decade, the counterinsurgent apparatus formed at the time of ALPRO waged a repressive campaign against the rising social movements and opposition parties. During the 1970s crisis that followed the Soccer War, the PCN governments infringed basic democratic procedures and elicited a veritable reign of terror in El Salvador. High-ranking military officers and PCN leaders rigged presidential elections in 1972 and 1977 and imposed Colonel Arturo A. Molina and Colonel Carlos H. Romero, respectively, as de facto presidents. Molina ordered the 1972 military occupation of the University of El Salvador campus in San Salvador. The National Guard conducted mass killings in rural communities in Chinamequita and La Cayetana in 1974 and in Tres Calles in 1975.[65] On July 30, 1975, army and security forces massacred participants in a student demonstration in downtown San Salvador in broad daylight. Many activists in this period considered this episode a declaration of war against the social movements and started calling the state forces "the enemy." Molina's timid agrarian transformation program, which had generated cautious expectations among Jesuit scholars at the Central American University, the PCS, and peasant activists, also came to an end in 1976. Molina and subsequently Romero mobilized the potent counterinsurgent apparatus to crush the rising social movements, the insurgency, and even the legal opposition. In doing so, the government created an internal enemy and led the country into a bloody civil war.

During the repressive government of President Carlos H. Romero (1977–1979), the Carter administration made US military aid contingent on respect for human rights. But in the aftermath of the Sandinista Revolution, the United States continued to support the Salvadoran military, despite its massive human rights violations. The Reagan administration fully restored military aid to the Christian Democrat–military junta that governed the country in the early 1980s. Between 1978 and 1983, US-backed military and public security forces in El Salvador murdered thousands of civilians.[66] In this period, the Salvadoran army conducted notorious massacres, such as El Mozote and El Sumpul, along with numerous lesser-known mass killings. Intellectuals who formed or supported the insurgencies in the 1970s had often advocated democratic reforms through legal, peaceful, and institutional means continuously since the early 1960s. The PCS joined the revolutionary war in 1979, but between 1966 and 1977, it participated directly or indirectly in three presidential elections and six elections of municipal governments and members of the National Assembly. The communists joined the insurgency as a result of the mass killings and electoral fraud conducted by the PCN governments.

This brief chronology of major events that preceded the civil war in El Salvador suggests that we must understand the trajectory and responsibility of the United States and other actors of the Cold War in Latin America in touching off the Salvadoran conflict, alongside narratives that reflect the complexity of the social and political forces, the ideas, and the events involved in this process. The use of labels such as "right- and left-wing extremists" to depict movements with intricate histories—unfortunately still far too common both in popular discourse and in scholarship—fails to do that.

Poets and Prophets of the Resistance utilizes archival sources in El Salvador and the United States, especially public and private archives that have preserved documentation about Catholic Church history, university politics, intellectuals, literary groups, social movements, insurgencies, and repression.[67] The book also relies on original interviews with men and women who took part in Salvadoran politics and cultural life in the 1950s, 1960s, and 1970s.[68] Many of those interviewed for this book resided in San Salvador or in neighboring cities and towns, but Chalatenango was the central locale for several reasons. This region was one of the major sites of peasant activism and rural insurgency in the 1970s. It also formed part of the Archdiocese of San Salvador, which promoted a number of pedagogical and rural development initiatives among peasant communities. Diocesan priests influenced by liberation theology, urban insurgents, and peasant leaders interacted in the context of pedagogical and pastoral activities promoted by the Catholic Church in the area in the early 1970s. These interactions enabled the emergence of the UTC in Chalatenango.[69] The book also draws on interviews with poets and activists who formed La Masacuata, a literary group in the city of San Vicente, who joined or supported the insurgency in the early 1970s. The interviewees were located through civil society organizations, human rights groups, universities, veterans' associations, and social movements.

The practice of oral history in postwar El Salvador poses certain challenges. Informants sometimes showed apprehension about discussing particular events related to the civil war; however, broadly speaking, they were willing to share their memories about the conflict. Most of the interviewees are survivors of state terror and a brutal civil war. They have endured extraordinarily difficult circumstances as former political dissidents, leaders of social movements, students, laypeople, and poets. Many are former political prisoners and survivors of torture. Some survived mass killings perpetrated by military forces. Others were insurgent leaders or combatants during the civil war. Many lost one or several family members who were either murdered or disappeared by state agents. In short, they have ample reasons to be hesitant to share some of their most painful memories. And yet, in telling their stories they exuded a sense of pride and accomplishment about their trying times as former activists and insurgents. Some even produced certificates the FMLN, now the official party in El Salvador, had granted them, which label them as "war heroes."[70] Their willingness to discuss their memories of the conflict and to be cited in this book is significant. If anything, it indicates their eagerness to claim agency of crucial facets of the civil war some fifteen years after the end of the hostilities.

The social violence and crime that characterize postwar El Salvador also create specific challenges to the practice of oral history. Some interviewees live in areas controlled by armed gangs or other criminal groups. I had to rely on the interviewees' advice to safely visit those neighborhoods. At a more substantial level, there is still a great deal of fear and uncertainty among Salvadorans. Politically motivated violence is uncommon in the neoliberal democracy that has taken hold in the country; nevertheless, social violence and crime, and the proliferation of small weapons generate a permanent level of anxiety among Salvadorans. Former activists and insurgents, on the other hand, also deal with the legacies of the civil war, including physical illnesses, war-related injuries, premature aging, family disintegration, poverty, social exclusion, unemployment, and not the least, the traumas generated by decades of state terror. Some of them are still active as public functionaries, politicians, social activists, professionals, and employees. This situation clearly informs the ways in which they remember the events this book recounts.

This book studies the origins of one of the most powerful insurgencies in the recent history of Latin America. It elucidates the trajectories of urban and peasant intellectuals who shaped the movement's ethos. These intellectuals drew on deeply rooted cultures of resistance in El Salvador and multiple international experiences to organize the revolutionary mobilizations that anticipated the civil war. The first chapter, entitled "Dreaming of Reform," analyzes the protest movement that emerged at the University of El Salvador against President José María Lemus at the time of the ousting of Venezuelan dictator Marcos Pérez Jiménez in January 1958 and the Cuban Revolution of January 1959. US State Department officials and diplomats assigned to San Salvador, and representatives of US labor unions played major roles in promoting anti-communist activities and repression against the growing opposition movement to Lemus. A crackdown against the university community ordered by Lemus in September 1960 with the purported objective of containing Cuban-sponsored subversion generated widespread protests in San Salvador. A reconfiguration of the authoritarian regime followed the ousting of Lemus in October 1960. In this context, communist intellectuals organized the United Front of Revolutionary Action

(FUAR), the first armed left movement that emerged in El Salvador after the 1932 insurrection. The chapter examines the early stages of the insurgent and counterinsurgent politics that characterized El Salvador in the subsequent three decades.

The second chapter, "University Apostles," explores the trajectory of the Salvadoran University Catholic Action, a conservative student organization in the 1950s that became the cradle of the New Left insurgency in the late 1960s. It shows that Catholic intellectuals adopted innovative approaches to religion and politics that constituted a rupture with a long-standing Catholic conservative tradition. The historical alliance between the authoritarian regime and the Salvadoran Catholic Church also crumbled at the time of the Second Vatican Council (1962–1965). The chapter also studies the pedagogical activities conducted by Catholic university intellectuals among urban and rural communities during the 1960s.

The third chapter, "Peasant Intellectuals in Chalatenango," examines the emergence of a cohort of peasant leaders in Chalatenango, which led anti-oligarchic mobilizations of the 1970s and early 1980s. Peasant intellectuals were teachers of the *escuelas radiofónicas* and members of rural cooperatives, two pedagogical initiatives sponsored by the Catholic Church among peasant communities in the central region of the country. During the 1970s, they founded the UTC, a peasant movement that posed an unprecedented challenge to the oligarchic-military regime in El Salvador, carrying out multiple land occupations; organizing strikes in large coffee, sugar cane, and cotton plantations; and undertaking political activism in both urban and rural areas. The chapter also studies the division between peasant communities that formed the emerging peasant movement and those that joined right-wing paramilitary forces, as well as the ensuing confrontations between these factions. Particular focus is given to the contribution of peasant leaders to the insurgency's massive expansion during the 1970s.

The fourth chapter, "La Masacuata's War," examines a little-known literary movement created in San Vicente, a provincial city in El Salvador, that later expanded to the capital. This group formed an artistic and political vanguard that blended long-standing cultural traditions in El Salvador and the insurgent spirit of the Global Sixties. The chapter considers the impact of the group's public performances, pedagogical activism, and efforts to create a revolutionary movement. La Masacuata formed multiple links with similar movements in Nicaragua as well as with countercultural groups in San Salvador and other cities in El Salvador. Members of La Masacuata rejected the reformist ethos they attributed to the Communist Party of El Salvador and joined El Grupo, the first insurgent movement formed in 1969.

The fifth chapter, "The Making of the Internal Enemy," studies the dialectics between counterinsurgency, social mobilization, and insurgency that heralded the civil war. It traces the formation of ANDES, the first independent teachers' union that defied authoritarian rule in El Salvador. Repression and psychological warfare against striking teachers in 1968 and 1971 were key events in the radicalization of the teachers' movement and the escalation of clashes between social movements and public security forces in the 1970s. A crackdown against university students carried out by the army and security forces took place in downtown San Salvador on July 30, 1975, an event that enabled the social and ideological articulation of several strata of intellectuals during the foundation of a coalition of social movements called the Popular Revolutionary Bloc (BPR). Public discourses and propaganda formulated by state agencies, official media outlets, business associations, and right-wing paramilitary groups (i.e., "death squads") portrayed teachers and peasant leaders as the "internal enemy" in an effort to justify the repression. The chapter also examines the first large-scale army operation against peasant communities in northern San Salvador in May 1977 as a turning point in the initiation of the armed conflict. The escalation of the repression in the 1960s and 1970s, which further polarized society and politics and ultimately led the country to civil war, has been less studied than human rights violations committed by government forces during the conflict.

The sixth chapter, "Insurgent Intellectuals," traces the origins and the political culture of the urban insurgents who first waged war against the state and the elites in the early 1970s. It analyzes the guerrillas' ideologies and politics, daily lives, intellectual production, political conflicts, ethics and practices of political violence, and pedagogical engagements.

Finally, chapter 7, "Crisis and Rural Insurgency," illustrates the fundamental roles that peasant leaders played in the transformation of the relatively small urban insurgency in the early 1970s into a massive rural insurgency by the end of the decade. The chapter also examines the political crisis that fueled the intensification of state terror, militant activism, and insurgency that led to the civil war.

Roque Dalton's poetics often alluded to the integration of writers into guerrilla organizations and derided the orthodoxy he attributed to communist intellectuals. For instance, he evoked the transformation of poets affiliated with La Masacuata into clandestine urban combatants in "Historia de una poética" (History of a poetics).[71] In a poem entitled "Qué le dijo el movimiento comunista internacional a Gramsci" (What the international communist movement told Gramsci), Dalton sardonically echoed the lyrics of a popular romantic song that asserted: "I am not old enough . . . to love you."[72] Dalton inferred that the social theory formulated by the Italian thinker Antonio Gramsci, which emphasized the centrality of intellectuals and cultural institutions in the functioning of state hegemony, was still anathema for communist leaders in the 1960s.[73]

Dalton's works illustrate the ways in which debates between Old and New Left intellectuals reverberated among Latin American writers in the 1960s and the early 1970s. At that time Dalton found himself at a political and intellectual crossroads insofar as he rejected the PCS's critique of guerrilla movements in Latin America. He became a dissident communist who embraced *guevarismo* and the countercultural sensibilities of the Salvadoran New Left. His poetry and social analyses echoed major cultural, political, and ideological transformations in the 1960s. Those transformations included the reverberations of the Cuban Revolution in Latin America; the rise of guerrilla movements in Guatemala, Venezuela, and the Southern Cone; the student mobilizations in Mexico, France, and the United States; the Vietnam War; and the growing participation of Catholics in revolutionary politics in El Salvador. Dalton's poetics mirrored long-standing cultures of resistance against oligarchic-military rule that crucially shaped the New Left's revolutionary ideals. He joined the first generation of urban intellectuals who relinquished institutional politics and declared war on the state and the elites in the early 1970s. The alliances formed between these urban intellectuals and peasant leaders from Chalatenango and other regions constituted the backbone of the insurgency during that decade and the civil war.

1

Dreaming of Reform

In 1962, Salvador Cayetano Carpio—a well-known Salvadoran communist leader—returned to El Salvador after a visit to the Soviet Union. Upon his return to the country, he faulted university intellectuals who led the party at that time for embarking on "a militaristic deviation." The organization these intellectuals had formed, the United Front of Revolutionary Action (FUAR), constituted the left's first attempt to carry out armed struggle in El Salvador since the disastrous 1932 uprising in the western region, which resulted in the massacre (*la matanza*) of thousands of indigenous peasants whom state forces labeled "communists." The creation of FUAR in 1961 was the left's response to the mounting state repression during the regime of President José María Lemus (1956–1960) and the ousting of the short-lived reformist Civic-Military Junta that replaced him. Carpio spent the next year working to dismantle FUAR, finally succeeding in 1963. In doing so, he echoed the Soviet foreign policy of "peaceful coexistence" with the United States, which firmly opposed the formation of armed revolutionary movements in Latin America in the 1960s.[1] Despite its fleeting existence, FUAR anticipated the emergence of guerrilla organizations in El Salvador at the end of that decade.

Lemus, a protégé of President Oscar Osorio (1950–1956), rose to power in 1956. Often remembered as an authoritarian ruler, Lemus at the outset of his presidency allowed the return of exiles and abolished the Law in Defense of Democratic and Constitutional Order, which sanctioned Osorio's anti-communist crackdown against trade union leaders, students, and public intellectuals in 1952.[2] Lemus governed El Salvador during a period of declining prosperity as coffee prices plunged in the international markets, forcing an economic restructuring that had particularly negative consequences for the poor. More important, the changing political landscape in Latin America posed enormous challenges for Lemus. The ousting of Venezuelan dictator Marcos Pérez Jiménez in January 1958 and the Cuban Revolution of January 1959 inspired a new wave of mobilization in El Salvador. The recently formed Revolutionary Party of April and May (PRAM) and National Front of Civic Orientation (FNOC) defied Lemus's authoritarian regime.[3] While the local press closely followed events in Cuba as reported by US press agencies, Lemus and the Revolutionary Party of Democratic Unification (PRUD), the official party, showed a renewed determination to prevent the spread of "Cuban-inspired subversion" in El Salvador. To this end, Sidney Mazzini, a representative of the PRUD at the National Assembly, envisioned the formation of what he termed *"un cordón sanitario"* (sanitary cordon) around Cuba.[4]

Although the ousting of the democratically elected Guatemalan president Jacobo Arbenz by the CIA has been considered a key event in the radicalization of Latin American Cold War politics, in El Salvador the Cuban Revolution marked a more important turning point.[5] Social democrats like the economist Jorge Sol Castellanos were eager to join Lemus's cabinet, which comprised several well-known technocrats, despite the fact that Lemus was considered a key US ally in the region.[6] Scholars at the University of El Salvador also maintained amicable communications with Lemus at that time.[7] The mild reaction of Salvadoran intellectuals vis-à-vis the coup against Arbenz can be attributed to the apparent neutrality of President Osorio in this affair and the political opening that prevailed in El Salvador before the Cuban Revolution.[8]

Since 1959, Lemus sought to contain the real and imaginary impacts of the Cuban Revolution in El Salvador. Backed by the US ambassador in El Salvador Thorsten Kalijarvi, Lemus repressed students and faculty at the University of El Salvador, which both men considered part of a Cuban-sponsored conspiracy to overthrow his regime. The reformist Civic-Military Junta deposed Lemus in October 1960. It conducted an unsuccessful plan to modernize the electoral system and demilitarize public security. US diplomats in San Salvador labeled university intellectuals who joined the Junta "communists" and opposed on those grounds granting diplomatic recognition to the new government. In spite of these views, the Eisenhower administration recognized the Junta in December, but in January 1961 a bloody coup encouraged by the US Military Group (MILGROUP) in El Salvador ousted the new government because it refused to break diplomatic relations with Cuba. These episodes of the early 1960s Cold War centrally informed the radicalization of university students and faculty who formed insurgent movements at the end of the decade. They marked the beginnings of the insurgent and counterinsurgent politics that characterized El Salvador in the subsequent three decades.[9]

This chapter examines the impact of US anti-communism in the politicization of university students and faculty in the early 1960s.[10] The radicalization of university intellectuals was largely a consequence of their failed attempts to challenge authoritarian rule through mass mobilization, electoral politics, and reforms. The unprecedented role that the United States played in El Salvador after the Cuban Revolution bolstered revolutionary nationalism among university intellectuals. A group of communist intellectuals in particular denounced a purported US plan to transform El Salvador into a "second Puerto Rico" or a "new colony of the United States" and created FUAR in 1961 to oppose this policy. According to FUAR's leaders, US government agencies took direct control of the Salvadoran state after the CIA orchestrated the January 1961 coup against the Civic-Military Junta, which had ousted President Lemus three months earlier.[11] These events left a deep imprint on the political culture of subsequent generations of university intellectuals, who saw the United States as a decisive internal actor in Salvadoran politics and intermittently debated the formation of armed revolutionary organizations.

"To Combat Communism in El Salvador"

After the Arbenz experience in Guatemala, US pundits and elites revived the specter of communist expansion in Central America and the Caribbean.[12] At that time, the Eisenhower administration showed a rising concern over Lemus's inability to fight "communism" in El Salvador, and it pressured the Salvadoran president to curtail the opposition movement against his government, particularly at the University of El Salvador.

In the late 1950s, El Salvador seemed to be a relatively stable nation amid the increasingly volatile situation in Central America and the Caribbean. In this context, the Lemus government became a showcase for US foreign policy in Latin America. In 1958, State Department officials prepared a "full state visit" for Lemus, partly to show that US–Latin American relations were not in such dire straits as Vice President Richard Nixon's rough reception in various South American capitals might have suggested.[13] State Department officials concocted an elaborate state visit for Lemus, which included an address by him to a joint session of Congress, a meeting with President Eisenhower, and private dinners with Nelson Rockefeller and other influential businessmen in New York City. But privately they harbored concerns about Lemus's apparent laxity fighting "communism" in El Salvador.[14] "Communists" had allegedly taken advantage of Lemus's political opening to gain substantial leverage at the University of El Salvador, in trade unions, and among the local press. Lemus "was shocked out of [his] complacency by large communist gains that became apparent at the national labor congress [sponsored by Lemus] in March 1957." At this time, according to a State Department report, "communists" had ostensibly gained control over a provisional committee in charge of drafting the bylaws of a new trade union confederation. Then, in August 1957, "top Communist labor leaders" organized a new labor congress and formed the General Confederation of Salvadoran Workers (CGTS). To counter them, Lemus supported the creation of the General Confederation of Salvadoran Unions (CGS) in May 1958.[15] He followed a similar line at the University of El Salvador, where he supported the formation of anti-communist student organizations at the law school, where "communist" influence was supposedly strong. Despite these efforts, the State Department officials remained doubtful about Lemus's capacity to effectively fight communism.[16]

Analysts at the State Department's Office of Central American and Panamanian Affairs (OCPA) had mixed readings of the strength of the PCS in the late 1950s. On the one hand, they believed that the PCS had been "an ineffectual, clandestine organization" for most of its history that "appear[ed] to lack the capability to seize power by force or to gain political control through democratic processes." On the other hand, they showed concern about the potential of the PCS to influence university and national politics. OCPA officials estimated that PCS membership was four thousand at that time.[17]

Thorsten Kalijarvi, the US ambassador in El Salvador, also expressed his dissatisfaction with Lemus's efforts "to combat communism in El Salvador." In this vein, State Department officials decided it was necessary to raise Lemus's apparent lack of resolve or skill in combating communism as a central issue during his state visit to the United States.[18]

US labor leaders were also directly involved in anti-communist activities during the Lemus regime. Serafino Romualdi, the international representative of the Inter-American Regional Organization of Workers, and Andrew McClellan, the Latin American representative of the International Federation of Food and Drink Workers, met Ambassador Kalijarvi in March 1959 to express their concern about Lemus's apparent lack of will to curtail the activities of the CGTS. The CGTS planned to hold a new congress in San Salvador in April 1960 that leaders of the pro-government union confederation bitterly opposed. CGS leaders thought that the CGTS meeting would not be a real labor congress but "a pro-Castro, anti–United States gathering in which left-wing student, political, and intellectual groups will participate." This event, according to Romualdi and McClellan, was part of a larger trend of "communist penetration" in Central America and the Caribbean. Anti-communist trade unions in the region were "on the verge of panic" with regard to events in Cuba, the growing outside support for communists in the labor movement, and the seemingly defensive attitudes of the Eisenhower administration and the Central American governments toward Fidel Castro. Communists, they warned, were "reacting with new boldness and confidence" inspired by Castro's defiant behavior toward the United States, and they expected to topple current governments and establish "Castro-type" regimes in the area. As an extension of this analysis, Romualdi and McClellan told Kalijarvi that the growing opposition movement against Lemus was in fact a centerpiece of a Cuban conspiracy to expand communism in Central America.[19]

Lemus's Crackdown on the University

Lemus's political opening allowed the formation or reorganization of social movements and political parties, which sought democratization through civic and electoral participation. The opposition movement against Lemus, chiefly made up of PRAM and FNOC, comprised a wide array of social and political forces. According to Héctor Dada—a founder of the Christian Democrat Party of El Salvador—PRAM "was a mixture of social democrats and radicalized liberals supported by the Communist Party."[20] PRAM was formed in 1959 to participate "in the parliamentary elections in 1960" and in the presidential elections set for 1962. It had a strong following at the university and was deeply influenced by the Cuban Revolution.[21] FNOC was a coalition of political parties and social movements, which aimed at orienting "people on civic rights, and by extension and logical consequence, political [rights]."[22]

Lemus considered the growing mobilizations against his government led by PRAM and FNOC as part of a Cuban conspiracy to topple him. In June 1960, he reportedly told C. Allan Stewart, the director of OCPA, and Donald P. Downs, the chargé d'affairs at the US embassy in San Salvador, that he had uncovered a plot against his government supported by Cuba, which was orchestrated by Salvadoran opposition leaders based in Costa Rica. Lemus allegedly announced to Stewart and Downs his intention to crack down on the opposition forces operating at the University of El Salvador. Lemus told them that "he had been patient" and had tried to conduct "a democratic government" and avert repression, but "that the limits have now been reached and that the time for action had arrived." He also informed them about the increasing "communist" influence at the university, in the trade unions, and among journalists.[23] Lemus declared PRAM illegal in July 1960, a decision that sparked widespread mobilization in San Salvador led by FNOC.[24] To counter FNOC demonstrations, Lemus announced a weak social program called the Metalío Plan.[25] The plan encompassed a symbolic land redistribution initiative among rural communities in the Acajutla area, which ostensibly epitomized an "orderly and democratic agrarian program." In August 1960, the Salvadoran government "trucked" some twenty thousand peasants to San Salvador to show support for this plan. Archbishop Luis Chávez y González, the head of the Salvadoran Catholic Church, officiated mass at the rally. The next day students demonstrated in downtown San Salvador. They criticized Lemus's authoritarianism and the Catholic Church's support for the government and hailed the Cuban Revolution. Public security forces cracked down on the pro-testers.[26] In the subsequent days, Lemus jailed and sent to exile members of the university community, including student leaders Schafik Hándal and José "Chepito" Vides.[27] In response, university students organized a new demon-stration on August 19, 1960. Again, the security forces attacked the student activists, who sought refuge at the facilities of the medical school in down-town San Salvador. State agents surrounded the medical school throughout the night as the demonstrators received food and staples from sympathizers. The following day, after Dr. Napoleón Rodríguez Ruiz, the university's rec-tor, held conversations with government officials, the activists left the medical school under the protection of the Red Cross.[28]

Tensions between the university community and Lemus grew, as the president accused the university authorities of plotting against his government to serve for-eign interests and openly threatened the university's autonomy.[29] On September 1, 1960, Lemus published an open letter addressed to Rector Rodríguez Ruiz, accusing the executive government of the university of "creating a climate of na-tional perturbation to serve international goals." Lemus stated that the univer-sity was gradually becoming "a true bastion of subversion and propagation of doctrinas disolventes" (doctrines leading to the dissolution of the state, ostensibly Marxism) due to the work of "audacious minorities." He claimed that he did not fear "any revolution" because his government was essentially revolutionary, but that "it pained him . . . to see the University become a focus of national perturba-tion. . . in a cold-blooded and mechanical agent of subversion . . . an importer of revolutions contrary to our history, our ideals, our aspirations, and our doctrine [i.e., the Cuban Revolution]." In this vein Lemus also lectured Rodríguez Ruiz on the responsibilities of the rectory and on those of the university's executive gov-ernment.[30] Subsequent military regimes invoked similar rationales to Lemus's to justify recurrent attacks against the university community and occupations of the university campuses over the following three decades.

On September 2, Lemus ordered troops to charge against the university in a crackdown that proved to be swift and brutal. Members of the National Police and National Guard entered the campus; beat to death Mauricio Esquivel Salguero, a university student and employee; and seriously injured faculty, stu-dents, and workers (figure 1.1). [31] Rector Rodríguez Ruiz, Dr. Roberto Emilio Cuellar Milla, the secretary general of the University, and other university offi-cials were also beaten and incarcerated.[32] Oscar Fernández recalled how his father, a professor of law at the University of El Salvador, returned home badly wounded after the police beat him during the raid.[33] Judge Ulises Salvador Alas estimated that damages of half a million colones (US$200,000) were inflicted on the university facilities during the raid. Police and National Guardsmen plundered the campus, even smashing a portrait of the Salvadoran literary icon

Figure 1.1 Mauricio Esquivel Salguero, a university student killed by security forces during the September 2, 1960, raid on the university campus in San Salvador ordered by President José María Lemus. The caption reads "Mauricio Esquivel Salguero. Diaphanous and dignified representative of all the martyrs of September 2!" *Opinión Estudiantil*, XV Epoch, September 1, 1961. Courtesy of Special Collections, University of El Salvador Library.

Francisco Gavidia. After the attack, the university closed down its activities and did not reopen until after Lemus's downfall.[34]

In the aftermath of the raid against the university, testimonies describing the multiple acts of brutality committed by the National Police and the National Guard emerged in the press.[35] Students organized a massive funeral for Mauricio Esquivel Salguero, the university student killed in the attack.[36] María Antonieta Rodríguez Arévalo told journalists that her husband, José Aristides Arévalo, an official at the municipal government of San Salvador, suffered "thirty cranial fractures" as a result of the police beatings. She and other women and children were also brutally beaten during the raid.[37]

By far the best-known case of repression was the detention of Roberto Edmundo Canessa, known as "El Cherito Canessa," President Osorio's minister of foreign affairs who ran as an opposition candidate against Lemus in 1956. Adrián Roberto Aldana, a photographer working at La Prensa Gráfica, a conservative newspaper, took a picture of Canessa being escorted by members of the notorious National Police's Directorate of Criminal Investigations that apparently saved Canessa from being disappeared or summarily executed.[38] But Canessa was beaten by members of the National Police and died as a consequence of these injuries within a few months. University students Roque Dalton García, Abel Salazar Rodezno, and José Luis Salcedo Gallegos were initially disappeared by the state security forces. The case of Dalton was particularly sensitive for Lemus, since Dalton was already a well-known poet and member of the PCS who lived in Chile during the Osorio regime. Lemus accused Dalton of promoting armed subversion and jailed him. A picture of Dalton, his wife, Aída Cañas, and four individuals labeled "Dalton's bodyguards" appeared in a one-page advertisement issued by Lemus's public relations office in a local newspaper to dismiss rumors that Dalton was disappeared by security forces. The advertisement also included a photo of Dalton standing near a pile of books allegedly published in the Soviet Union and a photo showing weapons, hand grenades, and dynamite. According to Lemus's public relations office, Dalton was captured, along with his "bodyguards," at Hacienda San Antonio near Rosario de la Paz on October 8, 1960.[39] Although it is unclear if Dalton and the other individuals who appeared in that government advertisement actually engaged in armed resistance, the PCS did form armed groups known as the Revolutionary Action Groups (GAR) in 1959 when Lemus's repression intensified.[40]

The US embassy in San Salvador tried to rally support for Lemus from the press and the Catholic Church during the final days of his regime. Roberto Dutriz, the manager of La Prensa Gráfica, one of the country's most influential newspapers, visited Robert Delaney, the US embassy public affairs officer in San Salvador, to express concern about the fate of his family newspaper after demonstrators attacked the La Prensa building. Demonstrators had pelted the newspaper's facilities with stones during a protest in August 1960. The next day's editorial exhorted Lemus to take strong action against demonstrators. In reference to this incident, Delaney wrote: "He [Dutriz] then launched into a lament admitting first that the paper's editorial policy had caused an economic boycott which had hurt, and second that the change in policy noticed last week had alienated the government. The paper felt alone, without protection, he said." Delaney told Dutriz that "Communists" considered La Prensa Gráfica, the

Catholic Church, and the state "the three institutions . . . they had to discredit and destroy before anarchy and a Communist thrust for final power could be assured. Thus <u>Prensa</u> had to stand firm in support of the State. They could not compromise; it would only bring more misery down on them. They simply had to fight."[41] According to Delaney, Dutriz showed "a sagging morale" and feared further attacks against his newspaper during a student demonstration planned for September 15, 1960. Delaney's advice to Dutriz was straightforward: he should fight back against those Delaney insisted on calling "the communists."[42] Delaney also visited Archbishop Chávez y Gónzalez to probe the Catholic Church's official position on the Lemus government. The archbishop, who mediated between Lemus and the opposition without success, ostensibly told Delaney that the Catholic Church supported Lemus's laws "governing public meetings and the universities" and also Lemus's "4 points" proposal to deal with the crisis. At the same time, Chávez y González also "wondered aloud whether the Communists were this involved in Salvador [sic]." To this Delaney retorted with the standard US bombast on the growing threat of a Cuban communist expansion in Central America. Delaney also wrote about the distancing between Chávez y González and the "rich families" who had traditionally funded the Catholic Church due to the archbishop's increasingly progressive social policy.[43]

While riots spread in San Salvador, US ambassador Kalijarvi offered Lemus advice and US military aid to deal with the unrest.[44] On September 15, Independence Day in El Salvador, the insurrectionary climate rose in the capital as the police shot at a large demonstration, killing Rodolfo Rivas Guardado and other unidentified individuals.[45] The next day, Ambassador Kalijarvi visited Lemus at the Presidential House. Responding to Lemus's sense of political isolation, Kalijarvi lectured him on the high responsibilities of the presidency. Kalijarvi reportedly told him: "Democracy must be defended by resort to force on occasion, and the high principles it seeks to attain can only be preserved by a readiness to defend it." Lemus allegedly responded by placing his hand on the statue of Abraham Lincoln in his office and saying: "Yes, I think of him often at this time. I realize fully that this [the willingness to defend democracy through force] is involved." Lemus and Kalijarvi also exchanged views on the "pattern of street fighting . . . and the evident importation of thugs from abroad and money supplied through Cuban channels," purportedly shown during demonstrations the previous day:[46]

> We agreed that the technique of disturbances and fighting that was followed yesterday was too sophisticated to have been devised in El Salvador. Police had picked up disturbers from Guatemala, Honduras, Nicaragua and Costa Rica. The President said that when a Costa Rican roughneck was interrogated, he spoke about the terrible hatred that

existed in Costa Rica for El Salvador. All kinds of provocation was [*sic*] spread in all directions.[47]

Kalijarvi did not mince words, encouraging Lemus to harden his position regarding the demonstrators. When the US ambassador asked why "the student organization AGEUS [the General Association of Salvadoran University Students] had not been disbanded," Lemus replied that this action would be futile, since there were a number of "illegal organizations such as the PRAM and the CGTS" that were also active. Kalijarvi criticized Lemus for exiling members of the opposition, arguing that this was a useless tactic. "The kind of men who were exiled [deem] . . . being thrown out . . . a mark of honor . . . they consider exile a further badge of honor when they returned home," he said. Instead, he advised Lemus to create legislation to incarcerate "agitators" for "from one to ten years." Lemus replied that Salvadoran law did not allow this kind of punishment and that only military tribunals could impose such a sentence. This last option, both men agreed, would only further the government's authoritarian image. Kalijarvi wrote that Lemus seemed indecisive on how to handle future demonstrations. However, Lemus showed interest in learning "how to handle tear gas and techniques for the use of other means to control mobs." Kalijarvi asserted that he bluntly asked Lemus: "What do you want?" "Do you want arms?" to which Lemus supposedly responded, "Yes I have already asked for arms." When Kalijarvi asked Lemus, "Do you want the U.S. army?" Lemus responded "no."[48]

Meanwhile, envoys of the Central American universities attempted to mediate between Lemus and the University of El Salvador. In October 1960, a delegation of rectors of Central American universities headed by Carlos Tunnermann, the rector of the University of Nicaragua, arrived in San Salvador to act as mediators.[49] Lemus offered to release members of the university community incarcerated during the September crackdown in exchange for a joint communiqué signed by Lemus and the rector announcing the normalization of relations between the government and the university. Rector Rodríguez Ruiz rejected Lemus's proposal, for he believed the government intended to use the agreement as a public relations prop. He told members of the university's executive government that the only document he was willing to sign was a unilateral declaration reiterating the apolitical nature of the University of El Salvador. In the end, the university authorities deemed negotiating with Lemus useless, for he not only failed to liberate political prisoners but also ordered the detention of Dr. Jorge Alberto Barriere, the general prosecutor of the University of El Salvador, on October 16, 1960.[50]

Ten days later, two members of the university's executive government, Dr. René Fortín Magaña, a lawyer, and Dr. Fabio Castillo Figueroa, the vice-dean

of the School of Medicine, joined sectors of the military loyal to former president Osorio in a coup against Lemus. Fortín Magaña and Castillo promised
to support the "economic autonomy" of the university, while the university
authorities congratulated their former colleagues on becoming members of the
newly formed Junta.[51] The university's executive government publicly declared
its support for the Junta, labeling it a "regime of freedom and optimism." Lemus's
despotism, they alleged, threatened to erase El Salvador "from the map of civi-
lized nations." Lemus's justification for the September raid—the elimination of
the communist menace—obscured the nature of the confrontation between the
military regime and the university, namely, the clash between "clumsiness and
ignorance" and "intelligence and culture" or the "open war between the forces
of right and the right of force."[52] In this case the forces of freedom and culture
incarnated in the University of El Salvador had won the day. In this struggle,
students "with their fine political sensibilities and their youthful breath assumed
the vanguard role in the defense of freedom, without other arms than their civic
rights facing machine guns and rifles."[53]

The ousting of Lemus produced popular fervor in San Salvador. Thousands
waited outside the National Penitentiary, where political prisoners, including
Roque Dalton and Abel Salazar Rodezno, were freed. Outside the penitentiary,
an exhausted Dalton told the press: "I did not receive physical torture, only
moral [torments]. . . . was slandered for something I did not commit. . . . I felt
very sick, because they treat us like dogs: the meals we received daily consisted
of two hard tortillas and sour beans."[54] A large crowd also gathered outside the
Presidential House, where members of the Civic-Military Junta gave their first
speeches. Salvadoran exiles living in Guatemala, Mexico, and elsewhere returned
home in the following weeks.

"Three Months of Democracy": The Ephemeral Civic-Military Junta

The Junta's existence constituted one of the three brief openings after the rise
of the military regimes in 1932.[55] The Civic-Military Junta, made up of three
civilians and three military men loyal to former president Osorio, took power
on October 26, 1960. The Junta vowed to set conditions for holding free elections and to restore public freedoms.[56] Dr. Mario Castrillo Zeledón, the new
general prosecutor, also declared his intention to promote the "demilitarization" of the National Police and the prosecution of policemen associated with
Lemus's repression.[57] One of the Junta's first official acts was to release the
National Police's secret files on those accused of "sedition and rebellion" during
the Lemus regime.[58] René Fortín Magaña, a member of the Junta, formulated a

democratization program that encompassed the dismantling of Lemus's repressive apparatus and the full restoration of civic and political rights. His proposal included the right to organize political parties, the creation of an independent electoral council, and the sanctioning of a new electoral law to ensure the transparency of elections scheduled for 1962.[59]

Fabio Castillo and other faculty who joined the Junta viewed education as a top priority of the new government. They deemed the persistence of oligarchic regimes in El Salvador a derivative of two closely related structures, namely, the semifeudal agrarian economy and the precarious educational system that excluded the vast majority of the population. Elites were uninterested in improving the country's educational system because their agrarian economy relied on the existence of a largely illiterate peasantry that constituted a cheap and massive labor force. According to Castillo, generations of university faculty and students before them had attempted to democratize the country's educational system. However, oligarchic elites tenaciously opposed these efforts. Among these attempts, Castillo analyzed one led by his great-grandfather Fabio Castillo. In 1865, Castillo's ancestor and other scholars founded a science and literature department (Facultad de Ciencias y Letras) at the university, which focused on the training of teachers. However President Rafael Zaldívar had suppressed the science and literature department headed by Castillo's predecessor, which Castillo deemed a major impediment to the democratization of the country's educational system. Castillo also discussed the contributions of Reynaldo Galindo Pohl, the president of the National Assembly during the Osorio government, and Carlos Llerena, the rector of the university between 1948 and 1950, to the democratization and modernization of university education.[60] He and Marina Rodríguez de Quezada, who headed the Ministry of Education at the time of the Civic-Military Junta, outlined an ambitious education program that echoed long-standing efforts to democratize education in El Salvador. The Junta declared 1961 and 1962 the Biennial of National Education.[61]

Social movements and opposition parties welcomed the Junta's political liberalization (figure 1.2). FNOC expectations of the new government were high. It publicly stated "its satisfaction for the ousting of the Prudist [PRUD] tyranny of José María Lemus" and considered the coup "a step toward the restoration of public freedoms . . . and the full restoration of the Constitutional order."[62]

Leaders of PRAM expressed enthusiastic support for the Junta but also warned the new government about the perils of the destabilizing activities of the "reaction."[63] Catholic intellectuals took advantage of the opening created by the Junta to form the Christian Democrat Party (PDC) in November 1960. Former and active members of Salvadoran University Catholic Action (ACUS), a conservative student organization led by Abraham Rodríguez, joined Roberto

Figure 1.2 University students celebrated the "burial" of the PRUD regime in 1961. In 1965, an editorialist of *Opinión Estudiantil* blasted the nefarious legacies of the PRUD governments, including the September 2, 1960, attack against the university community ordered by President Lemus. *Opinión Estudiantil*, XIX Epoch, no. 3, October, 1965, front page. Courtesy of Special Collections, University of El Salvador Library.

Lara Velado and other Catholic intellectuals to create the PDC, which became a major player in Salvadoran politics in the following three decades. Emerging from a series of conversations on Catholic social doctrine they held at the San José de La Montaña Seminary, the PDC sought to articulate a noncommunist reformist alternative to military rule. Rodríguez recalled that the founders envisioned the formation of a permanent and autonomous opposition party. Although legal opposition parties such as the Party of Renovating Action (PAR) existed in 1960, they were active only during elections and virtually ineffectual at challenging the official party. Founders of the PDC, according to Rodríguez, were eager to change this historical pattern, creating a thoughtful political alternative that drew on Catholic social doctrine and the pastoral letters of Archbishop Chávez y González to sustain a continuous activism among vast segments of Salvadoran society.[64] According to Héctor Dada, who was then a member of ACUS, the PDC generated substantial apprehension among existing political actors:

> The PDC was born on November 24, 1960, . . . at that time the PCS accused us of being CIA agents. [Conversely] the CIA feared political instability and the idea of withdrawing the army from politics and of not having an official party. . . . [The fact that the PDC] adopted the

pastoral letters of Monsignor Chávez [the archbishop of San Salvador] as [its] ideological base generated mistrust within the Church itself because Monsignor Chávez rejected a partisan commitment.[65]

State Department officials debated whether to grant diplomatic recognition to the Junta. Ambassador Kalijarvi firmly opposed this. The Junta, he contended, was formed by such "disparate" elements that it was doubtful that the new government could achieve stability and coherence. Moreover, there were persistent rumors about ongoing "conspiracies" and preparations for a countercoup. "Pro-communist or communist" elements such as "the Ministers of Justice and Labor" allegedly dominated the Junta.[66] The Junta allowed the broadcasting of "anti-American" messages on the radio and TV. The ambassador worried that US recognition would grant legitimacy to the Junta and encourage other groups in Central America to engage in similar actions against military regimes friendly to the United States. Finally, former president Osorio, the strongman behind the coup, who was considered friendly to the US government, could not control leftist members of the Junta.[67]

In contrast to Kalijarvi, Assistant Secretary of State Thomas C. Mann thought that the US government had better prospects of influencing political events in El Salvador by granting recognition to the Junta. According to Mann, liberals or leftists "who advocated change in the still largely semi-feudal social order in El Salvador" were often deemed communists. Mann wrote that the terms "leftist" and "communist" were often considered synonyms in El Salvador, positing that "it would be a grave mistake" to consider that the Junta was dominated by "pro-Communist individuals" without having "substantiating evidence." Mann alleged that the best deterrents for "pro-Castro or pro-Communist elements" in the Junta were the Osorista military (followers of former president Osorio), who were undoubtedly "pro-American." Moreover, Mann believed Osorio's claims to be able to control any "extreme Leftists" and "to bring unity to the coalition" behind the Junta. According to Mann, the Junta notified the US government and the Organization of American States (OAS) of its decision to honor international treaties and conventions, comply with the 1950 Constitution (approved under Osorio), "fulfill its obligations and commitments," and respect human rights. The Junta also told the US government that it represented a "strictly national and authentically democratic [movement], consistent with the basic principles of Western democracy, without any ties, whatsoever, with foreign powers or ideologies." Despite the growing rumors of a countercoup, Mann doubted that the US government's refusal to grant recognition to the Junta would ensure a successful right-wing coup. On the contrary, because Osorio enjoyed widespread support among the military, any such action could create a serious division among the military, weakening the strongest anti-communist institution in the country. In sum, Mann advised the secretary of state that granting diplomatic recognition would be the best means to deter communist influence in the new government.[68]

The participation of university intellectuals in the Junta was a serious concern for State Department officials. The matter of the political affiliation of Fabio Castillo, in particular, became the subject of State Department internal communications, as individuals acquainted with Castillo expressed solicited and unsolicited views about him. State Department preoccupations about Castillo's alleged anti-US activism at the School of Medicine were not new. Dr. José Kuri, the school's head, visited Ambassador Kalijarvi on September 29, 1959, to assure him that it did not engage in activities contrary to US interests. Kuri told Kalijarvi that Castillo was the leading advocate in adopting "U.S. teaching methods and technical procedures" at the School of Medicine and that Castillo also tried to persuade his colleagues that "the U.S. [educational] system was superior." Reflecting on the meeting, Kalijarvi wrote: "As Dr. Castillo's name had not been mentioned, Kuri's spirited defense of him was, in a way, an admission on his part that Castillo needs defending, that there are valid grounds for believing that he is the source of much of the present difficulties and that this is weighing on Dr. Kuri's conscience."[69]

US professionals who at one time resided in El Salvador also shared with the State Department their opinions about Castillo and other university intellectuals who joined the Junta. Blair Birdsall, an American engineer who supervised the construction of bridges in El Salvador in 1950, sent a memo to the State Department expressing unflattering views of Lemus and praising the clean liberal credentials of Castillo, Fortín Magaña, and other members of the Junta's cabinet, whom he knew either personally or by reference. Birdsall wrote about Castillo:

> He is a quiet unassuming professional man. He is extremely conscientious and all of his zeal has been brought to bear on a desire to improve the quality of medical education in El Salvador. In a few years, he accomplished a great deal in this direction. To the best of my knowledge, it was his capability, his singleness of purpose and his integrity which persuaded some of the large educational foundations here (I believe Guggenheim and Kellogg, but am not sure) to donate funds for a great deal of a new laboratory equipment. I believe it was this same equipment which was subjected to the greatest damage during the recent riots [probably the charge against the university ordered by Lemus in September 1960]. I had no direct word during the period, but can well imagine that this quiet young doctor became so desperate when he saw his life's work crumble around him, that he decided to risk his life in an attempt to do something about it.[70]

Birdsall categorized the Lemus regime as a typical Latin American dictatorship, "giving lip-service only to democracy supported by the ruling families
who have an interest in maintaining the feudal character of society." In his esti-
mation of the country's political climate he wrote: "The cancer that is Fidel
Castro has infected and inflamed the minds of much of the youth of Latin
America, manifested recently in El Salvador by student riots which resulted in
at least temporary closure of the National University and the establishment of
a form of martial law." Ultimately the "drastic measures" taken by the Lemus
government to counter the unrest created the conditions for the bloodless
coup in which Castillo, Fortín Magaña, and others were involved.[71] Dr. Jacob
Sacks of the University of Arkansas, a consultant with the OAS who worked
at the University of El Salvador between April and September 1960, also dismissed previous allegations made by one Dr. Barnett that the Medical School
was something of a communist haven. Instead, Sacks depicted Castillo as "an
intensely devoted patriot, but not chauvinistic," and unsympathetic to Fidel
Castro. "If Castillo was sometimes difficult to deal with, it is out of his intense
idealism rather than stubbornness," Sacks told State Department officials.
According to Sacks, Castillo had "no sympathy for [Fidel] Castro" and was
"a dedicated anti-communist . . . [who] look[ed] for Castro's political demise
within a year because of the anti-democratic actions he [had] taken since
assuming power."[72]

US embassy officials in San Salvador had tried to undermine the Junta
since its inception in October 1960. According to Fabio Castillo, the chargé
d'affaires Donald P. Downs, who substituted for Kalijarvi as the official US representative in El Salvador after the ambassador left the country that month,
challenged the Junta's democratization program during a private meeting
with him. Ricardo Quiñonez, a wealthy Salvadoran businessman who had
known Castillo since childhood, asked him to meet Downs in a "confidential
and unofficial place," since the US government did not recognize the Junta.
Downs, Castillo wrote, showed great concern about the Junta's decision to
allow the formation of independent political parties and organize free elections. He told Castillo that this course of action was "very dangerous for the
country and for Central America." In turn Castillo asked, "Is the United States
a democratic nation?" to which Downs replied, "Yes." Castillo further asked
if the US government "considered it appropriate and not dangerous holding
free elections in the United States," to which Downs responded, "Obviously
yes, but it is different, in the United States there are elections between two
candidates previously selected by the establishment and people freely elect
between two very similar apples." In this vein, Downs told Castillo that the
US government supported free elections in El Salvador "between two candidates previously selected by a common agreement between the US embassy

and the Salvadoran government." Castillo asserted that Downs told him that he "could be the chosen person," that is, one of the presidential candidates. Castillo replied that this suggestion was "contrary to the moral and ethical principles that sustained the Junta and its project of democratization" and flatly rejected it on behalf of the Junta. Moreover, Castillo called Downs's proposal "an act of corruption," which damaged any prospect of democratization in El Salvador.[73] Castillo also reported that Downs firmly opposed the Junta's education program. During a diplomatic reception held by the Junta on December 12, 1960, Downs asked Castillo if the Junta was serious about its recent statement on the "accelerated plan for the development of education." When Castillo replied that it was "a great necessity of the people," Downs retorted, "Don't you know that educated people demand bread?" Castillo in turn replied that "people had the right to education and to require human living conditions." Downs remarked in English, "You are crazy," tapped in a "military style, turned around, and left the reception." Castillo insisted throughout the years that after this conversation, Downs openly conspired to topple the Junta.[74] During the 1970s and 1980s Castillo wrote several testimonies retelling similar versions of these encounters, which suggests that these exchanges likely influenced Castillo's radicalization in crucial ways. After all, he witnessed firsthand brazen US support for illiberal forces in El Salvador and the fragility of the democratization project sponsored by the Civic-Military Junta. In the 1960s, he became increasingly active in left-wing politics. He was the presidential candidate of the PAR, a left-of-center coalition formed during the 1967 elections. As the state terror intensified in the 1970s, he became one of the initiators of the Central American Workers' Revolutionary Party (PRTC), a founding organization of the FMLN.

The US government ultimately decided to delay granting diplomatic recognition to the Junta based on the assumption that Osorio was unable to control the leftists in the Junta who harbored sympathy toward the Cuban Revolution. Evidence of the leadership's alleged pro-Castro leanings included a radio talk show that broadcast anti-US programming, the presence of a journalist from Prensa Latina (the Cuban press agency) in San Salvador, and the Junta's purported intention to create a popular militia.[75] On November 11, Kalijarvi, who was in Washington, DC, for consultations, argued that Osorio had lost control of the movement behind the October coup and advised the secretary of state to further delay recognition of the Junta.[76] The ambassador's views on this matter were largely based on a letter he received from Downs. In it, Downs argued that the anti-American inclinations of the Junta became apparent in the recent public criticisms of the US government and the US embassy in San Salvador articulated by some Junta leaders. Downs concluded that Osorio had been "double-crossed" and that consequently it would be "a very grave error to put our money on Mr. Osorio."[77] Later that month, Secretary of Defense Thomas S. Gates stated that the secretary of state should decide whether to recognize the Junta, since it was a matter that involved mainly "political judgment." Gates also recommended that various US government agencies consider "what feasibility actions can be taken to insure against a [communist] takeover" in El Salvador.[78] In the end, official recognition was granted in early December 1960, following that of several European and Latin American countries. Cuba also granted recognition at that time.[79]

On December 15, the Junta received the first news that members of the US MILGROUP in El Salvador were inciting their Salvadoran counterparts to topple the government. The US military warned Salvadoran military officers that "they won't see another Christmas" if they refused to oust the Junta. On December 18, Castillo asked the Junta to expel the US MILGROUP in El Salvador. Defense minister Colonel Alfonso Castillo Navarrete told the Junta that this expulsion was a necessary but impracticable decision. Castillo deemed that the Junta's incapacity to take this step "sealed [its] fate."[80]

The Junta tried to disband the remnants of the Lemus regime. It dismissed the municipal councils and mayors associated with Lemus, claiming that they were elected through fraudulent means and were rejected by the local population.[81] This action and the attempt to "demilitarize" the National Police, the Treasury Police, and the Fire Department reinforced right-wing opposition to the Junta.[82] On December 21, 1960, unidentified individuals machine-gunned the residence of General Prosecutor Castrillo Zeledón, nearly killing his ten-year-old son, Mario. Despite the attack against his house, Castrillo Zeledón vowed to continue prosecuting members of the National Police associated with Lemus's repression.[83] Leaders of PRAM had visited the Junta the previous day to express their support for its "democratic conduct." They warned the Junta that if it failed to respond, "with energetic measures," to the ongoing rightist plot against the government, "public freedoms would be gravely threatened and the country will be in danger of returning to the painful days of the tyranny." However, the Junta did not take any assertive action to prevent a new coup.[84]

On January 25, 1961, while members of the Junta participated in a seminar on the new electoral law, Colonels Julio Rivera and Anibal Portillo carried out a coup. Rivera and Portillo vowed to oust communists and Osoristas from the government and to restore order. The Junta, according to José Francisco Valiente, a civilian leader of the coup, created political instability and imperiled the country's international standing due to its close relation with the Cuban Revolution. He told US journalists who arrived in San Salvador the day of the coup that there were "definitive proofs" of Fidel Castro's support to "philo-communists" in El Salvador. The revolutionary propaganda Salvadorans traveling to Cuba brought back to the country and the presence of "communists" in the Junta were proof.[85] The San Carlos garrison, located in the northern area of San Salvador, became the coup plotters' headquarters. However, military officers loyal to the Junta remained in control of El Zapote garrison, near the Presidential House. A large crowd gathered outside El Zapote and marched toward the San Carlos garrison to protest the coup. As demonstrators walked down Avenue España, members of the National Guard shot at the march. Roughly twenty-one persons lost their lives.[86] As is the case with other similar episodes during this period, the circumstances of the massacre at Avenida España remain obscure. It is unclear who ordered these atrocities, who the officers who committed this mass killing were, and what repressive techniques the guardsmen used. In response, activists burned tires and buses in downtown San Salvador to protest the killings, while members of the Junta who led the demonstration and former president Osorio were captured and sent into exile.[87]

Dada, like other witnesses of these events, maintained that the leadership behind the coup was distinctly "North American." "That [was] a coup in the logic of avoiding the Cuban influence. That coup was conducted by a gringo colonel," Dada said.[88] Víctor Valle—a university intellectual in the 1960s—told a similar story.[89] Castillo testified before the US Congress in 1976 that "members of the U.S. Military Mission openly intensified their invitation to conspiracy and rebellion" against the Junta and that "members of the U.S. Military Mission were at the San Carlos Headquarters on the day of the coup."[90] For Dada it was clear that the Kennedy administration only rubber-stamped the coup. "Kennedy took over on January 20 [1961] and the coup happened on January 25 [1961]," recalled Dada. The coup in fact followed Eisenhower's decision to break off diplomatic relations with Cuba in early January 1961.[91] Dada's explication on the origins and authorship of the 1961 coup in El Salvador is consistent with the views of other participants and witnesses of these events and the available historical evidence. It was part of a US attempt to isolate Cuba in the inter-American system in preparation for a US-sponsored invasion of that country. On March 17, 1960, President Eisenhower had authorized the CIA to organize an attack on Cuba carried out by Cuban exiles, the beginning of a covert operation code-named "Operation Zapata." President Kennedy continued Eisenhower's plan against Cuba. He authorized a military operation against Cuba conducted by CIA-trained Cuban counterrevolutionaries on April 17, 1961, the so-called Bay of Pigs invasion, roughly three months after the start of his presidency.[92] The Junta's decision to maintain diplomatic relations between El Salvador and Cuba challenged US efforts to isolate Cuba in the Americas. Dada's recollection of this episode accentuated the logic behind US involvement in the coup that ousted the Civic-Military Junta in January 1961.

Political activists of the 1960s still had vivid memories of the Junta more than four decades later. In a 2007 interview, Dada emphatically denied that the Junta had anything to do with the Cuban Revolution, and he described members of the Junta, whom he knew personally, as university intellectuals who attempted to modernize the country's electoral system. He summarized the Junta's endgame as follows:

> [The Junta] should not be interpreted as a socialist initiative, because neither Ricardo Falla, nor René Fortín [Magaña] had ever been socialists. Fabio Castillo, at that time was not a socialist, nor was he a socialist when he was the rector of the university [between 1963 and 1967]. It should be remembered that the law [that sanctioned] the university reform was supported by [US] AID. But [the Junta] made an attempt to modernize the country. Another thing is that there were no organized political parties and that they rejected the creation of an official party or to take care of the PRUD, because their program was the electoral modernization of the country. Only one party supported them, the Revolutionary Party of April and May [PRAM]. [The Junta] gave the impression of being a left government, but as Ricardo Falla used to say until the time of his death: "When have I been a leftist?"[93]

Domingo Santacruz, who was then an FNOC activist, initially provided a blunt assessment of the Junta. "The Junta was the continuation of the political and military regime," he remembered.[94] But when I shared my impression, based on press accounts at that time, that the Junta harbored a reformist agenda, Santacruz reconsidered his argument. The Junta was not the continuation of the politico-military regime in the "conservative, reactionary character of the traditional dictatorship, so much so that it created mistrust and malaise" among the ruling class, and "that was the fundamental cause" for its downfall. Santacruz recalled that FNOC played the central role in the ousting of Lemus and it supported the Junta, but it was not represented in and "had no possibilities for influencing" the Junta. The Junta was, he concluded, a reformist government isolated from the social movements, and it achieved few changes. "A few laws were approved," but they were largely ineffectual. In the end, the Junta created "a little space, an opening" that allowed the mobilization of FNOC. The Civilian-Military Directorate that replaced the Junta closed down this opening. The ousting of the Junta constituted the final defeat of Osorio's reformist program.[95] In 2003, Castillo argued that the dismantling of the Junta's political liberalization in 1961 enabled the persistence of authoritarian governments in the following two decades. These governments intensified the conflicts that led to the country's civil war.[96]

In roughly eighteen months, the military-oligarchic regime was reorganized under US tutelage to fit the Alliance for Progress model of governance, which featured modernization, industrialization, political reforms, and national security.[97] The Civilian-Military Directorate constituted by Colonel Rivera, another colonel, and three civilians took over power and declared martial law in January 1961.[98] Dada considered the Directorate "the ideal Alliance for Progress regime" in that it combined an "intensely modernizing platform but before anything else, national security."[99] The leaders of the coup invited the Christian Democrat leader Abraham Rodríguez to join the Directorate and offered the PDC the chance to become the new official party. Rodríguez and the majority of PDC leaders rejected that deal as they contested the forming of new official parties after the recurrent military coups and considered the making of "permanent opposition parties" a precondition for the country's democratization. However, a conservative faction of the PDC left the party and joined members of the PRUD (the former official party) to create the National Conciliation Party (PCN), the new official party.[100] The Directorate called for the election of a constitutional assembly for December 17, 1961. While only the PCN and an obscure right-wing party participated in the election, the Directorate labeled the event "the country's first clean election since 1930."[101] In January 1962, the Constitutional Assembly amended the 1950 Constitution, appointed itself as a national assembly, "and scheduled a presidential election for April [1962]."[102] It gave the armed forces ample constitutional duties that included the defense of the national territory, law enforcement, and public security (i.e., "public order"). It also proclaimed the military the guarantors of "constitutional rights," particularly the defense of alternative access to "the Presidency of the Republic."[103] This last provision meant to preserve the right of competing military factions to access the presidency. These constitutional prerogatives further enabled the militarization of state and society during the next two decades. In this context, Rivera ran as the PCN candidate and won the presidency in an uncompetitive election. However, to avoid Lemus's fate, Rivera embarked on a series of political reforms at the advice of Murat Williams, Kennedy's ambassador in El Salvador.[104] Rivera's decision to tolerate opposition parties and to establish a new system of proportional representation at the National Assembly sought to limit the influence of the Cuban Revolution in El Salvador. Rivera also focused on the creation of the Central American Common Market (CACM) as his main strategy to generate employment, stimulate economic growth, and palliate the impending social crisis.[105] However, he was unable to conduct major socioeconomic reforms and instead implemented a limited "reform of agrarian property" along the lines of the Alliance for Progress.[106]

Fighting the Transformation of El Salvador into a "Second Puerto Rico"

Communist intellectuals created FUAR, a militant organization, to counter the Directorate's repression. The organization's brief existence overlapped with the formation of the Alliance for Progress regime headed by Colonel Julio Rivera. The movement also declared its intention to fight what it considered the imminent "transformation of El Salvador into a North American [US] colony."[107]

FUAR deemed the persistence of oligarchic and feudal labor relations and growing US investments in El Salvador the two major obstacles for "national development." Its platform stated that the increasing "penetration of US capital in El Salvador after World War II" reinforced the dependency of the Salvadoran economy on US markets, creating privileged conditions for US investments in El Salvador and limiting the expansion of the national industry. FUAR characterized Salvadoran elites as a mere "intermediary oligarchy" whose agro-export economy based on the superexploitation of labor was totally dependent on the fluctuations of the US market.[108] Like Dada, Valle, and Castillo, FUAR leaders deemed the 1961 coup the product of a US-sponsored conspiracy. However, they further read this event as the first step in the transformation of El Salvador into a "second Puerto Rico," that is, a new "colony" of the United States. Similarly, FUAR called the Alliance for Progress "a new method of Yankee colonization" in Latin America aimed at curtailing the growing influence of the Cuban Revolution.[109] The ongoing US colonization of El Salvador featured, according to FUAR, open involvement of US embassy officials in government affairs and social reforms conducted by the Directorate in accordance with the 1961 Punta del Este Charter—a document that originated at the special meeting of the OAS Inter-American Council held in Uruguay that ratified Kennedy's Alliance for Progress—which it labeled "a policy of crumbs and deception." It also deemed foreign loans "contrary to national interests" and the participation of US "technicians" in state institutions components of this plan. It claimed that the US MILGROUP and "Yankee policemen" in El Salvador exercised command over the army and security forces. They planned to "transform the National Army into a 'Nicaraguan Guard' [Somoza's National Guard] to serve as a colonial army of occupation."[110]

FUAR's blueprint comprised a set of socioeconomic, political, constitutional, and administrative reforms to conduct a "democratic, anti-imperialist and anti-feudal revolution."[111] Its focus was agrarian reform. FUAR asserted:

> The main internal task of the future government of the Revolution will be to conduct a deep Agrarian Reform, which liquidates the monopoly

over land, giving it to agricultural workers and landless peasants or peasants with small plots of land and at the same time liberates small and medium-sized farmers of oligarchic exploitation. . . . through Agrarian Reform, the Revolution will give a lethal definitive blow to feudalism in our country and will finish with monoculture and the colonial distortion of the economy, opening up a broad path for national industrialization and the complete liquidation of unemployment in the countryside and the city in a short time.[112]

FUAR was structured in six *columnas* (columns or sections) that engaged in "open and secret political and social struggle" and "some military training."[113] FUAR columns, organized in GAR, conducted actions such as agitation outside factories, "flash meetings" (street gatherings that lasted a few minutes), graffiti, "self-defense" (e.g., armed defense of demonstrations), and "even armed propaganda" (e.g., armed militants distributing flyers).[114] In his memoir, Victor Valle described in precise detail high-profile FUAR actions that generated "certain apprehension among the security forces." FUAR militants entered the Flor Blanca Stadium, the main soccer arena in San Salvador at that time, during the first game of a Central American soccer tournament "with a meter and half letters rolled to their bodies, lined up in an orderly fashion in the popular section of the stadium and at the culminating moment of the [official] ceremony they unfolded the letters that were the size of a person and it looked very good from the [opposite] section of the stadium . . . [The letters spelled out]'FUAR Welcomes You.'"[115] Valle commented: "It was a small propaganda action, amusing, but audacious. . . . the FUAR was an organization that at least did audacious things."[116] However, for Valle, FUAR's most emblematic action was a protest at the US embassy in San Salvador to repudiate Rivera's presidential inauguration held on July 1, 1962. On that occasion, a large group of FUAR demonstrators threw bottles of paint in FUAR's colors against the US embassy, breaking windows and staining the exterior walls. According to Valle, FUAR militants initially considered throwing Molotov cocktails instead of bottles of paint and entering the US embassy "to get files that supposedly contained personal information about Salvadoran politicians." However, on the eve of this action, FUAR leaders instructed demonstrators "to throw bottles of green and red paint instead of Molotov cocktails." This last-minute change of heart indicated, according to Valle, the ensuing tensions between sectors of the left that favored "violent solutions" and those that opposed them.[117]

Like their precursors, PCS intellectuals in the 1960s considered the "peasant question" a key problem of the Salvadoran revolution. For instance, Jorge Arias Gómez, a scholar affiliated with the PCS, analyzed the 1832 indigenous rebellion in La Paz and San Vicente led by Anastasio Aquino, an

indigenous worker at an indigo plantation. Arias Gómez saw continuities between Aquino's rebellion, the 1932 indigenous peasant uprising in western
El Salvador, and the land conflicts in the 1960s. He concluded his essay
on Aquino advocating for a "Democratic Bourgeois Revolution" that conducted an agrarian reform along the lines of the FUAR program.[118] FUAR
depicted in general terms the highly polarized agrarian structure during that
decade. Despite the rapid pace of industrialization in the 1950s and 1960s, El
Salvador remained, fundamentally, an agrarian society dominated by a small
landowner class that exploited roughly 50 percent of the arable land (some
754,000 hectares) and leased thousands of hectares to small or medium-sized
producers, while some 63,000 small landholders exploited roughly 4 percent
of the arable land (some 67,000 hectares). Coffee, sugar, and cotton producers hired a seasonal labor force made up of landless rural workers and small
landholders during the harvest seasons. Hundreds of thousands of rural workers lived in extreme poverty, deprived of the most basic public services. The
precarious living conditions of these rural workers in the early 1960s were
virtually unchanged from those of 1932 or earlier, making agrarian reform
the primary task of the Salvadoran revolution.[119] FUAR made a priority the
formation of a "peasant column," which was led by the survivors of the 1932
massacre such as Miguel Mármol, Daniel Castaneda, Modesto Ramírez, and
Segundo Ramírez.[120]

Castaneda, the PCS's secretary general between 1951 and 1964, Mármol,
Modesto Ramírez, and other survivors of the 1932 terror made repeated attempts
to organize peasant movements, but they were unable to do so due to the persecution of the ubiquitous repressive forces. Instead, they created small rural networks among peasant communities and workers at coffee farms in Ahuachapán,
Sonsonate, and Santa Ana, which promoted minimal labor demands. "The
National Guard was always after them.... there was a commissioner and a
patrulla cantonal (i.e., a paramilitary group) in every hamlet and rural settlement
[*caserío*]," said Santacruz.[121] They also organized networks among workers at
cotton plantations in Usulután and San Miguel and tried to form peasant unions.
According to Santacruz, "In the late 1950s there were worker organizations at
cotton plantations along the coastline but they never manage to create a union.
Several leaders ended up in jail."[122] They also met with workers at sugar haciendas owned by the Meléndez family near Apopa and Soyapango. Mármol and
Modesto Ramírez even produced a bulletin called *La Mazorca* (The Corncob)
that featured drawings depicting the history of land conflicts in El Salvador,
agrarian reform, and rural unionization, in order to "raise a little bit the consciousness of peasants about land struggles."[123] Members of these rural networks
constituted FUAR's peasant column.

In 1962, FUAR reached its greatest strength, but paradoxically it also started its quick decline as PCS intellectuals split over the issue of armed struggle. "The development of the revolutionary political consciousness of FUAR [militants] reached its finest moment in 1962," said Santacruz. FUAR leaders deemed the formation of the "feminine column" a great success. "The women's column developed an interesting organizational work, that is, combative struggle of women." FUAR militants often participated in "self-defense" activities and became increasingly radicalized as they confronted security forces or suffered imprisonment. FUAR was ready to start a "military option" in 1962 because some of its militants had basic military training. That same year, however, FUAR lost momentum at its clandestine Third Plenary held in San Salvador in 1962 due to Carpio's questioning of the party's engagement in armed struggle. "Since 1962 FUAR was undermined by that internal discussion [over armed struggle]. . . . the process of radicalization of FUAR stopped and consequently [the possibility] to take the step toward military action."[124] At that time, roughly two thousand militants made up FUAR, and the organization "continued growing."[125]

Carpio deemed the creation of FUAR a crass political error on the part of the PCS's political commission. He faulted Schafik Hándal, the coordinator of FUAR, Raúl Castellanos Figueroa, and other members of the PCS leadership for engaging in leftist extremism and militarism and for "educating FUAR militants in the idea that revolution was around the corner and that therefore the problem of power" was imminent.[126] Carpio maintained that the "subjective conditions" (i.e., widespread revolutionary consciousness and organization) that constitute, according to Lenin, a "revolutionary situation" were absent in El Salvador in 1962. More to the point, Carpio deemed that the "objective conditions [vast social inequalities, socioeconomic crisis, division among ruling classes, and so forth] for revolution were ripe in excess," but that "not even minimal [subjective conditions]" for revolution existed at that time. According to Santacruz, FUAR militants initially "misunderstood" Carpio's analysis, for in fact some thought that it reinforced Hándal's position on this matter. Hándal himself told FUAR militants that "there were discussions in the sense that perhaps [FUAR was] going too fast" in its plans to start armed struggle and that the "political situation was in fact changing." In the end, this debate "stopped the process of radicalization of FUAR," and the organization never engaged in military activity. Carpio's analysis prevailed within the PCS. Hándal was removed as coordinator of FUAR, and the movement itself demobilized in 1963. Carpio also shifted the party's focus on FUAR to the organization of the "new working class" that emerged from industrialization linked to the CACM. The Fifth Congress of the PCS held in March 1964 ratified the party's shift toward trade union politics articulated by Carpio.[127] However, the discussion on armed struggle initiated among PCS intellectuals at the time of FUAR became a dominant theme among left intellectuals throughout the 1960s.

President Lemus's crackdown on the university community constituted a clumsy attempt to curtail the influence of the Cuban Revolution in El Salvador. Although Lemus did not need a particular incentive to "combat communism," given that he was a "devoted anti-communist," State Department officials compelled him to close down the political opening of the early years of his administration. As the opposition to Lemus grew in San Salvador, he ordered repeated attacks on the university community and political opponents, which generated scores of victims. At this time, members of the university's executive government plotted with former president Osorio to topple Lemus.

The Civic-Military Junta that replaced Lemus outlined an ambitious plan for the democratization of the country, which included the demilitarization of the state and the restoration of civic and political rights, including the right to organize independent political parties. The Junta also promoted electoral reforms and planned to conduct democratic elections in 1962. Oligarchic elites and sectors of the army rejected the Junta's political liberalization, however, and orchestrated a reactionary coup as early as November 1960. The Junta's ambiguous political composition (i.e., liberal university intellectuals and Osorista military officers), its isolation from the emerging social movements and political parties, and its political miscalculations (e.g., the dismantling of Lemus's municipal councils) also contributed to its quick demise. However, US anti-communism and plans to conduct an attack on Cuba sealed the fate of the reformist Junta. The vacillations of State Department officials in granting diplomatic recognition to the Junta were motivated by concerns over the political affiliation of Castillo and other faculty who joined it, the Junta's relative opening toward the Cuban Revolution, and the US government's distrust of Osorio's capacity to control leftists in the Junta. Though coup forces had been brewing since November 1960, there are indications that the Eisenhower administration endorsed the coup in January 1961, after US embassy officials in San Salvador failed to persuade the civilians in the Junta to backtrack from their democratization program and to break diplomatic relations with Cuba. Arguably, the US government viewed the Junta's political liberalization as a process that might debilitate the armed forces and the official party, the strongest anti-communist institutions in the country, and allow the left to take power at a time when it tried to isolate Cuba in the inter-American system as part of its preparations to conduct the Bay of Pigs invasion.

The events of 1960 and 1961, with their international and internal dimensions, significantly altered the political awareness and political culture of university intellectuals in El Salvador. After these episodes, they considered the US government a crucial internal actor in Salvadoran politics. Unlike the crises of the military regimes of the 1940s and 1950s, which were largely resolved through intra-elite negotiations, the revamping of the military regimes, and the creation of new official parties, US participation in Salvadoran affairs became ubiquitous after 1959. This situation further radicalized left intellectuals in the 1960s. They harbored no doubts about the US authorship of the 1961 coup. Moreover, FUAR leaders deemed it the start of a new "colonization" under Kennedy's Alliance for Progress, which aimed at transforming El Salvador into a "second Puerto Rico." The university community's vigorous defense of its autonomy during Lemus's repression also strengthened the university as a center of political activity that gave impetus to the formation of opposition parties, student organizations, and social movements.[128] In the 1960s, university intellectuals renewed their efforts to create permanent opposition parties as key factors to promote the country's democratization. Lemus banned PRAM in 1960, but faculty and students strove to create a viable left political alternative throughout the 1960s (e.g., Fabio Castillo ran as a presidential candidate of PAR in 1967, and PCS intellectuals refurbished the Nationalist Democratic Union [UDN]). Members of ACUS, a Catholic conservative student organization, along with other Social Christian intellectuals, formed the PDC in 1960. PDC intellectuals articulated an anti-oligarchic discourse that gained widespread support among the rural population in the 1960s, largely due to their close alliance with reformist sectors of the Catholic Church. For the first time since the fateful 1932 insurrection, in 1961 communist intellectuals and leaders of social movements organized militant resistance against the authoritarian regime. Lemus's brutal crackdown on the university community, the social movements, and the opposition parties, as well as the January 1961 massacre at Avenida España, persuaded Hándal, Castellanos, and other PCS leaders to create FUAR. While it was not a guerrilla movement, because it never actually engaged in military activity, FUAR did mount a militant resistance against the oligarchic-military regime, which became part of the historical memory and practical experience of the insurgent organizations created in the 1970s. Moreover, the creation of FUAR marked the beginning of a prolonged debate over revolutionary strategies and tactics among university intellectuals in El Salvador.[129]

The Junta's democratization program had a lasting resonance in the country's political history. In fact, Castillo and other protagonists of this period became leaders of the New Left insurgency, who tackled similar issues to those included in the Junta's democratization plan during the peace negotiations that settled the civil war in 1992. They also viewed education as a central component of social and national emancipation, with ongoing reverberations among subsequent cohorts of university intellectuals who conducted pedagogical activities among peasant communities in the 1960s and 1970s.

Lemus's despotism and the Junta's failed reformist experiment, which ended in the bloody coup of January 1961, in the heyday of the Cold War in Latin America, pointed to the beginning of a discussion of armed struggle among left intellectuals. These events thus can be seen as the starting point of the insurgent and counterinsurgent politics that characterized El Salvador in the following three decades.

University Apostles

In 1958, Roque Dalton, a young poet affiliated with the Communist Party of El Salvador, won the first prize in a poetry contest at the University of El Salvador. A few days later, members of the student organization Salvadoran University Catholic Action (ACUS, a branch of Catholic Action) published a disparaging but carelessly written critique of Dalton.[1] The anonymous writer of an article titled "Bajo el imperio de la vulgaridad" (Under the empire of vulgarity) turned his disgust with the poem written by Dalton into a diatribe against Dalton's political persona.[2] Dalton's raw allusions to double standards in the sexual morality of priests and his remarks about the Catholic practice of fasting especially upset the leaders of ACUS.[3] A month later, ACUS published a rejoinder written by Dalton, along with excerpts of the controversial poem. In his retort, Dalton stated that ACUS dodged debates on substantial political and aesthetic issues by engaging in "insults, quick and facile judgments, and rude pigeonholing that closes all means of intellectual comprehension."[4]

What is telling about this episode between the ACUS intellectuals and Dalton, who were about the same age and came from similar social and educational backgrounds, is their contrasting aesthetic and political sensibilities. More important, this exchange shows that the leaders of ACUS took seriously their self-appointed role as arbiters and defenders of "decency" and "honor" in university life. ACUS publications often warned about the threat posed by an emerging "materialist morale in different orders of life" and called on Catholics to "safeguard their faith against the [anti-Catholic] prejudice skillfully promoted" by Marxists.[5] Although the ACUS is virtually unknown outside Catholic Church circles in El Salvador, it had a major impact in the political history of that country. Some of its members founded the PDC in 1960 and, later, in the early 1970s, two insurgent organizations: the ERP and the FPL. Together, these constituted the backbone of the FMLN during the civil war.

This chapter examines the roles that Catholic Action intellectuals played in the foundation of the New Left in El Salvador. It ponders how and why they adopted innovative approaches to religion and politics that constituted a rupture

with a long-standing conservative Catholic tradition in El Salvador. The radicalization of the young Catholic Action intellectuals was an unexpected result of the
profound theological transformations experienced by the Catholic Church in
the 1960s. From an institutional viewpoint these transformations were intended
to preserve the traditional influence of the Catholic Church in Latin America.[6]
Instead, they enabled the convergence between Catholic intellectuals and members of revolutionary movements who sought a structural transformation of capitalism.[7] Catholic intellectuals assimilated, often uncritically, the new theology of
the Catholic Church formulated by the Second Vatican Council and the Second
Conference of Latin American Bishops (CELAM) held in 1968, which they
learned through highly scripted pedagogical processes at a time of epochal political and institutional changes.[8] These changes included the growing polarization
of Salvadoran society and politics in the context of the 1960s Cold War, a major
reform at the University of El Salvador between 1963 and 1967, and the mobilizations of students in the United States, France, Mexico, and elsewhere. The
new theological leadership of the Catholic Church formulated a radical critique
of the core principles and ideology of liberal capitalism, the colonial past, and
"new forms of colonialism." It also undermined traditional Catholic anti-Marxist
attitudes, and it legitimized the use of revolutionary violence against tyranny,
echoing the Christian doctrine of the "just war."[9] These theological notions were
crucial in inspiring the young Catholic Action intellectuals who formed the New
Left insurgency in the early 1970s. The changing political and religious mentality of this cohort was also informed by what Michael Löwy calls the "negative
affinity" between "the Catholic ethic and capitalism." "Catholic anti-capitalism"
might be rooted in "the ethical and religious identification of Christ with the
poor" and communal traditions in Catholic Church history.[10] Catholic Action
in El Salvador increasingly embodied an anticapitalist ethos at the time of the
Second Vatican Council and in the years following. This emerging anticapitalist
culture influenced the increasing political and intellectual exchanges between
Catholic and Marxist university students and scholars at the University of El
Salvador, Catholic institutions, and political parties. This confluence between
Catholic and Marxists intellectuals, starting in the mid-1960s, shaped the politi-
cal cultures of the New Left prior to the emergence of liberation theology.

The decrees of the Second Vatican Council (1962–1965) changed in fundamental ways the roles that both men and women played within the Church and
in society.[11] In the case of El Salvador, scholars have examined the impact of
the Second Vatican Council on the pastoral work conducted by the archbishopric of San Salvador and its reverberations among the Catholic hierarchy and
among top Catholic intellectuals like the Jesuit Ignacio Ellacuría.[12] The sociologist Juan Ramón Vega asserts that a Church reform led by the archbishop of San
Salvador Luis Chávez y González (1938–1977) in the 1950s actually preceded

the council. The council's decrees ratified the Church reform conducted by
Chávez y González and encouraged him to disseminate the council's documents
among laypeople, priests, and nuns. The archbishop also penned several pastoral
letters inspired by the work of the council, particularly "On the Responsibility
of Laypeople over the Ordering of the Temporal," issued on August 6, 1966,
which steered the country's public opinion for several months and generated a
strong reaction among the Salvadoran elites.[13] Catholic Action intellectuals who
formed the New Left, like most sectors of the Salvadoran Catholic Church, experienced crucial ideological transformations in this period as they examined
the council's documents and increasingly realized the personal and collective
challenges implicit in its conclusions. ACUS and other Catholic Action groups
incarnated the socially committed theology of the council, breaking with the ritualistic and conservative Catholicism that prevailed in El Salvador in the 1960s.[14]

The Cuban Revolution, Christian democracy, and Cold War crises in El
Salvador centrally informed the politicization of Catholic Action intellectuals
in the 1960s. From the beginning of that decade, they accused Fidel Castro of
promoting a violent anticlericalism in Cuba and contributed to the emergence
of the PDC as a leading opposition party, which they viewed as a nonviolent
alternative to conduct social revolution in El Salvador. As the country's political
turmoil intensified in the late 1960s, members of ACUS and its sister organization, Catholic Student Youth (JEC), joined radical student movements at
the university inspired by the new Catholic theology and the countercultural
sensibilities of that period. In contrast to the prevalent narratives on the origins
of the New Left insurgency in El Salvador, I contend that a considerable number of the founders of both the ERP and the FPL were in fact members of a
cohort of middle-class students affiliated with Catholic Action. While dissident
Communist Party leaders and activists played an important role in the creation
of these movements, they constituted a small minority in the ranks of the first
guerrilla organizations. In the case of the FPL, for example, few communist
dissidents aside from Carpio remained active during the 1970s. Instead, I suggest that a precocious generation of university students affiliated with Catholic
Action, who came of age between 1967 and 1972, constituted the critical mass
of the nascent New Left insurgency. This cohort constituted a "rupture generation" that engaged in a long-term frontal struggle against the authoritarian
regime. Although most members of this generation had conservative Catholic
family backgrounds and educations, their radical politics were informed by the
rise of the social movements in El Salvador and the general climate of rebellion
against capitalism and colonialism in the late 1960s. They led a student movement that featured an unprecedented practice of direct democracy at the university; built multiple connections with similar movements in Central America,
Mexico, France, Spain, and other countries; challenged the Communist Party's

hegemony in university politics; and faced head-on the oligarchic-military regime through their radical activism. They also participated in pedagogical processes promoted by the Catholic Church, which enabled the first interactions between peasant leaders and university students that led to the expansion of the New Left insurgencies into rural areas. Unlike previous generations of ACUS intellectuals who were usually affiliated with the PDC and considered upward social mobility compatible with social activism and reformist politics, the Catholic Action youth of the late 1960s became the first generation of "professional revolutionaries" who emerged from the ranks of the Salvadoran Catholic middle class. Members of this generation fully embraced revolutionary lives, in the context of the growing confrontations between the social movements, the opposition parties, and the state at the height of the Cold War in Latin America.

In what follows I ponder the sinuous transformation of ACUS from a conservative student organization of the 1950s into the cradle of the New Left insurgency in the late 1960s.

Origins of ACUS (1949–1962)

When Abraham Rodríguez, a high school graduate from San Miguel, arrived in San Salvador to study law in 1948, strong anti-Catholic sentiments prevailed at the University of El Salvador.[15] Since 1949, students like Rodríguez had sought to create a Catholic political movement at the university, despite the opposition of students affiliated with the PCS who generally considered the Catholic Church a retrograde institution closely allied with the Salvadoran elites and the government of President Osorio.[16] Amid the intellectual and political activity of the moment, Rodríguez joined ACUS, aided by the Jesuit priest Isidro Iriarte, the rector of the San José de La Montaña Seminary.

Iriarte was particularly concerned about the absence of well-versed Catholic intellectuals at the constitutional assembly sponsored by President Osorio, which produced the country's first democratic constitution in 1950. He wanted to replicate the experience of the Cuban Catholic Church, which had trained several generations of Catholic university intellectuals since the 1930s, to address this issue. Iriarte advocated the creation of a Catholic Action group at the university among the Church hierarchy but also warned the bishops that they should not harbor illusions about quick successes in their pastoral work among university students. Forming a new generation of Catholic intellectuals at the university, according to Iriarte, was "not a matter of days or weeks but of years."[17]

ACUS was a specialized branch of Catholic Action, an international movement that endorsed a French theological and philosophical body of thought known as "integral humanism" or "Social Christianity." Catholic philosopher Jacques Maritain formulated Social Christianity in the 1930s and 1940s, largely as a response to the declining influence of Catholicism among the working classes in France and Belgium. Social Christianity constituted an alternative vision of the social order and a radical critique of unrestrained capitalism, which challenged the dominance of conservative sectors within the Catholic Church prior to the Second Vatican Council.[18] It inspired the creation of Christian Democrat parties and Catholic Action in Europe, and it first came to Latin America during the 1930s through the collaboration of the Vatican, Latin American bishops, and religious orders, all of whom wanted to counter the growing influence of secular ideologies (especially socialism and communism) among working-class and university intellectuals.[19] In El Salvador, it influenced the creation of social programs, institutions, media outlets, and Catholic Action organizations sponsored by the archbishop of San Salvador Luis Chávez y González that preceded the Church's renovation at the time of the council.

Catholic Action implemented a worldwide strategy to form Catholic intellectuals and workers. It created various organizations of university and high school students, peasant youth, and workers and formulated a pedagogy called "To see, to judge, and to act." This method comprised the depiction of the working and living conditions of the socially excluded, the analysis of such conditions from a Christian perspective, and the definition of practical actions to improve those conditions. Catholic Action was an influential movement in Brazil, Argentina, Chile, Venezuela, and Uruguay. It also set the basis for the foundation of Christian Democrat parties, and it influenced several cohorts of Catholic leaders who became important political and intellectual figures in those countries.[20] In the 1950s and 1960s, it was a well-established program in Central America, particularly in Guatemala and El Salvador. Deborah Levenson-Estrada studied the trajectory of the Catholic Worker Youth (JOC), a branch of Catholic Action, "in working-class neighborhoods" of Guatemala City. JOC activists played key roles in the reorganization of Guatemalan trade unions in the aftermath of the 1954 CIA coup against President Jacobo Arbenz.[21] In El Salvador, ACUS and JEC were particularly influential among middle-class students at the university and in high schools.

In the 1950s, ACUS was a conservative student organization that operated at the University of El Salvador, which served roughly seventeen hundred students.[22] It promoted a reformist anti-communist ideology, which gained considerable leverage among the mostly middle-class students, despite the fierce opposition of PCS affiliates to Catholic activism.[23] Members of ACUS designated themselves "university apostles" whose main mission consisted in promoting Christian values in leading sectors of society and "consciousness among Catholic university students about [their] responsibility and presence in the modern world."[24] In the 1950s, leaders of Catholic Action were still echoing *Rerum Novarum* (New Times), an encyclical sanctioned by Pope Leo XIII in 1891 that considered liberalism and Marxism two manifestations of Western materialism at odds with Catholic theology. They believed that nineteenth-century liberalism had created massive social exclusion (i.e., proletarians) in Europe and elsewhere and chastised communism as a form of "collective materialism" that brought grave social and religious consequences in countries where it prevailed. Catholics were committed to redeem proletarians, not necessarily by adopting a middle way between liberalism and communism but by assuming what they called "a firm equilibrium on justice." In this vein, Catholic Action called on "moderate Catholics" to promote long-overdue social transformations in the country.[25]

ACUS fully embraced the Cold War anti-communism prevalent in El Salvador in the 1950s. It showed particular concern for the Soviet persecution of nationalists and Catholics in the Eastern bloc. Catholic Action students strongly condemned the execution of Hungarian leaders Imre Nagy and Pal Maleter ordered by Nikita Khrushchev in June 1958, calling it "a new bloody page, written with traces of barbarism and cruelty . . . in the shameful annals of the Soviet Union."[26] They labeled the Soviet Union a tyrannical regime that curtailed religious freedoms in Poland and deemed Catholicism a major deterrent of communism in Eastern Europe. They ultimately described the Cold War as a decisive battle for the survival of "Western Christian civilization."[27] Communism, according to Catholic Action, constituted an unprecedented challenge to Christianity that embodied "a spirit of absolute violence," one that could not be "crush[ed] through brute force" but only "through a more powerful spiritual force."[28] But in contrast to their preoccupations about the future of democracy in distant Eastern Europe, ACUS leaders seemingly ignored the anti-communist crackdown ordered by President Osorio in 1952, which targeted hundreds of political opponents, public intellectuals, labor leaders, and students who advocated democratic rule in El Salvador. They also overlooked the 1954 CIA coup against the democratically elected president Jacobo Arbenz in neighboring Guatemala, a stand that was consistent with their anti-communism and the active role that the Catholic hierarchy and middle-class Catholic students in Guatemala played in the ousting of Arbenz. This is all the more notable because the coup against Arbenz was a key event in the radicalization of Latin American politics in the 1950s.[29] It motivated young leftists in several countries to engage in more militant responses to authoritarianism and US involvement in the region.[30]

The year 1960 was crucial in the history of the Cold War in Central America as the United States vigorously fought the real and imagined aftershocks of the Cuban Revolution in the region. The impact of the CIA coup against President Arbenz in Guatemala among university intellectuals in El Salvador had been limited, but the ousting of Venezuelan dictator Marcos Pérez Jiménez in January 1958 and the Cuban Revolution of January 1959 rekindled mobilization in San Salvador against the authoritarian government of President Lemus.[31] During the political opening created by the Civic-Military Junta that replaced Lemus, Catholic intellectuals founded the PDC, which became a decisive player in Salvadoran politics in the following three decades. Members of ACUS, reformist Catholic intellectuals, and affiliates of the Confederation of Latin American Christian Trade Unions (CLASC) founded the PDC in November 1960. According to Héctor Dada, who was then a member of ACUS, the foundation of the PDC and its "brutally anti-oligarchic" discourse generated anxieties among a range of political actors, including the PCS, US government agencies, ultraconservative sectors of the Catholic Church, and the Salvadoran oligarchy itself. The communists deemed the creation of the PDC a US government machination to undermine their influence among trade unions. The latter feared that the emergence of the Christian Democrats as an independent political force might debilitate the staunchly anti-communist oligarchic-military regime in El Salvador. The Salvadoran military and the elites viewed the Christian Democrats as a serious threat because they mobilized noncommunist middle-class intellectuals, as well as priests, teachers, and peasant leaders.[32]

In the aftermath of the Cuban Revolution and the transformative events of 1960 and 1961 in El Salvador, ACUS intellectuals were convinced that the highly polarized Salvadoran society faced a crucial dichotomy between "evolution and revolution." Despite their intense rejection of Fidel Castro and the Cuban Revolution, Catholic intellectuals depicted 1961, the year that the Civic Military Directorate took power in the bloody coup sanctioned by the Kennedy administration, as the "25th hour" to conduct social reforms to avert violent revolution in El Salvador.[33] Because of their anti-communist rhetoric, Catholic intellectuals called instead for revolution "under the Empire of Law." They claimed that the Catholic Church approved social revolution, without fomenting "violence, genocide, and class struggle as atheist communism proposes and practices."[34]

Besides their anti-communist activism, members of ACUS also conducted pastoral work in remote rural areas. Throughout the 1960s, they taught Catholic doctrine to laypeople in Chalatenango and other rural areas during Easter.[35] In 1963, Catholic Action affiliates joined Juan Ramón Vega, ACUS's ecclesiastical adviser, to celebrate Easter in Arcatao, Azacualpa, and Comalapa, three isolated towns in northeastern Chalatenango. During Lent, they engaged in spiritual and technical preparations to conduct pastoral work in rural areas.[36] Mario Efraín Callejas, a former Catholic Action affiliate, recalled that he and his peers conducted surveys on the living conditions of peasant communities in Chalatenango in the early 1960s. "It was disastrous. It was a miracle how those people [peasants in Chalatenango] survived without any governmental or institutional support.

They were conformists, they had not yet awakened, they were exploited and marginalized," commented Callejas.[37]

Catholic Action intellectuals viewed the PDC as a viable alternative for carrying out a nonviolent social revolution in El Salvador and decisively joined its ranks in the 1960s. During that decade, they drew on President Eduardo Frei's "Revolution in Freedom" in Chile (1964–1970) and the Christian Democrat tradition in Venezuela represented by Rafael Caldera and the Independent Political Electoral Organization Committee (COPEI) to devise a reformist program that positioned the PDC as the leading opposition party in the country. At that time members of ACUS became PDC activists, often as popular educators linked to Catholic Church pedagogical initiatives or as community organizers working with the municipal government of San Salvador under the first Christian Democrat major of the city, José Napoleón Duarte.

Transformation of Catholic Action (1962–1965)

On October 11, 1962, some ten thousand people of "all social strata" attended a "procession-vigil" in San Salvador to celebrate the start of the Second Vatican Council. In the following three years, Archbishop Chávez y González personally organized working groups of priests and laypeople to discuss the council documents, particularly *Gaudium and Spes*, the Pastoral Constitution on the Church in the Modern World sanctioned in 1965.[38] This document unambiguously declared that the Catholic Church had the foremost responsibility to side with the poor and the weak. *Gaudium and Spes* also appealed to the clergy and laypeople in developing nations to engage in ecclesiastical practices that addressed the renewed social concern of the Catholic Church.[39] ACUS intellectuals, like many other Salvadoran Catholics, experienced fundamental theological and political changes as a result of their examinations of the council's documents and interactions with priests and bishops cognizant of the new theology. Tomás Castillo wrote an eloquent article on the historical significance of the council that echoed the prevalent sentiment among Catholic intellectuals on this matter.[40] Castillo called on the Salvadoran Catholic Church to assume the resolutions of the Second Vatican Council with "courage and responsibility" to avoid "giving the sad spectacle of a Church that preaches what it does not do and that proclaims a faith of which it does not give true testimony." The post-council Church had to "dust off the lethargy of centuries" and to realize that the mission of Christians was to "build a world for God," something that could not "be achieved without being his true apostles."[41]

In 1964, Catholic Action started a process of ideological renewal under the guidance of two Belgian priests committed to the new Catholic theology. The arrival of Esteban Alliet and Jan De Planck, two clerics sponsored by the diocese of Bruges and the University of Louvain to serve as Catholic Action's new ecclesiastical advisers in San Salvador, was a turning point in the renovation of the organization. Their innovative pastoral work among the Catholic Action youth revitalized the organization and changed its negative image among the student population. Ignacio Paniagua, a former medical student who joined Catholic Action in 1964, recalled that at that time Catholic middle-class students generally had "very limited political baggage and little consciousness of social problems." Paniagua also remembered his initial skepticism about joining Catholic Action, an organization secular students usually considered reactionary. However, after meeting Alliet, Paniagua changed his mind. He recalled that Alliet did not wear a cassock and talked openly about the political participation of Catholics, social justice, and solidarity.[42] At that time, Catholic Action, like its Latin American counterparts associated with the International Movement of Catholic Students (based in Medellín, Colombia) and Pax Romana, was heavily invested in an effort to influence ongoing university reform on the continent, invoking the Second Vatican Council decrees.[43]

Priests, bishops, and members of Catholic Action reflected at length on the meaning of the Second Vatican Council for the university community. In a series of workshops and seminars, they discussed the multiple dimensions of the new Catholic theology. They debated a variety of topics, including pastoral work among university students, popular education, development, and agrarian reform. Bishop Arturo Rivera y Damas, a participant in the council meetings in Rome, and other members of the Church hierarchy met frequently with Catholic Action students and affiliates of the Movement of Catholic Intellectuals, a lesser-known group led by Guillermo Manuel Ungo, a social democrat intellectual formerly associated with Catholic Action, to discuss theological issues related to the council.[44] The legitimacy of violent resistance against tyranny implicit in the new Catholic theology was particularly controversial among the Catholic hierarchy. Bishop Marcos McGrath from Panama, a towering figure at the Second CELAM held in Medellín, Colombia, in 1968, commented on the Church's stand on this issue, citing Pope Paul VI's encyclical *Populorum Progressio* (On the Progress of Peoples) while lecturing Salvadoran Catholic students. A few months later, a conservative Salvadoran cleric accused McGrath of fomenting "a theology of violence." McGrath responded that he was interested solely in promoting "peaceful development" based on popular education. He stated that he had never preached "a theology of violence" as the cleric claimed but had only paraphrased the teachings of Paul VI that sanctioned the use of "violence as the last resort" in the face of tyrannical regimes. McGrath wrote emphatically: "And it is necessary to underline the word 'last' with great insistence." Indeed, he argued that Catholics needed "clearer theological principles that can orient those who feel tempted by violence."[45] McGrath's assertiveness on this matter reveals his concern about the danger that hasty interpretations of the new theology might encourage priests and laypeople to join guerrilla movements. After all, Camilo Torres Restrepo, a Colombian priest who joined the insurgent National Liberation Army (ELN) and was killed by the Colombian military in 1966, was an influential figure among Catholic intellectuals in El Salvador at that time.[46]

Esteban Alliet, the Belgian adviser of Catholic Action, also ruminated on the relevance of the new theology for Catholic students. During a seminar with members of Catholic Action held in La Palma, Chalatenango, in 1967, Alliet suggested that the social teachings of Pope Paul VI and the Second Vatican Council were not necessarily a new theology but rather a return to the roots of Christianity—that is, a search for the "true ideology and mission" of the Catholic Church, which ostensibly consisted in serving humanity, particularly the dispossessed, with a selfless and "humble attitude of love." The encyclical of Paul VI "On the Progress of Peoples" advocated the right of "equal participation" in society and the solution to "the physical and intellectual undernourishment" of the dispossessed, and not simply a technocratic approach aimed at increasing their levels of income. This meant that Catholic Action students had to envision practical ways to enhance the labor conditions of peasants and workers. In this vein Alliet asserted, "it is an evangelization of action but both had to complement each other. Whoever just talks but does not act, is not convincing; but whoever just acts without meditating, acts wrongly." This type of social activism also required conscientious planning or, in the words of Alliet, "a true spirit of efficacy." Members of ACUS had to carefully plan their activities, "to know what is the most urgent [task] to solve and to find the more just and effective means to achieve it." Alliet, like McGrath, also discussed the issue of violence as the last resort to fight tyranny, alluding to Pope Paul VI's encyclical. He added that once the decision to use violence as a method of self-defense had been made, it should be practiced "in a precise, planned and decisive" way. Ultimately, he believed that Catholic middle-class youth should play a fundamental role in the transformation of the social inequalities that characterized Latin American societies in the 1960s.[47]

Archbishop Chávez y González actively supported lay Catholic organizations during and after the Second Vatican Council. "Everything was integrated," recalled Ignacio Paniagua, "specialized groups [i.e., Catholic Action], the PDC, and the educational processes among workers and peasants, particularly peasants. However, the Catholic Church tried to [publicly] distance itself from [these efforts]."[48] Chávez y González, Bishop Rivera y Damas, and a team of diocesan priests supported the creation of a well-financed network of student organizations, cooperatives, peasant training centers, and a radio school program, which became the embodiments of the new Catholic Church envisioned by the council. Although Chávez y González is often remembered as a conservative archbishop who maintained a close alliance with the elites and the military regimes during his thirty-eight-year tenure, he in fact laid down the theological and organizational basis for the renovation of the Salvadoran Catholic Church in the 1960s.

Chávez y González and Rivera y Damas attended the Second Vatican Council representing the Salvadoran conference of bishops, and they witnessed the theological transformations of the Church promoted by European bishops and theologians.[49] At a more practical level, the archbishop also took advantage of his lengthy stay at Via Sant' Alessio 23 in Rome to raise funds for the projects of the Salvadoran Catholic Church. His funding priorities were the peasant cooperatives sponsored by the Church in Quezaltepeque and Chalatenango and the construction of the new Catholic Action headquarters in San Salvador.[50] The new ACUS building became the locus of Catholic activism among university intellectuals, high school students, peasants, and marginalized urban communities.[51]

Evoking the Second Vatican Council documents, Catholic intellectuals increasingly embraced an anticapitalist ethos that moved away from the moralistic questioning of liberalism inspired in *Rerum Novarum* and *Quadragesimo Anno* (Fortieth Year), two influential encyclicals among their peers in the early 1960s. Ricardo Sol, a young Catholic activist, hailed the integration of eighteen hundred new university students in 1967 but commented that most students remained excluded from higher education. Sol quoted extensively council documents stating that Christians must engage without reservation in struggles for justice, charity, and world peace. He made an "ardent and urgent" appeal to university students to participate in the creation of a just and humane social order and in "the annihilation of unmeasured" profit and power structures based on the "domination of men by men." He also criticized university professors who stayed on the sidelines of the university reform and those who opposed it. Sol also faulted Jesuits for fomenting class privilege by exclusively serving affluent students at their academic institutions. He cited Pedro Arrupe, the superior general of the Society of Jesus, who instructed Jesuits to relinquish an education that "domesticates and accommodates" students and instead to promote "the humanization of men domesticated" by mass society.[52] Ignacio Paniagua recalled that his views on private property changed after the council. In the past, Paniagua said, he had regarded private property as "inviolable," but after studying the council documents, he thought that "the common good and the right to land and life" should prevail over it. In the late 1960s, Paniagua and other members of ACUS regularly met with students of medicine affiliated with the PCS to discuss the potential convergence between the Marxist left and progressive Catholics at the University of El Salvador.[53] The frontal attacks on the ethics of capitalism embraced by Catholic intellectuals after the council weakened their traditional antagonism toward Marxists, enabling these first dialogues.

Revolutionary Pedagogy: Popular Education and the Emergence of the New Left

The pedagogy that enabled the formation of the unlikely alliance between urban and peasant leaders that led to the creation of the New Left insurgency emerged at the Center of Social Studies and Popular Promotion (CESPROP), a Church institution specializing in popular education, the cooperative training centers, the radio schools, and other Catholic educational initiatives during the late 1960s and early 1970s.[54] The priest-sociologist Juan Ramón Vega and Catholic students Alfonso Rivas Mira and Carlos Solórzano founded CESPROP in 1967.[55] It trained high school and university students to conduct literacy programs among marginalized communities, rural and urban, using the pedagogy of the Brazilian educator Paulo Freire.[56] Freire posited that subaltern groups must challenge what he termed the "banking education" in order to achieve social emancipation. By "banking education" Freire meant certain pedagogical practices that emphasize the unilateral and uncritical assimilation of knowledge, which can only serve to consolidate prevalent power structures. Freire argued that conscientious self-reflection and reciprocal and egalitarian educational interactions between teachers and students are preconditions for social change.[57] He wrote that ultimately social revolution is an "eminently pedagogical" process, for it requires the transformation of individual and collective consciousness, which can only be achieved through a critical educational process.[58]

In 1967, CESPROP trained dozens of high school graduates, mostly affiliates of JEC (the ACUS's high school sister organization) to conduct adult literacy training among urban marginalized communities. This generation of upper-middle-class male and female students at Catholic high schools from San Salvador such as Liceo Salvadoreño, Externado de San José, La Sagrada Familia, and La Asunción were substantially more politicized than their ACUS predecessors and soon challenged the organization's reformist politics.[59] Rafael Velásquez, a member of this cohort, remembered that he and his peers "shared left politics, enjoyed rock, movies, and parties; but first of all we were friends; politics came afterward." Velásquez also recalled that they were appalled to witness the precarious living conditions of socially excluded communities in San Salvador.[60] Miguel Huezo Mixco, a young poet and graduate of Colegio Don Bosco, a Salesian high school, remembered that there was a "symbiosis" among CESPROP, ACUS, and JEC affiliates, most of whom were also

Christian Democrat activists. Older Catholic intellectuals like the cofounder of CESPROP Carlos Solórzano became political mentors of younger Catholic Action students.[61]

CESPROP also conducted workshops among peasant communities in collaboration with diocesan priests and university students, training peasants on issues pertaining to agrarian reform, peasant unions, and a minimum wage. Rubén Zamora, a scholar and former Christian Democrat leader, recalled that CESPROP played a central role in the formation of peasant activists. In the late 1960s, Zamora and Lil Milagro Ramírez, a poet and a Social Christian activist, conducted popular education among peasant communities near Cojutepeque, a city east of San Salvador. Zamora and his peers produced educational materials aimed at rural workers that included biblical texts with short commentaries, news about the peasant movement, and articles on the national political situation. Zamora recalled that the content of these materials vividly reflected the activists' eclectic political ideology, which featured Social Christianity, Marxism, and Maoism. Echoing Mao, Zamora and his peers considered that the making of a socialist revolution required "the re-education of peasants," a task of primary importance for revolutionary intellectuals. Zamora and Ramírez also used the Catholic Action training method "To see, to judge, and to act " to conduct workshops with peasant communities in Cojutepeque. According to Zamora, between 1967 and 1969, Catholic students were "a machinery of ideological education" that organized hundreds of workshops in close collaboration with members of the Catholic Agrarian Youth (JAC). On May 1, 1968, Catholic activists organized the first peasant march held in Cojutepeque in decades. However, in order to avoid repression, they called it a procession in honor of Saint Joseph Worker (San José Obrero).[62] By the end of the decade, hundreds of peasants had attended the workshops and seminars on agrarian reform organized by Catholic students and priests in Cojutepeque. Nevertheless, the apparent success of this program ignited a repressive response of local authorities, who openly warned peasants to stop attending the training sessions.[63] At that time, the government accused CESPROP of promoting subversion among peasant communities. It sent "*orejas*" (snitches) to monitor the pedagogical activities conducted by the Circles of Popular Culture, study groups formed by CESPROP that enabled interactions between peasants, students, instructors, and diocesan priests, including their teaching materials, the workshops' content, and the identities of the lecturers and the participants. The authorities explicitly required the Catholic hierarchy to censure the teaching of protest songs to peasants during these pedagogical activities.[64]

In the late 1960s, Catholic Action openly embraced progressive politics, dispelling the prejudice that had prevailed against the organization among university students since the beginning of that decade. Paniagua recalled that in contrast to the conservatism of the "old ACUS" (ACUS in the 1950s), the "new ACUS" (ACUS between 1963 and 1970) considered social activism not only compatible with religion but also a fundamental aspect of Catholic life. Paniagua labeled the ACUS generation of the early 1960s "an intermediate generation" that joined the PDC and embraced reformist politics albeit with less intensity than his own generation. Paniagua asserted that after 1964, ACUS affiliates considered it "impossible to be Catholic or Christian without [assuming] a commitment to the social problematic."[65] Between 1965 and 1967, the "new ACUS" trained a generation of Catholic intellectuals who occupied a distinct political and ideological niche between the right-wing and Marxist student organizations at the university, particularly at the schools of medicine, architecture, and chemistry.[66] At that time, ACUS had a membership of roughly sixty well-rounded Catholic intellectuals who were cognizant of the theological reforms produced by the Second Vatican Council.[67] However, the 1967 JEC generation (i.e., the graduates of well-off Catholic high schools from San Salvador) who joined ACUS that same year did not fit well in the organization because most members of this cohort embraced radical left politics and were seriously planning the formation of insurgent groups.

University Reform and the Rise of the New Left

The emergence of the New Left in El Salvador had multiple foci and actors. It encompassed the entangled trajectories of student, teacher, and worker movements, literary groups, rock and folk bands, and political groups associated with the Catholic Church like Catholic Action and the PDC, as well as dissident Communist Party leaders. However, the university was by and large the main locus for the creation of the New Left insurgency. The multiple institutional, social, ideological, and political transformations generated by the university reform between 1963 and 1967 often motivated affiliates of Catholic Action to reconsider their roles in the changing university milieu and Salvadoran society. The belated university reform in El Salvador started in 1950, some thirty-two years after the 1918 reform at the University of Córdoba in Argentina, which inspired similar movements throughout Latin America. At that time, university students claimed the right to be part of the university government along with faculty. They also demanded university autonomy vis-à-vis the central government, which was sanctioned by the 1950 Constitution.[68] Nevertheless, a comprehensive academic and institutional reform of the university was only implemented until the 1960s. The university reform led by Rector Fabio Castillo, a professor of medicine and a former member of the Civic-Military Junta that ousted Lemus in 1960, aimed at "raising [the] scientific quality" of higher education to meet "the challenges that economic modernization posed [to the production of] knowledge." At the time of the reform, heated "social, political, economic, and cultural" debates on the country's future took place at the university campus in San Salvador. Numerous studies published during this period advocated "structural changes" aimed at improving the living conditions of peasants and urban workers.[69] The reform changed the university from an academic institution that served almost exclusively upper-middle-class students into a center of learning with a growing and socially diverse student body. The student population, which included students not only from San Salvador but also from cities and towns across the country, increased from three thousand in 1962 to roughly seventeen thousand by the early 1970s.[70] The reform also achieved major renovations in academic programs, teaching methods, research, administration, and infrastructure.[71] A salient feature of the reform was the creation of a two-year general studies program called Areas Comunes (General Studies) that incoming students were required to complete as a precondition for admission to a university department. The young Catholic Action students entering the university became leaders of a powerful student movement organized first in General Studies between 1967 and 1970; this was the Committee of Representatives of General Studies, better known as CRAC. It published a student newspaper called *CRAC the Onomatopoeic Voice of Rupture*.[72] In the aftermath of the university reform led by Castillo, successive authoritarian regimes increasingly challenged the university autonomy status. In the 1970s, military governments carried out several bloody occupations of the university campuses in San Salvador, Santa Ana, and San Miguel on the grounds that subversive elements sought to create a "state within the state" and to conduct war preparations against the government, taking advantage of university autonomy.

The General Studies program created by the university reform was "the nursery of the Salvadoran guerrillas," according to Rafael Velásquez, a former university student who joined the ERP in the early 1970s. Velásquez remembered that the founders of the insurgency were for the most part student activists in General Studies.[73] Students enrolled in General Studies elected classroom representatives who collectively formed CRAC. Through its practice of direct democracy, this organization mobilized thousands of General Studies students, who in fact constituted the majority of the student population at the university.[74] Among the affiliates of JEC, ACUS's sister organization, were students from elite Catholic high schools in San Salvador who later became top insurgent leaders; Rafael Arce Zablah, Joaquín Villalobos, Virginia Peña Mendoza, Ana Margarita Peña Mendoza, Felipe Peña Mendoza, Ana Sonia Medina, and Alejandro Solano initially were leaders of CRAC.[75]

The political and cultural gap between members of CRAC and students and faculty associated with the PCS (the "Old Left") grew steadily as the former began to exude greater defiance and express stronger antidogmatism. They plainly rejected attempts to "indoctrinate them using Soviet manuals," an effort purportedly conducted by Jorge Arias-Gómez, a lawyer-historian affiliated with the PCS, and other Communist intellectuals at the university.[76] Francisco Jovel, a former leader of CRAC who later became a top FMLN commander, summarized the collision between the PCS and the emerging New Left as follows:

> With all the events that came to bear on the debate, namely, the ANDES strike, Tlatelolco, "May 68" in France, the urban guerrillas in the Southern Cone, the [1969] war between El Salvador and Honduras, Vietnam, and the hippie movement, it was not an optimal environment to indoctrinate students when rebelliousness prevailed against docility.[77]

CRAC leaders viewed themselves as an integral part of the "Latin American Left" (that is, the Latin American New Left) allied with the Cuban Revolution in contraposition to the PCS, which they considered a dogmatic pro-Soviet organization. CRAC activists drew abundantly from dependency theory (a paradigm formulated by Latin American sociologists and economists that explicates the historical origins of Latin American underdevelopment, which they had studied with Argentinian sociologists teaching at the university in the time of the reform) to formulate alternative revolutionary theories to the PCS. They were closely linked to student movements in France, North Vietnam, Mexico, and Spain and actively supported the revolutionary left in Central America and the Southern Cone. CRAC leaders considered the experiences of the Tupamaros from Uruguay, the Left Revolutionary Movement from Chile, and the urban guerrillas led by Carlos Marighela in Brazil to articulate a new revolutionary strategy in El Salvador. They also supported the Fuerzas Armadas Rebeldes , a Guatemalan guerrilla movement, and the Sandinista National Liberation Front from Nicaragua; in fact, some CRAC activists joined the Guatemalan guerrillas in the late 1960s. They followed international events, particularly the mobilizations of students in France, Germany, and Mexico in 1968 and the Vietnam War, through multiple international publications that circulated clandestinely in El Salvador. Members of CRAC criticized the French Communist Party's negotiations with the French government in the aftermath of May 1968, which they viewed both as treason against the French unions and as an expression of the Soviet Union's policy of "peaceful coexistence" with the United States, which had grave consequences for revolutionary movements across the globe. They learned about the Tlatelolco massacre in Mexico City through the testimony of a Mexican professor of physics and mathematics who survived the killings and joined the University of El Salvador in 1968, only to be captured, disappeared,

Figure 2.1 "Vietnam Will Vanquish!" *Opinión Estudiantil*, Special Issue, November 1968, front page. Courtesy of Special Collections, University of El Salvador Library.

and assassinated by state agents in El Salvador the next year.[78] They were also highly informed about the Vietnam War and organized solidarity campaigns with North Vietnam and the National Liberation Front such as the "Solidarity Week with Vietnam" held at the university in November 1968 (figure 2.1).[79]

The emergence of CRAC was matched by a "cultural boom" at the university that featured the creation of literary groups, rock and folk bands, and theater groups, which incarnated the countercultural sensibilities of that period.[80] Important figures of the New Left (including some Catholic Action members) were in fact musicians, writers, and poets. Some were members of folk bands like La Banda del Sol (the Sun Band) and Mahucutah, and literary groups like

La Masacuata (a composite noun of Nahuat origin that means "deer-serpent"). While a careful discussion of the trajectories of these groups is beyond the scope of this chapter, it is fitting to note that like the Catholic Action intellectuals I discuss here, they were also active participants in the formation of the New Left.

The music scene in San Salvador and other cities was splendid at that time. Pop-rock bands formed in this period blended US, British, and Mexican rock with sounds and lyrics that revealed the imagination, concerns, and artistic creativity of Salvadoran youth. Los Supersónicos, Los Kiriaps, Los Vikings, Los Lovers, Los Juniors de Santa Tecla, Los Mustangs, Los Intocables, and (later) La Fiebre Amarilla, Hielo Ardiente, and many other bands emerged during that time. While these musicians were not organically linked to the New Left or the countercultural movements at the university, some of them in fact echoed in subtle (and sometimes poetic) ways the social concerns of the Salvadoran youth and occasionally joined forces with folk groups like La Banda del Sol. New Left activists and musicians like Carlos "Tamba" Aragón, the main composer and lead guitar player of La Banda del Sol, who later became a field commander in the FPL and died in combat at the start of the civil war, were also part of this musical scene.[81] In 1971, the year that the New Left insurgents declared war on the oligarchic-military regime, Estudio Doble V, a record label based in San Salvador, produced an anthology album called *Unidad*, which epitomized the sporadic cooperation between pop groups like La Fiebre Amarilla and Los Kiriaps, and the folkloric La Banda del Sol. Aragón authored the emblematic song of that album, called "El planeta de los cerdos" (Planet of the pigs). The song deprecated the tyrannical ethos, corruption, demagoguery, and virtual submission to the US government it attributed to the high-ranking military officers who ruled the country and anticipated an imminent uprising of Salvadoran youth inspired by "the light of love."[82] According to Manuel Sorto, a poet and actor who joined La Masacuata, this song "announced the . . . rebellion of Salvadoran youth. . . . [It] was in its epoch a club blow against the owners of maces and the military governments in Central America, an explosion of energy and clarity in its lyrics . . . the protest song . . . of that youth in transition from *hipismo* [hippiedom] to [becoming] guerrillas."[83]

In this period state agents often victimized with the same eagerness hippies, *mariguaneros* (marijuana smokers), men sporting long hair, and young women wearing jeans or short skirts, as well as poets, musicians, artists, and university activists whom they considered actual or potential insurgents. Clearly, from the perspective of the authoritarian regime, the countercultural movements, the student groups, and the New Left insurgency, as well as some rock and folk bands, incarnated the subversive spirit of the Global Sixties in El Salvador.

The intensification of state repression against the rising social movements and opposition parties in the late 1960s radicalized Catholic Action students.

The state crackdowns against the emerging teacher, worker, and student move-ments and opposition parties escalated significantly after 1967 as these forces seriously challenged the legitimacy of the PCN regime. At that time, the Party of Renovating Action (PAR), a center-left party formed by independent leftists and PCS intellectuals, and the PDC had significantly increased their electoral results despite the climate of intimidation against opposition voters generated by the official party and the counterinsurgent apparatus.

Abraham Rodríguez, a cofounder of ACUS in 1949 and the Christian Democrat presidential candidate in 1967, remembered that Alejandro Rivas Mira and Rafael Arce Zablah, two university students affiliated with the PDC and JEC, respectively, and later the founders of insurgent organizations, wit-nessed the brutal tactics that ORDEN paramilitaries and the National Guard deployed against peasant voters in San Miguel during those elections. According to Rodríguez, Rivas Mira and Arce Zablah "were in tears" when they told him about these occurrences during a meeting they held in the aftermath of the elections. Rivas Mira plainly told Rodríguez that the only alternative left to Social Christians was to take up arms against the dictatorship. Rodríguez com-mented: "If our [Social Christian] youth were thinking about that [starting an armed movement], just figure what the communists were thinking at this time."[84] In 1967, however, most communists were thinking about electoral politics, not armed struggle. Rivas Mira vanished from the university that year and traveled to East Germany and France. Little is known about his activities in Europe at that time, but apparently he, along with Venezuelan revolutionaries, participated in the 1968 insurgency in France.[85] In 1969, Rivas Mira returned to El Salvador to form an urban guerrilla cell known as El Grupo, a predecessor of the ERP.[86]

In 1970, CRAC organized a major student strike to protest an ongoing aca-demic crisis in General Studies. At that time, the program evidenced high levels of student failure and repetition, which created widespread frustration among students.[87] CRAC also orchestrated a "buffoon parade," a massive public protest that combined political critique and obscenity to ridicule the military govern-ment, the Catholic Church hierarchy, and even the country's beauty queen. This was probably the last public appearance of the former Catholic Action activists turned insurgents.

Between 1970 and 1972, leaders of CRAC founded several insurgent groups, which they called "politico-military organizations." A group led by Rafael Arce Zablah and Joaquín Villalobos created an armed organization they initially named Jaraguá, in reference to a resilient grass that grows in coastal areas in El Salvador and a peasant character in a novel by the Salvadoran writer Napoleón Rodríguez Ruiz who in Arce Zablah's view epitomized the purported rebelliousness of Salvadoran peasants. The Jaraguá group merged with survivors of El Grupo, the urban guerrilla cell founded by Alejandro

Rivas Mira, university activists without previous political affiliation, and former members of the Communist Youth to form the ERP in 1971.[88] Arce Zablah became the most influential intellectual of this cohort. Circa 1973 he penned *Golden Grain*, a Marxian analysis of the coffee economy in El Salvador that was widely studied by members of the New Left insurgency in the 1970s and 1980s.[89] Felipe Peña Mendoza and other militants led another group initially known as El Movimiento de Izquierda Revolucionaria (the Left Revolutionary Movement). In 1970 they joined Salvador Cayetano Carpio and other dissident communists, as well as students and faculty at the Instituto Obrero "José Celestino Castro," a high school that served workers and dwellers of shantytowns from San Salvador, to form a guerrilla organization. This organization remained anonymous until 1972, when it adopted the name FPL after it attacked the Argentinian embassy in San Salvador to repudiate the execution of political prisoners perpetrated by that country's military at the Admiral Marcos A. Zar naval airbase, near the city of Trelew, Chubut, earlier that year.[90]

The New Left's "Just War" (1972–1975)

The leaders of the New Left personified the blending of the Catholic anticapitalist thought that emerged in El Salvador at the time of the Second Vatican Council, the intellectual production and revolutionary experiences of the Latin American Left, and various Marxist-Leninist traditions, particularly Vietnamese Marxism in the case of the FPL and Maoism in that of the ERP. They were also cognizant of European New Left thought as formulated by Herbert Marcuse, Nicos Poulantzas, Louis Althusser, Daniel Cohn-Bendit, and others.

The social Catholic thought incarnated by ERP and FPL leaders formerly affiliated with Catholic Action (and CRAC) enabled the formation of long-lasting alliances between the New Left and peasant movements in Chalatenango, San Vicente, and Morazán, which constituted the backbone of the Salvadoran insurgency in the 1970s and throughout the civil war. However, this was not the typical case of the "unblocking of the peasants' consciousness" promoted by urban intellectuals; arguably, peasant leaders in those areas were already "politicized" by the time insurgents like Peña Mendoza and Arce Zablah first visited those regions in the early 1970s.[91] It was, instead, a dialogical process between urban insurgents, peasant leaders, and progressive Catholic priests that constituted a frontal challenge to the conservative Catholicism and the counterinsurgency apparatus that prevailed in the countryside in the 1970s.

The New Left insurgency sought to reinterpret the relation between religion and politics by bringing to the fore the Christian doctrine of the just war,

particularly in the case of the FPL. The Catholic background of the organization's top leadership informed its perspective on this matter. The FPL publicly
acknowledged the crucial role that Christians played in revolutionary politics
and envisioned the formation of an alliance among priests, Catholic communities, and the insurgency.[92] In 1975, it dedicated an entire edition of *Estrella Roja*
(Red Star), the organization's theoretical publication, to explicate its Marxist-
Leninist politics and ideology to "progressive priests."[93] *Estrella Roja 2* as the
document is known, stressed the legitimacy of revolutionary violence to combat
the oligarchic-military regime and to create a humane and just society, borrow-
ing from the Christian doctrine of the just war. It cited verbatim Pope Paul VI's
encyclical *Populorum Progressium* to make this point:[94]

> It is possible also that some might think that our revolutionary disci-
> pline (and even our revolutionary practice) does not duly consider the
> human character of the popular struggle. We believe that such a view
> would not match reality. All our activity aims at radically changing the
> situation of injustice, exploitation, and lack of humanism endured by
> the majority of workers. We are aware that such injustice can only be
> definitively liquidated through the deepening and intensification of the
> class struggle of the exploited to liberate themselves from the oppres-
> sion and exploitation of the ruling classes. And the revolutionary vi-
> olence of the masses is the crucial factor that will break the chain of
> oppression, vis-à-vis the stubborn resistance of the ruthless exploiters
> who are not willing to abandon their privileges and domination, neither
> through reasoning nor through appeals to their goodness, "charity," hu-
> manism, and religious beliefs. In this sense, we remember the acknowl-
> edgment of this fact contained in Pope Paul VI's encyclical *Populorum
> Progressium* when it says that revolutionary violence is justified "in case
> of evident and prolonged tyranny, which gravely threatens the funda-
> mental right of the person and dangerously damages the common good
> of the country."[95]

While the FPL has been often represented as the quintessential Marxist-Leninist
organization of the Salvadoran revolution, it also featured an influential Catholic
tradition embodied by former Catholic Action students like Felipe Peña
Mendoza, dissident Jesuits, diocesan priests, nuns, Catholic peasant leaders, and
laypeople. A similar argument can be made in the case of the ERP if we consider
the Catholic background of some of its most prominent leaders, among them
Rafael Arce Zablah, Joaquín Villalobos, Ana Sonia Medina, and others, as well as
the multiple alliances this organization forged with Catholic priests, nuns, and
Catholic communities in both rural and urban areas.[96]

Former affiliates of Catholic Action played fundamental roles in the creation of the New Left insurgency in El Salvador. In contrast to scholarship that has emphasized the participation of dissident communists and Christian Democrats in this process, the evidence presented here suggests that the ACUS-JEC cohort that came of age between 1967 and 1972 constituted a key component in the rising New Left. Multiple ideological, political, and cultural trends in the 1960s shaped this rupture generation, chiefly the Catholic anticapitalist thought that emerged in that period, dependency theory, and the revolutionary politics of the Latin American Left. In many ways, this group crystallized the rich eclecticism of the Global Sixties into innovative revolutionary theories and strategies that enabled the creation of one of the most potent insurgencies in twentieth-century Latin America, namely, the FMLN.

ACUS-JEC affiliates turned revolutionaries ultimately succeeded at what most urban radicals in Latin America in this period failed to do: create strategic alliances with peasant movements, which made up the core of the insurgency during the 1970s and throughout the civil war. As the reformist promise of the Alliance for Progress waned and the counterinsurgent state increasingly persecuted opposition parties like the PDC and PAR, the rising social movements, and dissident youth—especially after the 1967 presidential election—ACUS and JEC affiliates became leaders of CRAC, the radical student movement that emerged at General Studies at the time of the university reform. CRAC leaders formed clandestine revolutionary groups like Jaraguá and the Left Revolutionary Movement, which became the predecessors of the ERP and FPL, respectively. Drawing on Catholic social thought and the Christian doctrine of the just war, leaders of the New Left insurgency built long-lasting alliances with peasant communities in Morazán, Chalatenango, San Vicente, and other rural areas, and in doing so transformed this movement into a formidable political and military force that posed an unparalleled threat to oligarchic-military rule and US hegemony in El Salvador.

Based on his examination of the 1968 student mobilizations in Mexico, Brazil, and Uruguay, Jeffrey Gould posits that authoritarian governments in those countries repressed student and working-class movements before sectors of the New Left formed insurgencies in response to the escalating state terror.[97] He criticizes ex post facto explanations of the origins of the New Left insurgencies that omit a close examination of the trajectories of these movements and instead project "findings and analysis from other parts of the World onto Latin America," wrongly blaming the New Left for provoking state terror and undermining the Old Left's democratizing potential. Gould deems that state repression debilitated both the New Left and the Old Left and radicalized popular politics in Mexico and the Southern Cone after 1968.[98] My analysis of the radicalization of Catholic Action students in El Salvador reinforces Gould's perspective on this issue. Systematic state crackdowns against opposition parties, social movements, and dissident intellectuals that began in the early 1960s prompted the rise and rapid expansion of the New Left insurgencies, not vice versa.[99] Counterinsurgency ultimately created an internal enemy through its relentless persecution of the democratic movements formed in El Salvador in the 1960s and 1970s: its actions motivated dissidents of the PDC and PCS, leaders of social movements, and Catholic Action intellectuals, as well as youth affiliated with countercultural groups, to join or support the insurgency.[100]

The poet Roque Dalton relinquished his affiliation with the PCS circa 1967 due to the party's ambiguous and ambivalent stance on armed struggle and electoral politics. He joined the ERP in 1973, only to be murdered in May 1975 by a militaristic faction that commanded this group at the time. Like many other New Left intellectuals in El Salvador, Dalton objected to the PCS critique of the guerrilla movements at the meeting of the Organization of Latin American Solidarity held in Havana in August 1967 and to the party's rejection of Che Guevara's foco principles, published the same year. Dalton's resignation from the PCS, his endorsement of armed revolution in Latin America, and his (tragic) integration into the ERP epitomize the schism between the Old Left and the New Left in El Salvador.

While the ERP and the FPL developed different ideologies and politics, both produced virulent critiques of PCS reformism, particularly of its continued participation in electoral politics, which they deemed a legitimatization of the electoral frauds and repression conducted by the PCN governments in the 1970s. They also wrote theoretical works to disprove the PCS analyses of the Salvadoran economy, society, and politics. The cultural, political, and ideological gap between PCS and New Left intellectuals became a dominant characteristic of the Salvadoran left during the 1970s and 1980s.

The vital contributions of social Catholicism to the formation of the New Left ethos in El Salvador deserve serious reflection, as it conferred on this movement a distinct ideological endurance and potent organizational capabilities during the intensification of state terror in the 1970s and the civil war that devastated the country between 1980 and 1992.

3

Peasant Intellectuals in Chalatenango

In the early 1970s, Justo Mejía, a peasant leader in Chalatenango, a northern department in El Salvador, taught night classes to fellow residents from La Ceiba, a hamlet near the town of Las Vueltas.[1] He worked as a volunteer instructor at the *escuelas radiofónicas* (radio schools), a Catholic program that offered primary education to adult peasants.[2] There were approximately four hundred radio schools located in sixty-two parishes in the dioceses of San Salvador and San Vicente in the 1960s and early 1970s.[3] Peasant leaders like Mejía left an enduring cultural legacy among rural communities in the central region of the country. Between 1964 and 1970, the volunteer instructors of the radio schools taught night classes focused on primary subjects like reading and mathematics to roughly five thousand adult peasants per year.[4]

Peasants in Chalatenango also joined a cooperative movement sponsored by the Catholic Church that had a significant impact among rural communities in the area. In the 1970s, hundreds of peasant leaders from this region attended Chacalcoyo, a cooperative training center near La Nueva Concepción, which was part of a network of Catholic schools known as the "peasant universities." Nearly fifteen thousand peasant leaders studied at these institutions between 1967 and 1977.[5]

Educators and organizers like Justo Mejía founded one of the most powerful peasant movements in modern Latin American history. During the 1970s, it posed an unparalleled challenge to the oligarchic-military regime in El Salvador, carrying out multiple land occupations; strikes in large coffee, sugar cane, and cotton plantations; and political activism in both urban and rural areas. State forces conducted a relentless persecution of peasant leaders and eventually full-scale military operations against peasant communities in Aguilares, San Vicente, Chalatenango, and other rural areas. The peasant activists who survived the systematic repression in the 1970s formed the backbone of the insurgency during El Salvador's civil war, becoming combatants and officers in the FMLN's guerrilla army.

This chapter examines the cultural dimension of peasant politics. It argues that the leaders of rural cooperatives and the volunteer instructors of the radio schools (known as the "auxiliary professors") provided the foundation for the Union of Rural Workers (UTC), a potent peasant movement in Chalatenango. Scholars have generally considered university activists, teachers, and diocesan priests the catalysts of peasant mobilization in Chalatenango and in other rural areas of the country, partly reproducing urban-centered notions of popular politics.[6] However, the contribution of peasant leaders to this process has been greatly underestimated in the academic literature. During the 1970s, the peasant leaders became peasant intellectuals due to their multiple engagements in educational, leadership, and organizational activities—for example, as popular teachers and members of rural cooperatives. They led the mobilization of peasant communities across El Salvador through the articulation of a counter-hegemonic discourse and the formation of long-lasting alliances with Catholic priests, university students, and teachers.[7] Peasant leaders can be considered intellectuals in that they did the work of intellectuals: analyzing the situation of peasant communities, voicing their grievances and claims, and organizing an unprecedented peasant movement, all of which altered national politics in the 1970s.[8] The peasant intellectuals articulated a new vision of the relationship between the spiritual and the political, which crucially informed the ideology of the emergent peasant movement. In other words, the rapid transformation of the religious and political ideology of traditionally conservative peasant leaders in Chalatenango at the time of epochal changes in the 1960s and 1970s, which included major theological reforms in the Catholic Church, the rise of social and political movements, and exchanges between university activists, teachers, and peasant communities, enabled the creation of the UTC.

The formation of the UTC in Chalatenango was the peasants' response to a crisis that threatened their own survival. It addressed the extreme pauperization of rural communities generated by the oligarchic agro-export economy, which relied on a massive labor force made up of *jornaleros* (landless rural workers), *colonos* (workers living at large farms and haciendas), and campesinos mini-fundistas (small landholders or peasants) from Chalatenango and other regions.[9]

The profound socioeconomic and political crisis that followed the 1969 war between El Salvador and Honduras set the conditions for the radicalization of peasant politics in the country. The brief conflict between the two countries, known as the "Soccer War," had devastating effects on rural communities living on both sides of the border. The xenophobic attacks against Salvadorans living in Honduras carried out by La Mancha Brava, a paramilitary group, and civilians abetted or tolerated by the Honduran government preceded the Salvadoran army's invasion of that country in July of that year. Unsurprisingly, the military governments in both countries sponsored chauvinistic campaigns that stirred sheer hatred between the two nations to mobilize public support for their respective war efforts. In El Salvador, the media coverage of the massive displacement and dispossession of Salvadoran residents in Honduras matched the official discourse on the growing conflict. The government of President Fidel Sánchez Hernández organized a jingoistic campaign in support of the returning refugees it labeled the "Crusade for the National Dignity" and a war mobilization it called the "War of Legitimate Defense." Both campaigns gained widespread support in the country. Even the clandestine Communist Party of El Salvador declared its willingness to "paralyze class struggle" to foster national unity at the time of war.[10]

The Salvadoran military sacked Honduran towns and villages and forced Salvadoran peasant communities living near the border with Honduras to regularly feed the troops. "The sacking of the border towns in Honduras was brutal, bestial. They [El Salvador's armed forces] plundered communities in La Virtud, Valladolid, Guarita . . . they only left the houses' walls. Houses made up of good-quality clay bricks were dismantled. The army and the National Guard made sure that the plunder reached the military chiefs," said Facundo Guardado, a former resident of Arcatao, a Salvadoran town near the border with Honduras. The Salvadoran military also equipped paramilitaries in Chalatenango with weapons and gave them leeway to coerce their neighbors into becoming unwilling army collaborators.[11] The living conditions of peasant communities in Chalatenango deteriorated further due to the massive flow of Salvadoran refugees created by the war. Many refugees who were originally from Chalatenango and Cabañas had lost all their belongings in Honduras and returned to their communities empty-handed. Their arrival had a significant impact on the prices of arable land in those regions.[12] Overall, the conflict had a devastating effect on the Salvadoran economy. It dismantled the Central American Common Market, the centerpiece of the regional economy, produced tens of thousands of Salvadoran refugees, and worsened the country's sociopolitical crisis.[13]

Peasant communities in Chalatenango located at the edge of the country's agro-export economy were severely affected by this crisis. Small landholders in Chalatenango called minifundistas (peasant farmers who cultivated "less than ten hectares of land") could hardly make a living in the early 1970s.[14] In 1971, there were 18,989 farms of this type in Chalatenango, which accounted for "a quarter of the cultivated land in the department."[15] About 8,000 of those farms had less than one hectare (2.47 acres) of land.[16] Families cultivating "a land area between ten and 50 hectares" made up "the peasantry proper" in Chalatenango.[17] In 1971, there were 1,951 farms of this type, "covering a third of the cultivated land" in the area.[18] Minifundistas often cultivated barren soils, which required substantial investment to generate a surplus, which they were unable to make, since speculators who commercialized their limited production took most of the profit.[19] Small landholdings in Chalatenango were legacies of indigo production in the eighteenth and nineteenth centuries. Peasants and "small-scale farmers" steadily increased indigo production in Chalatenango between 1800 and 1852. In 1883, they accounted for 25 percent of the national production. Indian and Ladino (mestizo or Hispanicized) peasant communities in Tejutla and Chalatenango unsuccessfully resisted the privatization of community lands between 1886 and 1899, which resulted in the further fragmentation of the landholdings in the department.[20] Despite the decline of indigo production in El Salvador in the late nineteenth century, small landholders still cultivated and processed indigo in hamlets near La Nueva Trinidad and Arcatao in 1975.[21]

Minifundistas often worked at coffee farms and sugar and cotton haciendas to supplement their subsistence economy.[22] They usually faced harsh and perilous labor conditions at the plantations. They slept in the fields exposed to insect bites, rodents, snakes, and cold temperatures. They carried heavy sacks of coffee and cotton and ate meager rations of beans, rice, and tortillas.[23] Young women from Chalatenango were often victims of sexual violence during their stays at coffee farms.[24] This population was part of a vast reserve army of seasonal workers (466,000 people in 1971) made up of small landholders and landless workers, which kept salaries very low in the rural sector. More than half of these laborers (273,000 persons) could not find employment in "farms over ten hectares."[25] In other words, in the early 1970s, less than half of the reserve army of rural workers (roughly 193,000 persons) could find work at coffee, sugar, and cotton plantations.

Relations between the Church, the state, and the landed elites further deteriorated in the 1970s due to the latter's opposition to agrarian reform. These tensions centrally informed the radicalization of peasant politics during that decade. The conflict between the government of President Fidel Sánchez Hernández (1967–1972) and the Church intensified during the First National Congress on the Agrarian Reform, held in January 1970 at the National Assembly. The Church delegation to the Congress made up of Bishop Ricardo Urioste, José Romeo Maeda, Juan Ramón Vega, and José Inocencio Alas, three diocesan priests involved in the Church's social programs, and Ricardo Alvarado, a technical adviser, argued that the extremely unequal land distribution in the country had dismal impacts on rural and urban communities. The Church delegates estimated that 1,013 estates larger than 200 hectares occupied 38 percent of the arable land in the country (some 2 million hectares), while 175,615 small estates or *minifundios* of less than 3 hectares occupied only 11 percent of that land. *Minifundios* were typically located in inaccessible areas with depleted soils as in the case of peasant communities in northeast Chalatenango. Drawing on the theology of the Second Vatican Council and on Pope Paul VI's encyclical *Populorum Progressio*, they bluntly proposed the "massive expropriation" of large rural estates and the redistribution of land to peasants to correct this imbalance.[26] In an apparent response to the Church position at the Congress, state agents abducted and tortured Alas. Hundreds of peasants from Suchitoto, where he had worked for several years, demanded his release outside the National Assembly. A few days later, his captors released Alas. They left him drugged, blindfolded, and naked at the edge of a precipice near the town of Jayaque, La Libertad. Townspeople from Jayaque helped Alas during this ordeal.[27] This incident marked the start of the systematic state persecution against progressive Catholics in the 1970s.

The flooding of nearly 135 square kilometers of highly productive land as a result of the building of El Cerrón Grande, a hydroelectric dam in the Lempa River, created additional burdens for peasant communities living in the lowlands in Chalatenango. The construction of the dam also generated some fifteen thousand additional landless peasants in the area in the early 1970s.[28] The peasant mobilization against the construction of El Cerrón Grande preceded the foundation of the UTC. The government of President Arturo A. Molina (1972–1977) compensated the big landowners in the area for the lost land, but it threatened to forcibly evacuate peasants living and working in the area.[29] Peasant communities in Chalatenango and Suchitoto affected by the project formed a movement called "No to Cerrón Grande," which conducted demonstrations in San Salvador. Diocesan priests working in Chalatenango and Suchitoto, as well as teachers, university students, workers, and members of the opposition parties, also joined this movement.[30]

The meager wages they earned and the deplorable working conditions they endured as seasonal laborers at coffee, sugar, and cotton plantations made the precarious subsistence economy of rural communities in Chalatenango even more vulnerable. The founding of the UTC constituted an effort to improve the living and working conditions of small landholders and rural workers. It was also a response to authoritarian rule and the growing repression against peasant communities in San Vicente, Chalatenango, and other regions of the country. The demands of the UTC centered on access to land and credit for subsistence peasant farmers and the improvement of wages and labor conditions at coffee, sugar, and cotton plantations. The organization also called for the end of repression through the constant mobilization of peasant activists in the cities and the countryside.

"Agronomist of Liberation": The Emergence of the Cooperative Movement in Chalatenango

The rise of the peasant intellectuals in Chalatenango was closely linked to the formation of agricultural cooperatives sponsored by the Church. José Romero Maeda, a diocesan priest, played a leading role in this process. In the 1960s,

Maeda promoted the creation of twelve rural cooperatives in Chalatenango, which had roughly twenty-five hundred members, many of whom joined the UTC in 1974.[31] During that decade, Maeda regularly met with peasant leaders to discuss the principles of the cooperative movement. Since 1958, he had formed close bonds with small landholders from San Antonio Los Ranchos, Cancasque, Las Vueltas, Arcatao, and other towns in northeastern Chalatenango.[32] "I told them that the cooperatives were not only a means to resolve economic problems but also a means to achieve human development," said Maeda. He also advised peasants to "elect their best leaders [to manage the cooperatives] because they were risking their own money."[33] The peasant cooperatives in Chalatenango were part of a national cooperative movement sponsored by the Church called the Foundation for the Promotion of Cooperatives (FUNPROCOOP). It offered technical and humanistic education, low-interest credit, and advice on market strategies to peasant cooperatives in Chalatenango and other regions in the country. Peasant cooperatives were community associations constituted by small landholders, which fostered local socioeconomic development. Cooperatives elected leaders through direct democracy and offered access to cooperative training to male and, to a lesser extent, female members in an effort to improve the farming techniques, administrative skills, and commercial strategies implemented by small landholders.

In the late 1960s, peasant communities in Chalatenango joined the rural cooperatives to improve their fragile household economies, which depended on a combination of subsistence farming and seasonal work at coffee plantations. The case of the rural communities that inhabited La Ceiba, a hamlet near the town of Las Vueltas, at that time epitomizes this situation. La Ceiba is located in a mountainous area in northeastern Chalatenango, which remained at the fringes of the country's agro-export economy due to the poor quality of its soils. Three hundred closely related families lived at La Ceiba in the 1960s and 1970s. They bore combinations of six distinct family names: Mejía, Zamora, García, Delgado, Cartagena, and Palma. Small landholders from La Ceiba farmed sorghum, beans, and a local variety of maize that they called "Indian corn." Artisans from the hamlet specialized in the making of fishing nets, and a few families planted achiote, a spice, which they traded in local and regional markets. Some townspeople from La Ceiba were also seasonal workers at coffee plantations near Quezaltepeque and Santa Tecla.[34] In 1970, Justo Mejía led a group of small landholders from the hamlet to form La Esperanza, a rural cooperative that became highly successful in promoting community development. Approximately thirty, mostly male, adult peasants made up the cooperative at La Ceiba. They elected an executive committee (called La Directiva) and met regularly to discuss the cooperative business. They cultivated corn and beans in small plots they generally owned and were eligible to obtain low-interest credit from the

cooperative. They collectively marketed their agricultural production, bypass-
ing the traditional speculators who bought the peasants' crops cheaply and sold
them dearly in regional markets. The meetings of the cooperative were community events during which male and female inhabitants of La Ceiba discussed a
variety of issues, including from the cooperative's business, local development
projects, and politics.[35]

Members of rural cooperatives from Chalatenango and Santa Ana selected
peasant leaders to attend Chacalcoyo, a cooperative training center located near
La Nueva Concepción, Chalatenango. At the school they received a thorough
technical and humanistic education, taking a variety of courses on agricultural
techniques, cooperative administration, accounting, "the National Reality"
(studies on El Salvador's economy, society, and politics), the agrarian economy,
and Catholic social doctrine.[36] Ismael Merlos, one of the first peasant leaders to
attend Chacalcoyo, remembered his time at the school as follows: "We analyzed
the national reality [particularly] education, health care, nutrition, and [rural]
labor. This enabled me to become aware of the political reality of the country
and to have certain participation in the processes of organization and struggle."[37]

Chacalcoyo was part of a national network of Catholic schools that specialized in the formation of peasant leaders. The "centers for the promotion of peasants" or "peasant universities," as the peasant training centers were often called
(El Castaño, La Providencia, the Santa Ana Project, Los Naranjos, Chacalcoyo,
the Monsignor Luis Chávez y González School, San Lucas, the Guadalupe
Center, and the Guacotecti Center), trained thousands of peasant leaders between 1967 and 1977.[38] In the 1970s, Chacalcoyo trained approximately 150
students per year.[39]

The training at Chacalcoyo challenged traditional notions about society, religion, and politics prevalent among peasant communities in the early 1970s.
Mostly male peasant leaders attended the school while other members of the
rural cooperatives cared for their cornfields and domestic needs while they
were in training. The school provided peasant leaders with room and board for
the duration of their studies. Peasant leaders remembered that the training at
Chacalcoyo changed their "mentality," that is, it helped them to develop analytical skills to fully engage in social and political activism.[40]

The peasant leaders also created lasting political networks at Chacalcoyo.
Merlos recalled that at the school he met peasant leaders from Chalatenango
and other areas of the country, some of whom were killed by state agents in
the 1970s. He remembered fondly Antonio Morales and Antonio Zamora
from Upatoro, Facundo Guardado from Arcatao, and Manuel Serrano from
San José Las Flores, all of whom played central roles in the formation of the
UTC in Chalatenango.[41] Apolinario "Polín" Serrano, a leader of the Christian
Federation of Salvadoran Peasants (FECCAS), a peasant movement sponsored

by the Catholic Church, and Víctor Rivera, a leader of the Association of Agrarian Workers and Peasants of El Salvador (ATACES), lectured trainees on the recent history of the peasant movements in El Salvador. "Polín" Serrano in particular made a lasting impression on Merlos, who recalled: "Polín made an exceptional presentation. He had a very strong persuasive power. His words were simple. He was illiterate but his intellectual level was very good. Of course, I became friends with them [Serrano, Rivera, and other peasant leaders]. That contributed to the integration of the cooperative and the peasant movements."[42]

Peasant leaders and university intellectuals also created enduring political alliances at the school. Jesuits from the Central American University (UCA) taught peasant leaders an advanced course on the origins of the country's agrarian economy. This course, according to Merlos, helped him and other peasant leaders to develop a structural and historical interpretation of agrarian capitalism in El Salvador. It also allowed the integration of a cohort of cooperative and peasant leaders from Santa Ana, Chalatenango, and other regions, who became major political figures in the 1970s.[43] Facundo Guardado, a former peasant leader, recalled meeting at Chacalcoyo Antonio Cardenal and Alberto Enríquez, two Jesuit students who conducted workshops with peasant leaders in Aguilares. At that time Cardenal and Enríquez were also organizing a political movement they called simply El Movimiento (the Movement), which involved dozens of UCA students, seminarians, and upper-middle-class high school students. In 1975, the peasant leaders and the Jesuit students, along with leaders of ANDES–the main teachers' union—and student activists at the University of El Salvador, founded the Popular Revolutionary Bloc (BPR), the largest coalition of social movements in the 1970s.[44]

The peasant cooperatives in Chalatenango achieved a considerable level of economic self-sufficiency as a result of the cultivation of hybrid corn introduced by FUNPROCOOP in the late 1960s. Like many peasant leaders from Chalatenango, Justo Mejía and other members of La Esperanza learned to cultivate hybrid corn at Chacalcoyo.[45] Jesús Merino Argueta, a Salvadoran engineer, taught peasants techniques for the farming of "H1" and "H3," two hybrid corn species that he had recently developed. Merino played a major role in boosting the productivity of subsistence farming among rural cooperatives in Chalatenango. He suggested peasants from Las Vueltas plant the hybrid corn in *baldíos* (uncultivated areas) near the town. After his visit to Chalatenango in 1969, John Pino, an adviser to the Rockefeller Foundation, was so impressed with the apparent success of the farming of hybrid corn in the region that he recommended the foundation offer financial support to Chacalcoyo.[46]

In the 1970s, Catholic priests viewed the emerging cooperative movement in Chalatenango as the most effective model to overcome rural poverty in the country. At the closing ceremony of the first training course offered at Chacalcoyo, Martín Barahona, a diocesan priest and the director of the school at that time, asserted: "There will never be a deep change in the country's structures until we devote ourselves to educate in all aspects our men from the countryside."[47] In 1971, Nicolás González, a diocesan priest, hailed the success of the peasant cooperatives at La Ceiba and other hamlets near Las Vueltas. González commented that despite the remoteness of these hamlets and the poor quality of the soils in the area, the peasant cooperatives substantially improved the productivity of subsistence farming and raised the levels of community organization. He was elated to witness the success of hybrid corn cultivation at La Ceiba, which enabled the local community to reach an unprecedented level of economic self-sufficiency. González wrote: "It is pleasant to walk on the road looking at the cornfields [at La Ceiba], how they are moved by the wind, symbolizing the joy of peasants." He further asserted that members of the cooperative were much better off than workers at haciendas, where "systems of exploitation and barbarism" prevailed.[48] The cooperatives were "a true and complete solution" for small landholders and the basis for what he called "true Christianity," namely, a community way of life based on Christian values of compassion and solidarity. The Church had shown "that peasants, helped with sincerity, without political ends, become the agronomists of their liberation."[49]

"Tiniest Fireflies in the Darkness": The Radio Schools and the Auxiliary Professors

In the 1960s, the Catholic Church was keenly aware of the potential of mass media as a tool of popular education. The Second Vatican Council emphasized the centrality of high-quality media programming, particularly television and radio broadcasts, to reinforce Catholic values in modern societies.[50] Speaking in Bogotá in 1968 to a gathering of a half million peasants organized by the Colombian radio schools, Pope Paul VI stated that the radio schools greatly enhanced the living conditions of rural communities in Latin America. Members of the Salvadoran radio schools attended this event.[51]

In 1961, Archbishop Chávez y González sponsored the foundation of the radio schools in an effort to curb the high rates of rural illiteracy in El Salvador. The program was modeled after the radio schools in Colombia.[52] However, in contrast with the Colombian radio schools' emphasis on the formation of family study groups, the Salvadoran radio schools privileged the creation of local study groups called *núcleos radiofónicos* (radio nuclei), in hamlets, villages, haciendas, and towns in the central region of the country. Literate peasant leaders known as the "auxiliary professors" led the local study groups (figure 3.1).[53]

Promoción Humana a Través de Escuelas Radiofónicas

Grupo de Radioalumnos de la Escuela Radiofónica No. 15 del Cantón Mirandilla, jurisdicción de Suchitoto, con su Profesor Auxiliar Ricardo Acosta Rivera (2o. de izquierda a derecha).

Figure 3.1 Group of "radio students" of Radio School No. 15 at Mirandilla, a hamlet near Suchitoto. Second from left to right is the auxiliary professor Ricardo Acosta Rivera. *Orientación*, September 29, 1968, p. 4. Courtesy of the Historical Archive of the Archdiocese of San Salvador.

The radio schools offered marginalized rural communities access to primary education and technical and scientific knowledge. In the 1960s, the majority of the population in El Salvador (61 percent, or roughly 1,960,000 people) lived and worked in the countryside. Peasants generally did not have access to primary health care, lived in thatched houses, and endured high levels of malnutrition.[54] In 1961, 68.1 percent of the rural population more than ten years of age was outside of the school system, and at least 60 percent of the adult rural population was illiterate. In some hamlets, children under fourteen years of age attended primary school; however, neither adult education programs nor TV broadcasts were available in rural areas. Thus the radio schools became the most practical medium to promote adult education in the countryside.[55]

Some wealthy individuals and the government of President Julio Rivera supported the radio schools in the early 1960s. Ricardo Quiñonez, a benefactor of the Catholic radio station, YSAX, La Vox Panamericana (the Pan American Voice), served as the president of the board of directors of the radio schools from 1961 until his death in 1968.[56] The Ministry of Education granted official validation to the program. It administered a yearly test to *radio-alumnos* (radio students) who regularly attended the schools' study groups and issued diplomas to those who passed it. Each year an average of five thousand radio students successfully completed the courses and moved on to the next educational level offered by the program. In 1968, for instance, the Ministry of Education proctored final exams to radio students in nearly twenty towns and cities in the central region of El Salvador.[57]

The functioning of the radio schools encompassed carefully planned and supervised educational processes. The courses were structured in three cycles, each one corresponding to two grades of primary school. Specialized teachers based in San Salvador taught daily radio lessons on a variety of subjects, including mathematics, history, civic education, hygiene, household management, agricultural techniques, cooperative training, and Catholic doctrine. The program administrators also collected statistical data on the auxiliary professors, the registered students, the performance of each local study group, and the community activities promoted by radio schools. The radio schools produced textbooks, provided blackboards, and sold portable radios to auxiliary professors at subsidized prices. The Church imported a brand of portable radios called Peikard. In 1970, it bought five hundred radios and five thousand blackboards with the financial support of Dutch foundations.[58]

In theory, diocesan priests working in towns and hamlets were appointed "directors" of the radio schools, but in practice the auxiliary professors managed the daily activities of the program.[59] The auxiliary professors taught daily lessons to the radio students following the daily broadcasts of the radio schools. They also registered students, checked attendance, taught classes, graded the students' homework, administered tests, and gathered the statistical data required by the program.[60] In 1967, there were 355 auxiliary professors in the country.[61]

The radio schools had a significant impact among peasant communities in Chalatenango. In 1967, there were 981 radio students and 56 auxiliary professors in the department.[62] Justo Mejía organized a radio school at La Ceiba circa 1970; he had purchased "a small radio and copied on the blackboard" the radio schools' daily broadcasts.[63] Each year approximately forty men and women attended the daily lessons taught by Mejía, with some radio students attending his classes for several years. Mejía showed a remarkable charisma and patience in teaching illiterate students how to read and write.[64] Guadalupe Mejía, a former community leader from La Ceiba and Justo's widow, commented about her husband's role as a popular teacher:

> Learning how to read and write [as an adult] is very difficult when one doesn't have the skills for that. When one is illiterate one is simpleminded. It is easy for people to deceive you. That is why he [Justo Mejía] taught many people how to read and write. Since he was a young man he was willing to teach whoever needed it. It was his occupation Monday to Friday. He did that for several years. He was a popular teacher [*un maestro popular*]. There were no other teachers in the hamlet.[65]

The radio schools constituted a large social network in the central region of El Salvador. Radio students and diocesan priests organized public events to discuss the evolution of the program with Archbishop Chávez y González and other members of the Catholic hierarchy who regularly visited the radio schools on weekends. In June 1968, five hundred radio students led by Efraín López, a diocesan priest, met the archbishop in San Pedro Perulapán. That same month, two hundred radio students led by Salvador Interiano, a diocesan priest, met the archbishop in Candelaria Cuscatlán.[66]

The radio schools were also a community-building initiative. Men and women who attended the schools' study groups after working in the fields or at home for eight to ten hours were not interested only in obtaining a basic education but mostly in envisioning practical solutions to a variety of community issues. "Perhaps we learned just a little bit at the radio school but we talked a lot about many [community] issues," commented Hilda Mejía, a former resident of La Ceiba who attended the radio school led by Justo Mejía (who was her uncle) for several years.[67] The radio students and auxiliary professors organized reforestation campaigns, planted community gardens, and repaired roads.[68] In 1974, radio students from La Ceiba also discussed the creation of a new peasant organization, the Union of Rural Workers, after attending the daily radio lessons taught by Mejía.[69]

It is difficult to assess the overall cultural impact of the radio schools and the cooperatives sponsored by the Catholic Church in the 1960s and 1970s. However, testimonies from peasants published in the Catholic media suggest that the cooperative training, the radio education, and the cultivation of hybrid corn were key factors in raising the productivity of subsistence farming in Suchitoto and Chalatenango.[70] In the early 1970s, most rural cooperatives in northeastern Chalatenango achieved financial stability. Small landholders from Chalatenango affiliated with the Catholic cooperatives were able to create substantial reserves of beans, corn, and other grains at that time.[71] But, arguably, the most salient legacies of the rural cooperatives and the radio schools were the formation of a remarkable group of peasant intellectuals, the auxiliary professors and the cooperative leaders, and the creation of social networks that enabled the foundation of the UTC in November 1974.

Peasant Mobilization and Counterinsurgency

The founding of the UTC was the result of a process of biblical and political reflections and mobilizations that involved many peasant leaders and communities between 1972 and 1974. Justo Mejía, Gumercinda "Chinda" Zamora, José Santos Martínez, Facundo Guardado, and other peasant leaders organized dozens of meetings with members of rural cooperatives, radio students, *celebradores de la palabra* (lay preachers), and peasant communities across the region. They also conducted political exchanges with peasant leaders from San Vicente and other areas of the country.

In 1972, Mejía, Zamora, and other peasant leaders from Las Vueltas who had actively supported the PDC in the presidential election held in March of that same year met secretly to discuss the creation of a new peasant political organization. The peasant leaders who joined this process became increasingly frustrated with electoral politics after high-ranking military and the PCN, the official party, rigged the 1972 presidential elections. The Christian Democrat leader José Napoleón Duarte, the opposition candidate, won the election by a substantial margin, but military officers and state officials altered the electoral results in favor of the PCN candidate, Colonel Arturo Armando Molina. Francisco Mena Sandoval, a former captain in the Salvadoran army, claimed in 2008 that in 1972 his superiors ordered him and other commissioned officers to participate in the electoral fraud. Mena Sandoval, Roberto D'Aubuisson, an army major, and other army officers along with PCN leaders rigged the electoral results in San Miguel.[72] While Zamora, Mejía, and most of their relatives enthusiastically supported Duarte, the purported winner of the election, other neighbors from La Ceiba, like Pedro Zamora, supported the official party due to their close connection with the state security apparatus. This emerging pattern of political polarization at the local level later escalated into open paramilitary violence against peasant activists, fomenting the clandestine resistance of the peasant leaders.

Remembering the first secret meetings aimed at the creation of the peasant organization, Zamora stated:

> Justo [Mejía] usually came to my house very early in the morning and we discussed the work that we needed to do. We did that without any difficulty. I was a woman who was never afraid. The Lord had spared

me all this time. I was in a lot of danger. . . . we engaged in incredible work, organizing meetings and demonstrations in Arcatao, Las Flores, and San Salvador. We were the leaders of all that [the peasant movement].[73]

She also recalled Facundo Guardado as a young leader of the peasant movement: "Facundo, Justo, and I organized the movement. Facundo was a very smart comrade [*un compa tan resabido*]. He often came to my house and asked my daughter for a tortilla."[74]

The sheer savagery of the repression against the nascent peasant movement in San Vicente in 1974 produced shock waves among peasant communities in Chalatenango. A massacre at La Cayetana, a hamlet located on the slope of the San Vicente volcano, in November of that year motivated peasant leaders in Chalatenango to form the UTC. According to David Rodríguez, a former diocesan priest who worked in Tecoluca, a town near the site of the massacre, a group of landless peasants from La Cayetana formed a "pro-lease committee" in an effort to rent land for the cultivation of corn and beans. After the Ministry of Agriculture refused to support negotiations between the local landowners and the landless peasants, the latter organized a land occupation near La Cayetana. The next day, pro-government newspapers accused diocesan priests of promoting the land occupation. On July 25, 1974, unknown individuals gunned down the leader of the pro-lease committee. On November 29, dozens of National Guardsmen were transported in trucks to La Cayetana. They entered the hamlet, shooting at the inhabitants. Subsequently they captured the participants in the land occupation and moved them to the *ermita* (local chapel), where they tortured them. The guardsmen ordered the peasants to undress and lie down on the floor; they then jumped on the peasants' backs repeatedly singing "alleluia." As the guardsmen were leaving the hamlet, they encountered a group of workers who attempted to flee from the site. They murdered six of them and mutilated their bodies with machetes. The disfigured bodies of the six victims "appeared thrown in the streets near Tecoluca, destroyed by dogs."[75] In the aftermath of the mass killing at La Cayetana, peasant leaders from San Vicente led by Rafael Barrera met their peers from Chalatenango to create a new peasant organization they eventually called the UTC. They formed it as a radical peasant movement, but it was not an armed revolutionary organization proper. At that time, Facundo Guardado asked Romeo Maeda, the priest who sponsored the cooperative movement in Chalatenango, to offer courses on political theory at Chacalcoyo to support the formation of the new peasant organization. Maeda refused this request, stating that it was not the Church's role to promote the radicalization of peasant politics.[76]

Chinda Zamora, a resident of La Ceiba, played a crucial but often unacknowledged role in the foundation of the UTC. Zamora, the mother of nine children, a *rezadora* (a woman specializing in Catholic prayers and rituals), and a midwife, became one of the most charismatic leaders of the peasant movement. In 1980, she and her family fled La Ceiba and settled in Quezaltepeque, a city north of San Salvador in an area ravaged by heavy fighting between the insurgent and government forces during the civil war. Zamora compared the emergence of the peasant movement in Chalatenango with the construction of Noah's Ark: "I told them [her neighbors] that there were two contending forces [the peasant movement and the state forces] and that if they joined the Ark [the peasant movement], chances were that they will spare their lives but if they didn't, most likely they will perish."[77]

The story of Noah's Ark became a powerful metaphor in the mobilization of the peasant communities in Chalatenango. Zamora used it to persuade her neighbors and friends to join the peasant movement. This biblical narrative, in which God orders Noah, a just patriarch, to build an ark in order to save his family and all species of animals from an imminent universal flood, was particularly appealing for Catholic rural communities in Chalatenango. In Zamora's narrative, Justo Mejía embodied Noah, and the peasant communities represented his family. The UTC was the Ark, and the universal flood the ominous state terror, which threatened the peasant communities with total destruction.[78]

The existing network of rural cooperatives, the radio schools, and the religious associations in the area served as the initial bases for the emergence of the UTC. Members of rural cooperatives in particular were the first to join the nascent organization. They met in a variety of settings such as churches, convents, and other public places to form local committees. Many people from La Ceiba attended the general assemblies organized by La Esperanza to raise people's awareness about the causes of the "great poverty" in which they lived. Local committees of the emerging organization also held meetings at the hamlets near Las Vueltas to discuss "how Jesus Christ had struggled against the injustice." "This is how the local organization was expanded until the UTC was formed," said Guadalupe Mejía.[79] The nascent organization also held public events in Cancasque, San José Las Flores, and other towns.[80] In Arcatao, members of the cooperatives gathered at a convent near the local National Guard post. But despite the tensions between the peasant movement and the guardsmen in the town, the latter did not attack UTC activists prior to December 1976.[81]

As in the hamlets near Aguilares studied by the anthropologist Carlos R. Cabarrús in the 1970s, the peasant communities in northeastern Chalatenango experienced a deep fracture between those who supported the emerging peasant movement and those who joined ORDEN, a paramilitary anti-communist organization founded in 1965 by the Salvadoran general

Alberto "Chele" Medrano with the support of US Green Berets.[82] ORDEN paramilitaries in Chalatenango remained heavily armed after the war between El Salvador and Honduras in 1969.[83] They were under the control of ANSESAL, the state intelligence service, which comprised networks of informants and repressive forces.[84] The previous political affiliation of local peasant leaders with opposition parties (mainly the Christian Democrat Party) or the official party (the PCN), forms of integration into the state coercive apparatus, and kinship relations informed the schism within the peasant communities. In the case of La Ceiba, most members of the Mejía family joined the UTC, following the leadership of Justo Mejía, who was a former Christian Democrat activist, and most male members of the García and Cartagena families joined ORDEN, following the leadership of Pedro Zamora (aka Pedro Cartagena), who was previously affiliated with the PCN. Chinda Zamora, a sister-in-law of Justo Mejía, joined the UTC. She blamed Pedro Zamora, the local leader of ORDEN, who was also her relative, for the killing of many people in the area. "That man [Pedro Cartagena o Zamora] wanted to see us all dead. He destroyed our beautiful hamlet. He was responsible for the killing of many comrades [*compañeros*]. He wanted to see me dead. Only my Lord saved me," said Zamora.[85] Guadalupe Mejía also recalled Pedro Zamora as an "*oreja*" (snitch) who constantly reported the whereabouts of her husband, Justo Mejía, to the National Guard despite the fact that they were close relatives and neighbors.[86] Hilda Mejía, a niece of Justo Mejía, commented that the acute polarization of the communities at La Ceiba between 1974 and 1980 turned into a "very ugly melée [*un revoltijo bien feo*]," meaning that the growing paramilitary repression against UTC activists and the ensuing violent responses of the latter against ORDEN operatives generated numerous fatalities among closely related families.[87]

Members of *patrullas cantonales* (hamlet patrols), paramilitary forces under the jurisdiction of the army, and ORDEN operatives underwent intense anti-communist indoctrination through their contacts with local military commanders and members of the security forces after the 1969 war between El Salvador and Honduras. However, these organizations were far from being monolithic. Rank-and-file paramilitaries did not receive a salary. The mobilization of these forces ultimately relied on a combination of state coercion and control, a peculiar anti-communism prevalent among rural communities, and various incentives paramilitaries obtained as part of the repressive forces, such as permission to carry weapons and access to military and civilian authorities and local elites. Hence, it is not surprising that several founders of the UTC, including Justo Mejía and Santos Martínez, at one time served in the *patrullas cantonales*, and members of ORDEN secretly collaborated with the peasant movement.[88] These shifts from collaboration to resistance suggest that although subaltern groups play an active role in the functioning of state domination, their loyalty to community-based organizations such as the UTC often remains strong despite their multiple associations with the state repressive apparatus.[89]

Diocesan Priests, Urban Insurgents, and Peasant Intellectuals

Catholic priests who worked in rural areas of Chalatenango in the 1970s were active participants in the emerging "Popular Church," a growing network of rural and urban of Christian Base Communities (CBCs), local church groups formed by laypeople, nuns, and diocesan priests. They joined the First Pastoral Week in El Salvador, held at the San José de la Montaña Seminary in 1970, a forum that gathered diocesan priests, Catholic congregations, and bishops who conducted pastoral work among urban and rural communities. The First Pastoral Week was a crucial event in the history of the Salvadoran Catholic Church. It enabled the integration and renovation of the Church's pastoral work: the creation of the CBCs and the priests' full engagement with liberation theology. During this event, diocesan priests and members of the CBCs created a national coordinating committee that played a major role in the formation of the Popular Church movement in the 1970s.[90] Bishop Oscar A. Romero, who was then a conservative cleric, viewed the First Pastoral Week with apprehension. Romero refused to participate in the gathering and in fact sent his own critical observations about the event to the Vatican.[91] However, the Archdiocese of San Salvador (which was in charge of the Departments of San Salvador, Cuscatlán, La Libertad, and Chalatenango) supported the creation of the CBCs.[92]

Priests trained after the Second Vatican Council often challenged the traditional power relations between the Church, the state, and the elites. The experiences of Alfonso Navarro and Trinidad de Jesús Nieto, two diocesan priests ordained in 1967, illustrate this point. Navarro supported the formation of peasant cooperatives and CBCs and organized numerous workshops with peasants and students in Opico, a town in La Libertad. In turn, local elites and government officials harassed Navarro and his followers. While landowners in Opico labeled Navarro a "subversive priest," National Guardsmen visited hamlets in the area to warn peasants to ignore his homilies because "he was a communist." El Diario de Hoy, a conservative newspaper, falsely accused Navarro of tolerating drug consumption among the youth who frequented his church in Opico. Waldo Chávez Velasco, the head of the National Center of Information (CNI), a state propaganda apparatus under the direct authority of President Fidel Sánchez Hernández, summoned Navarro to an "informal" talk about his activities in Opico.[93] In October 1971, Navarro left the town due to the multiple threats he received from local elites and repressive forces during his tenure as parish priest. In his farewell address to Catholic peasants and youth in Opico, he asked them to persevere in their efforts to achieve "the Liberation in Christ" despite the "persecution, incarcerations, beatings, offenses, [and] slander" they endured at the hands of government forces. Navarro also announced his decision to honor Jesus's dictum "that guide[d] [his] life as a priest: Truth will make you free," even if that meant facing his own death.[94] In 1977, state agents murdered Navarro at his parish office in Colonia Miramonte, a middle-class neighborhood in San Salvador. In the early 1970s, Trinidad de Jesús Nieto was also in charge of the Catholic parish at Colonia Santa Lucía, a working-class neighborhood in Soyapango, a city east of San Salvador. He encouraged the formation of a CBC among the Catholic youth in the area. In 1971, the CBC in Santa Lucía supported striking teachers affiliated with ANDES with food and money. In the aftermath of this episode, Nieto received death threats from ORDEN paramilitaries, but he refused to leave the parish. Young Catholics from Santa Lucía joined the social movements and urban insurgent militias in the late 1970s.[95]

The connection between progressive diocesan priests and rural communities in Chalatenango was long-standing. Since 1958, Romeo Maeda and other priests had promoted the formation of rural cooperatives in the area. When Benito Tovar, Miguel Argueta, and Gregorio Landaverde, three young diocesan priests who had formed a "pastoral team," arrived in Chalatenango in 1973, they found a network of rural cooperatives that actively supported their new pastoralism. Drawing on the writings of prominent figures of liberation theology such as Gustavo Gutiérrez, Jon Sobrino, Juan Luis Segundo, and Leonardo Boff, which they had studied at the San José de la Montaña Seminary, they sought to promote "the peasants' dignity," that is, they advocated the labor and social rights of peasant communities. They had decided to undertake an "apostolate" in Chalatenango—a region that had produced numerous religious vocations despite the limited attention it had received from the Church—in order to assume the renewed Catholic social doctrine "not only with words." They were determined to work with peasant communities, students, and other sectors in the area despite their own fragile personal economies and the risk of being persecuted by state agents.[96] Diocesan priests had customarily assisted destitute rural communities and received very limited institutional support from the Church. They largely relied on the communities they attended to make a living. Some older priests working in Chalatenango were concerned about the potentially negative impact of the arrival of the pastoral team on their personal economies. "Poor old priests, they had to share their income with the pastoral team," said an anonymous informant who witnessed this process.[97]

The pastoral team fully embodied the emerging liberation theology in Chalatenango. They forcefully challenged the representations of Christ as a "bloody, non-living God prevalent in the area since colonial times" and instead promoted a new religious imaginary that depicted Christ "as a human God who suffers with the hungry and defends human dignity."[98] Unlike priests trained prior to the Second Vatican Council, who generally felt uncomfortable with the growing sense of entitlement and participation of laypeople in the Church, the young priests considered peasants fundamental actors of El Pueblo de Dios (the Community of God).[99] For roughly three years, Argueta, Tovar, and Landaverde promoted an intensive educational campaign among peasant communities in the area called the Cursillos de Cristiandad (Workshops on Christianity). Some eight hundred peasants from northeastern Chalatenango joined the workshops taught by the priests between 1973 and 1975.[100]

The vast Catholic pedagogical tradition in El Salvador informed the Cursillos de Cristiandad. The workshops combined three types of pedagogies: the Catholic Action method, Paulo Freire's Pedagogy of the Oppressed, and the Program for the Celebration of the Word, also known as the "Choluteca model." The Catholic Action pedagogy, known as "To see, to judge, and to act," developed by the Belgian cardinal Joseph Cardijn, comprised several techniques to analyze local sociopolitical conditions from a Catholic perspective and to formulate specific ideas to improve those conditions. This methodology was widely used by Catholic Action groups in El Salvador in the 1960s. Freire's method was first popularized in El Salvador in the 1960s and early 1970s by CESPROP, a research center founded by Catholic Action students and Juan Ramón Vega, a diocesan priest-sociologist. CESPROP created a network of popular schools known as the Centers of Popular Culture in parishes across the country. It conducted hundreds of workshops with peasants, workers, and students, drawing on the Freire's Pedagogy of the Oppressed.

The Program for the Celebration of the Word was taught initially at El Castaño, San Miguel, and then developed in other areas of the country. The Choluteca model focused on the formation of *celebradores de la palabra* and CBCs in hamlets and *caseríos* (small human settlements). However, progressive Catholics in El Salvador preferred the Catholic Action method due to its "practicality."[101] The *cursillistas*, as the individuals who attended the three-day Cursillos de Cristiandad were called, read passages of the Bible and reflected on the relevance of the Catholic social doctrine in their daily lives.[102] The workshops also included reflections on family relations and the need to "demand respect for the dignity of people."[103]

The workshops frontally challenged the conservative Catholicism prevalent in Chalatenango and promoted, according to one participant, a "Christian way of life from a humane and reasonable viewpoint."[104] They questioned the established Church teachings that preached social conformism and divine redemption in exchange for the everyday sufferings of peasant communities. They posited that the oppressed were entitled to organize and to fight for justice in the present. They also promoted the creation of autonomous peasant organizations, independent of the existent political parties.[105] The priests encouraged the lay preachers who attended the workshops to become active participants in national politics.[106] Participants in the workshops knew that the innovative Catholic social doctrine overtly challenged the power structures in the country and that to practice it entailed an imminent risk of persecution, torture, and even death at the hands of state agents.[107]

The new pastoralism generated a growing divide between conservative Catholics and the emerging CBCs.[108] Fidel Recinos, a diocesan priest, mobilized nearly one thousand peasants in Arcatao to protest the work of the pastoral team. The peasant supporters of Recinos marched in the town, chanting "Death to Cuba and Long Live Recinos," anticipating the ensuing confrontation between the CBCs and conservative peasants in the area.[109] However, members of traditional Catholic groups such as the societies of the Virgin Mary and various patron saints massively joined the CBCs. Prayer and ritual experts (i.e., *rezadores*) like Santos Martínez and Chinda Zamora, who had performed Catholic rituals among rural communities in the area since the 1950s or earlier, played a major role in the massive integration of peasants into the CBCs.[110]

Urban insurgents also formed alliances with peasant communities in Chalatenango from 1973 onward. FPL militants who first visited the area contacted peasant leaders through teachers and Benito Tovar, a diocesan priest.[111] The empathy between Tovar, Felipe Peña Mendoza, and Andrés Torres Sánchez, two university students affiliated with the FPL, enabled the organization's expansion in northeastern Chalatenango. Impressed by the modesty and sincerity that Peña and Torres showed toward the peasants who attended a workshop in Citalá, Chalatenango, in 1972, Tovar decided to cooperate with the FPL.[112]

The FPL first commissioned Torres, a sociology instructor, to form networks among peasant communities in the area. Unlike other university intellectuals who had joined the FPL in the early 1970s, Torres had humble social origins. He was born to a peasant family in Apaneca, Ahuachapán, in 1948. He had lost his parents at an early age and was adopted by a diocesan priest. He was an outstanding student who won a scholarship to attend the University of El Salvador in 1967.[113] At the university, Torres joined the student movement at General Studies (CRAC) and eventually the FPL.

The chemistry between peasant leaders and university activists in the early 1970s was often volatile. Alberto Enríquez, a Guatemalan Jesuit student who visited Aguilares, a neighboring region of Chalatenango in 1974, reported that peasants were generally friendly with him and his partner, Ana María Castillo, a psychology student. However, they were also suspicious of their real intentions and commitment to the peasants' struggles. Enríquez recalled that he and Castillo met FECCAS leaders at *cantón* El Líbano near Aguilares. During this meeting, Apolinario "Polín" Serrano, a leader of FECCAS, introduced the students to an audience of peasant leaders who gathered inside a small thatched house with a muddy floor. Polín told the FECCAS leaders:

> Here we have two UCA [Central American University] students who say they want to support FECCAS, but we have met several university students like them and they are *llamarada de tusa* [roughly, a "fleeting flame"], they come, they say they want to help us, and then when they realize the difficulties of our struggle, they leave. So I want these students to commit themselves in front of this assembly.[114]

Enríquez responded to Polín, "I don't know about other students, I can only speak for myself, but I am here to tell you that I am serious about my political commitment." In the following months, Enríquez, his fellow Jesuit students Antonio Cardenal and Fernando Áscoli, seminarians, and other members of El Movimiento organized workshops on social theory with the leaders of FECCAS. They trained nearly fifty peasant leaders in the 1970s who became important figures in the social movements and the insurgency, including Cirilo García, Patricia Puertas, Chepe López, one Luisón, Numas Escobar, and many others.[115]

In contrast with the rough reception that the FECCAS leaders initially gave Enríquez and Castillo, the peasant leaders in Chalatenango viewed Torres as one of their own, due to the latter's peasant background and demeanor. Moreover, the personality of Torres had a deep impact among the Catholic peasant leaders in the area.[116] Torres's deferential attitude toward the peasant leaders, most of whom were twice his age, gained him widespread appreciation among peasant communities in the area. José "Santos" Martínez depicted Torres as a humble and hard-working student who taught religion classes to peasant catechists and *rezadores*.[117] Facundo Guardado reminisced about him as a trustworthy and open-minded individual who provided valuable political advice to peasant leaders.[118] Torres helped the peasant leaders to organize dozens of meetings with members of rural cooperatives and other peasant communities in an effort to create the UTC.[119]

The encounter between the university activists and the liberation theology priests in Chalatenango was not always cordial. While some priests wholeheartedly supported the insurgent students, others clearly disliked them. Some priests labeled the student activists "recalcitrant" people who took advantage of "pious organizations" to promote their subversive ideas. "They wanted to have contact with people who struggled in favor of the peasants' dignity [i.e., diocesan priests] . . . they had a Marxist thought. . . . their slogan was that of death or life," said an anonymous informant. He vividly evoked the radicalism of the militants who worked in Chalatenango but vaguely remembered the organization's slogan. The FPL's motto, "Revolution or death, the armed people will vanquish," indeed became deeply ingrained among peasant communities in Chalatenango. The FPL found exceedingly favorable conditions to recruit peasant leaders into its ranks, as many of them were familiar with Church social doctrine, which apparently matched the organization's political culture. Selfless commitment to the poor, moral rectitude, social redemption, and notions of martyrdom constituted key aspects of the FPL ethos. "It was easy for them [the FPL militants] to recruit Church people who had a new consciousness," said an anonymous interviewee. On one occasion, a priest was deeply upset when a peasant informed him that the *muchachos* (the boys, as the peasants often called the insurgents) had told him: "Priests teach you about God and Heaven, we will teach you about the Earth, where you actually live." The insurgents often visited Catholic peasant communities and entered Catholic temples in northeastern Chalatenango without the consent of diocesan priests.[120] Eventually the FPL addressed these tensions between the organization's militants and the clergy in its policy documents.

The FPL's views on religion and politics enormously increased its prestige in Chalatenango, San Vicente, and other regions of the country. *Estrella Roja 2*, a document that summarized the FPL's elucidations on these matters, had an intense resonance among priests, nuns, and Catholic intellectuals in El Salvador and therefore is worth discussing at some length. It posited that the growing confrontations between the insurgency and the state and the militant activism of the peasant movement generated multiple speculations among the clergy concerning the FPL. Thus, it explicated the organization's ideology and politics, to clarify the "doubts and reservations" that priests might have about these issues. It stated that even reformist-minded individuals often misunderstood the unavoidable polarization generated by the revolutionary war in El Salvador and were prone to endorse reactionary politics. In contrast, progressive priests understood this process well and supported peasant movements despite the intensification of the armed conflict. The document offered an overview of the organization's strategy, the "Prolonged People's War," and its Marxist-Leninist ideology. It challenged intellectuals who considered Marxism a valid method of social analysis but rejected Leninism as a revolutionary theory. As a corollary to this point, it refuted individuals who deemed the FPL a dogmatic group. It claimed that dogmatism encompassed nonscientific or metaphysical approaches to revolution, which the organization clearly rejected.[121] It underscored the legitimacy of the revolutionary war conducted by the FPL in El Salvador, drawing on the Church's doctrine of the just war.[122]

The document also outlined the FPL's ideology, which resonated with Christian notions of self-sacrifice and martyrdom in defense of the dispossessed.[123] It also stated that the mobilization of the mostly Catholic "masses of workers and peasants" constituted the organization's most crucial political challenge. Responding to the criticism raised by some diocesan priests, who claimed that the FPL manipulated ecclesiastical work to expand its clandestine networks among peasant communities, the editors of *Estrella Roja 2* asserted that the organization was not "taking advantage of the other people's work" but merely exercising its right to promote revolutionary politics. They wrote that the FPL conducted organizational work in the countryside regardless of the presence of priests in a particular region and called upon clerics to respect the political freedom of Catholics who joined revolutionary organizations. The document also offered a brief assessment of the growing tensions between progressive and conservative Catholics, which it considered expressions of class polarization in El Salvador.[124] The FPL summarized its position on religion and revolutionary politics as follows: "Our revolutionary work is directed against the enemies of the people and it does not seek to undermine religion or religious work among the masses. The experience in this terrain indicates that religious work and revolutionary activity can be combined fruitfully in favor of people's interest."[125]

The new Catholic pastoralism and the FPL's revolutionary ideology blended in the personas of Benito Tovar and Andrés Torres. Since 1973, the priest and the revolutionary supported the formation of the peasant movement and created insurgent networks in the area, exchanging both religious and political roles. While Torres ably taught peasant communities religion classes for several years, drawing on his strong Catholic background, Tovar supported the formation of the first insurgent groups in the area. Tovar and Torres integrated the "Christian and revolutionary perspectives (united in space and time)" to promote the emergence of the revolutionary movement in the area. Tovar himself illuminates this point when he reminisced about Torres not as a hard-line guerrilla leader or a radicalized sociologist but as "a good Pastor":[126]

> Torres was a good Christian who managed to integrate the two things, his faith as Christian and Marxism. He was a man of faith who lived with the people of Chalatenango. He slept, ate, and lived the living conditions of peasants. . . . He participated in the Celebrations of the Word. He had a religious experience that helped him to promote popular organization. His work was the formation of the political consciousness of the people, and the organization . . . of the UTC in Chalatenango.[127]

Repression against peasants in Chalatenango escalated dramatically after the foundation of the UTC in 1974. The chronology of paramilitary violence against communities in La Ceiba, Las Vueltas, and other neighboring hamlets involves numerous cases of surveillance, threats, arbitrary detentions, torture, and summary executions.[128] National Guardsmen also persecuted UTC activists relentlessly after 1976. Peasant leaders left their homes and lived in the mountains, only to return at night, at dawn, or at times when the repressive forces withdrew from the area. They gradually developed a "clandestine culture": they learned methods and techniques to disguise their revolutionary activities and personal identities from state agents, as illustrated by the following anecdote. One night, Chinda Zamora, one of the most wanted peasant leaders in Chalatenango, encountered a National Guard patrol in the mountains near Las Vueltas. A guardsman asked her what was she doing so late at night in that desolated area. She responded, "I am on my way to assist a women in labor." The incredulous guardsman searched Chinda's bag and found only utensils and herbs commonly used by midwives (Chinda was in fact a midwife). When he asked her, "Do you know how to use these things?" she responded: "Of course I do." Finally, the guardsman ask her if she knew a woman named Gumersinda Zamora, known as "Chinda." To this, she calmly responded, "Yes, I do, I see her often, but I haven't seen her today." Chinda escaped on that occasion, but she was eventually imprisoned. She was placed in solitary confinement in a jail in Chalatenango, and her captors repeatedly threatened to throw her alive into the Lempa River wrapped inside a sack. However, she never admitted to being part of the peasant movement.[129]

The diocesan priests working in Chalatenango also endured intense persecution. In November 1970, Nicolás Rodríguez, a diocesan priest who worked in San Antonio Los Ranchos, was murdered near Cancasque. Rodríguez had supported one of the most successful peasant cooperatives in Chalatenango, called Santa Teresa, which was based in San Antonio Los Ranchos.[130] He disappeared for several days and was found horribly disfigured by machete blows and knife cuts. His corpse was missing one hand.[131] His homicide was initially attributed to common criminals, but people who knew him well have argued over the years that he was indeed the first Catholic priest murdered by state agents in the 1970s.[132] The state persecution against diocesan priests in Chalatenango was indeed relentless. National Guardsmen constantly monitored their activities, and spies routinely listened to their homilies and public talks. They were also photographed and their conversations secretly recorded by government spies. They feared being poisoned by paramilitaries during their visits to the hamlets. They received multiple death threats. Anonymous callers told them on repeated occasions: "We know you are visiting such a hamlet, we will kill you and throw [your body] into the river." A death squad called "The White Hand" printed a white hand on the door of the convent where they resided in Chalatenango, a common death threat used by state agents at that time. The military authorities in the region also tried to buy them off with offers of honorary military ranks and other perks. Once, a noncommissioned officer of the National Guard cryptically told a priest: "Protect our souls, we will protect your body."[133] According to one anonymous informant, "They [the diocesan priests] endured a terrible psychological warfare, but they never gave up. People guarded them. They gave them information, sent them horses, and fed them."[134] The priests suffered serious illnesses as a result of the persecution they experienced in Chalatenango. Some had to relinquish the priesthood to spare their lives. In the end, they left the area as the confrontations between the state forces and the peasant communities intensified in the late 1970s.

Peasant intellectuals became insurgents as they developed self-defense strategies in response to the mounting repression. In 1975, President Molina announced a limited agrarian reform program in response to the demands of the rural poor. However, it quickly failed as a result of a strong backlash orchestrated by landed elites. The fundamental state response to the emerging peasant movement was repression. US counterinsurgency crucially influenced the Salvadoran military's attempts to suppress the social movements in the 1970s. During the previous decade, hundreds of Salvadoran military officers and state bureaucrats had received counterinsurgency training in the United States and the Panama Canal Zone.[135] They incarnated a counterinsurgent ideology, which equated political opponents, social activists, and progressive priests with subversives, internal enemies, and terrorists. National Guardsmen and ORDEN operatives had also received counterinsurgency training. Paramilitaries, often motivated by a mix of anti-communism and personal grievances, harassed peasant activists and increasingly carried out summary executions and mass killings of neighbors and even relatives they considered UTC affiliates, whom they called "Utecianos." In turn, a cohort of peasant leaders formed a rural insurgency with the support of militants like Andrés Torres and others who followed him after his death in combat in 1976.

Given the severity of the repression in Chalatenango, it is not surprising that the cohort of peasant leaders who founded the UTC, most of whom were in their early forties in 1973, took seriously Torres and other young urban insurgents. Starting an armed movement at that age must have been trying for them. Besides, they had large families to feed and much to lose in an open clash with the government forces. But the growing state terror did not leave them much choice. They had to protect their communities from the repressive forces. In this context, they decided to wage war on the regime, aided by the urban insurgents.

Peasant Leaders as Revolutionary Intellectuals

Peasant leaders were the main promoters of revolutionary mobilizations in Chalatenango in their multiple roles as educators, organizers, and religious, political, and military leaders. By the time diocesan priests influenced by liberation theology and FPL insurgents arrived in Chalatenango in 1973, peasant leaders had already created rural cooperatives and study groups associated with the radio schools. They also led political networks, state paramilitary groups, and religious organizations that contributed to the formation of the UTC and the FPL insurgency. While urban insurgents and diocesan priests played auxiliary roles in the creation of the peasant movement and the insurgency, the decision to fight the repressive forces emerged from the peasant communities and their leaders.

The peasant intellectuals, the diocesan priests, and the insurgents built an enduring alliance drawing on a shared but heterogeneous anticapitalist ethos. It focused on the emancipation of the poor and the oppressed from capitalist exploitation and repression. This alliance encompassed an intricate confluence between the FPL's Marxist-Leninist ideology, liberation theology, and a distinct peasant culture that comprised traces of both anticapitalist and capitalist ideologies. Most peasant leaders in Chalatenango were small landholders who wanted first and foremost to dismantle military authoritarianism, to freely participate in electoral politics, and to advance the socioeconomic demands of the rural population.[136]

The charisma, pragmatism, and deeply rooted Catholicism that characterized peasant leaders in Chalatenango enabled the insurgency to substantially expand its influence among large segments of the rural population. Justo Mejía, Chinda Zamora, José Santos Martínez, Facundo Guardado, and other peasant intellectuals who emerged in the 1970s constituted a remarkable cohort of social and political leaders. Some, like Zamora and Martínez, had many followers among rural Catholic communities in Chalatenango. Others, like Mejía and Guardado, became national political figures. They articulated the peasant movement's views on issues ranging from agrarian reform to the demands of seasonal workers and minifundistas in public debates in San Salvador and other cities. They also played an important role in the formation of coalitions like the BPR, along with teachers, students, diocesan priests, and dwellers of shantytowns. They were pragmatic individuals with multiple agricultural occupations, as well as family and community responsibilities—people inclined to discuss politics and strategy rather than ideology and theory. The deep spirituality of *rezadores* like Zamora and Martínez who had performed Catholic rituals at funerals and other community events for decades or the selfless dedication of Mejía as a pro bono teacher of the radio schools and leader of rural cooperatives had created resilient bonds between these peasant leaders and rural communities in Chalatenango and beyond.

Peasant leaders in El Salvador advocated not the creation of a peasant utopia but a radical restructuring of capitalist society, politics, and political economy. They actively engaged in a frontal struggle against the oligarchic-military regime in rural areas and urban centers with the explicit goal of promoting "a popular revolution toward socialism."[137] However, their activism did not emulate mechanically the dogmatism that characterized urban FPL militants in the

1970s. Instead, these leaders articulated in very realistic terms the grievances of small landholders and seasonal workers at coffee farms and sugar and cotton haciendas. They demanded higher wages, better meals, and more bearable working conditions for rural workers. They drew on their expertise as small agricultural producers, leaders of rural cooperatives, and seasonal rural workers (i.e., semiproletarians) to make the demands of the peasant movement relevant to broad sectors of the rural population.

The peasant leaders penned or verbalized numerous assessments of the country's agrarian economy and labor rights. They also reflected on issues pertaining to religion and politics, the militarization of the countryside, counterinsurgency, and other topics, which university or high school students who collaborated with the peasant movement often transcribed.[138] Consider the labor demands for seasonal workers at coffee, sugar, and cotton plantations they articulated in the 1970s. They denounced the injustices and abuses committed by landowners and foremen against workers such as the alteration of scales or other inaccurate measuring techniques used to weigh or calculate the amount of cotton or coffee laborers collected during a workday. Similarly, the leaders condemned the "miserable salaries" and "mistreatment" seasonal workers endured at the plantations to make the point that rural workers had been "oppressed and humiliated" for too long. They also stated that in recent times peasant catechists who had denounced these injustices were sent to "rotten jails."[139] In December 1977, they demanded substantial wage increases for seasonal workers while they assessed the social impact of ongoing military operations and widespread repression against peasant communities near Zacatecoluca. During the harvest season of 1977–1978, they asked for 11 *colones* (US$4.4) per eight-hour workday. For workers who received compensation based on the amount of coffee or cotton they picked in a day, the leaders requested 2.75 *colones* (US$1.10) per twenty-five pounds of coffee (one *arroba*) and 11 colones per hundred pounds of cotton (one *quintal*). For workers at sugar cane haciendas who where paid by *tareas* (literally "tasks"), a cultivated area they were supposed to cut during a workday, they demanded 11 *colones* for a task of "six lanes of seven *brasadas* of eight quarter *varas*," roughly six sugar cane lanes, with each one measuring twenty-one feet in length. They also asked for 3 *colones* (US$1.20) to cover each worker's daily meals.[140] The peasant leaders summarized these and other demands such as access to clean water, adequate meals (i.e., well-cooked and sufficient amounts of rice, beans, and tortillas), and basic accommodations for workers at the plantations in a draft law they submitted to the Ministry of Labor in October 1977 entitled "Minimum salaries and better working conditions for the harvest season of coffee, cotton, and sugar cane 1977–78 law proposal."[141] They also formulated a similar set of demands for medium and small landholders. They requested more and better access to credit for small producers at state financial institutions like the Banco de Fomento Agropecuario (BFA). In the midst of the political crisis that preceded the civil war, they asked the BFA to stop requesting land property titles as collateral and to lower credit rates to small and medium-sized producers. They also made a list of pesticides, herbicides, chemical fertilizers, and hybrid corn seeds "H3" and "H5," which they considered necessary to increase the small landholders' productivity.[142]

The peasant leaders were keenly interested in the grievances of rural workers and small landholders but were chiefly preoccupied with the growing repression against the peasant movement. "Agrarian reform was a national demand, but in that area [Chalatenango] the main theme . . . was the abuse of the military and the lack of spaces for political participation. . . . the military were lords and masters who could use and abuse anybody . . . anything," said Facundo Guardado.[143] In this period, the peasant leaders denounced countless cases of torture, disappearances, illegal imprisonment, and summary executions of peasant activists committed by paramilitaries and public security forces. In fact, state agents murdered Justo Mejía, Apolinario Serrano, and other prominent peasant leaders in the late 1970s. Others, like Guardado, Martínez, and Zamora, endured illegal incarceration and torture at that time. An internal document produced by the peasant leaders in this period offers a glance at their views on counterinsurgency. Circa 1978, the National Executive Directorate of FECCAS-UTC, the top leaders of the most powerful peasant movements in the country, alerted the organization to the regime's intention to annihilate the peasant movement.[144] It termed this counterinsurgent effort the "criminal offensive" against rural communities. Such a plan featured three components: military repression, ideological repression, and reformist repression (reformism as a component of counterinsurgency). Military repression comprised the ongoing army operations and the persecution of peasant communities carried out by security forces and ORDEN paramilitaries in different areas of the country. Ideological repression consisted in the massive publicity and propaganda campaigns against the peasant organizations and other social movements orchestrated by government agencies and the Agrarian Front of the Eastern Region (FARO) and the National Association of the Private Enterprise (ANEP), a powerful coalition of big landowners and business leaders, in radio, television, and print media. These campaigns sought to "discredit the revolutionary movement" and to "distort the facts [about the ongoing peasant mobilizations] to confuse people." Lastly, reformist repression comprised President Molina's Agrarian Transformation program, which only superficially addressed the malformations of the country's agrarian structure; Acción Cívica Militar (Civic-Military Action), a minor social program conducted by the army among rural communities; and El Plan Bienestar para Todos (Well-Being for Everyone Plan), a palliative social program sponsored by the

Molina government. The peasant leaders called on their followers to vigorously fight counterinsurgency in all its incarnations.[145]

The peasant leaders also articulated their views on the relationship between
Catholicism and popular politics. In response to a pastoral letter penned by
four conservative Catholic bishops who called on priests and religious orders
not to cooperate with the peasant movement, they issued a pivotal document in
1978 entitled "UTC FECCAS a los Cristianos de El Salvador y Centroamérica"
("UTC FECCAS to the Christians of El Salvador and Central America").[146] In
it, the leaders of the newly formed alliance between UTC and FECCAS (later
renamed the Federation of Rural Workers) explained the origins and objectives
of the peasant movement and the activism they have conducted since 1974 to
advance the socioeconomic and political demands of rural workers and small
landholders. They also explicated the systematic state attacks against the peasant movement since the start of that decade. They condemned the military
operations against rural communities conducted by the army, security forces,
and ORDEN in Aguilares and San Pedro Perulapán in 1977, and in San Martín,
Cinquera, and Cojutepeque in 1978. They claimed that despite the repression,
the peasant movement "had demonstrated theoretically and practically" its
capacity to defend the rights of rural workers. UTC-FECCAS "had developed
without organic or political dependency from the government, the political
parties, the Catholic Church or any other institution."[147] They asserted that the
autonomy of the peasant leadership enabled the movement's swift expansion
between 1974 and 1978. In this context, they faulted the conservative bishops
for denying the peasant movement "the Church's protection" and for labeling
UTC-FECCAS "a left organization" in an attempt to erode its legitimacy.[148]
They accused the conservative bishops of protecting ORDEN paramilitaries
who had committed numerous crimes against peasant communities. In particular, they called the bishop of San Miguel Eduardo Álvarez, one of signers of the
pastoral letter who held the rank of colonel in the Salvadoran army, a member of the "repressive forces."[149] They indicated that the bishops' letter epitomized the growing division between conservative and progressive Catholics
in El Salvador. While it had produced fervor among conservative Catholics, it
had generated "sadness, frustration and even rejection among many Christians
and non-Christians."[150] They posited that the conservative bishops were either
uninformed about the new Catholic theology sanctioned by the Second Vatican
Council, which asserted the new social orientation of the Church, or plainly
rejected it. Paraphrasing the Bible, they wrote: "It is not possible to serve God
and money at the same time." They also invoked Pope Paul VI's message to
Latin American peasants issued during his 1968 visit to Colombia, in which he
stated that peasants had the right to demand more just living and working conditions. In this vein, they claimed that Christians would be able to differentiate

"the good pastors who give up their lives for their flock from those who are mere mercenaries who abandon them when they see the wolf coming or even join [it]."[151] Lastly, they stressed the secular character of the peasant movement but also acknowledged that most FECCAS-UTC affiliates and rural workers in El Salvador, for that matter, were Catholic. In doing this, they emphasized their will to strengthen the links between the peasant movement and Catholic peasant communities in El Salvador.

The secret interactions between the FPL militants and the peasant leaders who first joined the organization in 1975 created the basis for the emergence of the rural insurgency in Chalatenango. They often exchanged political analysis on national events and assessed the most important organizational developments of the UTC and the demands of the organization. Torres and other FPL activists who visited the area became trusted political advisers of the peasant leaders but were careful not to intervene in the decision-making processes of the peasant movement. In turn, the peasant leaders supplied Torres with valuable knowledge about the sociopolitical characteristics of the peasant communities in the region. They also guided Torres's explorations of the mountain ranges in Chalatenango.[152] Prior to Torres's initial contacts with the peasant intellectuals, the FPL leaders were utterly uninformed about the topography or the sociopolitical characteristics of rural communities in Chalatenango. In fact, the peasant leaders taught them how to effectively function in rural environments. "Before Andrés Torres went to Chalatenango we did not know there were mountains in Chalatenango . . . we could not even walk at night in the mountains. . . . had it not been for the peasants, we would not have survived," said Atilio Montalvo, one of the first insurgent commanders stationed in the area.[153]

On the threshold of the civil war, José Santos Martínez and Justo Mejía, arguably the most emblematic leaders of the peasant movement in Chalatenango, commented on the similarity of their personal stories. They were born in 1932, the year of La Matanza in western El Salvador, had extensive families, and made a living as small landholders who cultivated corn and beans in depleted soils in northeastern Chalatenango.[154] They had also participated in the Church-sponsored cooperative movement since the 1960s. Mejía had been a volunteer teacher at the radio schools for seven years and Martínez a *rezador* for roughly two decades. They had also been local commanders of the country's Servicio Territorial, a national paramilitary structure under the command of the army. In short, they were patriarchs whose deep spirituality and long-standing community service had earned them the respect of rural communities throughout the region.

Peasant leaders like Martínez and Mejía played key roles in the formation of the insurgency in Chalatenango. They shared with Andrés Torres and other urban militants their expertise as community leaders and paramilitary commanders.

For many years Martínez had commanded a force of twenty to forty men in El Portillo del Norte, a hamlet near San José Cancasque. They were in charge of securing the state territorial control in the area. They patrolled roads, provided security for community activities, recruited new members, gathered information, and controlled the whereabouts of the hamlet's inhabitants. Martínez supervised the attendance of teachers and other public functionaries at their respective jobs and even had to attest to the visits of National Guardsmen to the area. He was accountable only to the municipal commander (usually a civilian) based in Cancasque, the nearby town, and the departmental commander (an army colonel) stationed in Chalatenango city.[155] In short, Martínez had considerable experience following military orders and commanding local forces.

When the repression against peasant communities in Chalatenango began, Martínez ended his allegiance with the state security apparatus. Although he had enjoyed some perks as an unpaid local commander, such as having a permit to carry a handgun and certain access to the civilian and military authorities in the area, his clout in El Portillo del Norte emerged from his long-standing service as a *rezador* and community leader. On one occasion, he worked pro bono for eighteen months in the construction of a road to connect El Portillo del Norte with Cancasque. When I asked Martínez why someone like him who had been a member of state forces for a long time decided to join the peasant movement, he responded without hesitation: "Ever since I was a child I knew injustice. When I learned about an ORDEN document that discussed the [repressive] role I was supposed to play [as a local commander], I told myself: I will not betray my friends." He then added: "I played the two roles as I told you, I served twenty years as a commander [of the territorial service] and twenty years as a member of the organization [the FPL]."[156]

Five peasant leaders made up the first FPL guerrilla cell in Chalatenango. Mejía and Martínez were part of this first group.[157] They were not rookies in military matters. They knew the mountains in Chalatenango well, had experience commanding local forces, and were familiar with firearms. They also knew the workings of the state forces in the area, particularly the Territorial Service, ORDEN, and the National Guard. Martínez recalled the first drills he organized with Torres. "He came with a few handguns [*unas pistolitas*]. We went into a ravine. He told us: fire just one shot but don't tremble. [In his recreation of this conversation, Martínez riposted with a firm voice:] I don't tremble."[158] He probably felt a bit patronized by Torres, who was, after all, in his early twenties and had never commanded dozens of men as Martínez had done for two decades. Actually, Martínez shared his military expertise with Torres and the new peasant recruits. "We [the peasant leaders] taught them how to lie down on the floor, how to walk without leaving traces, shooting techniques. . . . they [the new recruits] were very excited. . . . I told them not to tell anyone about it."[159]

More important, the deep spirituality of peasant leaders like Martínez conferred on the rural insurgency in Chalatenango a powerful ethos that arguably sustained the movement for almost two decades (1975–1992). Martínez's religious convictions strengthened during his long trajectory as a *rezador*. He reminisced that as a child he used to recite the rosary with his mother and their neighbors in El Portillo del Norte. He claimed to have dreamed about the Virgin Mary on three occasions at that time. He remembered thinking: "Perhaps the Virgin wants me to learn how to pray." Initially he found it challenging to grasp and memorize the litanies of saints and holy places featured in Catholic prayers and the rosary's "glorious, painful, and joyful mysteries," but he soon became an expert on these matters.[160] This is how Martínez's trajectory as a *rezador* started in the 1940s. Since that time, he had recited prayers at innumerable Catholic rituals in Chalatenango and elsewhere. When I asked him to define a *rezador*, he swiftly responded: "I am Catholic. . . . I pray for the living and the dead."[161] He remembered fondly how he prayed in Latin at Catholic ceremonies in San Antonio Los Ranchos and other towns and hamlets in northeastern Chalatenango. Catholic communities near Zacatecoluca in La Paz, a central department in El Salvador, also invited him to pray during Easter. In gratitude for his services, they often presented Martínez with tamales and artisanal liquor.[162] Given that the Fifth Commandment in the Roman Catholic tradition stipulates that Catholics must not kill other human beings, I asked Martínez how he and other peasant leaders who joined the insurgency viewed the relationship between Catholic doctrine and their decision to take up arms against the dictatorship. He responded: "We had studied [the Catholic doctrine], we were clear [*estábamos claritos*], for a Catholic it was a sin to let them [state agents] kill him [her] if he [she] could defend himself [herself] . . . with handguns, machetes, sticks."[163]

Torres, the first FPL operative in Chalatenango, echoed the peasant leaders' ethics of violence to legitimize the insurgent mobilization. On one occasion, he and some peasants found the corpse of a man from Las Vueltas who was presumably killed by state forces. Torres commented: "Look at this comrade, he was Catholic, he wore a scapular but as the saying goes, 'Strike with thy rod while thou beg to thy God' [*a Dios rogando y con el mazo dando*]."[164] He implied that the dead man had not been able or willing to defend his own life from the repressive forces. Torres's message was clear: it was the peasants' duty to fight back against the state terror that threatened their communities with virtual annihilation.

The peasant intellectuals and leaders of urban social movements who joined the insurgency also held important conversations on revolutionary politics in the 1970s. Martínez often met with Mélida Anaya Montes, the leader of the teachers' union ANDES who later became the FPL's deputy commander, to discuss the contours of the national political crisis, peasant politics, and rural insurgency. During one exchange they held circa 1977, Anaya Montes advised

Martínez to counter the potential rise of "banditry [*bandolerismo*], opportun-
ism, and charlatanism" among rural communities, which she considered byproducts of the deep socioeconomic crisis and the ongoing conflict.[165] Martínez was
first skeptical about the relevance of these issues but soon realized that Anaya
Montes was right. As the peasant movement was becoming stronger both politically and militarily, certain groups that joined the insurgency resorted to banditry. They robbed and extorted peasant communities in the area on behalf of
the revolutionary movement. Other groups tried to profit from the chaotic situation. As the polarization between the insurgent and counterinsurgent forces in
Chalatenango grew, cattle rustlers and other petty delinquents in the area tried
to form their own political groups.[166] In this context, the peasant leaders concluded that they had to disarm the civilians living in the area to avoid the prospect of confronting multiple enemies during the imminent civil war.[167]

What did the peasant leaders teach the urban insurgents? What were their main
political and spiritual contributions to the movement? The answers to these
queries are manifold. The authority of the peasant intellectuals among rural
communities in Chalatenango motivated thousands of men and women to join
the peasant movement and eventually the insurgency. Zamora, Mejía, Martínez,
and other peasant leaders had deep-seated links with peasant communities in
the region, and their decision to join the insurgency had major repercussions
in Chalatenango. The diocesan priests and the urban insurgents were participants in this process, but they were ultimately external actors whose influence
among peasant communities was often mediated by the peasant intellectuals.
The peasant leaders' rationale to take up arms against the state had deep resonance in Chalatenango; after all, the idea that self-defense was a natural right of
Catholics, or anyone else for that matter, made sense to rural communities that
had endured countless atrocious deeds carried out by government forces. If anything, the presence of Torres and other urban insurgents in the area reinforced
this ethos. As small landholders and seasonal workers on farms and haciendas
across El Salvador, the peasant leaders from Chalatenango had expertise on a
range of agricultural and labor issues and knew the country well. They voiced
the concerns, sensibilities, and demands of large segments of the rural population. They also formed multiple alliances with the peasant, teacher, worker, and
student movements that constituted the BPR. In doing so, they transformed the
FPL from a small guerrilla group into a major political force. As former or active
members of the state security apparatus, the peasant leaders taught urban militants the workings of the repressive forces, the physical geography of the region,
and basic military techniques. Lastly, the peasant intellectuals' pragmatism (and
that of other leaders of social movements) gradually altered the rigidly dogmatic
political culture that characterized urban insurgents in the early 1970s. Their
lifelong experiences as agricultural producers, seasonal rural workers, heads of

households, leaders of rural cooperatives, midwives, educators, religious figures, political activists, and community leaders taught them that the poor and the oppressed do not have the luxury to play at war. They were obliged to fight the repressive forces in order to preserve their communities.

Martínez recalled that he found out about Torres's death in combat on October 12, 1976, the day he was to meet him in San Salvador. Upon his arrival in the city, Martínez learned that three insurgents had fought state forces that encircled a safe house in Santa Tecla, a city near San Salvador, on the night of October 10. Torres was one of them. He and two other university students affiliated with the FPL had apparently committed suicide in the early morning of October 11 after they had repelled hundreds of policemen for nearly eight hours. Recalling this episode, Martínez said proudly: "We worked with the sociologist Andrés Torres; he was a kind young man. He never had a bad gesture toward us [the peasant leaders]. He was all smiles, but he was formal, he treated us with much care [*con todo cariño*]. When I saw his picture in the newspaper I was unable to say [out loud]: this is my friend. He sacrificed himself until the end."[168] People like Martínez and Torres forged the alliance between the peasant intellectuals and the urban insurgents that sustained the revolutionary war in El Salvador for more than a decade.

4

La Masacuata's War

Poets, I declare you insubordinate of the established order . . .
Brigadas de La Masacuata (1970)

Crazy I am not,

Even if you see I wear my shoes on the wrong feet . . .

Don't be afraid

Words don't punch

Even if true hurts

Those who fear it

But, crazy I am not.
Emiliano Androski Flamenco, *On the Threshold of Silence*

Circa 1987 Eduardo Sancho (aka Fermán Cienfuegos), a top FMLN commander and a well-known poet, received a letter through the insurgency's clandestine channels from someone who addressed him colloquially as "Querido
Poeta" (Dear Poet). The sender had joined FMLN troops as they marched
toward Patamera, a remote hamlet in Chalatenango where Cienfuegos and
other rebel leaders conducted a meeting. In the letter, he reminded Sancho of
their mutual friendship with the poet Roque Dalton. Cienfuegos recalled that
the note caught his attention due to the "Dear Poet" salutation, which evoked
the informal tone of his communications with the insurgent commander and
fellow poet Alfonso Hernández.[1] Circa 1966, Sancho, Hernández, and other
poets had founded *La Masacuata*, a literary group that played an important role
in the formation of the first guerrilla movements in the early 1970s.[2] At first
Cienfuegos considered the author of the letter simply *abusivo* (rude) because
he had not addressed Cienfuegos by his military rank (i.e., commander) but on
second thought deemed him suspect as few individuals corresponded with him
using such familiar language. Near Patamera, FMLN forces captured the alleged
poet and author of the missive just as he was setting up radio communications

with the Salvadoran military. The man ostensibly confessed to FMLN combatants that he was indeed part of an army unit whose mission was to assassinate Cienfuegos and other rebel commanders. They apparently judged the man an enemy spy and summarily executed him. Sancho's recollection of his correspondence with Hernández, the most noted poet of La Masacuata, would alert him to the impostor, since he was the only person who addressed him as "Dear Poet" and not "Commander Fermán." By mimicking Hernández's tone in his correspondence with Sancho, the impostor had tried, and failed, to persuade Sancho that he was indeed one of the poets who joined the movement in the 1970s, in order to approach him and tip off the army about the rebel leaders' location in Chalatenango. This insight, according to Sancho, saved the FMLN leaders gathered at Patamera from being annihilated by the army special unit. Reflecting on this episode, he commented emphatically: "There is a legacy of the poets in the origins of the armed movement. . . . the news that there were poets in the guerrilla [forces] was a permanent motivator [for many people]."[3] Apparently, the counterinsurgent forces were also cognizant of this fact as they tried to ambush Cienfuegos by concocting a ruse that involved the unfortunate soldier posing as a rebel poet. This episode illustrates the centrality of poets in insurgent and counterinsurgent politics in El Salvador prior to and during the civil war.

Literary groups, artists, actors, and musicians played crucial roles in the formation of the New Left insurgency and in shaping the movement's ethos during the civil war.[4] The little-known history of La Masacuata elucidates the participation of countercultural movements in the creation of the first guerrilla groups that emerged in El Salvador in the early 1970s.[5] A cohort of poets from San Vicente and San Salvador created La Masacuata and joined El Grupo, an urban guerrilla cell, and eventually other insurgent groups like the ERP and the RN. La Masacuata sought to create both a political and a literary vanguard to fight the oligarchic-military regime in El Salvador. The Committed Generation, a literary movement created in the 1950s, and other literary groups formed in that country after the Cuban Revolution were also part of this same tradition. An intense rivalry between writers and intellectuals who envisioned the formation of a purely aesthetic vanguard like the Latin American boom and those who endorsed the creation of a political-aesthetic vanguard ensued in El Salvador in the 1960s.[6]

The founders of this literary movement adopted the noun concept La Masacuata to represent their connection with the country's history and culture, which centrally informed their artistic and political identities. *Masacuata* is a composite noun of Nahuat origin that literally means "deer-serpent" (i.e., a boa constrictor). For Sancho, "the mythology of the serpent" evoked the idea that "culture was in constant mutation . . . metamorphosis, the shedding of skin [*la muda de piel*]."[7] The poet Emiliano Androski Flamenco—a barber and small merchant from San Vicente who joined La Masacuata—explained the meaning of this noun concept as follows:

> La Masacuata is a nonpoisonous serpent, which adapts to any climatic environment. It shows its little head, it is humble. It bends, it hides, and it crawls. Surely our Masacuata grew horns. It became a deer. When they tried to hunt it, everyone had to come because La Masacuata was the insurrectionary expression of a people. In other words, La Masacuata was intimately nested in the revolutionary process that we lived. To speak of revolutionaries does not mean to speak about stone throwers but people who want a better world, to contribute to the evolution of human beings . . . who feel others' suffering as their own. That is [was?] La Masacuata.[8]

For Manuel Sorto, an actor and poet who joined the group in 1969, the term alluded to a serpent commonly found in peasant households in the 1960s. At that time, peasants living in thatched huts near his hometown of Sensuntepeque, Cabañas, used to have *masacuatas* as pets that ate "mice, rats, and insects." On one occasion, while he was visiting a rural home, Sorto was jolted when he saw a snake moving in the thatched roof. "Don't worry, it is part of the family, it belongs to our house," a member of the household told him. Thus, for Sorto, *masacuata* referred to "a nonpoisonous animal integrated into daily life," which is able "to coexist with humans, to help people." Under duress, however, it is also "able to asphyxiate" someone.[9] For Luisfelipe Minhero, a writer from San Vicente who joined the group, the poets did not attribute particular "esoteric, magical or mystical" qualities to the noun *masacuata*. "It was simply the Nahuatl-Castilian name with which a species of 'tamable' boa, an independent protector against certain vermin in rural households, is known in El Salvador." However, given "the great weight that Nahuatl culture, including the Pipil and mestizo cultures, have in El Salvador, it is possible" that some people thought that the name La Masacuata invoked "the myth of the plumed serpent, which is the representation of Quetzalcóatl, one of the supreme deities in the Nahuatl world." Most of all, this cohort of poets sought to break with the tradition of labeling "artistic groups" with derivative names such as the Committed Generation (which echoed Jean-Paul Sartre's idea of the "committed intellectual"), adopted by previous literary generations. Instead, they called themselves La Masacuata to "'prophesy' the imminent re-emergence of the vital revolutionary guerrilla in El Salvador."[10] Overall, for the members of this movement, the name La Masacuata suggested notions of power, adaptability, multiplicity, mutability, and defiance, which became principles of the group's unorthodox revolutionary strategy. When I asked Flamenco if the noun concept La Masacuata evoked pre-European Meso-American deities like Quetzalcóatl or Kukulkán, he responded without equivocation: "No, La Masacuata was a revolutionary strategy. . . . we looked crazy but we thrashed [*tetunteábamos*] in one way and the other."[11]

The group blended the countercultural sensibilities and revolutionary ethos of the 1960s with artistic and intellectual traditions of El Salvador, Latin America, and elsewhere. La Masacuata embraced with equal enthusiasm the Welsh lore of Dylan Thomas, the baroque poetics of José Lezama Lima's *Paradiso*, the revolutionary prose of Che Guevara, and the Salvadoran literary canon, particularly the writings of Claudia Lars, Salvador Salazar Arrué (Salarrué), and Roque Dalton.[12] As Alfonso Hernández once nonchalantly told Eduardo Sancho: "I read Ulysses of the Irishman James Joyce, ate yucca with *pepescas, totopostle,* [and drank] *shuco.*"[13] Unlike Dalton, who belittled the works of some of his predecessors like the writer and philosopher Alberto Masferrer, whom he famously called "*Viejuemierda*" (shitty old man) in a poem that disparaged the consecration of Masferrer as an icon of the official culture, the members of La Masacuata valued Masferrer and other Salvadoran writers.[14] They were also keenly interested in Central American history as a source of inspiration for their activism. They studied events like the 1932 indigenous peasant uprising in western El Salvador, the 1832 Nonualco rebellion led by Anastasio Aquino in La Paz and San Vicente, and major episodes in the history of Nicaragua and other neighboring countries. They were also fascinated by the legacies of famous artists and musicians who at one time resided in El Salvador, like the Paraguayan guitar master Agustín Barrios Mangoré, who taught at El Salvador's national conservatory between 1939 and 1944, establishing a new generation of guitar virtuosos in that country. In sum, the imaginaries of La Masacuata were not shallow attempts to revive a nationalist mythology but an expression of deep-seated cultural traditions in El Salvador, which were rekindled by artistic and literary trends and the insurgent spirit of the Global Sixties.

Politically, La Masacuata constituted a rupture. While Dalton and other members of his literary group, the Committed Generation, celebrated the rise of guerrilla movements in Latin America and advocated armed struggle in El Salvador both as poets and as left militants, they were not the initiators of the insurgency. In contrast, most members of La Masacuata bluntly rejected the Communist Party's reformism and cryptically declared war on the elites and the state in 1970. According to Flamenco, "La Masacuata was formed after Piedra y Siglo, a literary movement at the university, which emerged after the Committed Generation." While both "Piedra y Siglo and the Committed Generation cried out [revolution], we were going to cry out and to act."[15] La Masacuata formed a movement against the ruling system itself and not simply an oppositionist group. As Flamenco described it:

> La Masacuata came to frontally collide with the slave society [i.e., the authoritarian regime] that we faced as youth. . . . we had to show our

nonconformity with the system. The goal of La Masacuata was not to attack a government but a system. Anyone can attack a government but not a system because a system is complex. La Masacuata clashed with the system. . . . it became the voice of a revolution.[16]

Most members of this group were iconoclasts who derided the PCS pro-Soviet orthodoxy and created new insurgent identities drawing on their experiences as poets and activists. They constituted both an eclectic aesthetic vanguard and a semiclandestine radical group made up of young intellectuals of middle- and working-class origins that operated in provincial settings in San Vicente, Usulután, Zacatecoluca, Ilobasco, Sensuntepeque, and Cojutepeque, as well as in San Salvador. They epitomized the centrality of revolutionary cultural politics in the trajectory of the Salvadoran insurgency. Unlike the Catholic Action intellectuals discussed in chapter 2, they lacked the type of organic connections with the peasantry developed by ACUS-JEC activists through the Catholic Church pedagogical programs and diocesan priests. Instead, they conducted cultural activism in provincial cities and at the University of El Salvador's campus in San Salvador. They also met clandestinely to form networks among workers, artisans, peasants, and students in San Vicente. Between 1967 and 1970, Sancho, Hernández, and other poets affiliated with La Masacuata became insurgents through their connections with university students who formed El Grupo. However, not all members of La Masacuata joined insurgent groups in the 1970s. Some, like Flamenco, participated in electoral politics as members of the Nationalist Democratic Union (UDN), a legal political party led by the PCS. Others never joined insurgent movements or political parties and in fact became celebrated artists and poets or even icons of the official culture. Some even participated in the education reform promoted by Walter Béneke, the controversial minister of education of the Sánchez Hernández government, between 1967 and 1972.[17]

La Masacuata was made up of the poets Roberto Monterrosa, Eduardo Sancho, Alfonso Hernández, Mauricio Marquina, Rigoberto Góngora, Salvador "Chito" Silis, Manuel Sorto, Emiliano Androski Flamenco, Reyes Gilberto Arévalo, Luisfelipe Minhero, Salomón Rivera, Manuel Zelaya, Salvador Molina Cerritos, and Baltasar Carballo; the writer Carlos Eduardo Rico Mira; the painters Roberto Galicia, Roberto Huezo, and Pedro Portillo; and many unknown followers (figure 4.1).[18] As Minhero explained it, "Poets, painters, sculptors, musicians, short story writers, photographers, theater actors, and university students participated in La Masacuata Brigade, which was, let's say, the group's official name."[19]

La Masacuata conducted a pedagogical activism that sought to raise the intellectual and political awareness of underprivileged Salvadorans at a time of epochal social transformations. These transformations included

Figure 4.1 Members of La Masacuata at the house of Manuel Sorto in Colonia
La Rábida, San Salvador, circa 1970. From left to right, Eduardo Sancho, Roberto
Monterrosa, unidentified person, Rigoberto Góngora, Manuel Sorto, and Luisfelipe
Minhero. Photo by Roberto Salomón. Courtesy of Roberto Salomón.

industrialization, urbanization, and labor reforms generated by the Alliance for
Progress and the Central American Common Market, the increasing access to
higher education for students of modest social backgrounds promoted by the
university reform, and the multiple social impacts of the new Catholic theology.
La Masacuata featured activities such as poetry readings, public commemorations of revolutionary icons like Anastasio Aquino and Che Guevara, and demonstrations in support of unions organized by a network of writers, painters,
students, and workers in several provincial cities and San Salvador.[20] The group's
activism promoted a new vision of El Salvador's culture and history, as well as
the integration of artistic creativity and revolutionary action. In the words of
Flamenco, the pedagogy of La Masacuata

> sought the identification of Salvadoran society with its own culture.
> People had all the vices due to their bad education. Education had been
> eminently classist. Only the sons of the privileged [*fulanos y fulanotes*]
> were trained. The daughters of workers became prostitutes, the sons of
> peasants day laborers, the more brute, the better. We had to uplift the
> country. It wasn't easy. We bet our own skin [*apostamos con el pellejo*].[21]

La Masacuata was a quintessential cultural phenomenon of the Global
Sixties, which defied both oligarchic-military power and the Old Left in El

Salvador. It emerged in the midst of widespread anticapitalist mobilizations at home and abroad and the deep state crisis that followed the 1969 war between El Salvador and Honduras, which anticipated the acute polarization of society and politics and the start of the armed conflict between the military dictatorship and the guerrilla movements in the 1970s. As Luisfelipe Minhero put it, La Masacuata transpired in the context of

> the Cuban Revolution, the struggle of Che in Bolivia, May in France, the Night of Tlatelolco, the gringo hippy movement and its Woodstock Festival, the workers' strike at ACERO S.A. factory in Zacatecoluca, the 1968–1969 student-worker-teacher mobilizations in San Salvador, the Soccer War [the 1969 war between El Salvador and Honduras], and the revisionism of the PCS as the—then—only organic option of the "radical" left but established according to the system. All this prefigured the end of a historical period of domination and the start of the crisis of hegemony of the bourgeois state in El Salvador. It fermented the emergence of the military dictatorship that recreated certain aspects of fascism [la escalada fascista] but at the same time the re-apparition of the contrary antagonist, the revolutionary guerrilla.[22]

A comprehensive examination of the trajectory of La Masacuata requires an engagement with literary analysis as well as cultural and political history. This chapter focuses on the political saga of this group. It examines the early years of La Masacuata in San Vicente and San Salvador, its rupture with the Old Left, and the integration of some of its members into El Grupo and the ERP in the early 1970s.

San Vicente: "Town of Poets and Subversives"

Unlike most literary groups that emerged in San Salvador in the 1960s, La Masacuata was formed in San Vicente de Austria y Lorenzana, the provincial capital of the department of San Vicente. The city of San Vicente lies in the fertile Jiboa Valley under the imposing Chinchontepec, or San Vicente volcano (figure 4.2). An intense agricultural economy emerged in the Chinchontepec area in the 1880s when liberal elites gradually replaced the indigo plantations that had sustained the country's economy throughout the colonial and early republican periods with the new and more profitable coffee cultivation.[23] San Vicente, the center of gravity of La Masacuata, boasted a rich cultural and political tradition. Elites and high-ranking military from San Vicente played major roles in nineteenth-century Salvadoran politics.[24] The city was in fact the

Figure 4.2 Volcano of San Vicente, January 2015. Photo by the author.

country's capital between 1834 and 1840.[25] In the 1960s, it featured several local newspapers and magazines, including *El Heraldo Vicentino*, published by the poet Roberto Monterrosa, a cofounder of La Masacuata (who actually named the group).[26] Famous bands like Paquito Palaviccini's Orquesta Internacional Polío and La Orquesta Internacional de los Hermanos Flores often played in San Vicente. The city was also known for its Juegos Florales, a literary contest that received works from writers and poets from Central America and elsewhere. Poets like Francisco Esteban Galindo (1850–1896) and Antonia Galindo (1858–1893) and noted intellectuals like Sarbelio Navarrete (1879–1952), a former rector of the University of El Salvador, were Vicentinos.[27] La Masacuata was firmly rooted in San Vicente's vibrant cultural and intellectual life as its members entered the Juegos Florales, were students at the Sarbelio Navarrete Institute (the city's public high school), published local newspapers, and eventually created new institutions like La Casa de la Cultura (The House of Culture), a venue where they conducted poetry readings and other activities.

La Masacuata first emerged as the Círculo Literario Vicentino (Vicentino Literary Circle) formed by Monterrosa, Flamenco, and Hernández and later expanded to San Salvador through the contacts Monterrosa made with Sancho

Figure 4.3 Alfonso Hernández and Manuel Sorto, April 29, 1985, Tlalpan, Mexico City. Photo by Pantxika Cazaux. Courtesy of Manuel Sorto.

and other young intellectuals (figure 4.3).[28] They often met in public places such as high schools, the city hall, and the municipal park to conduct poetry readings and to discuss literary works and social theory.[29] They also held clandestine meetings in urban and rural settings to plan propaganda activities and to create a revolutionary movement. As Dylan Thomas sang to his "ugly, lovely town" Swansea, so Hernández reminisced about his native San Vicente and the formation of La Masacuata:[30]

> In towns, one has almost always to submerge oneself in sleep at ten at night, except on Fridays (which we call little Saturday) when one goes out to stroll in the streets or to visit the house of a Dulcinea girl or walk at the Cañas little park, drink a guava or coconut drink at Menche Santana's or at Mátal Cat's mom's place. . . . We had formed a group of young poets very integrated to literature, a poetic-literary movement. . . . [The poet Mauricio] Marquina and the poet [Eduardo] Sancho came every Friday to [attend] the clandestine meetings we organized. We planned *las pegas* [the posting of propaganda] at the Cañas little park, the headquarters of the Infantry Brigade, the Penitentiary or the market, in every street there was always a place for revolutionary slogans. We also met with construction workers, shoemakers . . . and all the artisans that we have managed to organize. That gave the town a revolutionary splendor. Yes, Town of poets and subversives, as people said.[31]

The poetics of La Masacuata celebrated the lives of common folk in the city. It exalted the sensibilities, language, and representations of marginalized people, the mentally ill, and delinquents as well as workers, vendors, and artisans. It vividly recreated daily life in San Vicente: the voices, the smells, the colors, and the shapes. Hernández, for instance, wrote a poem called "Por el ojo de mi ventana vi pasar mi infancia" (Through my window's eye I saw my childhood passed) which illustrates this point:

Through the streets of the barrio passed the charioteer
He looked at me and showed me his tongue . . .
It passed crazy Carlota, scruffy,
Kicking her hunger over the cobbled paving . . .
It passed Chente Pelota with his archbishop's hat
Whistling with a bird in his mouth.
Through the eye of the window the universe of the street was extracted
People floated on the landscape
The chariots and the oxen floated completely
(Forests where extraordinary
events took place) . . .
Through the sky in the lock I saw don Chico Santana
With a tyrannosaurus' belly and legs of a skunk.
La niña Tencha passed,
The seller of *chilate con nuégados*, murmuring:
What a fuck-up life!
The street with flowers and girls who brighten their faces
                                         Like a mirror
Who flexed their legs at the rhythm of their fifteen years.
A concave dream that fitted all the world's love
The screams of the markets
The cry of life
Everything (even the laughter of don Abrahám Mena and his spitting).
In that marvelous world I discovered that
           My grandma's left eye turned 360 degrees . . .
It passed Copinillo through the streets reflected in my grandma's little house
Mincho Malacate the cobbler and Juan Paloma
                            The stabber
Pata de Cuma the seller of newspapers
Piruja with his lame leg like a British merchant
In a Tarzan movie . . .[32]

This poetics of daily life in San Vicente and a poetics of revolution inspired by local narratives of indigenous resistance to colonial and postcolonial oppression were two dominant themes in the group's literary creation. In particular,

Figure 4.4 Memorialization of Anastasio Aquino, January 2015. Mural by Maestras y Maestros, Grupo de Artes Plásticas MINED, San Vicente. Photo by the author.

La Masacuata venerated Anastasio Aquino, an indigenous worker at an indigo plantation who led the 1832 Nonualco rebellion (figure 4.4). Like other intellectuals in El Salvador in the 1960s and 1970s, they memorialized this episode as part of a historical continuum that had shaped their ongoing antidictatorial struggles.[33] The Nonualcos—an indigenous group of Nahuat origin—resisted the harsh working conditions at the indigo plantations and the conscription of young indigenous males conducted by the Salvadoran army during the endemic wars between liberals and conservatives that plagued Central America between 1821 and 1838. During the Nonualco rebellion, Aquino routed the Salvadoran army in several battles and occupied San Vicente after the local elites had fled east toward San Miguel. Narratives of the rebellion that circulated in the 1960s held that Aquino had declared himself the "king of Nonualcos" at El Pilar Church—a colonial building in San Vicente—while he wore the crown of Saint Joseph he found at that place. In 1962, the historian Julio A. Domínguez Sosa challenged the veracity of this story, which he attributed to Vicentino elites who tried to demonize Aquino.[34] Flamenco, himself cognizant of San Vicente lore, also held that Aquino never meant to proclaim himself a king but entered El Pilar to confiscate the weapons and treasure abandoned by the city's merchants and landowners who had fled to San Miguel.[35] Whatever the case, the poets of La Masacuata deemed this episode a quintessential act of subaltern defiance in Salvadoran history.

Flamenco described Aquino as a revolutionary hero who challenged the power of the "fifty Spanish families from San Vicente," elites of Spanish ancestry who were still royalists a decade after the country had declared independence in 1821.[36] He wrote the poem "Anastacio Amigo" (Anastacio friend), which epitomizes the ways in which the rebel poets from San Vicente matched Aquino's uprising with their own struggles. It posited that in the twentieth century the poor in El Salvador still endured the oppression that had caused the Nonualco rebellion:

> I write to you on behalf of all the poor
> In the name of all those who suffer
> From the deepest darkness of the night my voice rises
> To the clear explosion of dawn
> I want to tell the truth and only the truth
> We are slaves
> The injustice, the misery, the pain
> And the cold hurt us in the midst of the twentieth century
> We keep vigilant in the tranquil wait
> To punish and revile all the traitors
> We wait everywhere
> At the public plaza we wait
> There we confess our sins of resented men
> Because we are slaves in the daily wait
> Humiliated, battered, and hungry
> A sad drum agitates our bodies
> Because in the north, a fearful crushing
> A blustery storm howls.
> Here is the clear landscape
> The beautiful Jiboa Valley and the Cuesta de Monteros
> Here, your voice is alive, a hundred up, a hundred down
> Attack my Santiagueños
> The country breeze still sings your song of liberty
> And at the Cuesta they exhibit your head
> Aquino Anastacio Brother

Giant like the great Chinchontepec
Here your voice sounds in the mouth of humble
Peasants
The stones have the living history of the path
The moss is green still
Your steps live at El Pilar Church.[37]

The memories of Aquino articulated by Flamenco and other members of the group crucially informed La Masacuata's revolutionary politics. Aquino had demonstrated that Salvadoran independence "was a farce." He became, in Flamenco's parlance, "the authentic voice of a frustrated people," who took up arms in 1832 against the racism and tyranny of the Salvadoran elites: "Aquino rebelled because he realized that despite independence there was more slavery because they [the elites] started to recruit Indians to turn them into soldiers so that they could repress people. Anastacio freed the conscripted Indian. He and his brother Blas were condemned to the stocks and then the war started."[38]

Flamenco was emphatic: Aquino's rebellion was not "a fantasy." Aquino had built an unprecedented multiethnic army made up of Nonualcos and members of other indigenous groups as well as Ladinos (i.e., mestizos or Hispanicized persons), which instilled fear among the Salvadoran elites. He had indeed defeated the Salvadoran army at several battles and forced the government to evacuate the capital. Aquino won the war but remained unaware of this fact. As Flamenco described it, "This is not a fantasy. Aquino won the war. Anastacio made bombs out of bamboo shoots. He organized people from Lempa, San Vicente, Cojutepeque, Los Nonualcos to San Salvador. He won the war but he did not realize it."[39] In this vein, the poets of La Masacuata considered the 1832 Nonualco rebellion a key "referent" in their efforts to initiate a guerrilla war.[40]

One of the most memorable episodes in the history of La Masacuata was a poetry reading and public gathering to honor Che Guevara's legacy the poets held in 1968, which generated a negative response of the ultraconservative bishop of San Vicente, Pedro Arnoldo Aparicio Quintanilla. The city's mayor—a member of the official party, the PCN—oddly supported the event, probably out of respect for San Vicente's diverse cultural tradition. However, the Catholic hierarchy in San Vicente did not take La Masacuata's boldness lightly. While Hernández, Sancho, Flamenco, and other poets read their work outside the main Catholic church in the city, Bishop Aparicio and the members of a paramilitary group called Los Caballeros de Cristo Rey that he had formed violently dispersed the gathering.[41] In the aftermath of this event, Aparicio, a militant anti-communist, excommunicated the poets and artists affiliated with La Masacuata.[42] The poets were not hostile to the Church, but Aparicio likely viewed them as rebels who posed a cultural, ideological, and political threat to Catholic conservatism in El Salvador.

Town politics can be deeply personal. Aparicio, who was nicknamed "Tamagás" (a poisonous snake), became a sworn enemy of "Los Masacuatudos," as town people often called the poets of La Masacuata. He warned Catholics in San Vicente to stay away from Los Masacuatudos, whom he considered dangerous subversives. In a sermon Aparicio told his parishioners: "Don't listen to them [the rebel poets]. They are trying to sicken the minds of Salvadorans not only in San Vicente but all over El Salvador. They are subversives."[43] This antipathy was mutual. Minhero recalled that he had a "direct, personal, and written confrontation" with Bishop Aparicio, whom he depicted as "one of the most reactionary individuals ever in El Salvador."[44] Flamenco remembered Aparicio as a "terribly corrupt" individual who played an active role in the repression of the 1960s as the chief of Los Caballeros de Cristo Rey. "El Tamagás was the antithesis of La Masacuata," said Flamenco.[45]

Members of La Masacuata also conducted demonstrations in support of unions and other social movements, which they unofficially represented in the city. They gathered banners of unions, student movements, and the University of El Salvador, which they displayed according to the occasion. Flamenco recalled a colorful march organized by La Masacuata in 1968 during which the poets ingeniously used the banners to increase the visual impact of the small number of participants:

> La Masacuata worked very nicely, wonderfully. We always had almost all the [union] banners FUSS, FESTIAVCES, FESINCONSTRANS, and the university's banner. We had a lot of banners. We were just a few. Once we organized a demonstration from the train station to the [Cañas] park. To each guy [*curioso*] who joined we gave a banner and sent him [her] ahead. The demonstration was moving. Carlos Alfonso [Hernández] wore his long MacArthur pants [baggy khaki pants]. He was a tall guy. He was ahead of the demonstration, chanting: "The people united will never be defeated." We arrived at the park and held a meeting. [When the gathering ended] we rolled our banners as if we were vendors and went home around 1:00 p.m..[46]

The interactions between La Masacuata and young Nicaraguan writers and poets who visited San Vicente constituted pivotal moments in the trajectory of this movement. The Nicaraguan writer and historian Jorge Eduardo Arellano met with members of the group in 1969.[47] "Jorge Arellano was not a Sandinista but became a renowned historian of Sandinismo. [When] he came [to San Vicente] he was surprised to learn what we [La Masacuata] did at the time of the dictatorship," commented Sancho. Arellano told Sancho about his idea to promote a dialogue between Sandinistas and Christians in Nicaragua.[48] Leonel Rugama, a young Nicaraguan poet who became an icon of the Sandinista Revolution, also visited La Masacuata in San Vicente in December 1969, a few weeks before his death in combat on January 15, 1970.[49] Rugama talked about the Sandinista insurgency in Nicaragua with Hernández and other poets. In turn, Hernández told Rugama about La Masacuata's plan to start an armed movement in the near future.[50]

Sancho, Flamenco, Monterrosa, Minhero, and possibly Hernández also visited Nicaragua in 1969 to continue their conversations with the Nicaraguan poets and to seek out support for their revolutionary activism.[51] The trip substantially expanded the political and cultural horizons of the group. "We went because we did not have money [to build the movement]. We went to Nicaragua to look for contacts," recalled Flamenco.[52] They actually made the considerably long trip between San Vicente and Managua by hitchhiking (roughly 532 kilometers). "La Masacuata meandered in Nicaragua [salió a pegar un corcón a Nicaragua]. All the crazy boys went there."[53] During their sojourn in Managua, they met poets who were sympathetic with the Sandinistas and a writer known as the "Carpenter Poet," a figure affiliated with Somoza's Liberal Party.[54] They also met young Sandinista leaders, including Daniel Ortega, and prominent Nicaraguan poets like José Coronel Urtecho: "We met this gentleman who is now president of Nicaragua, Daniel Ortega. We were daring, we were just [a bunch of] little high school graduates but we met the big guys in Nicaragua [la macizada de Nicaragua]: Coronel Urtecho [and other] poets of great stature."[55] But as it turned out, their stay in Nicaragua was brief because the National Guard expelled them from that country after they spoke out publicly against Somoza.[56] "That trip was a decisive flight for the future that awaited La Masacuata," wrote Minhero.[57]

One wonders why the repressive apparatus in El Salvador did not crack down on La Masacuata in the late 1960s, as the group's revolutionary activism was public. The answer to this query is probably that it did not take the rebel poets seriously. The National Guard routinely monitored Sancho's activities in San Vicente but never arrested him. They followed his steps closely during his frequent visits to the city from San Salvador. "They waited for me at the bus stops, but then I took the train," remembered Sancho jokingly. On one occasion, Flamenco, who was then in his early twenties, publicly displayed some books by Lenin at his barbershop in downtown San Vicente. Sancho, who had brought the Marxist-Leninist literature from San Salvador to start a "clandestine library" in San Vicente, asked Flamenco why he had exhibited the books. The latter replied to the baffled Sancho that he wanted to "raise people's consciousness" about the struggle. Another time, Flamenco allegedly invited a personal friend who turned out to be a police detective to a secret meeting of La Masacuata that brought together roughly forty people. Sancho remarked that the detective "made his day" collecting the identities of many of the group's affili-ates.[58] Flamenco corroborated these incidents and emphasized that in the 1960s he indeed believed that the public display of Marxist-Leninist literature was a way to show "a historical truth" and the validity of working-class struggles else-where to the people of San Vicente. The unconventional Flamenco commented about this episode: "I did display the books [by Lenin at the barbershop]. It did not make sense to hide them. If we did we were hiding a truth, a historical truth. Lenin had been the promoter of the proletarian revolution in the world. Why hide it? Let them know."[59] He also clarified that he had not personally invited the detective to the La Masacuata meeting but rather had told a young carpenter and poet to invite "all his friends" to the gathering. When Flamenco asked the poet why he had brought the detective to the meeting, he simply responded that the detective was indeed his friend.[60] But despite the many security gaffes Sancho, Flamenco, and other members of La Masacuata committed, the state forces did not suppress them in the 1960s. Perhaps the naiveté they showed at that time puzzled the authorities, causing them to underestimate the group's capacity to pose a serious threat to the state.[61] For Minhero, state and economic elites simply "ignored" the movement. Privately they "considered it a harmless expression of unruly petit bourgeois youth of both sexes."[62] As Flamenco put it:

> They [the state agents] saw us as an expression of juvenile rebellion, they did not think we were the youth that had collided with the system; but as young thinkers, as intellectuals we had to break with all that and open a new road for the new generations. They have it now. We crashed with a system that had generated many corrupt governments and had massacred people.[63]

At any rate, it is still surprising to consider how and why La Masacuata was able to organize a political movement, as it were, under the noses of the highly organized repressive apparatus in San Vicente. During the counterinsur-gent buildup of the mid-1960s, San Vicente had a tight security structure that involved an army Infantry Brigade, the National Guard, the Treasury Police, the National Police, and the local paramilitary structures. The latter included not only the state paramilitary network (El Servicio Territorial) led by local com-manders and commissioners stationed in each hamlet but also Los Caballeros de Cristo Rey, the paramilitary group commanded by Bishop Aparicio. Both the state paramilitaries, which were integrated into ORDEN circa 1965, and Los Caballeros formed spy networks in hamlets, which reported the whereabouts of local residents they labeled "atheist communist" subversives to the depart-mental commander stationed at army brigade in San Vicente.[64] This situation illustrates the close collaboration between the repressive apparatus of the state and conservative sectors of the Catholic Church in the 1960s.[65] But despite the insidious repressive network in San Vicente, La Masacuata conducted meetings with a group of peasant activists in the late 1960s. They convened at an abandoned house at a place called La Gloria located on the outskirts of the city. Left political leaders and intellectuals visited San Vicente to interact with the poets and the peasant activists who regularly gathered at that place. Schafik Hándal (an influential communist intellectual), Fabio Castillo (the former rector of the University of El Salvador and the PAR presidential candidate in 1967), and poets of earlier generations such as José Roberto Cea, Tirso Canales, Manlio Argueta, and Alfonso Quijada Urías visited the activists at La Gloria. These meetings enabled the articulation of multiple trans-class urban-rural alliances, including the formation of a nucleus of the UDN—the legal opposition party sponsored by the PCS—in San Vicente. Some members of La Masacuata actually joined the UDN. Flamenco, for instance, became the party's first candidate from San Vicente for the 1970 Legislative Assembly election. Although he was not elected for that post, he received a few hundred votes. In the intensely repressive environment of that period, Flamenco's ticket helped La Masacuata (and the PCS) to test the waters of electoral politics.[66]

La Masacuata in San Salvador

Besides conducting an intense activism in San Vicente, La Masacuata also influenced the cultural life in San Salvador in multiple ways. Hernández and other poets from San Vicente were also student activists at the University of El Salvador at the time of the reform initiated by Castillo. The reform greatly expanded access to higher education to students from cities and towns across the country, such as Hernández. The poets of La Masacuata found a space at the university library where they planned their activism in San Salvador. They lived both at *pupilajes* (boarding houses) and in the university's student housing.[67] Flamenco also moved to San Salvador, hoping to expand the organization in the capital. Because he was not a university student and did not have a permanent job, he lived a precarious existence in the city. He usually ate simple meals at friends' homes, as well as fruit he picked up in parks or other public spaces.[68] Salvador "Chito" Silis, a member of the group from Usulután, who was more affluent than his peers from San Vicente, started a bookstore in San Salvador that offered a selection of literature that was usually unavailable in the city.[69]

The poets distributed *Brigada La Masacuata* (the group's magazine) and pamphlets like *Seudópodo primero* and *Los Masacuatines* in San Salvador and other cities.[70] The magazine featured the cultural and political views of the movement, as well as poetry from Cuba, Nicaragua, and El Salvador. It scorned the alleged pedantry of earlier literary generations and announced a "cultural offensive" against "the bloodsuckers of labor":

> We are youth [*somos juventud*] and that is the best way to define us before stiff brains [*cerebros anquilosados*]. We start this cultural offensive [*embestida cultural*], just like that, because we think that to define La Masacuata would be too difficult, because we are as complicated as life itself. . . . someone expected a manifesto like other previous movements have done it or a publicity campaign or that we consider ourselves the most genial artists. . . . well, no, we don't do those pantomimes or romantic posturing of a buried and unburied epoch. . . . we will do those tasks that are fitting for us without drumming or a triumphal march. . . . we no longer have the hope of integrating ourselves into the army you belong to, the army of conformists, of peaceful beings vis-à-vis the atrocities . . . moneymakers [*tragamonedas*] with spiritual thirst. . . . we defend everything that culturally liberates humanity from the bloodsuckers of labor.[71]

Notwithstanding their rebelliousness, the poets of La Masacuata were keenly interested in writers of previous generations whom they considered guiding figures for their art and activism. Sancho, for instance, considered himself a "neo-Marxist" in the late 1960s, but he was equally interested in Alberto Masferrer. "I was a Marxist at that time, but I was not a popularizer of Marxism as I did not have a defined political line, I [also] joined Los Círculos Masferrerianos," recalled Sancho.[72] These were study groups specializing in the works of Masferrer, a prolific cultural figure in the early twentieth century who penned influential essays such as *The Minimum Vital, Dammed Money, To Read and to Write, Letter to a Worker*, and the novel *A Life at the Cinema*, among other works.[73] He formulated a moralistic discourse on the evils of agrarian capitalism, alcoholism, illiteracy, lack of education, class and gender oppression, and the high levels of social violence and crime that characterized Salvadoran society at that time. Dalton and other poets of earlier generations disparaged Masferrer's utopian doctrine as presented in *The Minimum Vital*, which advocated restraint for profit-making capitalists and conformism for workers to avert social conflicts and to ensure prosperity, but curiously La Masacuata never criticized it.

In the late 1960s, members of La Masacuata also developed a strong connection with the journal *La Pájara Pinta*, which at that time was directed by the poet Claudia Lars, a major literary figure in the country. After an initial clash between Sancho and Lars, the latter opened *La Pájara Pinta* to Hernández and other members of the group. Sancho had accused the venerable Lars of refusing to publish the work of young poets and labeled her "a censor." The poet Roberto

Armijo—a member of the Committed Generation—facilitated a conversation between Sancho and Lars to work out this issue. In the meeting Lars allegedly told Sancho: "You don't know me. I am of Irish descent. My grandfather was an industrial worker in New York. I belong to an immigrant family. I know. Visit me again." The remorseful Sancho apologized to Lars. He commented about this incident: "I did *a bandazo* [an erratic political move] with Claudia, but I promptly rectified it."[74] La Masacuata also made attempts to connect young poets with writers of earlier generations, who often kept their distance from their peers. Sancho organized a memorable dinner party at his upper-middle-class family house in Colonia Flor Blanca in San Salvador for young and seasoned writers and poets. To his surprise, the who's who of Salvadoran literature showed up at the gathering.[75] These episodes indicate that La Masacuata constituted a generation that represented a rupture, while at the same time honoring the work of its predecessors. As the Brigada La Masacuata put it: "We recognized every previous [literary] work."[76]

La Masacuata took Salvadoran and Central American history seriously. "The seed is deep because they [the poets of La Masacuata] all loved the country's history," recalled Sancho.[77] David Luna—a professor of history at the University of El Salvador—was an influential figure among this cohort. He taught Sancho and other members of La Masacuata the social and economic history of Central America and research methodologies that shaped their views on society and politics in the 1960s. As Sancho explained it:

> My professor David Luna was a multifaceted man. He was a historian and filmmaker. . . . He taught me historical [research] methodology. I learned about the history of the Chamorro-Brian Treaty [the interoceanic canal treaty signed between the United States and Nicaragua in 1914], the Panama Canal, the liberal revolutions in El Salvador and Costa Rica of 1948. . . . we had a regional vision.[78]

In contrast to Sancho and other poets of his generation who respected Luna, PCS activists at the university labeled the historian "bohemian and crazy" because Luna was an eccentric scholar who did not subscribe to the party's pro-Soviet views.[79] The contrasting attitudes between the poets of La Masacuata and the communist activists toward independent intellectuals like Luna reveal the growing cultural and political rift between these groups. This fissure grew steadily as emerging New Left intellectuals like Sancho and Hernández defied the PCS's reformist politics and the communist leaders objected to the poets' radical activism. Although at one time Sancho and other members of the group had had a working relationship with the Patriotic Youth (the Communist Youth) in San Vicente, they never joined the PCS. The communist activists in

San Vicente considered the rebel poets "untrustworthy petit bourgeois" (i.e., middle-class) intellectuals, and the latter were simply uninterested in joining a party they deemed reformist. The PCS engagement in electoral politics despite the prevailing authoritarianism seemed objectionable to the young poets.[80] This is consistent with the views on the increasing political participation of middle-class intellectuals formulated by the PCS in 1968. Hándal, the party's most influential intellectual, deemed that the "infantile radicalism" inherent in the massive integration of middle-class sectors to the revolutionary organizations created further obstacles for revolution in Latin America, and that "a great ideological effort" was in fact necessary to reorient them "to sane revolutionary motives."[81] In practical terms, Hándal wanted young intellectuals like the members of La Masacuata to endorse the PCS's electoral politics, not to start an armed insurgency.

The age and cultural differences between these cohorts were also important. The poets were in their early twenties, the communist leaders in their late thirties. Hándal and other communist intellectuals had historical links with the Soviet Union, Cuba, and other socialist countries. They had been active in union and university politics, formed alliances with legal opposition parties, and participated in electoral politics for several years. They had briefly engaged in militant activism at the time of FUAR. The poets, on the other hand, were emerging actors of the Global Sixties and embodied the countercultural inclinations, avant-garde aesthetics, and radical politics of that period. They were eager to defy the Old Left (i.e., the PCS) conventions in their efforts to articulate a new revolutionary strategy, particularly after the murder of Che Guevara in Bolivia in 1967.

The tensions between La Masacuata and the PCS intensified during the war between El Salvador and Honduras in July 1969. At that time, the poet Eduardo Sancho, Fabio Castillo, and other well-established left intellectuals in El Salvador faulted the PCS for endorsing the Salvadoran government's war effort against Honduras. Sancho, along with Castillo and the Honduran scholar Jorge Arturo Reina, actively opposed the war between the two countries. Amid the nationalistic hysteria that permeated Salvadoran society during the war, which included an intoxicating anti-Honduran radio and television campaign sponsored by the Sánchez Hernández government that featured songs like "El Pájaro Picón Picón," which exalted Salvadoran machismo and denigrated Hondurans, Sancho, Castillo, and Reina went to San Vicente to conduct an antiwar rally at the city's plaza. They called the conflagration between the two neighboring countries "an unjust war" and denounced the *patrioterismo* (false patriotism) they attributed to the official party and the PCS. As they returned to San Salvador, a group of paramilitaries seized them near Tecoluca. The thugs forced them to lie face down on the pavement while they held machetes against their throats and told them: "You are already dead communist asses."[82] Remembering this incident, Sancho stated: "There was a real hatred against the University of El Salvador [among the paramilitaries]." Hernández and other members of La Masacuata also conducted protests in San Vicente against the 1969 war between El Salvador and Honduras. "We are conducting cultural activities [against the war], . . . activities related to political culture," Hernández jokingly told Sancho.[83]

La Masacuata Wages War

Four out of the ten founders of El Grupo—the first urban guerrilla cell formed in 1969—were poets and writers, and three of them were members of La Masacuata. The poets Lil Milagro Ramírez, Alfonso Hernández, and Eduardo Sancho and the writer Carlos Eduardo Rico Mira were among the founders of the Salvadoran guerrillas.[84] This was no coincidence. El Grupo emerged in the midst of an "intense and deep" cultural milieu in San Salvador, which gathered writers, poets, painters, students, and hippies, who routinely met at the university campus and the city's cafes to discuss culture and politics. "They formed groups of lively young intellectuals with very high cultural levels," recalled Sancho.[85]

The origins of El Grupo have remained relatively obscure until recently.[86] Who, in fact, were the founders of this movement? What were their personal, political, and religious backgrounds? What were their international connections? What roles did the rebels poets play in this process? El Grupo emerged at the University of El Salvador. Sancho and Alejandro Rivas Mira, the main leaders of the cell, first met at the university campus in San Salvador circa 1969. The latter had recently returned to El Salvador after spending nearly two years studying in Germany. Rivas Mira was—perhaps still is—an elusive figure of the Salvadoran New Left.[87] His cousin, the writer Rico Mira, one of the first guerrilla operatives in El Salvador, was obviously baffled to find him in Havana circa 1972 transformed into a leader of the Salvadoran guerrillas. He remembered him as a teenage Nazi sympathizer who morphed into a Marxist revolutionary.[88] Rivas Mira had initially joined a group at the university called the Social Christian Revolutionary University Federation also known as Social Christians, and possibly Catholic Action. He was also a Christian Democrat Party (PDC) activist. After he witnessed how National Guardsmen in San Miguel assaulted peasant voters during the presidential elections held in 1967, he announced to Abraham Rodríguez—the PDC presidential candidate—his intention to form a guerrilla group.[89] According to Sancho, Rivas Mira joined or collaborated with the Baader-Meinhof Group in Germany and participated in the French insurgency of 1968. Upon his return to El Salvador, he contacted university students mostly affiliated with the PDC and Catholic Action whom he considered qualified to form a guerrilla group in El Salvador. Although Sancho was not connected with those groups, Rivas Mira approached him probably due to his well-established revolutionary credentials as a member of La Masacuata. Curiously, Sancho recalled his first encounter with Rivas Mira as an ordinary event. During their first interaction, Rivas Mira told Sancho: "I want to speak with you. We are thinking about this [forming an armed group]." To which Sancho responded: "Yes, let's do it."[90] Sancho spent roughly two decades operating as a guerrilla commander in urban and rural milieux in El Salvador. Possibly, he remembered this foundational episode in the history of the Salvadoran insurgency simply as an affirmation of the young revolutionaries' will to initiate hostilities against the state, nothing more.

Another major figure in the creation of El Grupo was Lil Milagro Ramírez. Rivas Mira had also asked Ramírez, a Catholic poet and activist who had conducted workshops among peasant communities since the mid-1960s, to join the movement. She had recently returned to El Salvador from Chile, where she had witnessed the "Revolution in Freedom" led by the Christian Democrat president Eduardo Frei. Sancho remembered Ramírez as a sisterly or motherly figure who instilled cohesiveness among the mostly male members of El Grupo thanks to her intellect, personality, and devotion to her fellow combatants (she was twenty-four years old in 1970). Sancho recalled fondly that she was the only leader of El Grupo who had leverage over Joaquín Villalobos, Rafael Arce Zablah, and other former Catholic Action affiliates who had joined the guerrillas, whom Sancho and Rivas Mira deemed an unruly group. They often asked Ramírez to put "her children [*tus niños*], the enfants terribles of ACUS," under control. While Villalobos and Arce were more conversant in Marxist theory than Ramírez, they honored her authority due to her acumen and allure. On a more mundane level, Sancho recalled that Ramírez enjoyed cooking meals for the leaders of El Grupo and tried to help a collaborator of the organization to overcome alcoholism. Sancho recalled telling Ramírez: "The revolution is not for helping drunks [*bolos*]."[91] Rico Mira also wrote about his interactions with Ramírez during his brief participation in the ERP—the offspring organization of El Grupo—circa 1973. Like Sancho, he depicted her as a cordial and mature woman with a "great human sensibility." According to Rico Mira, Ramírez enjoyed reading *Mafalda*—a comic by the Argentinian artist Quino—and had a keen interest in art, literature, women's rights, and metaphysics. He described her as an affectionate woman who wiped the faces of destitute children who wandered in the market where she usually ate. He also deemed her an accomplished intellectual who devised self-defense strategies for the social movements influenced by the National Resistance (RN)—a faction of the ERP. Ramírez envisioned the creation of armed self-defense groups among student, worker, and peasant movements, which faced increasing attacks from government forces in the early 1970s. Nevertheless, Rico Mira was also critical of her rigid ideas on military discipline during the internal crisis in the ERP in 1973, which motivated him to leave the organization.[92]

The formation of El Grupo took place in social gatherings organized by the Social Christian activists. According to Sancho, those who participated in these meetings were "defined" from the beginning.[93] That is, they were committed to declare war on the state without further delay. They were an eclectic group made up of Social Christian intellectuals like Ramírez, "neo-Marxists" like Sancho, writers from San Vicente like Hernández and Rico Mira, and university intellectuals like Rivas Mira who were conversant in Marxist theory and Catholic intellectual traditions. They deemed Rivas Mira the most gifted intellectual of this cohort and chose him as their main leader. "He was [a] top [intellectual]. He articulated the critique of the PCS. We told him you are the [chosen] one," said Sancho.[94]

In the early 1970s, La Masacuata experienced a rapid transformation, as the rebel poets became insurgents. At that time, Hernández, Rico Mira (aka "Pancho"), and Sancho turned into combatants while other affiliates of the group became collaborators of the nascent insurgency. The poets were also among the first recruiters of the guerrillas in San Vicente and San Salvador. Because they often performed at public venues and high schools, they were able to enlist other poets, writers, and artists. "The poets from San Vicente are founders of the guerrillas. . . . they recruited many poets, that is why during the first wave [of the insurgency in the 1970s] many poets died," remarked Sancho.[95] Pondering the simultaneous transformation of La Masacuata and the creation of El Grupo, Sancho stated: "La Masacuata was about denouncing [the dictatorship]. At the university El Grupo was emerging. . . . La Masacuata meant mutation [into a revolutionary movement], not simply the shedding of the skin."[96] Flamenco commented about this process:

> The poets of La Masacuata formed El Grupo. They joined the Rivas Mira brothers from Apastepeque [a town in San Vicente]. The entire Masacuata became rebellious: some [collaborated] in logistics, some collected information; others conducted [poetry] readings. Everyone contributed to the advancement of the thing [they supported or participated in the insurgency]. La Masacuata became subversive.[97]

The historical record bears Sancho and Flamenco out. In June 1970, while El Grupo was forming, La Masacuata produced its own cryptic declaration of war against the state and the elites. The group critiqued communist intellectuals like Hándal who opposed the insurgency ("those firemen with special attire, with neutral positions") and called on the Brigades of La Masacuata—their followers in San Vicente, San Salvador, and other cities—to organize for the start of the guerrilla war ("to prepare their little cultural cannons"):

> We have decided to reach the fire, to make the most convenient use [of it] against those who don't let live the human plenitude or those whose task is to stop or extinguish the fire. Those firemen with special attire, with neutral positions. The fire that we use to throw is the result of the enthusiasm and devotion to cultural work, because if there is no creative artistic [and] organizational work there is no fire, no flame that produces heat. Thus we tell the groups that make up the BRIGADES to prepare their little cultural cannons [*sus cañoncitos culturales*], to store powder fused with the Latin American tradition, to start distinguishing the mediocre, the parasites, the dominant pedantic [*los encopeta-dos dominantes*], the troubled recessive [*los enfrascados recesivos*], the bureaucrats, the vulgar imitators.[98]

La Masacuata called on its brigades to orient the rebel Salvadoran youth in the fight against the dictatorship and to embrace an unbending insurgent spirit:

> The role of the BRIGADES OF LA MASACUATA . . . is to be on the side of the nonconformist youth, rebels with a cause, with interest for the new. Only that could transform the Brigades into cultural guides. We have always been willing to fall on our noses.
>
> We are with this youth that "has said enough," which wants to assault the walls, the walls that will create obstacles for our work, but to take care of this we have ladders, tin cans, lamps to illuminate. . . . We will build a new horizon for us, we will open gaps, trenches.[99]

These statements illustrate the measure of La Masacuata's ambition. The poets sought to mobilize the nonconformist Salvadoran youth into battle with the state and the elites through their revolutionary cultural politics. They posed a crucial albeit unacknowledged challenge to authoritarian rule. They rejected the PCS's reformism, which in their view, attempted to channel the rebelliousness of Salvadoran youth into electoral politics.

On March 2, 1972, Alfonso Hernández (aka Arturo Buendía), Rico Mira, and seven other militants initiated the hostilities against the state.[100] They carried out one of the first act of war against the regime the Salvadoran left had conducted since the fateful 1932 uprising. They formed two insurgent commando units armed with handguns that attacked National Guardsmen stationed at the city's children hospital in order to confiscate their G-3 German-made rifles.[101] In 2003, Rico Mira published a memoir about his time as a guerrilla combatant; he passed away soon after. Unlike most practitioners of this genre, who usually are still active in public life and produce trite narratives about their personal trajectories, he wrote a poignant account about traumatic events he witnessed during the conflict.[102] In Rico Mira's narrative, only Hernández and Carlos Menjívar, another combatant, were able to open fire against the guardsmen stationed at the hospital. He claimed that several years after this episode, Hernández told him that Menjívar shot a guardsman, killing him almost instantly. During the attack, Hernández bent to avoid the exchange of gunfire (because he was a tall individual). He shot at a guardsman, but as the latter surrendered his G-3 rifle, he spared him. Hernández was clearly traumatized by this event. He told Rico Mira that he would never forget the passing of the guardsman killed by Menjívar who "clung to his rifle as if he was clinging to life itself."[103] In the aftermath of the guerrilla attack, the ERP (the new organization formed in March 1972 by survivors of El Grupo) issued a communiqué announcing: "The peace of the rich has ended. The war of the people has started."[104]

Flamenco did not join El Grupo because he had a large family to feed. Instead, he remained active in electoral politics as a member of the Nationalist Democratic Union during the 1970s. He also supported the FMLN throughout the civil war. Twice state agents kidnapped him in the 1980s. He worked closely with Schafik Hándal and other Communist Party leaders who visited San Vicente in the early 1970s. However, he did not consider his electoral activism inconsistent with armed struggle but rather as one of several means to weaken the authoritarian regime. In his view, both the poets of La Masacuata who had joined the guerrillas and those like him who remained active in electoral politics were part of the same movement. "We formed a kind of fan [un abanico]; we kept in touch," Flamenco stated. For him, the Salvadoran elites' genocidal trajectory, which started at the time of Aquino's rebellion in 1832 or even earlier, informed the brutal repression in the 1970s and ultimately united the fractious Salvadoran left.[105] At the height of the left's sour and bloody ideological disputes in the 1970s, which resulted in the murder of Roque Dalton carried out by a militaristic faction of the ERP led by Rivas Mira in 1975, Flamenco tried to persuade his associates in the PCS and the insurgency to unite to avoid being exterminated by the dictatorship. He told his comrades that in fact "Colonel [Arturo A.] Molina"—who became president of El Salvador after the 1972 electoral fraud—was "more revolutionary than Schafik Hándal":

> My function was to convince them [the guerrillas and the PCS] that we should not work separately that we had to unite because the enemy did not ask what organization do you belong to? [And then figured] I will pardon you. I will not pardon you. They killed everyone [nos daban parejo]. The comrades jokingly told me: Emiliano is crazy. He says that

Colonel Molina is more revolutionary than Schafik Hándal. Yes, I told
them. You see, you don't want to follow Schafik's parliamentary way but
Colonel Molina will unite us by force [*a pura verga*]. And that was how
it happened. They repressed us and thus ignited the war. Many people
became revolutionary guerrillas not out of conviction but out of con-
venience. If they did not join [the guerrillas] [the military] killed them
because they killed everyone who did not think as the regime did.[106]

In contrast with Sancho, who was highly critical of the PCS politics in the
1960s and 1970s, Flamenco had a different recollection. He considered Hándal
a brilliant strategist and not "a revisionist" as most New Left intellectuals of this
period would have it. Echoing contemporary visions circulated by the FMLN
that portray Hándal as the most visionary leader of the Salvadoran Revolution,
Flamenco stated:

Schafik was accused of being a revisionist because he rejected the guerrillas [in the 1960s and 1970s]. No, he was a great strategist, brilliant.
He knew perfectly well that he had to let dialectics work, to exhaust
the legal means. Once it was demonstrated that [the dictatorship] did
not respect anything [it rigged the 1972 and 1977 presidential elections
and escalated repression], then people had to accept that the only way
out was an armed insurrection. And it was like that.[107]

However, Flamenco quietly but clearly affirmed that La Masacuata (not even
El Grupo and much less the PCS) started the revolutionary war in El Salvador
by combining "action and emotion" to spark people's consciousness:

We combined action and emotion in the process of change. We worked
with that mentality. The war started then. As simple as that, the war
started like that. Our [La Masacuata's] position caused others who
were more advanced than ourselves who had money [to take up arms].
They told me so: the boys are right but they do not have the capacity to
implement a project of such magnitude. A very important revolutionary Schafik Hándal [also] told me so. . . . There has not been another literary movement that turned into a [revolutionary] vanguard. We tried
to be dialectic.[108]

Minhero's recollection of the roles that La Masacuata played in the formation
of the guerrillas echoed Flamenco's. For him, state agents were "clumsy," in that
they failed to carefully read La Masacuata's publications and to realize what were
the group's intentions. Thus, they did not persecute "those who appeared as

masacuatos [affiliates of La Masacuata]." Had they done that, "possibly the civil war would not have started, because the majority of *masacuatos* joined the revolutionary guerrilla, some were its founders."[109]

La Masacuata was part of a cultural boom that occurred in El Salvador in the late 1960s and early 1970s. The poet and theater director Manuel Sorto, a former member of the group, described that period as a "marvelous epoch." He was one of the last poets to integrate La Masacuata while he was an actor in a theater group called El Taller de los Vagos (the Vagrants' Workshop). For him, La Masacuata was part of a powerful "wave" (*una marea que viene y ahí va*) that deeply transformed poets, artists, musicians, and actors in El Salvador. It was also "a kind of laboratory" that produced the "founders of the guerrillas and new cultural movements" that had a major impact on the country's cultural politics in the 1970s and beyond.[110]

Like the poets of La Masacuata, other countercultural movements, public intellectuals, peasant leaders, priests, students, and teachers across El Salvador also debated multiple revolutionary strategies to confront the political crisis in the 1970s, which preceded the civil war. The state sought to contain these emerging actors using all the legal and illegal means at its disposal.

5

The Making of the Internal Enemy

Beauty queens from five continents attended the Miss Universe pageant contest held in San Salvador in July 1975. The show, choreographed at an awkward-looking structure resembling a Mayan pyramid, was broadcast to millions of TV viewers around the world in a daunting attempt to invigorate the tourist industry of a country on the brink of civil war. The day after the head of the Salvadoran tourist institute announced the government's intention "to utilize Anne Pohtamo," Miss Universe 1975, to promote the country's image, army and security forces massacred participants in a student demonstration in downtown San Salvador that protested a crackdown against university students in Santa Ana earlier that month.[1] The widely documented incident, which recalled the Tlatelolco massacre in Mexico City in 1968, took place on July 30 at a busy intersection of the city, when army troops and security forces, supported by armored vehicles, opened fire on the demonstrators, killing, injuring, and disappearing scores of protesters (figure 5.1).[2] For several months, the emerging popular movements vigorously protested the attack and demanded the release of those who had been captured and disappeared.

The rural and urban massacres perpetrated by the state forces in the 1970s, most notably the mass killing of university students on July 30, 1975, in downtown San Salvador, became episodes that allowed the convergence of various strata of intellectuals. The massacres sought to terrorize subaltern groups and intellectuals into submission. However, these efforts turned counterproductive as intellectuals represented the horrific events as "declarations of war" against the social movements, thus eroding the regime's repressive strategy. Ultimately, urban and peasant intellectuals transformed these acts of state terror into symbols of popular rebellion that nurtured several generations of activists and insurgents.

The July 30 crackdown against university students is an event about which we know much, and yet we understand very little. Although its basic chronology has been clearly established, there are huge open questions about the decision-making process that led to the killings, the direct authorship of the massacre, the

Figure 5.1 "Colonel Molina Where Are These Students?" The headline alludes to the victims of the July 30, 1975, massacre in downtown San Salvador carried out by army and security forces during the government of President Arturo Armando Molina. *Opinión Estudiantil*, August 14, 1975, p. 3. Courtesy of CIDAI, Biblioteca "P. Florentino Idoate, S.J." of the Central American University "José Simeón Cañas."

repressive techniques utilized, and the crackdown's sociopolitical consequences. This event was a conjuncture that enabled the social and ideological articulation of teachers, peasant leaders, and university activists, during the formation of the Revolutionary Popular Bloc (BPR), a coalition of social movements. A large-scale army operation against peasant communities in Aguilares in 1977 also became a turning point in the conflict between state forces and the growing rural and urban social movements.

During the 1970s, the teacher and peasant movements became crucial components of the left's strategy to unsettle oligarchic-military hegemony. The National Association of Salvadoran Educators June 21 (ANDES), which was founded in 1965, seriously undermined the traditional power base of the authoritarian regime, generating a movement that attracted thousands of disaffected educators and fostered student and peasant organizing. ANDES featured national teachers' strikes in 1968 and 1971 to reject the government's education reform and to demand basic labor rights, which drew widespread support from high school students and other sectors. It also denounced the blatant discrepancy between the idyllic representation of the country promoted by the organizers of the 1975 Miss Universe contest, who called El Salvador "El País de la Sonrisa" (the Country with a Smile), and the oppressive sociopolitical conditions endured by the majority of Salvadorans.[3] The organization labeled the Miss Universe contest a "trivial affair," which epitomized the aesthetics and notions of female beauty of international elites and silenced the exploitation of Salvadoran working-class women. According to ANDES, the event constituted a deliberate attempt to divert worldwide attention from the growing movement that opposed the authoritarian government of President Molina.[4] The association's stance on Miss Universe was an expression of its public pedagogy, which encompassed a critique of "dependent capitalism" in El Salvador. In particular, ANDES engaged debates on the shortcomings of the educational system and the government's agrarian reform program during its yearly national assemblies called "congresses."[5] The peasant movement also became a major factor in the shifting power dynamics in the 1970s. The magnitude of peasant mobilizations in urban areas and in key sectors of the agrarian economy at that time vastly surpassed that of the indigenous peasant uprising that had occurred in the central and western regions of the country in 1932.

Autonomous peasant mobilization receded after state forces massacred thousands of indigenous peasants and their urban allies (mostly Communist Party intellectuals and union activists) in the aftermath of the 1932 revolt.[6] In contrast with the despotic regime of Rafael L. Trujillo in the Dominican Republic (1930–1961), which promoted land distribution processes in an effort to create a strong peasant constituency, the dictatorship of General Maximiliano Hernández Martínez (December 1931–May 1944) and the subsequent military regimes that governed El Salvador until 1979 did not engage in any significant transformation of the highly polarized agrarian structure in the country.[7] Instead, authoritarian rule in the countryside relied mostly on the deployment of public security and paramilitary forces that maintained a tight social and political control of the rural population between 1932 and 1979.[8] President Molina attempted to conduct an "Agrarian Transformation Program," but ultimately a coalition of landed and business elites boycotted his agrarian policies. In the 1970s, the highly organized peasant mobilization shook up the very basis of oligarchic power in El Salvador. As in the case of the teachers' union, UTC and FECCAS, the largest peasant organizations in the country, which fused into the Federation of Rural Workers (FTC), became a powerful "party association"—a social movement that functioned as a revolutionary party, which mobilized thousands of peasants across the country.[9] The teachers' union and the peasant federation crucially contributed to the formation of the BPR in 1975.

Responding to the challenge posed by the rising social movements, government forces and clandestine paramilitary groups (i.e., the "death squads") targeted intellectuals (i.e., peasant leaders, teachers, students, and priests) who performed critical leadership and organizational roles within these movements. Between 1971 and 1980, state forces systematically murdered, imprisoned, tortured, and disappeared hundreds of intellectuals. Although the Truth Commission report on El Salvador issued in 1993 provides a general account of the human rights violations committed in El Salvador during the civil war, the extent and the characteristics of state terror in the 1970s have not been sufficiently studied. State terror matched by propaganda campaigns conducted by government agencies, business associations, anonymous right-wing groups, and death squads in the official media and clandestine publications legitimized the persecution of intellectuals whom they considered instigators of subversion. In the 1970s, autonomous peasant mobilizations were "unthinkable" for Salvadoran elites, who generally viewed peasants as submissive and uninformed individuals incapable of organizing social or political movements without the external support of the state, the Church, or the traditional political parties.[10] The copious propaganda produced by state agencies, paramilitary groups, and business associations in the 1970s generally blamed Catholic priests, teachers, and university intellectuals for initiating peasant mobilizations. This set of political discourses and public opinion campaigns, which I call the "pedagogy of terror," aimed at framing intellectuals as "the internal enemy," or the incarnation of an international conspiracy promoted by the Soviet Union and Cuba to subvert the "democratic institutions" in El Salvador.[11] While the "pedagogy of revolution" sponsored by urban and peasant intellectuals sought to create active historical subjects able to transform the world, the "pedagogy of terror" aimed at forming objects rendered passive by the world.[12]

Since the early 1970s, the public discourses formulated by government agencies such as the National Center of Information, business associations, and death squads featured several rhetorical strategies and purposes and had different audiences, but they all framed progressive intellectuals as the "internal enemy." These discourses portrayed activists, political opponents, and Catholic priests as "subversives" or "terrorists," and they equated the social mobilizations with the escalating guerrilla operations in the 1970s. They constituted a set of symbiotic discourses that sought to justify acts of terror against social activists. More to the point, while state agencies defamed them vis-à-vis their potential allies and supporters among the poor and the middle class, business associations pressured the government to crack down on social movements. In turn, death squads derided intellectuals and threatened them with summary executions in clandestine publications issued by countless anonymous groups. In conjunction, these discourses construed the rise of the teacher and the peasant movements as the emergence of the "internal enemy." They conflated the realms of social activism, legal opposition, and insurgency. They subsumed every form of mobilization that challenged the elites' economic and political interests and authoritarian rule into the categories of communist subversion and terrorism. Drawing on this rationale, state forces carried out systematic human rights violations in the 1970s. State terror motivated teachers and other intellectuals to join or support the insurgency. While the emergence of the teacher and the peasant movements as major political actors in the 1970s paralleled the rise of the insurgency, they constituted movements with substantially different histories, politics, and ideologies. However, the mounting repression in the 1970s produced a spiral of political violence that heralded the civil war. Counterinsurgency aimed first and foremost at dismantling the emerging peasant movement. Between 1974 and 1978, security forces and paramilitaries persecuted, incarcerated, tortured, and murdered peasant leaders and activists. These forces also conducted mass killings in rural communities they considered foci of the insurgency. Between 1979 and 1981, they carried out scorched earth campaigns against peasant communities in northeastern Chalatenango, San Vicente, Morazán, and other regions, which sparked the armed conflict.

Claiming the "Teachers' Dignity"

Teachers created a formidable social and political movement in the 1960s. The foundation of ANDES, an independent teachers' union, posed a major challenge to the government of president Fidel Sánchez Hernández (1967–1972). It mobilized thousands of primary and high school teachers, students, and parents across the country during the national strikes it carried out in 1968 and 1971. ANDES advocated a set of labor rights and vigorously opposed Sánchez Hernández's education reform, which they deemed an effort to consolidate US cultural hegemony in El Salvador. Public security forces and paramilitaries battered teachers and their supporters during the 1968 strike. However, the repression against the striking teachers in 1971 was much more brutal. Paramilitaries and security forces attacked teachers who had peacefully gathered at schools in San Salvador and other cities and the homes of leaders of ANDES.

The counterinsurgent apparatus grossly misrepresented the rising labor conflicts during that decade. The National Center of Information (CNI), a state propaganda agency, and the official media depicted the teachers' strike as part of an insurgent offensive to destabilize the Sánchez Hernández government. They portrayed the leaders of ANDES as communist militants who manipulated naive rank-and-file teachers on behalf of the insurgents. The 1971 teachers' strike became a template of the "making of the internal enemy." It was a carefully orchestrated effort of the Salvadoran state and the official media to equate social activism with communist subversion and terrorism to legitimize the repression against the teachers' union. The 1971 crackdown was a watershed in the radicalization of popular politics insofar as several teachers joined or supported the rising guerrilla groups in the aftermath of this event.

In 1965, Carlos López, a newly graduated teacher from Suchitoto, arrived in Chalatenango to start his first job assignment. López remembered that job openings were available only at primary schools in the "towns where nobody wanted to go because of the risky conditions." López first taught at a local school in an isolated village near the Lempa River called Potonico. Although López had a modest rural background, he was appalled when he first experienced the living conditions in the impoverished town. Potonico lacked electricity, running water, and other basic services, and the food supplies were very limited.[13] During the following three years, López taught first grade to barefoot children who suffered high levels of malnutrition and parasite infections, and he walked long distances to get to his job site at the start of the school week. Female teachers working in similar locations also feared being sexually harassed or raped.[14]

In the early 1960s, an unprecedented grass-roots movement emerged to address the deplorable living and labor conditions endured by the majority of teachers. Because the hiring process of teachers was based on political affiliation, the recent graduates of *las escuelas normales* (teachers' schools) often faced serious difficulties obtaining job assignments. To access suitable jobs, teachers joined the PCN, the official party, or the Frentes Magisteriales (Teachers' Fronts) it created during electoral periods. Officials in charge of public education often sent teachers who lacked connections with the military establishment, the official party, or the government to schools in remote villages or hamlets where living and labor conditions were particularly harsh. Teachers were also poorly paid, lacked access to medical care, and often bore the abuse of principals or government supervisors. In the 1960s, teachers earned 200 *colones* (US$80) a month and were only eligible for a salary raise of 10 *colones* (US$4) every five years.[15] They had to work "thirty long years" to be able to earn a monthly salary of 270 *colones* (US$108).[16] At that time in neighboring Honduras, teachers earned 200 *lempiras* (US$100) as a starting salary and 300 *lempiras* (US$175) after twenty-five years of service.[17] In 1963, Mélida Anaya Montes, José Mario López, Arnoldo Vaquerano, Mario González Medrano, and other teachers embarked on the formation of a new movement that promoted *la dignificación del magisterio* (teachers' dignity). The movement was not originally part of the opposition to the government because it dealt exclusively with the teachers' demands, namely, job stability, salary increases, healthcare, and legal rights. For two years, the leaders of this movement, along with government supervisors known as "circuit supervisors," organized teachers' assemblies in towns and hamlets across the country to discuss the formation of a new teachers' organization that they named ANDES in December 1965.[18] ANDES became the first autonomous teachers' union in the country's history.

Carlos López's account of the origins of the teachers' union in Chalatenango revolves around the meetings between Mélida Anaya Montes, a leader of ANDES, and teachers working in the area, held in 1966. At that time, teachers were "unorganized and each one dealt individually" with their challenging living and working conditions. Anaya's explanations for the critical working conditions of teachers made perfect sense to teachers who for the most part were "disoriented" about alternatives to promote their labor rights.[19] According to López, Anaya told an audience of teachers meeting in Chalatenango city in 1966,

> Well, teacher comrades, as a guild we have been disorganized for twenty or thirty years, but now our intention is that teachers go and organize other teachers in order to defend our rights. Chalatenango has thirty-two municipalities, and it is necessary that you go to San Luis del Carmen, Las Flores, and other towns and meet more teachers.[20]

Anaya's call received a warm response among primary school teachers working in the area. Starting in 1966, Carlos López, Roberto Escalante, Roberto Córdova, and other teachers joined an "ANDES collective" to promote the teachers' union in northeastern Chalatenango. Embodying the organization's radical spirit, López and his peers traveled once a week to Cancasque, San Miguel de Mercedes, and San Antonio Los Ranchos, three neighboring towns, to conduct organizational work among teachers and students' parents. "ANDES's influence became widespread because we were disciplined, ANDES's mystique was not a joke. You got it through hard work and political education," said López.[21]

The majority of the roughly fourteen thousand primary school teachers in the country supported ANDES's vigorous campaign to obtain legal recognition as a union and new legislation to protect teachers' labor rights in 1967 and 1968.[22] ANDES organized local assemblies all over the country, a massive teachers' demonstration in San Salvador on June 21, 1967, and a national teachers' strike at the start of 1968. Teachers working in hamlets across Chalatenango participated in meetings led by Anaya Montes and Mario López in Chalatenango city and San Salvador. They actively supported the creation of the teachers' union in order to end "the marginalization, the mistreatment, the low salaries, and the lack of medical care" of teachers. Nearly four hundred teachers working in Chalatenango joined the first national teachers' demonstration held in San Salvador on June 21 to demand the legalization of ANDES.[23]

The two-month teachers' strike in 1968 became the first major confrontation between the emerging teachers' union and the Sánchez Hernández government. The striking teachers camped outside the new building of the Ministry of Education at a place they called the "plaza of the teachers' dignity." The plaza became a symbolic space where teachers, workers, students, and vendors from local markets gathered every day for "58 days" to denounce the "humiliation[s], the selling of [teacher's] degrees," and other practices linked to the "partisan politics" that dominated the profession.[24] As a result of the strike, the government sanctioned the Ley de Escalafón (Law of the Teaching Profession), which created a system of promotion for teachers; but, more important, ANDES affiliates became keenly aware of the organization's huge political clout.[25]

ANDES's antihegemonic discourse featured a radical critique of the educational reform conducted by the Sánchez Hernández government between 1968 and 1972. Modernization, mass media, and development theories that circulated in the United States, Japan, and other countries during that decade inspired Sánchez Hernández's education reform.[26] The reform virtually revamped the country's education system. It introduced educational television, administrative reforms, teacher training programs, methods of school supervision, and new curricula. It also promoted a substantial expansion of primary education and created a diversified high school system.[27] Teachers objected to several components of the reform but found educational television especially jarring because it altered traditional classroom dynamics between teachers and students. *Telemaestros* (TV teachers) who incarnated the technocratic ethos of the reform lectured students on subjects including new mathematics, sciences, and English during the daily broadcasts of the educational television, rendering actual teachers into passive figures in the classroom. Teachers also criticized the automatic promotion of students to the next grade featured in the reform, which they believed contrary to cultural values implicit in traditional education, and new math, which they found "unnecessary" and unpractical.[28] The unionized teachers also articulated a political critique of the reform. ANDES's Tenth Congress, held in December 1974, emphatically declared, "It is not possible to conduct a new education radically different from that to which the exploiting class aspires while the capitalist system prevails. Therefore, the struggle for the new education must be contained in the global strategy to defeat Capitalism and to construct a new society."[29] ANDES intellectuals deemed the official educational reform antithetical to the "liberation pedagogy" formulated by the Brazilian educator Paulo Freire, which they considered one of the most fitting educational models for the emancipation of the Latin American poor. The government's educational reform deepened the "scientific, technological, cultural, economic, and political dependency" of El Salvador on the United States and other developed nations. Moreover, in their view, it pursued the creation of a cheap and ideologically tamed labor force to fulfill the needs of international capitalist markets. In contrast with the official educational reform, ANDES championed an alternative educational model they simply called the "new education." ANDES declared that the new education should promote first and foremost "the emergence of the new man, combative, responsible, and critical"; the study of the "country's reality"; and the "organization and action" toward "total liberation."[30] ANDES affiliates had a twofold responsibility in this enterprise. As teachers, they had to encourage critical thinking among students, challenging imperialist and oligarchic ideologies as well as obsolete and nonscientific contents in the schools' study programs. As "advisers and organizers of other social sectors," teachers had "to live near the students' parents and peasants," engaging specific "work programs" to encourage student and peasant organizing.[31]

"Sometimes the Words and the Reasons Are Worthless": The Crackdown on the Teachers' Movement in 1971

The government's reluctance to consider ANDES's proposal to amend the Law of the Teaching Profession originated the strike. ANDES posited that the PCN representatives, who dominated the National Assembly, disregarded the teachers' proposal despite their initial promise to analyze it over a three-month period. Teachers considered this law crucial to end the politicization of the teaching profession enabled by the regime and to defend their labor rights.[32] They overwhelmingly supported the strike that started on July 7, 1971. According to the minister of education, Walter Béneke, 175 public schools were closed, 131 partially functioned, and 103 worked normally during the strike.[33] Nearly eleven thousand primary school teachers joined the strike (figure 5.2).[34]

In contrast to the 1968 ANDES strike, which featured a two-month public gathering outside the main building of the Ministry of Education in downtown San Salvador, in 1971 the striking teachers occupied numerous schools

Figure 5.2 Teachers affiliated with ANDES at Escuela República de Paraguay in San Salvador during the 1971 strike. *El Tiempo*, Third Week of July, 1971, p. 3. Courtesy of CIDAI, Biblioteca "P.Florentino Idoate, S.J." of the Central American University "José Simeón Cañas."

throughout the country with the support of students and their parents. The government offered the teachers some concessions, but it rejected their basic demands, namely, a salary increase and various reforms concerning the Law of the Teaching Profession, particularly the forming of a joint council (Consejo Nacional de Escalafón) made up of representatives of ANDES and the Ministry of Education.[35] On July 16, thousands of teachers and students marched peacefully outside the National Assembly in support of ANDES's demands, while paramilitaries who pretended to be "groups of concerned parents" entered the National Assembly to batter teachers who lobbied congressmen.[36] The security forces attacked a demonstration outside the Assembly while protesters sang the "hymn to teachers" to show their support for ANDES.[37] They caused numerous victims among the demonstrators.[38] Several students, faculty members, and university professionals lost their lives during the 1971 crackdown.[39]

In the following days, state forces unleashed an unprecedented persecution of teachers and their supporters. Teachers and activists endured beatings, kidnappings, and torture during the 1971 ANDES strike. Public security and paramilitary forces violently displaced teachers from several schools, attacked their homes, and murdered several teachers. On the night of July 28, some thirty striking teachers at the Daniel Hernández School in Santa Tecla welcomed a group of self-identified supporters of the strike who were in fact ORDEN paramilitaries. As the individuals entered the school, they pulled out machetes while their leader shouted at the baffled teachers: "If you sons of bitches don't leave [the school] . . . we'll cut you into small pieces right here." The paramilitaries beat the teachers while they rushed out of the school, leaving behind their personal belongings.[40] Similar incidents took place at schools in Chalatenango, Santa Ana, Chalchuapa, San Miguel, and San Vicente. Government forces staged a major assault against some four hundred teachers and their supporters who gathered at the Néstor Salazar School in Cojutepeque. A motley crew of paramilitaries, PCN activists, guards from the local prison, and "musicians of the Regimental Band" threw a "rain of stones" at the school, destroyed the school's furniture with machetes, and stole the teachers' food and utensils.[41] Paramilitaries and state agents also pelted with stones and machined-gunned or threw incendiary bombs at the homes of ANDES leaders (figure 5.3).[42] They also killed Francisco Hernández Urbina, the leader of ANDES in San Vicente.[43] Carlos López remembered that Roberto Córdova and other teachers working in Chalatenango were also victims of the repression.[44] In the aftermath of the strike, many teachers relinquished their affiliation with ANDES. Only those with a stronger political commitment remained active in the organization.[45]

A state propaganda campaign matched the attacks against the striking teachers. It was a raw attempt to portray the leaders of the teachers' movement as communist militants who ruthlessly manipulated well-meaning but naive teachers.

Figure 5.3 "More Than Fourteen Thousand Teachers Strike." Images of José Mario López, secretary general of ANDES, and Mélida Anaya Montes, secretary of labor conflicts of that same organization, two major figures in the history of the Salvadoran insurgency. López was a cofounder of the Revolutionary Party of the Central American Workers (PRTC), and Anaya Montes became the deputy commander of the FPL in the late 1970s. *El Tiempo*, Third Week of July, 1971, p. 8. Courtesy of CIDAI, Biblioteca "P. Florentino Idoate, S.J." of the Central American University "José Simeón Cañas."

A series of anonymous advertisements titled "Dear Teacher" published in *La Prensa Gráfica*, apparently by the CNI, a propaganda apparatus under the direct authority of President Sánchez Hernández, sought to create a split between the rank-and-file teachers and the leaders of the strike. The government argued that it was in fact willing to approve the Law of the Teaching Profession and a salary increase for public workers (including teachers), which rendered the teachers' strike "useless." It rhetorically asked the striking teachers, "Dear Teacher, why do you abandon your students and your own responsibilities?" while it threatened them with monetary penalties and other sanctions. It depicted the leaders of the strike as a privileged stratum of intellectuals who were immune to government reprisals, since they were either university faculty (Anaya Montes was indeed a professor at the University of El Salvador) or union bosses on the ANDES payroll.[46] The campaign against ANDES focused its attack on the political persona of Anaya Montes. It contrasted the supposed virtues of traditional female teachers, namely, rectitude, modesty, and submission, with Anaya's ostensibly subversive political and cultural values. Another series of anonymous advertisements titled "What Kids Think about Their Teachers," which were attributed to a primary school student, created a female teacher character called "La Niña Menchita."[47] The author of the invective wrote that La Niña Menchita had a "humble appearance," did not "use any makeup," and "NEVER MISSES WORK."[48]

In contrast with La Niña Menchita, the government propaganda described Anaya as a perfidious, cold-blooded, and childless communist ideologue who manipulated the teachers' union following the guidelines of the emerging insurgency. Anaya herself commented that La Niña Menchita was in fact a real teacher who supported the strike at Escuela República del Paraguay in San Salvador.[49] A full-page advertisement signed by three individuals who self-identified as teachers, published in *La Prensa Gráfica*, accused Anaya of manipulating the teachers' union on behalf of the Communist Party. The authors of this diatribe were apparently uninformed or simply did not care about the fact that the PCS was closely associated with the Soviet Union and critical of China. They called Anaya a militant of "Beijing's hard line." The piece quoted extensively an article it attributed to Anaya in which she reportedly advocated armed struggle. Anaya had argued that the CIA coup against President Jacobo Arbenz in Guatemala in 1954 proved that nonviolent revolutions in Latin America were simply impossible. To this her critics countered that the example of the democratically elected socialist president Salvador Allende in Chile proved Anaya wrong (Allende was ousted by another US-backed coup in September 1973). Anaya had praised the guerrillas in Latin America, crediting them with "raising the consciousness of millions of inhabitants in such a short time (more directly after the Cuban triumph in 1959)—twelve years—as the left parties that trusted the verbal struggle have not done it in various decades." Anaya's critics posited that the 1971 ANDES strike was not motivated by the teachers' legitimate grievances but by her machinations on behalf of the insurgency.[50] The government accused Anaya of promoting violence as a means to achieve the teachers' demands and depicted her as a childless woman who was ultimately responsible for thousands of children missing classes due to the teachers' strike.[51]

Another facet of the government campaign against ANDES suggested the existence of direct links between the teachers' strike and El Grupo, the guerrilla group founded by Alejandro Rivas Mira, Eduardo Sancho, and other militants. Judge Ricardo Avila Moreira charged Jorge Cáceres Prendes, a twenty-eight-year-old lawyer, with participating in the kidnapping and murder of the Salvadoran industrialist Ernesto Regalado Dueñas in February 1971, a day before the initiation of the teachers' strike.[52] The prosecutor accused Cáceres and other Social Christian intellectuals of belonging to El Grupo. In the following days, the official press matched the coverage of the teachers' strike and the trial against Cáceres. *La Prensa Gráfica* published pictures of alleged members of El Grupo and gave extensive coverage to the witnesses in the case against Cáceres.[53] On July 14, the CNI claimed that policemen had captured Juan Humberto González, a leader of ANDES, at the national airport, for carrying "subversive literature." The police had ostensibly confiscated from González copies of "The Minimanual of [the Urban] Guerrilla of Carlos Marighella and the handbook of the National Brigade of Socialist Teachers from Chile, which contain[ed] basic points for the penetration of parties and trade unions."[54] In the following days, an anonymous advertisement published in *La Prensa* cited Marighella's "[The] Minimanual of the Urban Guerrilla" indicating that it offered specific instructions for the organization of strikes in "places of work or learning to affect those who study," as well as kidnappings, and assassinations of public officials and businessmen. The text concluded that both "Marighella and Mélida Anaya Montes" incited "our youth and our teachers" to revolutionary violence.[55] General Fidel Torres, the minister of defense, publicly accused the leaders of ANDES of being members of the clandestine PCS and of fomenting political violence.[56]

Public intellectuals vigorously challenged the government attacks against the teachers' movement, considering them part of an effort to establish a brazen military tyranny in El Salvador. They accused Waldo Chávez Velasco, the head of the National Center of Information, of orchestrating the smear campaign against the striking teachers.[57] Fabio Castillo, the former rector of the University of El Salvador and the presidential candidate of the Party of Renovating Action (PAR), a left-to-center party, in 1967 called Chávez Velasco and minister of education Walter Béneke "fascists" at the service of the "foreigners who run the National Center of Infamy (wrongly called National Center of Information)" (figure 5.4).[58] Castillo, whose daughter Luisa Eugenia Castillo and son-in-law Ricardo Sol Arriaza were accused by the government of belonging to El Grupo, also rejected Judge Avila Moreira's request to serve as a witness in the case and blamed *La Prensa* for twisting his public statements on the subject.[59] He deemed the trial against Cáceres a political charade

Figure 5.4 Fabio Castillo Figueroa, a pivotal figure in the history of the Salvadoran left. He was a professor of medicine at the University of El Salvador in the 1950s, a member of the reformist Civic-Military Junta (October 1960 through January 1961), the rector of the university between 1963 and 1967, the PAR presidential candidate in 1967, and a cofounder of the PRTC, a founding organization of the FMLN. Castillo denounced the trial against Jorge Cáceres Prendes as a "judicial farce" of the Sánchez Hernández government. *El Tiempo*, Third Week of July, 1971, p. 3. Courtesy of CIDAI, Biblioteca "P. Florentino Idoate, S.J." of the Central American University "José Simeón Cañas."

mounted by the Sánchez Hernández government to obscure the consolidation of the military dictatorship:

> In the country a terrible dictatorship is being established or better said a fierce and terrible dictatorship is deepening. Most people don't see

it, are not able or don't want to understand it. It is a despotic and criminal dictatorship, which will not stop at [committing] any crime that
[enables it] to reach its objective of terrorizing people.

It is not a personal dictatorship of Sánchez Hernández. It is a dictatorship established by a military regime and a system: the dictatorship
of the oligarchy to maintain its privileges; it is a dictatorship of economic and military power[s] supported by the forces of the Pentagon.
The government of Sánchez Hernández is weak, but instead the military
regime is strong. Sánchez Hernández is a puppet of the dictatorship....

The case against Cáceres Prendes is a manifestation of that dictatorship. A judicial process of an essentially political nature ... with a
totally corrupt trial, in which nobody believed, the government tried
to justify the murder of the engineer Rosales Araujo and the massacre
at tunnel no. 1 [at the coastal highway; these killings were attributed to
the National Guard].... Jorge Cáceres Prendes, under terrible physical and moral torture, was forced to tell the story that the Guard had
crafted.[60]

On July 16, Rafael Menjívar, the rector of the University of El Salvador, told
parliamentarians who had hastily approved the General Law of Education on
July 8 and were debating the Law of the Teaching Profession that the government of President Sánchez Hernández had declared "a state of siege at the back
of the [National] Assembly," that is, the president had ostensibly annulled basic
civic and political rights without the explicit authorization of the legislative
branch of government. That same day, ANDES's secretary general José Mario
López told the assemblymen that his plea in favor of ANDES's proposal on the
Law of the Teaching Profession would be brief, for "sometimes the words and
the reasons are worthless." He claimed that the previous night paramilitaries
had attacked the "homes and the properties" of all members of the ANDES
Executive Council, including his own. López accused the government of trying "to defeat the guild by hunger," alluding to the pecuniary reprisals against
the striking teachers. He also declared: "The venomous campaign of the official
sector through the press, prepares the repression.... We are at the doors of a
repressive confrontation."[61]

Mélida Anaya Montes, the slandered teacher leader, argued that the repression against the teacher movement in 1971 was mainly informed by US counterinsurgency, which sought to prevent the emergence of guerrillas by cracking
down on the growing social movements:

In El Salvador proper methods of counterinsurgency warfare are being
applied before there is really an offensive of revolutionary groups

willing to use arms as a method of struggle to conquer political power. The preventative aspect of the government's measures motivates them to attempt the destruction of any peaceful popular movement that is independent of the government and the traditional left. ANDES is a peaceful association, and the government knows it better than anybody else, but it is considered dangerous due to its strict independence.[62]

In her memoir about the 1971 teachers' strike, Anaya wrote that she and her colleagues were totally unprepared psychologically, politically, and logistically to face the crackdown:

> Such an element [the repression] had been used in El Salvador against workers and peasants in the past, but not with teachers. The reason is very simple: teachers had never combated [the regime]. During the 1968 strike [the government] pressured [the teachers] in other ways, that is why perhaps [they] had the audacity to rise up again. . . . [In 1971] the government [was] willing to give [them] an exemplary lesson.[63]

In the aftermath of the 1971 teachers' strike, Anaya publicly advocated revolutionary violence and faulted the PCS for its unwillingness to initiate armed struggle against the authoritarian regime.[64] In her distinctive rhetorical style, she wrote a vignette that illustrates this point. When policemen laid a siege to La Casa del Maestro (the Teacher's House, ANDES headquarters in downtown San Salvador) during the 1971 strike, Anaya asked the leaders of ANDES who met at the site if anyone had at least a "shaving blade" to defend themselves, to which "they responded in unison, no." "I only had a 30-centimeter pin attached to my dress. Outside there were thirty machine guns pointing at the Teacher's House. We [the leaders of ANDES] continued our discussion. We had words they had weapons," Anaya concluded.[65] Carlos López recalled that the strike became a turning point in the radicalization of the teachers' movement. After the event many teachers started labeling the government, the security forces, and the army "the enemy." While some teachers joined the official party to preserve their job stability, other ANDES affiliates joined the insurgency.[66]

Other actors sympathetic to the striking teachers also commented on the origins of the conflict and on the disproportionate use of state violence against them. According to the professors of the Escuela Normal Alberto Masferrer, the main teachers' school in the country, the strike was motivated by the marginalization of teachers and by their deeply felt sense of duty as intellectuals committed to social analysis and social change. "When institutional mechanisms show negligence or indifference to resolve the problems of teachers . . . the guild is obliged to prove that its demands are felt and supported by each one of its members," stated the professors.[67] University students deemed the repression against the teachers and their supporters an expression of the structural violence endured by Salvadorans in their everyday existences. After the government attack against the July 16 demonstration, an editorialist of *Opinión Estudiantil*, a student newspaper at the University of El Salvador, wrote that the crackdown on the striking teachers had generated widespread indignation, but that it "should not surprise anyone . . . we live in a country where violence has deep roots, where the violence of the rich against the poor is institutionalized, legalized, and morally justified . . . and when the indignation against it is transformed into a decision to struggle, the government violence becomes specialized and more defined: murders"[68]

"The July 30 Massacre": The Intellectuals' Crucible

In 1975, peasant leaders, teachers, and university students created the BPR, a popular front that posed an unparalleled challenge to the authoritarian regime. Other intellectuals and activists had previously founded a similar movement called the Unified Front of Popular Action (FAPU).[69] The formation of the BPR was the intellectuals' response to the mounting repression that culminated in the July 30 massacre.

Given the crucial reverberations that the July 30 massacre had in Salvadoran society and politics in the 1970s, it is necessary to discuss this event in some detail. The General Association of Salvadoran University Students (AGEUS) and other student groups that organized the protest sought to denounce a previous crackdown on university students carried out by government forces in Santa Ana on July 25. They gathered at the university campus at around 2:00 p.m. to stage a large protest in downtown San Salvador.[70] Participants in the march recalled that they feared a particularly harsh repression against the protest because government officials had made several public warnings against it.[71] As the demonstrators walked southward on Twenty-Fifth Avenue, a major artery in downtown San Salvador, at around 5:20 p.m., they noticed a large contingent of soldiers, National Guardsmen, and members of the Treasury Police supported by armored vehicles, which blocked the avenue at an intersection near the city's main public hospital.[72] As the demonstrators approached the state forces, the latter opened fire on them while armored vehicles moved toward the marchers. Civilians in the protest (likely agents provocateurs) fired small arms in various directions.[73] Carlos Evaristo Hernández, a former economics student who witnessed the massacre, claimed that the soldiers initially fired over the students' heads and subsequently aimed at their bodies. Another participant had told

Hernández not to worry about the shooting because the soldiers were "firing rubber bullets," but in fact they used live ammunition.[74] As the protesters ran in several directions, guardsmen and policemen chased them on foot in the surrounding areas. Atilio Montalvo, a former university student, recalled how he miraculously escaped a Treasury Police patrol that followed him several blocks after he jumped off a ten-meter bridge and hid in an empty lot.[75] Oscar Miranda, another former student, recalled that an elderly women living in a nearby shantytown hid him at her home while guardsmen searched the area.[76] Several students climbed over the wall that surrounds the Salvadoran Institute of Social Security (ISSS) hospital on Twenty-Fifth Avenue, where medical personnel sheltered them from the security forces. Other participants were able to escape by running in the opposite direction of the advancing state forces or sprinting down alleys or adjacent streets. Nevertheless, some demonstrators could not escape. Many were hit by the soldiers' gunfire and died on the spot or were seriously injured. Others received deadly machete wounds or were victims of serious beatings as they tried to climb the walls of the ISSS hospital. Ibalmore Córtez Vasquez, a university student who was hit by bullets and then attacked with a machete or a bayonet, lay in agony for nine days at a local hospital and finally died as a consequence of his wounds.[77] Eleven students lost their lives, and roughly fifty people were victims of "gunfire, cutting weapons and grave contusions" as a result of the crackdown.[78] After the attackers cleared the area, they loaded the dead bodies and the injured students into military trucks while firemen hosed down the site of the bloodbath. Mirna Antonieta Perla, a survivor of the massacre, asserted that it was a carefully planned "military operation," which involved army units, armored vehicles, specialized security forces, and firefighters who "wash[ed] the blood of the injured and erase[d] any evidence [of the killings]."[79] Dozens of social movements, institutions, and opposition parties condemned the massacre and blamed it on President Arturo Armando Molina and other high-ranking military officers. However, to this day it is still unclear who ordered the massacre, who planned it, and which commanding officers executed it. Because the mandate of the Truth Commission created as a result of the peace negotiations between the FMLN and the Salvadoran government (1990–1992) was restricted to the investigation of politically motivated crimes carried out during the civil war (1980–1992), the human rights violations committed by the state agents in the 1970s and earlier remain obscure. At any rate, the Molina government publicly admitted that the military fired at the students, but it maintained that the soldiers had reacted to a previous armed attack by the demonstrators. It also claimed that ten soldiers and many civilians were injured as a result of the "fire exchange" between the state forces and the demonstrators.[80] Whatever the case, student leaders unequivocally viewed the July 30 massacre, as this event has been labeled ever since, as the state's declaration of war against the social movements. After enumerating the repressive actions conducted by the state forces against peasant and student organizations between 1973 and 1975, an anonymous editorialist of *Opinión Estudiantil* compared the July 30 killings with similar crackdowns perpetrated during the Hernández Martínez dictatorship (1931–1944) and called the Salvadoran elites the "enemy."[81]

> This is a new stage in the struggle in which the oligarchy [assumes] new political objectives with new techniques and with the planned use of reactionary violence aimed at destroying the popular organizations. . . . The enemy is not acting in a improvised way. It is acting under plans to impede the advance of the popular struggle and therefore is "working" to devastate every popular organization and political subversive "foci."[82]

AGEUS claimed that the massacre had rendered elections obsolete. "Extralegal, extraparliamentary, and combative struggles of the popular masses constitute the main form of struggle of the people," the student movement declared.[83] It also labeled Carlos Alfaro Castillo, the rector appointed by the Molina government after the military occupation of the university campus in 1972, a collaborator of the repressive forces. "His servility to [the government's] interventionist interest had made him dig his own tomb within the university. . . . His complicity with the events in Santa Ana on July 25 and San Salvador on July 30 has been clearly demonstrated."[84] A commando of the insurgent FPL assassinated Alfaro Castillo in August 1977. At that time, a heavily armed university police known as Los Grises (the Grays) made up of members of the state security forces, which operated under the direct authority of Alfaro, managed the university campus. The FPL called the rector "a well-known cadre of the counterinsurgency" who transformed the university into a "garrison and an appendix" of the military dictatorship. The insurgents claimed that Alfaro had led the repression against students, workers, and faculty and ordered the university police to shoot at the students who evaded the state forces during the July 30 massacre.[85] Alfaro became the first rector murdered for political reasons in the 1970s.

Amid the widespread condemnations of the July 30 massacre, a self-described "Group of Christians" for the first time in the country's history occupied the cathedral in downtown San Salvador to protest the killings. Students who made up a group they called El Movimiento (the Movement), peasant leaders, and diocesan priests led the occupation of the Catholic church. Alberto Enríquez, one of the participants in this event recalled:

> We planned the takeover. I remember that the decision was to attend the funeral mass for the slain [students], wait until people left, . . . and then close the doors of the Cathedral. The second decision was to figure

out who will stay inside and who will remain outside [the church]. Most members of the Movement stayed inside. Ana María [Castillo] [a university student] and I [Alberto Enríquez] stayed outside. Many peasant leaders [leaders of FECCAS] joined the action, including Netón, Chepe López, Patricia Puertas, Félix García, Numas Escobar, and Mardoqueo. Three diocesan priests also joined. Netón became the chief of security. Without knowing what would happen we took over the cathedral (figures 5.5 and 5.6).[86]

The activists denounced the repression for six days and asked San Salvador archbishop Chávez y González to form a commission to investigate the July 30 killings.[87] They called for the liberation of the disappeared students and the dismissal of the defense minister, the heads of the security forces, and Alfaro Castillo, the rector of the University of El Salvador. They also demanded compensations for the victims of the repression and their families. Various social movements supported the activists at the cathedral.[88] In response to the "Group

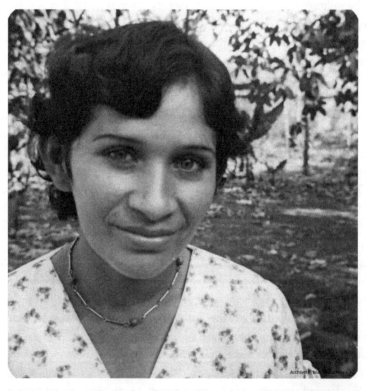

Figure 5.5 Patricia Puertas, a leader of FECCAS, Aguilares, 1976. Archivo del Padre Marcelino Pérez, S.J. Courtesy of P. José Aníbal Meza Tejada S.J., rector of Externado de San José, San Salvador, El Salvador.

Figure 5.6 Patricia Puertas and Félix García, leaders of FECCAS, Aguilares, 1976.
Archivo del Padre Marcelino Pérez, S.J. Courtesy of P. José Aníbal Meza Tejada S.J., rector
of Externado de San José, San Salvador, El Salvador.

of Christians," the government published a one-page notice stressing that it had
never accepted the mediation of the archbishop of San Salvador and the rector
of the Central American University (UCA) as the group had publicly claimed.
However, this time, it refrained from attacking the demonstrators.[89]

The founding of the BPR took place at the Teacher's House during the occupation of the cathedral. It was a political process that brought together crucial
strata of intellectuals, chiefly the leaders of the teacher and the peasant movements and university students. Over several days, they met to envision a movement they originally called the "Bloc of Organizations" that mainly combined
the political, intellectual, and organizational strength of ANDES and the peasant
movement. It also included university students, a rapidly growing high school
student movement, and several smaller organizations.[90] The creation of the BPR
enabled a systematic political dialogue among clandestine FPL intellectuals
such as Salvador Cayetano Carpio, Felipe Peña Mendoza, and Clara Elizabeth
Ramírez and the leaders of the social movements. It also became a remarkable political school. Urban and peasant intellectuals shared their expertise as

Figure 5.7 BPR activists march in San Salvador, undated. Courtesy of Museo de la Palabra y la Imagen.

members of the new organization. It also allowed the integration of the socio-economic and political demands of the most potent social movements in the country, as well as the implementation of unprecedented forms of militant protest (figure 5.7).

The First Military Operation in *Aguilares* and the Peasant Mobilizations in the City

During the 1970s, the peasant organizations that joined the BPR, namely, FECCAS and UTC, displayed a vibrant activism in cities and key sectors of the agrarian economy, posing a strategic challenge to the regime. They fused into the FTC, which was largely constituted by small landowners from various regions of the country. They perfected the art of *lucha reivindicativa*: the articulation of the socioeconomic and political demands of peasants and seasonal rural workers, which they promoted through a combination of grass-roots organizing, media campaigns, workshops, and urban and rural mobilizations supported by teachers, diocesan priests, and students. They built a network of "experienced teachers and peasant leaders" that facilitated peasant mobilization in urban areas, as well as the active support of teachers in cities and towns across the country. Teachers and students routinely accompanied peasant mobilizations in urban and rural areas after 1975.[91]

The peasant movement featured an intensely ideological discourse, which openly advocated the overthrow of the oligarchic-military regime, the destruction of capitalism, and the foundation of a popular revolutionary government.[92] However, its mobilizing potential derived mainly from its ability to promote sensitive socioeconomic demands of peasants and landless rural workers. Starting in 1975, FECCAS-UTC articulated yearly campaigns demanding salary increases and the improvement of working conditions of seasonal laborers at coffee, cotton, and sugar plantations, as well as lower prices for agricultural products and more affordable land rents for small and medium-sized cultivators. They denounced violations of labor laws committed by landowners and organized strikes at coffee farms and sugar and cotton haciendas. For instance, in November 1977, FECCAS-UTC organized a strike at Hacienda El Recuerdo, which involved the participation of 150 workers, to denounce Gustavo Denis, a cotton producer who purportedly altered scales used to weigh the cotton workers picked at his property.[93] They also denounced Nicolasa Quintanilla de Sánchez, the owner of El Guajoyo, a large hacienda near Tecoluca, San Vicente, who allegedly asked security forces to displace the *colonos*, rural workers residing at the hacienda.[94] They joined the national debate on the Agrarian Transformation Program sponsored by the Molina government in 1975 to appease the growing social pressures around this issue. Apolinario "Polín" Serrano, Facundo Guardado, Justo Mejía, Patricia Puertas, Félix García, and other peasant leaders gained national attention at that time through their eloquent public engagements in university halls, plazas, and other public spaces. Guardado recalled that in 1976 he commented on the "counterinsurgent nature" of Molina's Agrarian Transformation in front of an audience of students, professors, and activists at the University of El Salvador.[95] The peasant leaders became ubiquitous political figures and public intellectuals between 1975 and 1980.

Molina's Agrarian Transformation received lukewarm support from state bureaucrats, the clandestine PCS, and the UCA, but it generated a fierce backlash from the landed elites and business sectors that formed FARO-ANEP.[96] These groups publicly challenged Molina on this issue. While Molina had initially promised not to yield to pressures from the right, FARO-ANEP managed to halt the incipient Agrarian Transformation. Ignacio Ellacuría, a Jesuit scholar at the UCA, wrote a caustic piece criticizing Molina for giving in to the right's campaign to boycott the agrarian reform, titled "A sus órdenes mi capital" (At your orders my capital), which incensed the reactionary military and economic elites. Ellacuría faulted ANEP for promoting a smear campaign and threats against government officials in charge of the Agrarian Transformation and all those who "purportedly supported a social change." He believed that a "dictatorship of the bourgeoisie" was implanted in the country after this episode.[97] While

FECCAS-UTC leaders were highly critical of Molina's Agrarian Transformation and Ellacuría's support for it, privately, they wished it could offer enough land at reasonable prices to landless peasants to avoid further confrontations between the peasant movement and the state.[98]

After the failure of Molina's Agrarian Transformation, the peasant movements carried out land occupations in April and May 1977. The government responded with full-fledged military operations. Participants in land occupations in Chalatenango, Aguilares, Cinquera, Tecoluca, and Zacatecoluca were subsistence farmers who were unable to obtain land through normal leasing procedures due to the intransigence of big landowners.[99] The military operations against peasant communities started in full force in May 1977 with an attack against a land occupation near Aguilares, a town that sits on a large plain cultivated with sugar cane, roughly thirty kilometers north of San Salvador. The assassination of Rutilio Grande (a Jesuit priest who promoted a liberationist pastoral in the area), Manuel Solorzano (an elderly man), and Nelson Rutilio Lemus (a child who accompanied Grande), committed by National Guardsmen and paramilitaries near the neighboring town of El Paisnal in March of that same year, had provoked a rift between President Molina and the recently appointed archbishop of San Salvador, Oscar A. Romero.[100] It had also substantially escalated the tensions between the security forces and the peasant movement in the region. In the early morning of May 17, 1977, some two thousand soldiers and members of the security forces supported by armored vehicles, artillery, planes, and helicopters entered the area to dismantle the FECCAS network in the region. Two days later the soldiers machine-gunned the Catholic church in Aguilares and captured José Luis Ortega, Salvador Carranza, and Marcelino Pérez, three Jesuit priests working in the area. They also attacked peasants who occupied Hacienda Los Gramales near Cantón San Lucas in Suchitoto. The peasant leaders blamed the Molina government and the big landowners in the area for waging a "war against the people."[101] Members of ORDEN and the Union of White Warriors (UGB), a recently formed death squad, operated with total impunity in the region with the backing of security forces. Death squads were clandestine right-wing paramilitary groups (i.e., armed illegal groups) formed by landowners, wealthy individuals, and members of the state security apparatus. They perpetrated numerous crimes against peasant communities in Aguilares and El Paisnal, including theft, destruction of crops, burning of houses, arbitrary detentions, assassinations, and "beatings of women, elderly men and children."[102] In the aftermath of the military operation in Aguilares, the peasant leaders warned the recently formed alliance of landed elites and big business associations FARO-ANEP:

> The exploiters must know that if today they have massacred hundreds
> of humble workers, the day is near when neither the CONDECA [the

Central American Defense Council] nor the Yankee marines will be able to submit millions of Salvadorans when they decide to turn into dust [*hacer polvo*] the regime of plunder, oppression, and misery and its supporters.[103]

The peasant leaders also accused FARO-ANEP and the Molina government of orchestrating a media campaign against the peasant movement to match the military operation in Aguilares.[104] They also used war slogans against the government, and against "Yankee imperialism," after the events in Aguilares.[105]

The repression in Aguilares was a turning point in the start of the civil war. ANDES called it the "Aguilares nightmare." After describing the one-month military occupation of Aguilares, leaders of ANDES argued that the elites attempted "to crush" the popular organizations by "jailing [and] killing" peasant activists and "engaging in psychological warfare" against the rural population. "The people have developed a class conscience . . . and live an irreversible revolutionary process," they asserted.[106] In fact, peasant activism steadily increased throughout the country over the next three years despite the constant military operations in areas of incipient rural insurgency. For instance, in 1978, peasants who occupied land near Cinquera and on the slopes of the San Vicente volcano gained certain concessions from local landowners and the government. Alberto Martínez, a landowner in Azacualpa, a hamlet near Cinquera, "signed a 3-year lease contract . . . for [the period] 1978–1981" with peasants who occupied his property, which was backed by the Ministry of Agriculture. At Hacienda Tehuacán near Paz Opico, San Vicente, the Institute of Rural Transformation leased roughly "420 *manzanas*" (840 acres) to peasants from "La Cayetana, La India, and San Luis La Loma." Parallel to this process, army and security forces intensified their military operations in the area. On April 27, security forces occupied "El Perical, La India, Paz Opico, La Cayetana, León de Piedra, [and] San Luis La Loma"—peasant communities located on the slopes of the San Vicente volcano—killing José Vicente Belloso, a sixteen-year-old boy, and Julio César Osorio a thirty-year-old man with physical disabilities. They also burned a peasant's home in León de Piedra.[107]

The initiation of war involves the transformation of hostile intention into hostile action.[108] In El Salvador, peasants became insurgents driven by their efforts to obtain arable land, to resist the increasing attacks of state forces against their communities, and to undermine the authoritarian regime. While the peasants' grievances against the repressive forces had been brewing in different areas of the country since the early 1970s, one of the first armed clashes between peasant activists and public security forces occurred in April 1977, during a land occupation near Cancasque, a town in northeastern Chalatenango. José Santos Martínez and Justo Mejía, two peasant leaders from Chalatenango whose trajectories I discussed in chapter 3, led the land occupation. Martínez recalled that UTC activists had occupied state-owned land at a place called Tempisque, near the Lempa River, due to the scarcity of arable land in the region. They had not planned to attack the repressive forces; instead, the armed confrontation occurred when a Treasury Police unit attempted to oust the activists from the state land. "They chased us out and then we returned," said Martínez. At one time, five peasants from El Portillo del Norte, El Jicarito, and Concepción-Guillenes, three hamlets near Cancasque, who carried small weapons, clashed with a Treasury Police patrol that tried to force them off of the occupied land. They killed one policeman and wounded another. "They [the policemen] were heavily armed. We were not," recalled Martínez. "I was not at the land occupation that day, but the comrades [*compañeros*] had one shotgun and a couple of small .38 handguns [*un par de pistolitas .38*]. They opened fire [against the policemen] with those. They confiscated a G-3 [German made] rifle but lost the shotgun. It was practically an exchange," said Martínez.[109] One can think of this incident as the first act of the peasant war in El Salvador.

As the war in the countryside intensified, the peasant movement also increased its urban activism. On July 25, 1977, representatives of FECCAS-UTC submitted a set of demands on behalf of seasonal workers to the minister of agriculture, Colonel Roberto Escobar García. They demanded 9 *colones* (US$3.60) as a daily wage for adults and 7 *colones* (US$ 2.80) for children, a seven-hour workday, better working conditions, social security, life insurance for rural workers, a collective contract, and freedom of organization at the worksites. The minister promised to respond to the plea by August 7.[110] In October 1977, representatives of FECCAS-UTC introduced another "proposal to improve the salaries and the working conditions" for the 1977–1978 harvest of coffee, cotton, and sugar cane to the Ministry of Labor and the Council on Minimum Wage. The petition denounced the rural workers' "miserable salaries," the fraudulent techniques used by growers to calculate the amount of coffee and cotton picked by workers on a daily basis, the arbitrary firings, the "miserable and dirty food" landowners provided to workers, and the inhumane living conditions prevalent at the farms. FECCAS-UTC claimed that seasonal workers slept "in the open under trees [in areas infected] with snakes, rats and all sorts of insects. In the best cases [they slept] inside unhealthy installations."[111] It also formulated a similar "proposal to lower the rent of land and the prices of fertilizers, [agricultural] products, and herbicides," claiming that large coffee, cotton, and sugar producers monopolized all the productive land in the country, leaving small farmers only arid land that required vast amounts of fertilizers and other agricultural products to generate subsistence crops. This situation rendered small landowners unable to pay back high-interest loans to the state banking system.[112]

In November 1977, the tensions between the state and the peasant movement reached a new level as hundreds of BPR activists led by the peasant leader

Facundo Guardado occupied the Ministry of Labor. On November 10, they announced a "peaceful takeover" of the ministry's installations to protest the government's failure to address the labor demands of seasonal rural workers and to support two ongoing strikes at the local industries El León and Inca. The activists detained the minister and the undersecretary of labor, the minister of economy, and an OAS official who happened to be at the ministry that day, along with two hundred employees. The official press called the event unprecedented in the country's history.[113] The activists displayed new forms of militancy and organization, including the use of colorful propaganda, high-quality sound systems, and rudimentary tools to block traffic such as multiple-edge spikes known as *miguelitos*. They also occupied the street adjacent to the Ministry of Labor, improvising collective kitchens and other facilities to support the activists inside the building. Guardado told journalists who entered the ministry that before this incident the peasant leaders had unsuccessfully attempted to conduct a dialogue with the minister of labor. They had "explained the labor problems to the minister [of labor] but he maintained a total silence," which they interpreted as a "total no" to the workers' demands. Guardado also asked Archbishop Romero to mediate between the government and the BPR to resolve the crisis.[114] During the occupation of the Ministry of Labor, peasant activists composed a song called "Lucha Reivindicativa" (Raising labor demands), which alluded to their grievances, the intransigence of landowners, and widespread repression in the countryside. The song, which incited activists to wage war on the regime and asserted that the military and the elites had tremendous fear of the guerrillas and the BPR, became emblematic among BPR militants:

> Come join comrade [*compañero*]
> To demand your salary
> Because it's what
> All revolutionaries demand
>
> War! To the tyranny
> Trembles! Before the guerrilla
>
> What we demand
> Is an eleven-*colones* salary
> And also demand
> Rice, tortilla, and beans
>
> War! To the tyranny
> Trembles! Before the guerrilla
>
> The lords up above
> Are very scared

> Because here is all the Bloque
> Willing to strike
>
> War! To the tyranny
> Trembles! Before the guerrilla
>
> The lords of the [coffee] farms
> Are calling up even the guard
> So that we don't demand
> Our salary increase
>
> War! To the tyranny
> Trembles! Before the guerrilla.[115]

The defiant attitude of the peasant leaders puzzled the high-ranking military in charge of public security. General Federico Castillo Yanes, the minister of defense, declared that the "government [does] not negotiate with delinquents." He considered the occupation of the Ministry of Labor part of a scheme sponsored by "International Communism" to escalate "violence" in El Salvador, Latin America, and "other areas of the world." The undersecretary of defense, Colonel José Eduardo Iraheta, accused Mélida Anaya Montes, a leader of ANDES, of masterminding the occupation.[116] For Castillo and Iraheta, it was unthinkable that peasant leaders had orchestrated the action on their own, without the intervention of external actors. These military leaders had to invoke the phantom of international communism to account for the grievances of peasant communities in El Salvador and could not imagine or at least were not willing to publicly admit that peasants were political actors in their own right. However, the minister of labor and the other public officials who were held at the ministry negotiated with the BPR activists to end the occupation. They sponsored a dialogue between labor leaders and business representatives of El León and Inca and promised to consider the peasants' demands regarding salary increases and the improvement of working conditions for seasonal laborers.[117]

In 2007, Guardado maintained that the decision to "peacefully" occupy the Ministry of Labor in 1977 was the result of a political discussion between peasant and BPR leaders and not the outcome of a dogmatic decision imposed on them by the insurgent FPL, with which both movements had close links. "We embarked on a process of organization and mobilization and tried to use the institutional mechanism . . . to present our proposals prior to the occupation," said Guardado. He asserted that the relationship between peasant, BPR, and FPL leaders consisted in a dialogue among equals: "I did not owe anything to Mélida [Anaya Montes] or to Marcial [the pseudonym of Salvador Cayetano

Carpio, the founder of the FPL], neither Mélida or Marcial owed anything to me or to Polín [Apolinario Serrano, another peasant leader]. We were all leaders in our own right [*éramos gente hecha y derecha*]."[118] Guardado also insisted that the peasant leaders were autonomous historical actors who decided to fight the regime as a result of the electoral frauds in 1972 and 1977 and the mounting repression against the peasant movement:

> The only thing I am adamant about the peasant leaders in the 1970s, is that we had all attended school, had access to information, and had food on the table every day. We did not go to war because one day our mother told us, son, there is no food on the table. But they [the state and the elites] killed a whole generation [of peasant leaders], only a few survived. We, Justo [Mejía], Antonio Morales, Apolinario Serrano, and others [i.e., peasant leaders] had a different school [than the urban insurgents]. We did not grow in a sect or the nucleus of a sect or in a farm or an island. We were mostly small landowners from the northern region in Chalatenango, San Vicente, and Usulután. Only a few wage laborers joined the movement.[119]

The fierce state persecution against the peasant leaders sparked the peasant rebellion in Chalatenango. The torture and summary execution of Justo Mejía at the hands of ORDEN paramilitaries on November 9, 1977, was a turning point in this process. The paramilitaries captured Mejía in Dulce Nombre de María at dawn. They tortured and killed him near San Fernando, a neighboring town. The paramilitaries gouged out Mejía's eyes and forced him to walk toward San Fernando while he bled to death. They told peasants living in the area that Mejía was a dangerous thief and subversive. Mejía died near 2:00 p.m. that same day and was buried by his executioners. Two weeks later, hundreds of peasant activists marched to San Fernando, exhumed Mejía's body, and brought it back to his hometown La Ceiba, the hamlet near Las Vueltas where Mejía had taught his neighbors how to read and write and formed a thriving peasant cooperative. During Mejía's wake and funeral, thousands of peasants from Chalatenango and other areas in the country as well as scores of urban activists packed the main plaza in Las Vueltas. Guadalupe Mejía, Justo's widow, and their children led the funeral.[120] Peasant militias closely guarded the massive gathering, while the vastly outnumbered National Guardsmen in the town watched the event from afar. A few days later, the militias ambushed a National Guard patrol stationed in Las Vueltas at the curving dirt road that connects the town and the nearby city of Chalatenango along the banks of the Tamulasco River. In August 1978, ORDEN paramilitaries killed six children and two women, in an incident known as the Massacre of La Ceiba. The victims were close relatives of Justo Mejía and also of their alleged murderers. In turn, the peasant militias tried to assassinate Pedro Cartagena, the leader of ORDEN, at La Ceiba, but instead they gunned down— by mistake—another relative of Justo Mejía who happened to be at Cartagena's house that day.[121] Remembering the murder of Mejía, Chinda Zamora said:

> Justo and I worked together. A few days before he died, he told me, "It will be sad for you the first days after I am gone from this world. But I have decided [to fight] because the military tyranny persecutes us too much. I told him, "God willing you won't die because you will leave us all very sad." He was such a helpful [*colaborativo*] and wise [*alcanza-tivo*] man. Nobody told him what to do. He knew the work that needed to be done. He came to my house often and said, "I have a task [*una tarea*]. God willing we will be able to complete it." I told him yes, and we planned the work without any difficulty. I was a woman who was never afraid. The Lord has spared me all this time, but I was in great danger all the time.[122]

Chinda Zamora, Facundo Guardado, José Santos Martínez, and Justo Mejía were part of a cohort of peasant leaders who created an unprecedented peasant movement, which radically altered the dynamics of the conflict in El Salvador. As the state waged war on the social movements in the 1970s, they became peas-ant militants who formed vast political and military networks, which constituted the backbone of the FMLN insurgency during the civil war. After the murder of Mejía, they prepared to conduct a protracted armed conflict with the state and the elites.

During the 1970s, state terror sought to dismantle the rising social move-ments, but, instead, it created a formidable internal enemy: an urban and rural insurgency that waged a twelve-year revolutionary war, which deeply trans-formed El Salvador's society and politics. The deep spirituality that character-ized most peasant leaders in Chalatenango, their political and military expertise, the Catholic education initiatives in which they participated, and the alliances they formed with the teacher union ANDES and other social movements that constituted the BPR, and with the FPL, shaped the ethos of rural insurgency in Chalatenango. The next chapter explores the imaginaries of revolution articu-lated by urban and peasant intellectuals during that decade.

6

Insurgent Intellectuals

In facing armed brutes, there are no valid laws or reasons.
Lil Milagro Ramírez (1972), guerrilla leader

The night of October 10, 1976, Clara Elizabeth Ramírez, José Alejandro Solano, and Andrés Torres, three young militants, engaged in a protracted battle with security forces at Residencial Don Bosco, a neighborhood in Santa Tecla, a city near San Salvador. At around eleven thirty that night, police contingents besieged a safe house where insurgent leaders had recently met to discuss plans to counter the growing repression against the social movements.[1] Armed with three shotguns and three pistols, the insurgents repelled the policemen for nearly eight hours. Throughout that night, the security forces failed to take over the place despite their massive firepower and overwhelming numerical superiority over the rebels. At dawn, police officers found the insurgents dead inside the virtually demolished house. Apparently they had committed suicide after they incinerated documents and inscribed the organization's acronym on a wall with their own blood.[2] The conservative media in El Salvador reported this episode with trepidation. On October 12, 1976, *El Diario de Hoy* reported, "Three Terrorists Commit Suicide after 8 Hours of Fighting." A hastily written article in the paper described the prolonged and unequal combat between the policemen and the rebels.[3]

Since 1976, left movements in El Salvador have honored "Eva," "Chico," and "Toño"—as Ramírez, Solano, and Torres were respectively known in the ranks of the insurgency—as precursors of the Salvadoran revolution. Like other intellectuals of their generation, Ramírez and Solano, two students of sociology at the University of El Salvador, and Torres, an instructor of sociology at that same institution, became actively engaged in popular politics at a young age. Ramírez was born in 1949 in Ciudad Delgado to a middle-class family. She joined the university at the height of the student mobilizations in 1969 and became a leader of the Sociedad de Estudiantes de Áreas Comunes (Society of General Studies Students) along with Catholic Action activists who became founders of the insurgency. Solano also had middle-class origins. He was born in San Salvador in 1952. Both of his parents were teachers. He was a promising piano player and a jovial individual whom his friends affectionately called "El Ejote" (the Green Bean), due to his tall, slender physique. He was a Catholic Action activist who joined the student movement in the late 1960s. Ramírez and Solano met at the university and married in 1972.

Torres, on the other hand, had more modest social origins. He was born in Apaneca, a city in Ahuachapán, in 1948. He worked at coffee farms near that city

Figure 6.1 Image of Clara Elizabeth Ramírez issued by the FPL in 1977. The caption reads: "Comrades Eva, Chico, and Toño, Present in the Peoples' Heart! Eternal Glory to the Heroes of October." FPL, *El Rebelde*, October 1977, Year 5, no. 60, pp. 7–8. Courtesy of CIDAI, Biblioteca "P. Florentino Idoate, S.J." of the Central American University "José Simeón Cañas."

to pay for his education at a Catholic parish high school. He won a scholarship to study sociology at the university and joined the student movement at General Studies. Between 1973 and 1975, he was the liaison between the insurgency and peasant leaders in northeastern Chalatenango. In the early 1970s, Ramírez, Solano, and Torres were part of the first generation of "armed commandos" formed by the FPL to conduct guerrilla warfare in San Salvador and other cities (figure 6.1).[4] They were also insurgent intellectuals who played a major role in the formulation of the organization's strategy.[5] Ramírez and Torres, for instance, were coeditors of *Estrella Roja* (Red Star), the FPL's theoretical publication. In fact, the organization posthumously attributed *Estrella Roja 3*, published in January 1977, to them.[6]

Over time, the meaning of the battle at Residencial Don Bosco has changed dramatically among former insurgents now reconverted into public officials, politicians, business persons, and professionals. During the civil war, Ramírez, Solano, and Torres were celebrated as quintessential revolutionary icons. For instance, the FPL named one of its most combative guerrilla battalions after Torres.[7] In 2006, the sister of Clara Elizabeth Ramírez, Victoria Ramírez—a former FPL militant who is currently an architect—commented on the changing significance of this event in recent years. She was concerned about the potentially negative social impact that the yearly commemorations of this episode sponsored by veterans of the insurgency, civil society institutions, and the municipality of Santa Tecla, an FMLN electoral stronghold since the mid-1990s, might have. The tributes to the militants who perished in Santa Tecla in 1976 inevitably involved the glorification of an act of political violence, at a time when Victoria Ramírez and other former rebels turned into public officials were coping with rampant social violence and crime in El Salvador. However, she still considered this event a crucial juncture in the resistance against authoritarian rule, which also epitomizes the tensions between the guerrilla organizations and the PCS in the 1970s:

> I don't want to make an apology for violence [during the commemorations of the battle in Santa Tecla]. . . . [To state] that they [Ramírez, Solano, and Torres] fought [eight] hours is somewhat contradictory with the culture of peace we [FMLN leaders] want to implement. Now we see it like that, but at that time . . . perhaps because we were fighting a military tyranny that responded only with repression . . . we were convinced that that [armed struggle] was the only path. Moreover, those who privileged electoral politics we called "revis," [shorthand for] revisionists. For instance, Schafik [Hándal, the secretary general of the PCS] advocated for a long time electoral politics. Our [the FPL's] conflict with the PCS was precisely about that. The PCS privileged for roughly ten years [1966–1977] electoral struggle. They remained

unconvinced [about the need to conduct armed struggle]. We [FPL leaders] used to say that they [PCS leaders] were the last ones to board the train [to join the revolutionary war].[8]

I asked Ramírez if she thought armed struggle had become dogma for New Left intellectuals in the 1970s. She responded affirmatively. When I inquired why, she stated:

> We did not even question ourselves if armed struggle was valid. That was the path. There was no other path. It became a dogma perhaps because the Cuban Revolution had seized power that way. For the Latin American [revolutionary] left, that was the only way. . . . we considered pacifists allies of the bourgeoisie. We believed that no people had seized power through peaceful means. There was the Bolshevik Revolution, the Chinese Revolution, and Vietnam. . . . It was a world paradigm, armed struggle was the path.[9]

Intellectuals featured prominently in the history of the Cold War in Latin America. In the 1960s, the notion of a "Latin American intellectual" was commonly associated with poets and writers sympathetic with the Cuban Revolution and the left more broadly.[10] Latin American writers and poets constituted an intellectual community that conducted frequent literary and political exchanges during congresses and other meetings they held in Chile, Cuba, and Mexico.[11] At that time, Havana became not only the focal point of revolutionary politics in the Americas and to a certain extent the Global South but also a major cultural and literary center. Casa de Las Américas, a cultural institution founded in the aftermath of the Cuban Revolution, was the site of important dialogues among intellectuals from Mexico, the Caribbean, Central and South America, Europe, and the United States.[12] Literary figures like Julio Cortázar, Carlos Fuentes, Miguel Ángel Asturias, Mario Benedetti, René Depestre, Javier Heraud, Enrique Lihn, and Ernesto Sábato—to name a few—at one time collaborated with Casa de Las Américas.[13] Roque Dalton became a ubiquitous figure in Havana's cultural life in those years.[14] He contributed to multiple discussions on the roles that intellectuals played in revolutionary politics, held in Havana, Prague, and other places in the 1960s.[15] Dalton's poetics recurrently engaged the political and aesthetic debates that preoccupied left intellectuals in this period. For instance, he echoed the conversations he and other Latin American and European intellectuals conducted at Prague's U Fleků tavern between 1966 and 1967, in a poem called "Taberna."[16]

The idea of the "revolutionary intellectual," a writer/public figure turned into an insurgent militant, became more prevalent among Latin American intellectuals in the aftermath of Che Guevara's murder in Bolivia in 1967. At that time, a strong anti-intellectualist current emerged among intellectuals associated with the Cuban Revolution. This anti-intellectualism, a paradoxical contempt for the alleged social privilege of intellectuals and a simultaneous revalorization of "action" (i.e., revolutionary activism), adopted by Latin American intellectuals in this period, demanded a militant commitment on the part of intellectuals and a clear subordination to the moral and political authority of revolutionary vanguards (i.e., guerrilla movements) and ultimately to that of the Cuban Revolution.[17] As part of this trend, intellectuals allied with the Cuban Revolution blasted poets and writers who established relations with cultural institutions in the United States, which they viewed as part of US efforts to infiltrate the community of Latin American intellectuals.[18] They censured the bourgeois ethos they attributed to intellectuals of middle- or upper-class origins (e.g., their vanity, pedantry, and cosmopolitanism) and contrasted it with the alleged revolutionary ethos that characterized working-class militants and guerrilla combatants.[19] While a thorough discussion of this phenomenon is beyond the scope of this book, it is fitting to emphasize that it crucially informed cultural and political debates conducted by intellectuals, left movements, and guerrilla organizations in the late 1960s and the 1970s.[20] Anti-intellectualism acquired a deadly potency in the Salvadoran insurgency. It was a recurrent and spurious argument that insurgent leaders often invoked to deprecate intellectuals like Roque Dalton. They considered Dalton's cosmopolitanism, solid theoretical formation, and creativity a threat to their authority and power. While the origins of this tradition can be traced to earlier periods in the history of the Salvadoran left, it is apparent that the murder of Dalton, conducted by ERP leaders in 1975, was a decisive episode in the trajectory of the New Left anti-intellectualism. It also acquired a lethal force in the ranks of other insurgent organizations, particularly in the FPL, ultimately producing persecutions and victims among left activists in the 1970s and during the civil war.

Guevarismo and other intellectual and political traditions in vogue in the 1960s informed the debates over electoral politics and armed struggle between communist and New Left intellectuals. Their contrasting analyses of Salvadoran society and politics, particularly their ideas on the consolidation of fascism in El Salvador, also shaped their strategies and tactics in the 1970s.

Imagining Revolution at the Time of *Guevarismo*

Like their counterparts across Latin America, insurgent intellectuals in El Salvador forcefully debated theories of revolution in the 1960s and 1970s. They often criticized the PCS's ambiguous discourses on electoral politics and armed

struggle, and they advocated new paradigms of revolution they considered fitting to El Salvador. They celebrated Ernesto "Che" Guevara's ethos and trajectory but were hesitant to embrace his revolutionary strategy. In turn, communist
intellectuals (i.e., the Old Left) showed concern for the massive incorporation of
"middle sectors" (i.e., students, university professors, teachers, employees, and
professionals) into insurgent movements, which they deemed anarchists, popu-
lists, and left-wing extremists. These acrimonious discussions between Old Left
and New Left intellectuals shaped the ethos of social activists and insurgents in
this period.

After the fleeting existence of the United Front of Revolutionary Action
(FUAR), the militant movement formed by the PCS between 1961 and 1963,
the party focused on electoral politics and union organizing, and its engagement with armed struggle lagged. Nevertheless, throughout that decade, communist leaders often pondered the future of revolution in Latin America. In
1967, the PCS, then led by Salvador Cayetano Carpio, publicly criticized Che
Guevara's "foco theory" for its militaristic vision of revolutionary politics. This
theory held that small guerrilla detachments (i.e., guerrilla vanguards) fighting
in isolated mountainous areas could ignite revolutionary mobilizations in several Latin American countries. The PCS attributed Guevara's defeat in Bolivia
to fundamental flaws in his strategy, particularly its disregard of "political struggle."[21] It contrasted the widespread peasant support for the July 26 Movement
in the Sierra Maestra during the struggles against the dictator Fulgencio Batista
in Cuba with the virtual isolation of the guerrillas led by Guevara in Bolivia,
to point out the flaws of the foco theory.[22] A number of Salvadoran activists
rejected the PCS's criticism of Guevara's strategy in the aftermath of his assassination in Bolivia.[23] Some left the party to join nascent revolutionary movements.[24] A conversation between Carpio and Guevara held in Havana in the
1960s further illustrates the evolution of the Salvadoran left's vision of armed
struggle. Che reportedly told Carpio that El Salvador could play only a second-
ary role in his imaginings of guerrilla warfare in Central America because the
country had only a few densely cultivated, deforested, and highly populated
mountainous areas, which could hardly become a strategic rearguard for the
guerrillas. In contrast, Guevara believed that it would be feasible to sustain large
guerrilla forces in remote mountain ranges in Guatemala and Nicaragua. Carpio
rejected Che's assessment of the limited revolutionary potential of El Salvador.
He often asserted: "Our mountains are the masses."[25] Indeed, the two men had
divergent strategic visions about armed revolutionary struggle in Latin America.
Differing with Guevara, Carpio believed that unionized workers, peasant movements, and their grass-roots leaders, in alliance with radicalized teachers, university students, and other middle-class intellectuals, could potentially form
an unparalleled revolutionary movement in El Salvador. As Marta Harnecker,

a Chilean intellectual, put it, the FPL, the insurgent organization founded by Carpio in 1970, "was born immunized against *foquismo* [i.e., the foco theory]."[26] In other words, the FPL was one of the first insurgent movements in Latin America to formulate an alternative revolutionary paradigm to Guevara's foco. It devised an integrated politico-military strategy, which combined the formation of urban and rural guerrillas, broad-based social movements, and a new type of Marxist-Leninist party.

Schafik Hándal, a prominent communist leader, also reflected at length on the future of revolution in Latin America in the 1960s. In 1968, he reported that the communist parties and the emergent revolutionary movements actively debated the contours of a new theory of revolution.[27] Hándal wrote:

> It is evident that in Latin America there is an open debate about revo-
> lutionary notions on fundamental problems of contemporary history.
> This discussion emerges . . . in newspapers and magazines, in parlia-
> ments and universities, in trade unions and other mass organizations, in
> jails, and in the mountains. . . . at the outset there is a tendency to ques-
> tion or doubt all or almost all the strategic and tactical systems that have
> informed the development of the Latin American revolution, in . . .
> the last forty years . . . [or alternatively] since the start of the postwar
> [i.e., the post–World War II period] or since the triumph of the Chinese
> Revolution. The real and growing interest in search of new answers is
> mixed. . . . [It involves] the confrontation between old and new dog-
> matic theses, between schemes devoid of life.[28]

According to Hándal, the political trends that had shaped revolutionary mobilizations in Latin America in the 1960s originated in two distinct historical processes. "The first trend of polemic tension," as he called it, had its origins in a variety of reformist, revolutionary, and nationalist movements that took center stage in Latin America since the 1930s. This trend was shaped by the progressive government of Lázaro Cárdenas in Mexico, the mobilizations against the military dictatorships in El Salvador and Guatemala in 1944, the anticolonial movement led by Chedi Yagan in Guyana, and the emerging liberal peasant guerrillas in Colombia. The election of President Gabriel González Videla in Chile in 1946 and the subsequent persecution of Chilean communists who had supported him, the overthrow of the democratic-reformist government of President Rafael A. Calderón Guardia in Costa Rica in 1948, and the democratic revolutions in Guatemala and Bolivia were also part of that historical process.[29] In other words, revolutionary, nationalist, and popular movements with diverse political and ideological orientations made up the first trend. In contrast, the Cuban Revolution and the Marxist guerrillas who emerged in Latin America in

the 1960s neatly defined the second trend, which materialized during the ousting of the Venezuelan dictator Marcos Pérez Jiménez in 1958 and the triumph
of the July 26 Movement in Cuba in 1959. In the 1960s, guerrilla movements in
Venezuela, Guatemala, Bolivia, and Colombia and potent social movements in
Chile, Uruguay, Mexico, and other Latin American nations constituted the vital
components of this revolutionary wave. According to Hándal, a crucial feature
of this trend was the massive integration of "middle sectors" (i.e., employees,
professionals, students, and teachers) to the new revolutionary organizations
that challenged the communist parties' traditional leadership in popular politics.[30] Hándal favored an open ideological debate with these rising forces, which
he termed "leftists" or the "naive left," but he also warned communists leaders
in Latin America not to blame them for "throwing a windfall of doubts over
old truths" because "life itself . . . is unfolding in unexpected directions, very
different from those foreseen in our conceptions." He wrote that the Cuban
Revolution had challenged US domination in the Americas and inspired revolutionary mobilizations across the region. In the early 1960s, the United States
responded to this challenge by promoting a continental counterrevolution,
dubbed "counterinsurgency." Repression, limited political openings, modernization, and direct military interventions like the US Marines' invasion of the
Dominican Republic in 1965 constituted the toolbox of US imperialism in Latin
America in the 1960s.[31] Nevertheless, Hándal deemed the Cuban Revolution
the exception that confirmed the rule, for the rest of the Latin American left
had failed to advance democracy and revolution in the continent through armed
struggle, or electoral politics, for that matter.[32]

The Salvadoran communists' soul-searching echoed the conundrums of the
Latin American left in the 1960s. The party sought to reconcile its rhetorical
support for armed struggle with its exclusive engagement in electoral politics at
a time when the authoritarian regime in El Salvador drastically escalated the repression against the opposition parties, the teacher movement, and the unions.
Hándal asserted that revolutionary violence in Latin America was in fact unavoidable due to the prevalence of authoritarian governments and the US-sponsored
counterrevolution, which ultimately sought to "smash the Cuban Revolution"
and bring back "the history of the Continent to 1954, the year of the ousting
of Jacobo Arbenz in Guatemala." Hándal wrote that violence in Latin America
(i.e., crime, political unrest, and poverty) was the result of a structural crisis of
capitalism. Revolutionary violence, in particular, constituted an expression of
popular resistance against oligarchic-military rule and US hegemony in the region. While Hándal explicitly defended the legitimacy of revolutionary violence
in Latin America, he also chastised the "infantile radicalism" of the New Left in
1960s. He wrote that the massive incorporation of "middle sectors" within the
emerging revolutionary organizations "had revived many features of anarchism

and populism" and deemed this process an obstacle to revolution.[33] However, he was also adamant about the need to dismiss any "illusions . . . about the real possibility of the so-called <u>peaceful takeover of power by the revolution.</u>"[34] *La Verdad*, the official newspaper of the PCS's central committee, which circulated widely at the university and other venues in the 1960s, often contained analyses and information about ongoing debates in the Latin American left (figure 6.2).

A number of left intellectuals ended their communist affiliation due to the party's ambiguous and ambivalent stance on armed struggle and electoral politics in the 1960s. Roque Dalton was one of the first to do so. The PCS's criticism

Figure 6.2 "For a True Independence." *La Verdad*, official organ of the Central Committee of the Communist Party of El Salvador, Second Epoch, September 15, 1966, no. 5. Courtesy of CIDAI, Biblioteca "P. Florentino Idoate, S.J." of the Central American University "José Simeón Cañas."

of the guerrilla movements at the first meeting of the Organization of Latin American Solidarity (OLAS), a gathering of communist parties and revolutionary movements held in Havana in August 1967, apparently informed Dalton's decision.[35] The PCS distanced itself from the OLAS resolution, which categorically declared, "Armed revolutionary struggle constitutes the fundamental course of the Revolution in Latin America."[36] The PCS delegation to the OLAS meeting echoed Hándal's analysis of Latin American revolutions.[37] Domingo Santacruz, a PCS delegate to the OLAS gathering who befriended Dalton at the time, recalled, "Roque [Dalton] considered that the PCS was no longer a revolutionary alternative and the party did not show the capacity to persuade him of the contrary."[38] Dalton wrote *A Revolution in the Revolution? And the Right's Critique*, a rejoinder to the French intellectual Régis Debray's book *Revolution in the Revolution? Armed Struggle and Political Struggle in Latin America*, which summarized his criticisms of the Latin American communist parties.[39] Subsequently, he tried to join the guerrillas in El Salvador. Carpio turned down Dalton's request to join the FPL because he considered Dalton "a desk intellectual," that is, a left dilettante, not a militant. Carpio's opinion of Dalton epitomized the persistent anti-intellectualism in the Salvadoran left. He also deemed Hándal, Raúl Castellanos, and other communist leaders with middle-class backgrounds "petit bourgeois intellectuals" who undermined proletarian hegemony in the party, despite the fact that "Carpio himself was also [a working-class] intellectual."[40]

The renovation of European and Latin American Marxism in the 1960s and 1970s crucially informed the insurgent New Left's thinking. Louis Althusser's critique of Stalinism, the Soviet domination over Eastern Europe, and the Soviet Communist Party's influence over the French Communist Party resonated in particular ways with the New Left's criticism of the PCS. Althusser's "defense of Marxism as a science," analyses of modes of production and social formations, and views on the "relative autonomy" of politics and ideology also shaped the insurgent intellectuals' interpretations of Salvadoran society, economy, and politics.[41] Two disciples of Althusser had a special resonance in the Salvadoran left: the Chilean sociologist Marta Harnecker and the French philosopher Régis Debray. Harnecker wrote *Elemental Concepts of Historical Materialism*, a text that popularized Althusser's ideas, which circulated widely in El Salvador and elsewhere in Latin America in the 1970s.[42] Debray joined Che Guevara in Bolivia and penned the influential book *Revolution in the Revolution?* In that text he drew on the experiences of the Cuban Revolution and advocated a revolutionary strategy centered on guerrilla warfare, armed struggle, and the creation of revolutionary vanguards. He deemed the traditional communist parties outdated, reformist organizations influenced by bourgeois states that pursued ineffective political strategies. As a militant of the National Liberation Army led by Guevara in Bolivia, he promoted the foco as the chief strategy to "catalyze revolution" and overcome "illusory and obsolete" political and intellectual debates in the left.[43]

Debray's book offered a sketchy rendering of the trajectory of colonial and modern insurgencies in Latin America, but it masterfully captured the sensibilities of the 1960s revolutionary left. In the aftermath of the Cuban Revolution, guerrilla movements in Guatemala, Venezuela, Nicaragua, Peru, and other countries explicitly or implicitly challenged the leadership of Latin American communist parties. Debray called the "armed self-defense" strategies of peasant guerrillas in Colombia and workers and miners in Bolivia weak, but he praised the efficacy of rural guerrilla warfare in Cuba, Venezuela, and Guatemala.[44] In the midst of the climactic student mobilizations in France, Germany, the United States, Mexico, and elsewhere, and the rise of the Latin American guerrillas, the communist parties seemed unable to guide the rebellious student youth and other radicalized sectors. Instead, they often invoked Marxist-Leninist orthodoxy to counter those who considered them bureaucratic pro-Soviet organizations, which had lost touch with social realities in Latin America. In this frame, Debray challenged fundamental aspects of the communist parties' ideology and politics. The guerrilla vanguards and not the communist parties were to play the leading roles in Latin American revolutions.[45] Rural guerrillas—not labor and electoral politics, or urban insurrections for that matter—were the key to defeating oligarchic-military regimes in the region. Debray even commented on the generational gap between seasoned communist leaders and young revolutionaries to make the case that in Latin America there was a crucial link between "biology and ideology." Despite their ideological zeal, elderly communist leaders accustomed to urban life were unfit to command rural guerrillas in Latin America. This was a task for young revolutionaries.[46] Not surprisingly, Debray's influential book produced shock waves among communist parties in the region. While numerous communist parties and leaders met it with skepticism or outright rejection, the Argentinian Communist Party (PCA) and Pompeyo Márquez, a leader of the Venezuelan Communist Party (PCV), produced two of the most acrid critiques of Debray. Márquez in particular faulted him for summarily disregarding the histories of Latin American communist parties. He emphatically disputed Debray's assertion that the July 26 Movement had formed the core of the Communist Party of Cuba at the time of the 1953 Moncada barracks attack, which in his view silenced the legacies of the Partido Socialista Popular (the traditional Cuban Communist Party) in the Cuban Revolution.[47] He also considered dubious Debray's idea of constituting the "rural guerrillas" as the "sole revolutionary instrument" that displaced the authority of the communist parties to create new revolutionary vanguards. Márquez called such policy *"la desviación guerrillerista"* (guerrilla deviation). "The Venezuelan revolution without the PCV and against the PCV is inconceivable. The Latin American

Revolution without the participation of CPs [communist parties] and the socialist world where communist parties rule does not have a prospect of victory.
Cuba is the most relevant example of this assertion," wrote Márquez.[48] Márquez,
like Hándal, was adamant about the exceptionality of the Cuban Revolution.
Armed struggle and the guerrilla vanguard (i.e., the July 26 Movement) proved
efficacious in Cuba, but this experience did not necessarily match the sociopolitical conditions in the rest of Latin America, as Debray argued.

In the midst of this debate, Dalton wrote a "defense and a critique" of
Debray: *Revolution in the Revolution? And the Right's Critique.* In it, he pondered
Márquez's critique of Debrary and also assessed the impact of Debray's book
in Latin America. Dalton claimed that Márquez had dodged Debray's core argument in his attempt to defend the legacies and authority of the communist
parties, namely, what was the main strategy to "take power and to make the revolution in our countries?" Was it feasible to make revolution without eroding
the military power of the state or even confronting a direct US military intervention? Was it possible to achieve those objectives without forming a revolutionary
army that emerged from the rural guerrillas?[49] Ultimately, Dalton reinforced
Debray's critique of the communist parties. In his view, the Latin American
communists had relinquished the objective of taking power and had instead focused on electoral politics. Their mechanical attempts to replicate Soviet policies
in Latin America had discredited them. The persistent legacies of Stalinism had
made them dogmatic organizations, incapable of interpreting Latin American
societies on their own terms. Their views on "the exceptionality of the Cuban
Revolution" had hindered their potential to articulate revolutionary strategies
in other regional settings. Dalton also criticized Debray on two counts. He had
failed to understand the importance of creating "a political revolutionary organization" able to orient emerging "revolutionary actors" (i.e., social movements)
and did not elaborate a viable politico-military strategy. During his brief participation in the ERP, Dalton, along with Sancho, Lil Milagro Ramírez, and other
militants who founded the National Resistance (RN), tried precisely to create
such a political revolutionary movement. While none of the insurgent groups
formed in El Salvador in the early 1970s followed Debray's dicta, the polemic
around his book informed their own ruminations on strategy.[50]

The PCS split in 1970 over the debate on armed struggle and electoral politics and its apparent endorsement of the Salvadoran government's chauvinistic
campaign during the 1969 war between El Salvador and Honduras.[51] A new insurgent organization led by Carpio, the FPL, emerged as a result of the party's
division. According to Santacruz, who was then a leader of the PCS, in the late
1960s Carpio organized unionists affiliated with the party into a distinct faction,
which promoted the party's *proletarización,* that is, the hegemony of working-
class communist leaders, taking advantage of his position as the party's secretary

general. The Celestino Castro School, a night school that served urban work-
ers, became in fact a "nursery of FPL cadres." Carpio also recruited the "Frank
País cell," a PCS collective made up of medical students at the University of
El Salvador, as the first members of the new organization.[52] On April 1, 1970,
Carpio and other union activists formally broke with the party and formed the
new guerrilla group.[53] The FPL's version of the PCS division in 1970 highlights
Carpio's rejection of the party's "chauvinism" during the war between El Salvador
and Honduras in 1969, its bureaucratic practices in union and university politics,
and its reluctance to lead the armed struggle against the dictatorship.[54] However,
"Valentín" (aka "Gerson Martínez"), a leader of the FPL in the 1970s, posited
that the rise of the insurgency during that decade had more structural reasons.
The rise of "new [social] subjects," particularly, the unions and the teacher and
student movements, and the growing repression against such movements, motivated "left [intellectuals]" and "other honest democrats . . . humanitarian and
Christian people," to create the guerrilla organizations in the early 1970s.[55]

La Masacuata also embraced Guevarismo in the late 1960s. Che Guevara's
murder and the PCS critique of the foco theory constituted a watershed in the
radicalization of the group. The poets of La Masacuata did not take lightly the
PCS's devastating critique of Guevara's strategy in the aftermath of his murder.[56]
They openly denounced the PCS's stance and became, in the words of Sancho,
"mouthpieces of Guevarismo."[57] They shared the views of José Domingo Mira,
a university intellectual who had attended the OLAS meeting in Havana and
became a founding figure of the New Left in El Salvador. Upon his return to
El Salvador, Mira published *The Bolivian Diary of 'Che' Guevara* and actively
promoted Guevara's thesis on armed struggle among university students. Mira
argued that "Che was right" about the need to conduct armed struggle against
the military dictatorships in Latin America. According to Sancho, Mira was the
first intellectual "to break [with the PCS] but he did not form any group."[58]

In response to Mira's publication, the PCS published *The Bolivian Diary of
'Che' Guevara* with an epilogue endorsed by the party's political commission,
which questioned the validity of the foco theory but not the legitimacy of armed
struggle in Latin America.[59] At that time, the poets of La Masacuata became serious students of Guevara's writings. They read "the complete works of Guevara
and started forgetting about literature [i.e., they joined the insurgency]. . . . the
desperate petit bourgeoisie [as communists often labeled the rebel poets] was
radicalized. . . . La Masacuata shed its skin, experienced a metamorphosis. . . .
the ethical component was Che," said Sancho.[60] This makes sense. Guevara
incarnated the prophetic aura of Dalton's poetics, which the rebel poets deeply
admired (figure 6.3).[61] He evoked the romanticizing of revolutionary violence
promoted by the Cuban state and the Latin American guerrillas since the early
1960s, as well as notions of social justice and ethical renewal implicit in the

Figure 6.3 "A Year after His Death CHE LIVES! Guiding with His Example the Youth of the Americas." *Opinión Estudiantil*, Epoch 26, October 8, "Day of the Heroic Guerrilla," 1968, front page. Courtesy of Special Collections, University of El Salvador Library.

ongoing Catholic theological reform. He also echoed ideas on the emancipating power of anticolonial violence, articulated chiefly by Franz Fanon in *Wretched of the Earth*, a book that circulated widely among New Left intellectuals in El Salvador in the 1960s.[62]

The leaders of El Grupo, the guerrilla cell founded by Rivas Mira and Sancho, debated the applicability of Guevara's strategy to the socioeconomic and political context of El Salvador but mostly were anxious to initiate guerrilla warfare largely to thwart the PCS's vehement opposition to the insurgency. Sancho attended a historic meeting with the central figures of the Old Left that illustrates this point. On December 24, 1969, he met Carpio and Hándal at the university campus. A professor of sociology at the university with close ties with the New Left mediated the exchange. Sancho recalled that Carpio, the secretary general of the PCS, "spoke on behalf of the working class" and argued in favor of starting armed struggle in El Salvador, a position that clearly contradicted the party's official line.[63] Hándal, on the other hand, "brought some ten [Marxist] books" to the meeting to question the feasibility of armed struggle in the country and called the founders of El Grupo "ultraleftists." He also endorsed the 1968 Soviet invasion of Czechoslovakia and the USSR's views on the Sino-Soviet conflict.[64] Sancho's recollection of this exchange is consistent with Hándal's opinions about El Grupo. He deemed the young revolutionaries militarists with a simplistic view of politics. From his vantage point, Rivas Mira had instilled a militaristic culture among the founders of El Grupo, likely as a product of his clandestine experience in Germany.[65]

Carpio did not trust El Grupo either. He considered its members a blend of middle-class Christian Democrats, "neo-Marxists," communist dissidents, and anarchists influenced by Marcuse, Cohn-Bendit, and other New Left thinkers, which he reviled. For him, they constituted a faction made up of militarists, anti-communists, and pragmatists, able to engage in complex political maneuvering and deception to achieve their objectives.[66] At any rate, Sancho approached Carpio after the meeting and sardonically told him, "You are trying to convert the PCS [into a guerrilla movement]," to which Carpio replied, "There will be a shift within the PCS." "But we were not waiting for that, we were already doing other things [forming the insurgency]," recalled Sancho.[67]

"The Secret Societies": Precursors of Urban Guerrilla Warfare

In December 1969, Sancho, Alejandro Rivas Mira, Lil Milagro Ramírez, and other Social Christian activists and the poets of La Masacuata formed El Grupo.[68] This organization kidnapped and murdered the Salvadoran industrialist Ernesto Regalado Dueñas in February 1971. The Salvadoran authorities first blamed "a band of Guatemalan guerrillas" for Regalado's abduction. But as it turned out, Regalado, the heir of the two most powerful clans of the Salvadoran oligarchy, was the first of several Salvadoran and foreign businessmen targeted by the Salvadoran insurgents in the 1970s.[69] While the security forces dismantled El Grupo after Regalado's murder, the survivors of the cell became cofounders of two guerrilla organizations in the 1970s, the ERP and the RN. El Grupo initially mutated into the ERP.[70] In turn, the ERP split at the time of Roque Dalton's murder. Rivas Mira (a former Social Christian activist), Rafael Arce Zablah and Joaquín Villalobos (two former members of Catholic Action), and other militants led the ERP after this event. Sancho and Lil Milagro Ramírez became leaders of the RN. The two organizations developed contrasting revolutionary strategies. Drawing on Maoism, the ERP carried out a militaristic strategy and created extensive networks among peasant communities across the country. In 1977, it conducted a major political turn. It formed the Popular Leagues February 28 (LP-28), a coalition of social movements that played an important role in the national political crisis that unfolded at the end of that decade. In contrast, the RN combined armed struggle, broad front politics, and labor activism since its formation in 1975. It became an influential organization among peasant communities in Suchitoto and other rural areas, university students, and unionized urban workers.

The insurgent intellectuals' lives in the early 1970s were exacting. Their daily routines usually comprised political and military training sessions, the planning and execution of urban military operations, the construction of political networks, and intense intellectual activity (e.g., the formulation of social analyses, revolutionary strategies and tactics, and clandestine publications). Atilio Montalvo, a former university student who joined the FPL in the early 1970s, recalled that at that time he inhabited safe houses in San Salvador, facing a precarious existence. "Our basic diet was rice and beans. We sometimes lacked even cooking pots and utensils and had to cook our meals using milk cans and other containers," said Montalvo.[71] Sonia Aguiñada, a former high school student who joined the ERP in the early 1970s, recalled that she and her fellow combatants had a militarized daily routine, which included drills, political and military studies, the planning of military operations, and the construction of support networks among activists, friends, and relatives.[72] Ana Sonia Medina, a former leader of the ERP, had similar recollections about her clandestine life in the early 1970s.[73] The combatants were also subject to disciplinary sanctions of various degrees of severity. Montalvo recalled that on one occasion, his superiors in the FPL ordered him to walk fifty kilometers as a penalty for allegedly failing to follow safety precautions while he vacated a safe house in San Salvador.[74] In his most recent memoir, Sancho offered a poignant account of his trying life as an insurgent commander in the 1970s. On top of the constant persecution by the state forces, he endured extreme poverty, several accidents, and serious illnesses and was even stabbed by a thief during his life as an urban combatant.[75] He drew a comparison between the lives of militants in the early 1970s and ancient "secret societies":

> The founding group . . . is a secret society like the Church of the catacombs, to conspire against the oligarchic crown of Central America, in the second independence. It is a kind of sodality [*cofradía*] with disciplinary rules that serve to survive . . . to preserve its nucleus it takes

measures, thus it uses cyanide. Between 1971 and 1974, if one [was] captured or wounded, one must ingest the venom. That military order lasted four years.[76]

The founders of the insurgency were acutely aware of the country's recent political conflicts and viewed themselves as conscious actors in an ongoing historical process. Lil Milagro Ramírez defended the legitimacy of the insurgency in a letter she wrote to her mother in March 1972. To make her case, she recalled the failed experience of the Civic-Military Junta that governed El Salvador between October 1960 and January 1961, which advocated electoral democracy and civilian rule. Reactionary military officers sponsored by the United States perpetrated the bloody coup that ousted the Junta in 1961, effectively closing the path for peaceful reform. Ramírez also blamed them for rigging the 1972 presidential election, which was won by Duarte, the National Opposition Union's candidate. The military officers who supported the reformist Civic Military Junta and those who rejected the electoral fraud in 1972 had committed the "same mistake . . . they feared arming the people." Thus the reactionary military backed by the United States had easily routed them. In concluding the letter, Ramírez wrote: "In facing armed brutes, there are no valid laws or reasons."[77] This statement summarizes a widely held conviction among the insurgent intellectuals: the closing of political spaces, the electoral frauds, and the mounting state terror had made armed struggle the only viable alternative to promote social revolution and democracy in El Salvador.

The insurgent intellectuals carefully studied the contours of politics, society, and economy in El Salvador to formulate revolutionary strategies. The ubiquitous debates on dependency theory that permeated the Salvadoran academy at that time centrally informed their intellectual production throughout the 1970s. Montalvo summarized this perspective as follows:

> Neocolonialism was the word that expressed the way in which we saw the phenomenon of dependency of El Salvador to the United States. Not the traditional form of colonialism but a new type of relationship between the underdeveloped countries and the metropolis. We deemed that the ruling class, the right-wing political party [the PCN, the official party], and the military dictatorship had partners in the metropolis, which ultimately would not allow that the problem [the conflict] be resolved through free elections. It was convenient for the metropolis, quote unquote, to support a military dictatorship because they [US elites] thought it was the easiest and cheapest way to defeat the insurgency or any political attempt to change [the system]. It was a way of maintaining [the status quo] in Central America, which

they [US elites] considered "banana republics." In the 1960s, this view changed a bit, with the Alliance for Progress, but ultimately, it was the same approach.[78]

The intellectual production of insurgent leaders in the 1970s was considerable. The politico-military organizations left a vast paper trail that merits a comprehensive engagement with the intellectual history of these movements. Although this is not the place to offer a detailed review of this literature, it is worth mentioning some insurgent publications that had greater resonance during that decade. The ERP published a caustic critique of the March 1972 presidential elections in a pamphlet titled *Is Your Vote Your Weapon?* The pamphlet, which argued that the regime's fraudulent electoral practices rendered elections obsolete as a method to promote social change and democracy in the country, circulated widely in El Salvador. Rafael Arce Zablah, the most influential ERP intellectual, wrote *Grano de oro* (Golden grain), a structural analysis of the coffee economy in El Salvador, which accounted for the patterns of capital accumulation of the landed agro-exporter elites. The Party of the Salvadoran Revolution (PRS)-ERP, the revolutionary party that directed the ERP, also published *Prensa Comunista* (Communist Press), a periodical that featured political analyses and information about the organization's activities (figure 6.4).[79] The last two publications circulated mainly among ERP militants and supporters.[80]

FPL intellectuals Felipe Peña Mendoza, Clara Elizabeth Ramírez, Andrés Torres, Atilio Montalvo, and Cayetano Carpio authored *Estrella Roja* (Red Star), a serial publication, which explicated the organization's policies, strategy, and tactics.[81] *Estrella Roja 2* in particular had important reverberations among Catholic priests, nuns, and laypeople. It elucidated the organization's views on religion and politics and advocated an alliance between Catholics and Marxists.[82] *Estrella Roja* circulated among FPL members and supporters. The FPL also published *El Rebelde* (The Rebel) a clandestine newspaper that circulated widely in El Salvador in the 1970s. The organization regularly produced thousands of copies of this publication. The RN put out *Por La Causa Proletaria* (For the Proletarian Cause), also a periodical that featured social and political analyses and discussions of political and military strategies and that had a massive circulation in El Salvador.[83] The corpus formulated by the insurgent intellectuals in the 1970s, which included works on politics, political economy, revolution, guerrilla warfare, mass movements, and socialism, deserves careful consideration. As a whole this literature constituted a vital component of the insurgents' "pedagogy of revolution" as it helped them to train thousands of activists during the 1970s and into the revolutionary war.

In the early 1970s, the urban guerrillas launched a series of attacks against the public security forces (i.e., the National Guard, the National Police, and the

Figure 6.4 "El Salvador: A Revolutionary Perspective." PRS-ERP, *Prensa Comunista*, Special Publications, May 1977, front page. Courtesy of CIDAI, Biblioteca "P. Florentino Idoate, S.J." of the Central American University "José Simeón Cañas."

Treasury Police). The ERP and the RN centered their offensives on the public security forces and not the army, as they deemed them bastions of the dictatorship and envisioned the creation of alliances with what they called the "democratic con-stitutionalist sector" of the military.[84] The ERP guerrillas who carried out the first attack against two National Guardsmen stationed at the main children's hospital in San Salvador, on March 2, 1972, had virtually no military training and in fact relied on their readings of Carlos Marighella's "[The] Minimanual of the Urban Guerrilla" and the experiences of the Uruguayan Tupamaros to conduct the attack. However, for weeks they were unable to disassemble the guns and could do so only with the help of army officers who secretly collaborated with the insurgency.[85]

Communist intellectuals readily condemned the first urban guerrilla attacks in the 1970s. They labeled the guerrillas "Maoists, Trotskyites, left extremists" and even agents provocateurs at the service of the state intelligence and the CIA.[86] In turn, the insurgents chastised the PCS for its participation in electoral politics, which they considered a blatant legitimizing of authoritarian rule and repression. In 1974, the Organization of Revolutionary Workers (ORT)—a predecessor of the Central American Workers' Revolutionary Party (PRTC), a founding organization of the FMLN—labeled communist intellectuals "social opportunists" and added them to a list of purported accomplices of the dictatorship, which included "legalists . . . the working class aristocracy . . . and the renegades of socialism."[87] In 2003, Carlos E. Rico Mira, a member of La Masacuata who became one of the first guerrilla operatives in El Salvador, offered a more benevolent reading of the PCS's condemnation of the insurgencies in the 1970s. The party was simply unable to realize that armed struggle had become a central component of the antifascist resistance during that decade. It erroneously believed that the guerrillas were trying to replicate Guevara's strategy in El Salvador, which it vigorously rejected. Instead, according to Rico, the insurgents sought to combine armed struggle and mass collective action, a path that ultimately enabled the formation of the FMLN in 1980.[88] At any rate, the dispute between the insurgent and the communist intellectuals continued until 1977, when the PCS relinquished electoral politics in the aftermath of the February 28 massacre in downtown San Salvador. During that episode, the army attacked unarmed activists who protested the electoral fraud orchestrated by the PCN government against the National Opposition Union's presidential candidate, Colonel Ernesto Claramount.

The insurgent intellectuals were also profoundly divided over a number of ideological, political, and strategic issues. El Grupo made an unsuccessful attempt to unify the guerrilla movements in 1971. Sancho reported that he, Carpio, and Fabio Castillo, who led other nascent insurgencies, conducted a meeting to discuss El Grupo's initiative. Carpio, whom the younger insurgents considered a living legend due to his participation in antidictatorial struggles for nearly three decades, utterly rejected the unification of the guerrilla groups. He plainly told Sancho that he "did not trust the group of Christians" who made up El Grupo.[89] (While several Social Christian activists formed El Grupo, Sancho, the poets of La Masacuata, and other cofounders of the cell were secular individuals.) Drawing on Vietnamese Marxism, the FPL adopted a strategy it called "prolonged people's warfare." In Carpio's view, the centerpiece of this strategy was the construction of the "true Communist Party." He clearly did not consider the PCS a communist organization and thought that the other insurgent movements were not militant enough. They were all unfit to complete that task. Carpio deemed the pure communist party of his imagination the cornerstone for the development of popular movements, the creation of a guerrilla army, and ultimately the formation of "a popular government" that set the basis of socialism.[90] The dominant faction in the ERP, led by Rivas Mira (aka "Captain Sebastián Urquilla"), Arce Zablah, and Villalobos, embraced certain aspects of Maoism in the early 1970s.[91] They privileged the formation of a guerrilla army (thus the organization's name: People's Revolutionary Army) and the planning of insurrections with the collaboration of army officers over the creation of mass political movements.[92] Another faction in the ERP, which self-identified as the National Resistance, led by Lil Milagro Ramírez and Sancho, focused on the creation of a broad-based alliance formed by emerging social movements, legal political parties, and members of the state army.[93] Upon his clandestine arrival in El Salvador in December 1973, Roque Dalton joined Ramírez, Sancho, and other intellectuals affiliated with the RN.[94] The tensions that prevailed among ERP intellectuals in the early 1970s led to a bloody internal conflict in 1975, which resulted in the assassination of Dalton and Armando Arteaga (aka "Pancho"), an ERP combatant, committed by the faction led by Rivas Mira, Vladimir Rogel (aka "Portillo"), and other individuals.[95]

The Deaths of Roque Dalton and Armando Arteaga and the New Left's Paradoxical Anti-intellectualism

The iconoclastic Roque Dalton made dogmatists of various kinds feel deeply uncomfortable. In 1958, the leaders of ACUS, then a conservative Catholic student organization, considered him a provocateur due to his sarcastic commentaries on Catholic priests' sexual morals and the romantic ideas about class conflict that prevailed among middle-class Catholic students.[96] In 1960, President José María Lemus, a Cold War anti-communist, incarcerated Dalton for his participation in the mobilizations of that period, accusing him of "rebellion and sedition."[97] In May 1975, the dominant faction in the ERP ordered the murder of Dalton and Armando Arteaga (aka "Pancho") in an incident that has traumatized the Salvadoran left ever since.[98] Much has been written and debated about the specifics of Dalton's assassination.[99] In recent years Sancho added an important contextual reference about the circumstances in which these events unfolded. He reported that in 1975 the ERP had militarized its party structure because it was planning to launch an insurrection with the support of a group of army officers. The militarization of the Party of the Salvadoran Revolution (PRS), the ERP's political structure, enabled Rivas Mira, according to Sancho, to charge Dalton with insubordination and to accuse him of being a Cuban and a CIA agent.[100]

Dalton's decision to join the insurgency in 1973 reflected his ethics as a revolutionary intellectual. He lived in exile in Cuba and Czechoslovakia in the 1960s, but his writings, particularly those on the roles that intellectuals played in Latin American revolutions, had resonance among university students in El Salvador.[101] He harshly criticized what he deemed the political and ethical inconsistencies of left intellectuals in Latin America. In his view, most Latin American writers and artists subjectively identified with the poor and the oppressed, but their cultural production was exclusively geared toward elite consumption. Dalton deemed the Peruvian Marxist thinker José Carlos Mariátegui one of the few exceptions to his dictum. Mariátegui was, according to Dalton, a true revolutionary intellectual.[102]

Historically, left intellectuals had joined social movements as a means to connect with popular culture, but they were unable to bridge the cultural and educational abyss that alienated them from the urban and rural poor. Thus, to bridge this gap, left intellectuals in the 1960s had to meet two crucial challenges: to strengthen the theoretical foundations of the insurgencies in Central and South America and to enhance the cultural and educational levels of the oppressed.[103] Dalton summarized his own ethos, citing an aphorism coined by the Guatemalan writer Miguel Angel Asturias: "El Poeta es una conducta moral" (The poet incarnates a moral conduct). According to Dalton, the political and intellectual trajectory of the Guatemalan poet Otto René Castillo (1934–1967) incarnated the spirit condensed in Asturias's dictum.[104] Castillo, who was tortured and murdered by the Guatemalan military in 1967, was, according to Dalton, the quintessential "revolutionary hero." Dalton sharply contrasted the paths of Castillo and the Nobel laureate Asturias to make this point. The first embodied the moral conduct of a revolutionary poet; the latter betrayed the ethics contained in his own maxim by becoming the ambassador in Paris of the dictatorship that murdered Castillo.[105]

Dalton also evoked the martyred poets Leonel Rugama and Roberto Obregón Morales, from Nicaragua and Guatemala, respectively, to argue that revolutionary politics had become an irreversible feature of Central American arts and culture.[106]

Informed by these intellectual and ethical views, Dalton left his exile in Cuba at a time when his literary fame peaked, after he was awarded the Casa de Las Américas Prize in Havana in 1969, a prestigious Cuban literary prize, to join the guerrillas in El Salvador. Dalton's ideas about the historical calling of revolutionary intellectuals in Latin America became a parable of his life and death. He was a cosmopolitan intellectual, a poet of the resistance, who consciously prepared to join the Salvadoran insurgency for nearly a decade. However, the leaders of the ERP repudiated his politics, demeanor, and literary endeavors, articulating an anti-intellectualist discourse, and finally ordered his execution on May 10, 1975 (Mother's Day in El Salvador).

The ERP qualified Dalton's brief participation in the insurgency in 1974 and 1975 as an expression of the "insidious influence of petit bourgeois intellectualism in the revolutionary movement."[107] The First Congress of the PRS-ERP, held in October 1977, considered the decision to execute Dalton "a grave political and ideological mistake."[108] It also dismissed Rivas Mira's accusation against Dalton, who had labeled him a "CIA agent" in order to justify his execution. However, the congress stated that Dalton's intellectualism and his bureaucratic and conspiratorial methods contributed to the "fratricidal struggle" in the ERP and to his own demise.[109] It deemed the execution of Dalton and Arteaga in 1975 a manifestation of a conflict between the faction headed by Rivas Mira and the RN, the movement led by Lil Milagro Ramírez, Sancho, and Dalton. It faulted the RN and Dalton for advocating forms of representative democracy, which it considered unfitting for the functioning of a clandestine revolutionary movement. In other words, the RN had allegedly tried to incorporate leaders of social movements into the ERP leadership (i.e., representatives of peasant, worker, and student movements) to augment its clout in the organization. The congress labeled the RN leaders, and Dalton in particular, "the maximum exponents of bureaucratic and inconsequential tendencies, which considered themselves an intellectualist sector, which thought too much and worked little. . . . their lack of initiative provoked political mistakes . . . [that originated] . . . from their lack of energy and liberalism." It also faulted them for their lack of capacity to organize "military activities," which ostensibly emanated from their "ideological vacillation" and unwillingness to "risk their valuable lives."[110]

The PRS-ERP Congress sought to attenuate the serious implications of Dalton's execution by maligning his political reputation and minimizing his intellectual contributions to the organization (although it probably managed to do the contrary by detailing Dalton's intellectual production during his brief participation in the group).[111] First and foremost, it questioned Dalton's motives for joining the organization. It claimed that he had joined the ERP as part of a "maneuver of international revisionism to intervene and influence decisively the organization"—in other words, as part of an effort of the Cuban state to control the ERP. It also asserted that the Soviet Union considered revolutionary movements in Latin America as "fifth columns" in its fight against the United States and therefore sought to "influence and control them." Dalton, according to the PRS-ERP, was a "firm defender of such policy of revisionism" and had at times admitted that he "had conducted special works" for the KGB and the Cuban state security. In sum, the PRS-ERP concluded, without presenting any evidence, that Dalton joined the ERP as part of a conspiracy of "international revisionism" to infiltrate the organization.[112]

The PRS-ERP Congress also criticized Dalton's lack of discipline and his "liberalism" (i.e., lack of ideological rigor), self-promotion, and purported ambition to become "a revolutionary caudillo."[113] It also made a spurious contrast between the alleged value of the lives of working-class militants and Dalton's life to diminish the significance of the poet's murder. It argued that the lives of the "humble" revolutionaries who had perished fighting the dictatorship in the 1970s were "100 times more" valuable than Dalton's life.[114] It depicted Arteaga as a model of proletarian virtue and Dalton as the proverbial hesitant petit bourgeois intellectual. It considered the decision to execute Arteaga an "unjust measure." While Arteaga had supported the RN, he showed a "high morale and ideological quality," even in facing his imminent execution. Vladimir Rogel (aka "Portillo"), one of Arteaga's purported killers, gave him the opportunity to recant his affiliation with the RN, but he plainly refused to do so. Rogel ostensibly told Arteaga that Dalton himself had already recanted his political views by stating that the conflict between the two factions was simply due to a "lack of communication." Arteaga allegedly responded to Rogel: "Julio [Dalton's nom de guerre] is a petit bourgeois and he fears dying and that is why he doesn't defend his ideas. I am not [a petit bourgeois], I will not change my way of thinking from night to day. . . . I won't argue with those who are pointing [their guns] at me. . . . I will never aim [a gun] against a comrade."[115]

The PRS-ERP claimed that it truthfully reproduced this dialogue between Rogel and Arteaga in an attempt to clarify the circumstances of the latter's death and to vindicate his memory. It also maintained that Dalton was not "a coward but [rather] a petit bourgeois pragmatist consequent with his petit bourgeois positions, who was never a revolutionary." The contrasting conduct ostensibly shown by Arteaga and Dalton at the time of their executions illustrated, according to the organization, the "deep ideological abyss that separate[d] the militant proletarian from the adventurer."[116]

The PRS-ERP also responded to Latin American intellectuals who strongly condemned Dalton's assassination with a solid diatribe. In the aftermath of the poet's death, the French-Argentinian writer Julio Cortázar wrote that Dalton's murderers had made good on a threat made to Dalton by a CIA agent who interrogated him during his illegal imprisonment in El Salvador in 1964. The agent allegedly had warned Dalton that the CIA had enough documentation to frame him as a traitor to the left even after his death.[117] The PRS-ERP stated:

> Dalton's execution unleashed a rabid campaign of the petit bourgeois "intellectuals" that little by little became a work aimed at transforming Dalton into a political banner [of] the most low and obscure positions of the inconsequential petit bourgeois intelligentsia, which consider itself the thinking head, leaders, critics . . . rectors of the Latin American revolutionary processes. These gentlemen [who] elaborate their judgments, their essays and poems, from their comfortable

parasitic exiles, from the banality of their existentialist lifestyle or from academic positions, have seen in Dalton the possibility not only of their auto-justification as the petit bourgeois intelligentsia, which considers [itself] father and mother of the revolutionary left. By transforming Dalton into a "revolutionary" of "great qualities," [and] failing to tell the truth about his role in the Salvadoran revolutionary process and sublimating his ephemeral militancy, they attempt to position themselves as a sector through the banner of Dalton the poet and writer. . . . this is what makes his death important and transforms him into a hero when truly he was the victim and author of his own death.[118]

In 2006, Ana Sonia Medina (aka "Commander Mariana"), a leader of the ERP in the 1970s and during the civil war, argued that the circumstances that led to Dalton's assassination were the result of an intergenerational, political, and cultural conflict between the younger ERP leaders and the older and bohemian Dalton:

The fundamental nucleus [of the ERP] was made up of very young men and women [*muchachos muy jóvenes*] formed in ideas of revolutionary consequence, sacrifice, and discipline. Unfortunately Roque [Dalton] did not have that [those ideas]. They questioned him a lot because of ideological things, for instance while we were all obliged to get up for drills at 5:00 a.m. every day, Roque did not get up. He was an old man [he turned forty in 1975], much older than Sebastián [Rivas Mira, the ERP's main leader who at that time was probably in his late twenties]. He liked drinking [alcohol], being lazy. He did not like to do domestic work. Those were minor things in his dimension as a poet, but for those of us who were forming a revolutionary organization whose goal was to overthrow a dictatorship supported by the [US] imperialism, those things were unacceptable. That is probably why it was not hard for us to accept the arguments [articulated by Rivas Mira] in the problem with Roque. In the nucleus of the [ERP] leadership the conflict was clear, the arguments apparently revolved around issues related to the military struggle and the work with the masses. But in the end, Roque did not have enough clout in the leadership to express his conceptions with clarity, instead he wrote documents and worked at a conspiratorial level. The members of the [ERP] leadership were Sebastián, Joaquín Villalobos, Jonás [Jorge Meléndez], Lil Milagro [Ramírez], and [Eduardo] Sancho. The advisers [of the ERP leadership] were Lito [Rafael Arce Zablah], Roque [Dalton], and I [Ana Sonia Medina]. The balance of power clearly favored Sebastián.[119]

Sancho, on the other hand, flatly rejected the version that Dalton was an undisciplined bohemian combatant. "Concerning the myths [that he was] a bohemian, they are not real, during his short participation in the guerrilla [movement] from December 24, 1973, to May 1975, that theme is out of question and does not have the least foundation," wrote Sancho.[120] Instead, he presents us with a stoic Dalton who trusted until his final hour that he would be able to negotiate the end of his unjust imprisonment with the ERP leaders. Dalton apparently refused an offer made by Sancho and Lil Milagro Ramírez to free him with the help of his jailers and to split from the organization. Sancho viewed Dalton's murder as one more case in a long list of political assassinations perpetrated by left- and right-wing extremists and military tyrants in the history of El Salvador, who embodied a shared "authoritarian culture."[121] The strict secrecy, dogmatism, and militarized discipline that characterized the ERP at the time of Dalton's assassination were not exclusive features of this particular group. In the early 1970s, the FPL and other insurgent organizations had similar clandestine cultures. The insurgent intellectuals' political culture became, to a certain extent, more open as a result of their growing interactions with peasant leaders, teachers, and other social activists who joined the revolutionary left in large numbers from the mid-1970s onward.

Resisting "Fascism"

The eclecticism of the insurgent intellectuals constituted their greatest strength and challenge. They blended multiple and often conflictive intellectual and political traditions to fight what they labeled the fascist regime in El Salvador. They had different interpretations of the historical origins, social composition, and economic interests of the fascist forces in El Salvador. But they concurred that in the 1970s the oligarchic-military regime incorporated distinctive attributes of fascism, chiefly, state terror, recurrent electoral frauds, mass propaganda, psychological warfare, and the vast militarization of society and politics. They labeled it with terms such as the "fascist-like military tyranny," "Salvadoran fascism," and the "fascist escalade." They considered oligarchic elites, high-ranking military officers, and PCN officials the core fascist forces in El Salvador. Ultraconservative sectors of the Catholic Church, ORDEN paramilitaries, members of the security forces, sectors of the army, and PCN followers made up the social base of Salvadoran fascism.[122] In their view, the Communist Party's participation in electoral politics was a form of right-wing revisionism, which enabled the fascist regime to create a veneer of democratic legitimacy.

Communist intellectuals, on the other hand, also viewed the consolidation of fascism as a real threat but contended that broad front politics, not armed struggle, was the most expedient way to fight it. In this vein, the PCS advocated the creation of a *poder democrático de transición* (transitional democratic power; i.e., a broad democratic front), as a means to defeat the fascist regime and to create a liberal democracy. Such power was inherently unstable for it comprised both capitalist elites allied with the United States and anti-imperialist and socialist forces. Therefore, for the PCS it was not an end in itself but rather a path to isolate fascists and to eventually form a democratic anti-imperialist government. For Hándal, the guerrilla groups and the revolutionary social movements undermined this policy through their radical activism. In Hándal's words, "ultra-left groups" promoted "the artificial radicalization of the transitional democratic power" through "expropriation[s]," "land occupations," and "the seizure of factories and houses."[123]

In the 1970s, the PCS viewed electoral politics as the fundamental means to create a transitional democratic power in El Salvador. Although the party had practiced revolutionary violence, most notably during the disastrous 1932 uprising and between 1961 and 1963, communist intellectuals believed that modernization and the limited political opening promoted by President Rivera since 1962, in the context of the Alliance for Progress, had rendered armed struggle unviable as a revolutionary strategy in El Salvador. During Rivera's tenure, opposition parties like the PDC and PAR operated legally. They made substantial electoral gains and obtained considerable representation at the National Assembly. The PDC had governed San Salvador and other cities since 1964. The country experienced rapid industrialization and high rates of economic growth throughout the 1960s. A new industrial working class emerged. The professional middle class and the university student population also grew substantially in this period. In sum, while repression was still prevalent, electoral participation was indeed possible and necessary. Under these assumptions the PCS joined two legal opposition parties, the PDC and the National Revolutionary Movement (MNR), a social democratic party, to create the National Opposition Union (UNO) in 1971. Hándal flatly rejected insurgent politics. In his view, the guerrilla groups' strategies did not match the political consciousness of the majority of Salvadorans, who still considered elections relevant despite the repression and vehemently defended the legitimacy of the party's endorsement of UNO in the 1972 election. Electoral politics showed "the masses through their own experience . . . the fraudulent character of the elections and the falsehood and hypocrisy of the famous [*tan vitoreada*] 'representative democracy' defended by the ruling classes and the government."[124]

The insurgent intellectuals wrote poignant critiques of the PCS. A few months before their deaths in combat in October 1976, Clara Elizabeth Ramírez and Andrés Torres penned *Estrella Roja 3*, a synthesis of the FPL strategy in the 1970s, which featured a detailed analysis of the PCS's politics.[125] It claimed that

the Salvadoran insurgencies emerged in the context of "the new historical conditions" generated by the Cuban Revolution in Latin America. Since the early
1960s, the Cuban Revolution had profoundly altered continental politics. The
Cuban revolutionary experience had shaped in decisive ways the "development of revolutionary movement[s]" in the region and forced the US and Latin
American elites to adjust their methods of "global domination."[126] In the aftermath of the Cuban Revolution, President Kennedy's counterinsurgency sought
to defeat revolutionary movements and popular insurrections through a series
of interrelated political, economic, and military strategies. *Desarrollismo* (development policies), which included foreign aid, investment, and socioeconomic
reforms aimed at softening the image of authoritarian regimes, broadened their
base of support and "neutralize[d] the influence of revolutionary organizations." They matched the purely repressive aspects of counterinsurgency. The
FPL asserted that the Cuban Revolution had elevated the fighting morale of
revolutionary forces in the continent. It had also challenged basic dogmas held
by communist parties in this period, namely, the impossibility of taking power
through armed struggle and building a "popular socialist alternative" in Latin
America. These dogmas, according to the FPL, had informed the communist
parties' "conciliatory and collaborationists" policies toward "the local bourgeoi-
sies" and their "erroneous thesis" on the linear or gradual accumulation of forces
"through exclusively peaceful means." In other words, the communist parties'
focus on electoral politics, the formation of alliances with what they deemed
progressive economic elites, and other nonviolent forms of political mobilization were counterintuitive.[127] In the 1960s, the party had relinquished "the
seizure of power by the people" as its strategic objective and reaffirmed the "conservative and yielding [*claudicante*]" policy toward the "bourgeoisie" it had held
since 1932. It ultimately underestimated the revolutionary potential of workers,
peasants, and other sectors of Salvadoran society.[128] The PCS strategy created
obstacles for the development of revolutionary social movements for it considered worker mobilizations a component of the party's electoral politics, which
centered on the formation of alliances with bourgeois parties like the PDC.[129]

   Estrella Roja 3 acknowledged that the PCS had formulated a policy on revolutionary violence. Such policy considered organizing revolutionary uprisings during critical political junctures, but it also maintained that the guerrillas
prevented the expansion of social mobilizations, put at risk basic democratic
freedoms, provoked repression, and ultimately "caused the destruction of the
popular movement." Therefore, it rejected insurgent politics and engaged exclusively in elections.[130] The Cuban Revolution had also questioned the PCS's
views on the formation of revolutionary vanguards. It had proved that the creation of guerrilla movements did not require fully mature revolutionary conditions as the PCS claimed but "some sufficient objective conditions" (i.e., certain

sociopolitical and economic conditions) and a "degree of subjective conditions
. . . particularly the existence of a serious revolutionary organization." It had also
shown that the emergence of the guerrillas and mass political mobilizations
were instrumental in raising "the revolutionary awareness of large popular sectors" and became "the basic element . . . to change the balance of political and
military forces" that enabled the triumph of the Cuban Revolution.[131]

The insurgent intellectuals also attempted to disprove the PCS's social and
economic analyses by drawing on dependency theory.[132] As students at the
University of El Salvador, the founders of the insurgencies studied dependency
theory with Argentinian sociologists who taught at that institution in the late
1960s. Drawing on this tradition, they viewed capitalism as a world system in
which imperialist metropolises had historically exploited the natural resources
and cheap labor of peripheral countries and prevented their industrial and
technological development. In other words, they considered the underdevelopment of Latin America a result of European colonialism and US neocoloni-
alism. Echoing dependency theory, they rejected the PCS's characterization of
Salvadoran society as "feudal" or "semifeudal" and the need to conduct a "bourgeois revolution" in alliance with sectors of the "national bourgeoisie." Instead
they posited that the agrarian capitalism that emerged in El Salvador in the late
nineteenth century was fully integrated into the world capitalist economy and
relied fundamentally on capitalist labor relations.[133] In the 1970s, El Salvador was
a dependent capitalist country ruled by a small agrarian-industrial-financial elite
firmly under US political and economic tutelage. In contrast with the PCS, the
insurgent intellectuals maintained that the landowning class and the industrial-
financial bourgeoisie were one and the same. El Salvador lacked a "national
bourgeoisie," as the PCS argued, and thus a "democratic bourgeois revolution"
was simply unviable. Instead, an oligarchic elite with strong fascist proclivities,
which was fully subordinated to US interests, ruled the country. Development
was only possible as a result of a popular democratic revolution. In this vein,
insurgent intellectuals advocated a political rupture with the United States and
its local allies, the formation of a popular democratic government, and a gradual
transition to socialism.[134]

Grano de oro, a Marxian analysis that examined the origins of the coffee economy in El Salvador, penned by Rafael Arce Zablah, the most influential ERP
intellectual, offers further insights about the discrepancies between New Left
and communist intellectuals in this period. Arce analyzed the workings of differ-
ential land productivity, labor, and other mechanisms that enabled the massive
capital accumulation among Salvadoran coffee growers in the twentieth century.
He pondered the limits of the country's agrarian economy to promote sustained
growth and development due to its high degree of dependency and vulner-
ability to the fluctuations of international markets. In contrast with communist

intellectuals in the 1960s who deemed the agricultural economy in El Salvador feudal or semifeudal, Arce maintained that coffee production at large estates (called *fincas*) did not show "any sign of feudal serfdom." On the contrary, he argued that coffee production, processing, and export (i.e., the country's agro-export economy) constituted pure agrarian capitalism.[135] Arce criticized the PCS intellectuals' analysis of the Salvadoran agrarian economy. He refuted the PCS's thesis on the existence of a historical tension between feudal landowners and other capitalist sectors. According to Arce, such tensions characterized the trajectories of capitalism in other latitudes and periods, like nineteenth-century England, where distinct capitalists and landowning classes existed. In twentieth-century El Salvador, however, the capitalists and the landowners formed an oligarchy that dominated the country's agro-export coffee economy. The capitalist and the landowner were in fact one and the same historical subject in El Salvador.[136]

These divergent characterizations of agrarian capitalism in El Salvador had substantial political ramifications for both the PCS and the New Left. Drawing on the purported existence of separate and antagonistic feudal or semifeudal landed and capitalist classes, the PCS emphasized the desirability of forming political alliances with modernizing elites or legal political parties like the Christian Democrats that opposed fascism (i.e., the formation of the "transitional democratic power" discussed earlier). In contrast, Arce posited that the imminent failure of the agro-export model in the early 1970s, in the aftermath of the Soccer War (i.e., the war between El Salvador and Honduras) and the collapse of the Central American Common Market in 1969, enabled the emergence of Salvadoran fascism. In the end, according to Arce, "dependent capitalism" in El Salvador had failed to promote sustained economic growth and development due to two major factors. First, the limits of land productivity in El Salvador put the country at a great disadvantage in relation to other major coffee producers like Brazil, which set international production standards. Second, the transition from the oligarchic agro-export model to financial capitalism with an agro-export base, or in Arce's words, "the hegemony of [the] financial sector with an oligarchic agro-export base," ("la hegemonía [del] sector financiero con base oligárquica agroexportadora"), which sectors of the Salvadoran elites attempted to conduct in this period, failed due to restrictions imposed on the Salvadoran economy by "international monopolistic capital."[137] This failed economic transition had negative effects among landowners and capitalists, but more important, it devastated the precarious economies of rural workers and small landholders (also called at that time "poor peasants" or minifundistas) whose livelihoods depended partially or fully on the agro-export economy. These circumstances brewed fascism in El Salvador, for the elites had limited capacities to address the growing demands of rural and urban workers and increasingly privileged state terror to contain social mobilizations. Arce's theoretical formulations on the limits of agrarian capitalism and the emergence of fascism crucially influenced the New Left's politics in the 1970s.

Despite contemporary attempts to silence, minimize, or read backward the history of the FMLN, there is no denying that communist and New Left intellectuals were immersed in ruthless power disputes in the 1970s, for they embodied conflicting political cultures and ideologies and represented multiple social actors. The PCS was a political organization that had endured the 1932 massacre, underwent several incarnations, and promoted mainly peaceful resistance against authoritarian rule for nearly four decades. In the 1960s, it was made up of university intellectuals, students, union leaders, and politicians who advocated a "National Liberation, Agrarian, Democratic, and Popular" revolution.[138] They embraced a reformist strategy that echoed the Soviet policy of peaceful coexistence with the United States. They imagined the "transitional democratic power" as a means to consolidate the legal opposition parties and to defeat the authoritarian regime. As a corollary of this policy, they formed alliances with sectors of the military they deemed progressive. In 1977, they endorsed Colonel Ernesto Claramount as UNO's presidential candidate. The electoral fraud against Claramount conducted by the Molina government and the subsequent massacre against UNO activists in downtown San Salvador on February 28 effectively ended the PCS participation in electoral politics.

The New Left insurgency, on the other hand, was a conjunction of guerrilla organizations and social movements firmly rooted in emerging social actors, chiefly, the Catholic peasantry, the teacher and student movements, and to a lesser extent the urban working class. Drawing on the experiences of the Cuban Revolution, the revolutionary left in Latin America, Vietnamese Marxism, Maoism, dependency theory, and Catholic social thought (as discussed in chapter 2), they developed highly eclectic political cultures. Their intellectual production, daily immersion in social and political struggles, and sustained military activity enabled the transformation of the small urban guerrillas that emerged in the early 1970s into powerful rural and urban insurgencies at the end of that decade, which posed an unprecedented challenge to oligarchic-military rule and US hegemony in El Salvador.

The insurgent intellectuals carefully pondered the future of revolution in El Salvador and Latin America. They were invested, as it were, body and soul in their efforts to oust the authoritarian regime and to transform Salvadoran society. That type of commitment likely informed the conduct of Ramírez, Solano, and Torres, the night of October 10, 1976.

Between 1977 and 1979, President Carlos H. Romero, Molina's successor, implanted a veritable reign of terror in El Salvador. The horrific repression perpetrated by state forces in this period put the country on the path toward civil war. In the end, the Old and the New Left started a sinuous process of integration in the context of a major political crisis. At that time the civil war in El Salvador became a centerpiece of the regional conflict that emerged in the aftermath of the 1979 Sandinista Revolution in neighboring Nicaragua. Such conflict involved multiple international actors, chiefly the United States, Nicaragua, and Cuba, as well as several Latin American and European countries that promoted the negotiated solution of the Central American crisis in the 1980s.

7

Crisis and Rural Insurgency

We have to form a single body in this battle against the rich.
Gabriel Cienfuegos (1980), forty-seven-year-old
worker marching in San Salvador

On January 22, 1980, the left showed decisively its political might. It mobilized no fewer than one hundred thousand people in San Salvador to commemorate the forty-eighth anniversary of the 1932 massacre and the unification of revolutionary social movements.[1] The demonstrators demanded the end of repression and the liberation of political prisoners. The protest frightened tremendously the ruling elites and the military.[2] Despite the intense repression and psychological warfare against social activists conducted by the government of President Carlos H. Romero (June 1977–October 1979) and the first Revolutionary Government Junta (October 1979–January 1980) that replaced him, the newly established Revolutionary Coordination of the Masses (CRM), a coordinating committee formed by the merger of revolutionary social movements, organized what is still considered the largest demonstration in the country's history.[3] The conservative elites' response to the demonstration was ferocious. In the days that preceded the march, right-wing groups like the Broad Nationalist Front orchestrated a radio and television campaign to discredit it and to threaten the potential participants.[4] They also promoted a transportation stoppage to create obstacles for the mobilization of people from rural areas, cities, and towns to San Salvador. Security forces also set up checkpoints to crack down on activists who traveled to the capital. During the event, witnesses reported that unidentified small aircraft sprayed insecticide on the demonstrators. But more ominously, government forces planned to carry out a bloodbath in broad daylight as they had done recurrently in the 1970s.[5] At dawn on January 22, plainclothesmen organized in groups of twenty individuals took positions on the top floors or terraces of roughly twelve public and private buildings in downtown San Salvador.[6]

Francisco Andrés Escobar, a poet and professor of literature at the Central American University (UCA) who witnessed the demonstration, wrote a poignant account of this episode. He depicted the colorful, festive contingents of activists that joined the march. Early the day of the event, a Tuesday, the city was empty. Gradually tens of thousands of demonstrators occupied key arteries, including Avenida Roosevelt, 25th Avenida Norte y Sur, Calle Arce, and Calle Rubén Darío (figures 7.1–7.3). The CRM had intended to conduct a massive rally in downtown San Salvador, but as it turned out, the demonstrators were so numerous that most of them were still standing at the starting point when those who led the march reached that area. As they stepped into downtown San Salvador, they were sprayed with bullets from the sharpshooters stationed at the top of buildings. The total number of victims was never clearly established. Escobar estimated that 20 people were killed and 120 injured by the sharpshooters. But despite the attack, most demonstrators retreated to the university campus while others took refuge in churches, private homes, and businesses. In some instances, armed groups formed by peasant and urban militants exchanged fire with the sharpshooters to allow activists to leave the area.[7] In the aftermath of the massacre, the Junta denied the involvement of security forces in the repression and called for a judicial investigation, which never occurred. It also ordered a *cadena de radio y televisión* (official broadcast) to silence the independent media that covered the event. That night *Radio Nacional de El Salvador*, the official state radio station, aired children's songs in the midst of the sorrow and

Figure 7.1 Activists distribute leaflets in Mejicanos, January 22, 1980. Courtesy of Museo de la Palabra y la Imagen.

Figure 7.2 Activists march in San Salvador, 1980. Courtesy of Museo de la Palabra y la Imagen.

Figure 7.3 BPR leaders during the foundation of the Coordinadora Revolucionaria de Masas (CRM), January 1980. From left to right, Francisco Figueroa, a leader of the UTC; Juan Chacón, a union leader and the last secretary general of the BPR; and Julio Flores, a leader of the teachers' union ANDES. Courtesy of the Museo de la Palabra y la Imagen.

dread produced by the massacre.[8] Escobar pondered the ramifications of this episode:

> The extreme right has lost another battle. . . . [It failed to] induce an insurrectionary response that could originate and justify a massive extermination, people's prudence and spirit of sacrifice have vanquished. Prudence does not mean cowardice. The spirit of sacrifice is not synonymous with irresponsibility and deafness toward the blood of assassinated brothers [and sisters]. . . . we are living one of the most tense moments in our history . . . and the cord will break. . . . it is just a matter . . . of time.[9]

It did. Soon the civil war ravaged El Salvador.

During the political crisis that preceded the civil war, the peasant movement turned into a potent rural insurgency. Peasant intellectuals, local communities, and the peasant movement in Chalatenango played crucial roles in this process. They created self-defense groups and militias to fight government forces in rural and urban areas. Like their urban counterparts, peasant insurgents in the late 1970s articulated a distinct revolutionary ideology and an ethics of violence that drew on Catholic notions of justice, exchanges with urban militants, and local political traditions. They sought the destruction of the authoritarian regime and the subsequent instauration of a revolutionary government. This "vision of total victory" echoed the experiences of the Cuban Revolution of 1959 and the Sandinista Revolution of 1979. It informed the ideology and politics of urban and peasant insurgents until the mid-1980s. The trajectory of the war on the ground thereafter, the escalation of the Central American conflicts (i.e., the Contra war in Nicaragua, the civil war in Guatemala, and the militarization of Honduras), the peace initiatives sponsored by the Catholic hierarchy and civil society groups in El Salvador, diplomatic proposals formulated by Latin American and Western European countries to scale down the regional conflicts, and above all, the growing pragmatism of the insurgent FMLN rendered obsolete any dream of total victory.

The Sandinista Revolution in Nicaragua made the possibility of an insurgent victory in El Salvador appeared within reach.[10] It raised the fighting morale of the revolutionary social movements and the guerrillas and accelerated their processes of unification. It also hastened preparations for a coup against the repressive Romero government, which sought, as it were, to steal the thunder from the insurgents and to create a reformist alternative to revolution. Insurgent and counterinsurgent mobilizations also reached unprecedented levels at that time. The state and the elites matched the intensification of social mobilizations and guerrilla warfare in urban and rural areas with outright terror. They conducted a war of extermination against social activists, progressive Catholics, political opponents, public intellectuals, and insurgents, which was abetted, albeit somewhat hesitantly, by the Carter administration (1976–1980) and more decisively by the first Reagan administration (1980–1984).[11] This campaign claimed the lives of thousands of civilians between 1979 and 1983.[12] The "Genocide Option" carried out by the Reagan administration in El Salvador had devastating sociopolitical, psychosocial, and cultural reverberations that remain to be fully understood.[13] However, this terror drove the country, irreversibly, into the twelve-year civil war. It further radicalized politics and society and shattered the prospects of an institutional solution to the crisis promoted by progressive sectors of the army, opposition parties, segments of the left, Jesuit scholars, and the Catholic Church hierarchy, particularly the archbishop of San Salvador, Oscar A. Romero.[14]

The 1979–1981 crisis generated a profound realignment in the country's political system.[15] On October 15, 1979, a group of military officers who called themselves the Movement of the Military Youth, who had formulated a reformist program with the help of Jesuit scholars at the UCA, overthrew President Romero and constituted the Revolutionary Government Junta.[16] The Military Youth was a hybrid movement made up of progressive officers who carried out a last-ditch attempt to avoid a civil war.[17] They appointed Colonel Adolfo A. Majano to represent them in the Junta.[18] They promised to halt repression, to respect human rights, to end government corruption, and to conduct major democratic and socioeconomic reforms. They vowed to organize free elections with the participation of the entire spectrum of political forces in the country, including the left, to re-establish diplomatic relations with Honduras, which were broken at the time of the 1969 war, and to promote amicable relations with the Sandinista government in Nicaragua.[19] They invited leaders of the opposition, professionals, and public intellectuals to join the Junta. Prestigious figures such as the social democrat leader Guillermo Manuel Ungo, Napoleón Duarte's running mate in 1972, and Román Mayorga Quiroz, the rector of UCA, joined the first Junta.[20]

Another movement formed by an amalgamation of conservative military officers, some of them backed by the US government, also joined the coup against Romero. Colonel Jaime Abdul Gutiérrez, a member of the Junta, was a leader of this sector. High-ranking military officers associated with the repressive Molina and Romero governments also supported the coup. The roles that sectors of the military played in the coup are still debated, but there is little doubt that the Carter administration tolerated or encouraged it.[21] Whatever the origins and intentions of the coup leaders, in December 1979 reactionary military officers displaced reformist leaders in the Junta and intensified the terror. They announced to members of the Junta their intention to conduct a massive extermination of civilians as part of their efforts to contain the left's offensive.[22] In January 1980 progressive civilians in the government collectively resigned their posts. At that time, Christian Democrat leaders made a pact with the military to form a new government, the second Revolutionary Government Junta (January–December 1980). An envoy of the Carter administration who visited El Salvador at that time asked the Christian Democrat leaders to ally with the military to create the new government. He also informed them about US plans to support a massive counterinsurgency program in El Salvador. Rubén Zamora, a Christian Democrat leader who attended this meeting, recalled an exchange he had with the US envoy as follows:

US ENVOY: There is no doubt that we face a guerrilla threat and there is a need to conduct counterinsurgent struggle. That is the premise. But we distinguish two types of counterinsurgencies, which we call white counterinsurgency and black counterinsurgency. The military here [in El Salvador] practice black counterinsurgency. The role of Christian Democrats is to teach [them] white counterinsurgency and [ensure] that black counterinsurgency is abandoned. . . . the purging of the armed forces and the introduction of standards of respect for human rights and education [on human rights were part of this process].

ZAMORA: Look . . . white counterinsurgency sounds interesting. This is the first time I hear about it. Could you mention a case where it has been used?

US ENVOY: Of course, Indonesia.

ZAMORA: I don't see the difference.

US ENVOY: Of course there is a difference. . . . one agrees with the rule of law and the other not.[23]

Zamora was baffled by this conversation. "Indonesia!" he said. "Where nearly one million 'communists' were murdered by the so-called white counterinsurgency and now people are outraged. . . . we were not going anywhere as Christian Democrats. We were lost. It was clear the position of the North Americans [the US government] and it was the Carter administration, it wasn't [yet] Reagan."[24]

The Christian Democrats soon split over the party's alliance with the United States and the military and the repression against their own party affiliates. During the first months of 1980, security forces cracked down on Christian Democrat activists across El Salvador. "Between January and March 1980, the Christian Democrats endured more deaths than all the previous seven years combined," said Zamora.[25] The reactionary military in the Junta were apparently playing a double game: they associated with the top Christian Democrat leaders in the government, while they decimated the party activists.[26] Progressive

Christian Democrats like Zamora confronted the minister of defense, Colonel José Guillermo García, and other military officers on this matter. Duarte and other conservative Christian Democrats sidelined the issue.[27] Duarte had returned from his exile in Venezuela the previous year. He made a political comeback not as the charismatic populist leader that he was in the 1960s and early 1970s but as an ally of US counterinsurgency and the military. The left denounced him and other conservative Christian Democrats as demagogues and apologists of counterinsurgent terror and US intervention in El Salvador.[28] The Christian Democrat–Military Junta indeed implemented a US-financed counterinsurgency program, which combined socioeconomic reforms, particularly agrarian reform, and sheer terror. The country descended into a brutal spiral of violence in this period. The army committed numerous mass killings at that time, most notably the massacres at El Sumpul River in Chalatenango in May 1980, and El Mozote in Morazán, in December 1981, which claimed the lives of approximately six hundred and a thousand victims, respectively.[29] Security forces and right-wing paramilitaries also murdered thousands of civilians in this period.[30] This terror increasingly legitimized the left insurgency among vast segments of Salvadoran society and ultimately drove the country into the civil war.

The first Junta failed to create a democratic alternative to the crisis. This outcome produced a tectonic power shift in the left.[31] The PCS and the RN had conditionally supported the first Junta, but the ERP and the FPL waged war on it. The PCS had initially joined El Foro Popular, a loose coalition of parties and social movements formed at the time of President Romero, which advocated democratic reforms. Professionals affiliated with the party joined the first Junta's cabinet. In recent years, Eduardo Sancho, the top leader of the RN, revealed that the Movement of the Military Youth that conducted the 1979 coup was, to a certain extent, a continuation of a similar movement formed in 1975, which had conspired with the ERP and the RN to mount a frustrated insurrection against President Molina and to carry out a reformist program. Thus the RN decided to "critically" endorse the first Junta. It adopted a unilateral ceasefire and only encouraged political mobilizations in this period.[32]

The ERP and the FPL, on the other hand, deemed the coup against Romero and the Junta byproducts of US machinations to avert revolution in El Salvador.[33] Beginning in October, they launched political and military offensives against the new government. However, the FPL also signaled a minor opening to the Junta.[34] In the end, the Junta's inability to stop the repression and to carry out democratic reforms due to the displacement of progressive figures in the government by the reactionary military led the communists and the RN to reconsider their openings to the Junta. This scenario shifted the balance of power in the left to the most radical organization, the FPL, which advocated a protracted war strategy to topple the regime.[35] The FPL stated the following about the collapse of the first Junta:

> Very little time has gone by since . . . October 15, when from the gar-risons of the tyranny a coup d'état was announced, which inaugurated a bourgeois reformist model of government . . . to save the regime from the grave crisis and stop the advance of the Popular Revolution. . . . But only 75 days after, the counterrevolutionary political maneuver has been unmasked . . . the cabinet is . . . falling apart as a consequence of the manipulation to which they were submitted by the Oligarchy and the assassin officers [*mandos*] of the Army to carry out at any cost their reactionary and antipopular plans.[36]

In December 1979, the PCS relinquished its affiliation with the first Junta and joined the revolutionary left as the reactionary military took power.[37] That same month, the FPL, the RN, and the PCS formed a historical alliance they originally called La Coordinadora Político-Militar (Political-Military Coordination).[38] Shortly after, the ERP joined that initiative, and a second body, La Dirección Revolucionaria Unificada-Político-Militar the (Unified Revolutionary Direc-torate of Political-Military Organizations [DRU-PM]), emerged.[39] This proc-ess resulted in the founding of the FMLN in October 1980.[40] This confluence between the Old and New Left marked the start of an intricate process of inte-gration of various intellectual traditions, political cultures, ideologies, strategies, and historical experiences, which transformed the FMLN into a formidable political and military movement during the civil war.

The right also experienced a major realignment between 1979 and 1981. A new right-wing coalition made up of businessmen, middle-class activists, mili-tary officers, and paramilitaries formed the Nationalist Republican Alliance (ARENA), which effectively displaced the PCN, the official party created in 1962, as the main political force of Salvadoran conservatives. ARENA became a key player in Salvadoran politics during the civil war and beyond. It uni-fied different currents in the right and filled up the power vacuum created by the downfall of the PCN in 1979. Several movements and organizations con-verged in the formation of ARENA, mainly the Broad Nationalist Front and the Nationalist Democratic Organization (ORDEN). The Broad Nationalist Front was a political movement, which controlled a network of paramilitary groups made up of civilians and military.[41] ORDEN was a paramilitary and intelligence network formed by US Green Berets and Salvadoran military in 1965. Business persons, professionals, and activists headed by Ricardo Mena Lagos and Armando Calderón Sol also formed the Nationalist Salvadoran Movement which also joined ARENA. This movement denounced the prevalent "social disorder" and called on the state and the military to crack down on the left.[42]

Roberto D'Aubuisson, an army major and intelligence officer, became the leader of ARENA. D'Aubuisson and his followers replicated to a certain extent the organizational model of the left insurgencies. They formed a political movement (the Broad Nationalist Front), "civil defense" groups to protect affluent neighborhoods, and clandestine paramilitary groups (i.e., "death squads"), which sought to exterminate social activists and opposition figures.[43] D'Aubuisson drew on intelligence information to wage a war of extermination against legal opposition parties, social movements, and the revolutionary left. He took control of the secret archives of the Salvadoran National Security Agency (ANSESAL), the state intelligence agency, at the time of the first Junta. It is still unclear how and why high-ranking military officers in the Junta enabled D'Abuisson to manage the ANSESAL archives, but apparently he extracted information from them to denounce people he labeled "communists" who were later murdered by death squads.[44] He also presented part of this information to leaders of the Nationalist Salvadoran Movement to show his allegiance to the group.[45] His multiple connections with military officers, members of the security forces, the state intelligence, the paramilitary network ORDEN, and business elites, as well as his profile as an anti-communist figure who articulated a chauvinistic discourse to deprecate progressive Catholics, Archbishop Oscar A. Romero, his enemies on the left, and his political adversaries, the Christian Democrats, transformed D'Aubuisson into the uncontested leader of the Salvadoran right.

Archbishop Romero vigorously condemned the state terror and the persecution against the Catholic Church from February 1977 until his assassination in March 1980. The relations between the Church and the state were seriously strained after National Guardsmen assassinated Rutilio Grande, a Jesuit priest who worked in Aguilares and El Paisnal in March 1977.[46] On May 11, the Union of White Warriors (UGB), a death squad, murdered Alfonso Navarro, a Catholic priest, in San Salvador. In June that same group publicly "invited" Jesuits to leave the country within one month under the threat of being considered "military targets" after that time. The archbishop refused to participate in official state ceremonies, including the inauguration of President Romero, after these events.[47] Death squads murdered two diocesan priests, Rafael Palacios Campos, in Santa Tecla in June 1979, and Alirio Napoleón Macías Rodríguez, in San Esteban Catarina in August.[48] The conflict between the Church and the state reached a breaking point after these murders. Reflecting on the assassination of Palacios, the archbishop stated:

> It is painful that this persecution against our church is taken to such excesses of violence. . . . it is unacceptable to think about violence or

vengeance. . . . nobody thinks that retribution is Christian. . . . The Lord has taught us another path: to forgive, to pray for those who persecute and slander us, to ask the Lord [for] the grace of conversion for the grave sin against the fifth commandment—NOT TO KILL—and against the sacrilege that supposes to have put violent hands over a blessed of the Lord [*un ungido del Señor*, the Catholic priest Rafael Palacios Campos].[49]

The divisions within the Church intensified during the political crisis of the late 1970s. Conservative bishops, who constituted the majority in the Episcopal Council, condemned the peasant organizations and called on priests and laymen not to cooperate with them.[50] Archbishop Romero and Bishop Arturo Rivera y Damas, the auxiliary bishop of San Salvador, issued a joint pastoral letter called "The Church and the Popular Organizations," in which they defended on theological grounds the social and political rights of peasants. In the letter, the bishops condemned the mounting paramilitary violence against members of peasant organizations: "In order to overcome misery, some [peasants] are seduced by the advantages that the pro-government organizations offer them. In exchange for these, they are used in various repressive activities, which often include denouncing, terrorizing, capturing, and in some cases and circumstances killing their own fellow peasants." Romero and Rivera y Damas also pondered the types of violence that prevailed in El Salvador in the late 1970s. They readily censured state and "seditious or terrorist" violence (i.e., insurgent violence) but also acknowledged that the growing repression compelled activists to engage in what they termed "spontaneous violence." The bishops argued that the constant state attacks against the "demands, demonstrations, just strikes" and other forms of social mobilizations motivated activists to engage in improvised and ultimately ineffective forms of self-defense. They also explained that the Church sanctioned the use of "violence in legitimate defense" under extreme circumstances:[51]

> The Church permits violence in legitimate defense under the following conditions: a) the defense should not exceed the degree of the unjust aggression (for instance, if it is enough to use the hands it is not licit to shoot the aggressor); b) to engage in proportionate violence after exhausting all possible peaceful means; c) that the violent defense does not bring as a consequence a worse evil than the one against which it is defending: for example, more violence, more injustice.[52]

As the state terror escalated in March 1980, Archbishop Romero made a public appeal to members of the security forces and the army to disobey orders to murder civilians. During the last Sunday mass he officiated on March 23 at the Metropolitan Cathedral of San Salvador, Romero articulated his most remarkable homily. He acknowledged the presence of members of Catholic and Protestant churches from the United States at the mass. In his view they incarnated the "solidarity of North America in its Christian thought." The archbishop commented that "Christian groups" in the United States had publicly supported the letter he had recently addressed to President James Carter in which he demanded the end of US military aid to the government of El Salvador, arguing that it resulted "in repression against our people." After enumerating the atrocious human rights violations committed by government forces the previous week, Romero stated:

> I would like to make an appeal in an especial manner to the men of the army and concretely to the bases of the National Guard, the Police, of the garrisons.
>
> Brothers, you are part of our own people, you kill your own peasant brothers and in the face of an order to kill given by a man, the law of God that says: DO NOT KILL must prevail. . . . No soldier is obliged to obey an order against the law of God. . . . Nobody has to abide by an immoral law. . . . It is time that you recover your consciousness and that you first obey your consciousness than the order of sin. . . . The Church, defender of the rights of God, of the law of God, of human dignity, of the person, cannot be silenced before so much abomination. We want that the government takes seriously that reforms are worthless if they are tainted with so much blood. . . . In the name of God, then, and in the name of this suffering people whose laments rise to heaven each day more tumultuous, I beg you, I implore you, I order you in the name of God: Stop the repression . . . ![53]

Archbishop Romero's admonition constituted a fundamental threat to the power and authority of military and oligarchic elites insofar as it openly called on members of the public security forces to disobey orders to murder civilians. The next day a death squad assassinated Romero while he officiated mass. Security forces also attacked Romero's funeral in downtown San Salvador, murdering and injuring scores of civilians. These events further radicalized progressive Catholics and persuaded many of them to take up arms against the state.

Rural areas in Chalatenango, Aguilares, Guazapa, Cinquera, San Vicente, Usulután, and Morazán had become war zones by the late 1970s. Army units, security forces, and paramilitaries conducted numerous operations against peasant communities at that time. For instance, they committed fifteen mass killings (each involving ten or more victims) in northern Morazán prior to the 1981 El Mozote massacre, causing nearly four hundred victims, mostly in the municipalities of Villa El Rosario and Cacaopera. They also carried out fifteen summary executions at El Mozote between January 1980 and December 1981.[54] The army also attempted to massacre civilians at Villa El Rosario, a town in Morazán, which it considered a bastion of the ERP guerrillas. Army units forced people living in the area to gather at that place, using the "hammer and the anvil," a tactic they deployed repeatedly to conduct mass killings in the early 1980s. This scorched-earth tactic involved the mobilization of large army units (i.e., several battalions) in a relatively small area with the objective of surrounding and exterminating civilians whom army commanders deemed supporters of the insurgency. Army commanders apparently had planned to destroy the entire town using artillery fire. Fortunately for the inhabitants of Villa El Rosario, two army captains who later joined the insurgency, Francisco Mena Sandoval and Marcelo Cruz Cruz, disobeyed orders they had received from a commanding officer to assassinate civilians who had been coerced by the army to assemble in the town.[55]

Army and security forces carried out similar mass killings and summary executions in Chalatenango and other rural areas in this period. In December 1978, a group of orphans and peasants visited *La Crónica del Pueblo*, an independent newspaper in San Salvador, to denounce the disappearance and murder of forty-four peasant activists who left ninety-nine orphan children in hamlets in northeastern Chalatenango.[56] Between 1978 and 1980, official and independent newspapers were full of similar news and *campos pagados*, paid advertisements sponsored by social movements, human rights organizations, and relatives of victims of the repression. They demanded President Romero and subsequently the first Revolutionary Government Junta and the Christian Democrat–Military Junta to halt the crackdowns on strikes and demonstrations, the mass killings, the summary executions, and the incarceration and torture of activists and regular citizens. They also asked the government to reveal the whereabouts of the disappeared and to free all political prisoners.[57]

As the political crisis deepened in the late 1970s, peasant activists initiated hostilities against public security forces and paramilitaries in Chalatenango. They formed self-defense structures and militias to counter the attacks of repressive forces against peasant mobilizations in rural and urban areas. The Church's teachings on the practice of "violence in legitimate defense," the peasant leaders' own views about revolutionary violence, and the insurgency's guidelines on this matter informed the growing peasant insurgency in Chalatenango.

The Emergence of Rural Insurgency in Chalatenango

Inhabitants of *cantones* (hamlets) in northeastern Chalatenango formed the backbone of the emerging insurgent forces. Hamlets were small rural settlements formed by closely related families. A few hundred families who lived in adobe or brick houses constituted a typical hamlet in this region. Small landholders who owned an average of two acres and cultivated subsistence crops and their relatives lived in these hamlets. Many of them were practicing Catholics whose lives revolved around religious events and festivities. Both the state and the Church had an important presence in these communities. Paramilitary forces known as *patrullas cantonales* operated in every hamlet, and military and civilian authorities in the area often relied on local paramilitary leaders (i.e., *comandantes locales*) to exercise state power. Diocesan priests routinely visited hamlets to perform mass and other religious rituals. *Rezadores* and *rezadoras* (prayer and ritual experts), as well as individuals affiliated with religious associations, were influential members of these communities.

Since the mid-1970s, dwellers of hamlets in northeastern Chalatenango joined en masse the UTC and subsequently the BPR (the coalition of social movements to which the UTC belonged to). In turn, paramilitary and public security forces, particularly the National Guard, callously persecuted peasant activists and their families. Largely in response to the growing state terror, entire hamlets joined the FPL insurgency in the late 1970s. The increasing confrontations between peasants integrated into the paramilitary structures and those who joined the revolutionary movement preceded the initiation of the civil war in 1980.

The trajectories of residents of Corral Falso, a hamlet near Potonico, illustrate the emergence of rural insurgency in northwestern Chalatenango. They were among the first peasant activists who became insurgents in the midst of land conflicts that pitted the peasant movement against government forces in the area. In the early 1970s, Corral Falso was home to three hundred families. Small landowners who possessed "at least one *manzana* [two acres] of land" and cultivated subsistence crops lived there. Most of them were affiliates of the PCN, the official party, who supported local right-wing candidates. In 1974, peasants from Corral Falso occupied a fertile strip of state-owned land along the banks of the Lempa River. For nearly two years they cultivated watermelons in that area without compensating the Hydroelectric Executive Commission of the Lempa River, the state company that owned the land, and probably because of their membership in the official party, the security forces did not bother them. "People came in boats to buy the watermelons because there was no land access to the hamlet in those days," remembered Héctor Martínez, a peasant activist.[58] At that time, peasants from Corral Falso also formed Christian Base Communities (CBCs) and attended a "biblical course" taught by two diocesan priests. They became part of the first generation of peasant activists who joined the UTC in Chalatenango.[59]

Peasant activists from Corral Falso and other neighboring towns worked closely with Andrés Torres, one of the insurgents who perished in Santa Tecla in 1976, to address the grievances of marginalized rural communities in the area. Martínez vividly recalled Torres's arrival in Corral Falso in 1974. He described

Torres as "a great guy [un tipazo], very kind, . . . very skillful, attentive to detail. He paid attention to people . . . a lucid guy." [60] Irma Serrano, an activist from Potonico, depicted Torres as a "short, chubby, and quiet [man], someone who knew when to speak."[61] Martínez and Serrano relied on their own clout among peasant communities and Torres's advice to expand the UTC networks in the area. Martínez recalled attending numerous meetings with peasant leaders in neighboring hamlets and towns at that time:

> I had meetings with people from El Portillo del Norte, Cancasque, Arcatao, we held meetings and wrote regional guidelines and discussed how to implement them. It was a nice experience. We grew up in very poor places and had low academic levels. [Torres] knew he was work- ing with people with zero academic levels and encouraged them to learn how to read and write. That is how the coordination of the masses started.[62]

Martínez and Serrano joined the movement at a time of major political trans- formations in the peasant organizations. In 1978, FECCAS-UTC conducted a gathering of top peasant leaders it called the First Departmental Council Heroes and Martyrs of Chalatenango.[63] The event memorialized the victims of the repression in the area and assessed the organization's potential to intensify its mobilizations in rural and urban areas. The peasant leaders distributed suc- cinct biographies of peasant activists murdered by ORDEN paramilitaries in Chalatenango in the 1970s. For instance, the following account was given for Pedro Guardado, a peasant activist from El Conacaste, a hamlet near Las Vueltas:

> Pedro joined the U.T.C. in 1975. . . . Hunger and misery forced him to search for a response to the system of exploitation, which he fought until the last minute of his death [life]. On January 29 [1978], com- rade Pedro joined an important demonstration of the BPR [in San Salvador] to demand the liberation of political prisoners. Near Hospital Rosales he was run over by a car, which left at a great velocity. . . . he died eight days later. Pedro had much love for Revolution, which is why he worked tirelessly so that the Exploited Class also understood its sit- uation of poverty. Pedro was much loved and appreciated at the hamlet [El Conacaste] and the surroundings, since his revolutionary mystique inspired friendship and trust.[64]

The peasant leaders also described the intricate kinship networks that made up the repressive forces in the area. For example, they blamed one "Chepe Leonés," the leader of a clan known as " Los Leoneses," for the murders of several peasant activists. They claimed that one Abraham Guardado fatally shot Salvador Guardado, a peasant activist, in Chalatenango city following the orders of Chepe Leonés. They wrote: "This criminal henchman [*esbirro*] . . . also murdered comrade Isabel Nuñez in the municipality of Las Flores. . . . he also has tried to murder and displace honest and working peasant families."[65]

Above all, the peasant leaders who attended the council declared war on the state and the elites, paraphrasing Ho Chi Minh to do so: "In the hard struggle against the class enemy . . . it is necessary to oppose the revolutionary violence to counterrevolutionary violence, to take power and to defend it."[66] Eventually, the UTC and FECCAS, the most powerful peasant organizations in El Salvador, merged to form the Federation of Rural Workers (FTC), which constituted the backbone of the BPR. In one of its first public statements issued in July 1978, the FTC announced its intention to conduct an effort to educate and to "combatively" mobilize rural workers to demand that their "most urgent needs" be met and to fight for the country's "definitive liberation." It also denounced the counterinsurgent efforts conducted by the Romero government or, in FTC's parlance, the "plans of repression and reforms" carried out by "US imperialism, the creole bourgeoisie, and its criminal military tyranny."[67] In this setting, peasant militants in Chalatenango such as Martínez and Serrano increasingly identified as BPR activists in the late 1970s. Martínez recalled about this period:

> Facundo [Guardado—a peasant leader from Arcatao and the secretary general of the BPR], Andrés [Torres], and the priests planted this seed [the peasant movement]. We [peasants from Corral Falso] formed a BPR directive and joined a regional coordination with people from Potonico, Los Ranchos, Las Vueltas, Arcatao, a few from Nueva Trinidad, and San José Las Flores. [In the latter case] people who joined were not from the town but from the hamlets.[68]

The BPR local committees were tightly organized. They were structures made up of elected leaders and their respective teams (i.e., a secretary general and secretaries of organization, conflicts, propaganda, security, and so forth). "That is how we met many people. . . . We integrated very well, there were meetings at El Portillo del Norte, Corral Falso, El Conacaste, Los Rachos. Those places were very combative. People participated massively," said Martínez, [69]

To counter the growing repression, peasant leaders first created armed structures made up of peasant activists they called *grupos de autodefensa* (self-defense groups) in 1975. They operated under the authority of peasant leaders such as Facundo Guardado, José Santos Martínez, and Justo Mejía. Martínez and Mejía were older community leaders and former commanders of the *patrullas cantonales*, a paramilitary structure managed by the army's territorial service.[70] Mejía was mobilized by the Salvadoran army during the 1969 war between El Salvador and Honduras and probably had combat experience.[71] Guardado, on the other hand, was a young leader of the Church-sponsored cooperative movement in his native town of Arcatao. Like many peasant leaders in the area, he had studied at Chacalcoyo, the cooperative training center run by the Church near La Nueva Concepción. Guardado explained that his decision to join the UTC and to form armed peasant groups was informed by the mass killings and assassinations of peasants, students, and teachers carried out by state forces during the Molina government (1972–1977).

> We [the peasant leaders in Chalatenango] took the decision to form the UTC in 1974 in response to the killings [committed by National Guardsmen] in León de Piedra and La Cayetana [San Vicente].... Then [the] July 30 [massacre against students in San Salvador in 1975] was an alarm bell [*un campanazo*] for us; they [the Molina government] had decided to crack down on us. But if one thinks about it, in those years it was not yet a policy of systematic extermination but rather a repressive policy aimed at [undermining] the [social] movements. When they [the Molina government] realized that the movements were strong, then they reacted in a virulent manner, closing [political spaces] and eliminating the leaderships. It was a deliberate policy. They killed 401 teachers in the 1970s. The same happened with the rest of [social movements]. In the case of the peasant leaders, I don't think there was a national list [of peasant leaders whom the state planned to eliminate], so to speak, but it was clear for us that they had a policy of identifying the regional leaders. The [repressive] actions were clearly planned; they were not casual. They pointed at one person and then they killed her, they killed the leaders. The idea was to strike at the head [of the movement]. ORDEN paramilitaries [in Chalatenango] roamed heavily armed. They looked at you in the face and fired their guns into the air with total impunity. The affair was getting more and more complicated.[72]

Jose Santos Martínez also argued that state terror compelled him and other Catholic peasant leaders in Chalatenango to resort to violence as a self-defense mechanism:

> I participated in the labor struggles. We went to San Salvador with bare hands, they [security forces] shot at us, then we desired to take up arms even if we were Catholics. They taught us [to be violent].... we knew that the Catholic Church prohibits killing but what were we supposed to do? We were forced to be violent otherwise we would not be at this

level [living peacefully in their communities]. . . . It was necessary to do anything possible to defend oneself, even to kill [state agents] because it is a sin to let yourself be killed.[73]

Former or active local commanders and members of the *patrullas cantonales* such as Santos Martínez and Justo Mejía played an important role in the formation of peasant self-defense groups. The *patrullas cantonales* were structures of territorial control (and to a lesser extent population control) in charge of crime prevention, particularly moonshining and cattle rustling. In Chalatenango, *patrulleros* were often less indoctrinated than ORDEN paramilitaries, a parallel anti-communist structure created in 1965 with specific counterinsurgency functions. The *patrullas cantonales* were deeply ingrained in rural communities. At times they provided unpaid public services (e.g., maintenance of public roads), and some of their leaders were respected local figures.[74] It is thus not surprising that certain local commanders joined the peasant insurgency, which after all, was also formed by community leaders. They used their military expertise to form the armed self-defense groups. According to Guardado:

> Santos Martínez and Justo Mejía were not the only paramilitary commanders who joined the UTC. There were more cases. In Arcatao, in the Orellanas hamlet, we created the UTC based on the *patrulla cantonal*. The leader of the paramilitaries organized a meeting. He introduced me, saying, "We have invited this person, so that you learn about the repression against students that took place on July 30."[75]

In addition to the self-defense groups created by the peasant leaders, the FPL also formed clandestine peasant militias in Chalatenango. Mostly young and combative peasant leaders in the area joined the militias. "We were a selective militia," said Héctor Martínez. They were in charge of protecting peasant mobilizations in rural and urban settings. They also distributed propaganda and carried out minor attacks against public security and paramilitary forces.[76] In theory the FPL conceived of the militias as a separate force from the self-defense groups, but in practice they intermingled and performed similar functions in Chalatenango. The militias were clandestine regional forces under FPL command; the self-defense groups were local forces under the authority of peasant leaders. However, the self-defense groups expanded at a much faster pace than the militias. Most combatants who first joined the guerrilla army in 1980 were members of the self-defense groups and the militias.[77]

The peasant militias formed clandestine groups in towns and hamlets in northeastern Chalatenango. They relied on community leaders, members of Catholic groups, young activists, and in some cases paramilitaries to create local networks. They developed a stern combat morale and rapidly enhanced their capacity to fight local state forces and to make their presence known to people in the region. Héctor Martínez joined this force in 1976, when he was barely seventeen years old. He was first commissioned to detonate a propaganda device in San Antonio Los Ranchos. "I felt my feet were swollen but I detonated 'a mushroom' [*un hongo*] [guerrilla slang for a propaganda explosive device] full of *Rebeldes* [the FPL clandestine newspaper] and I felt proud of what I was doing," said Martínez.[78] He had eagerly joined the militias, but he was startled when he first learned about the organization's rigorous discipline, which included notions of self-sacrifice and martyrdom:

> Once my immediate chief told me when we were preparing an operation: "You are carrying this much ammunition, but remember you will not use it all, you will save yours" [your bullet]. Mine? I asked him. [He responded:] "If you find yourself in a desperate situation, you must not hesitate to shoot yourself." I was shocked. They were interested in protecting the confidentiality of the organization. But I did not like that.[79]

Over the next four years, Martínez and other militants from Corral Falso conducted numerous propaganda operations in towns and hamlets in the region.[80]

Residents of hamlets and towns in northeastern Chalatenango often joined the peasant militias because of the moral indignation they experienced after witnessing atrocities committed by security forces in the area. That was the case for Irma Serrano, a former member of a Catholic community in Potonico. She routinely saw corpses of peasants reportedly murdered by National Guard and Treasury Police patrols while she traveled to her job site at the nearby Cerrón Grande hydroelectric dam between 1976 and 1978.[81] Likely because of Serrano's influence among Catholic communities in the area, the FPL commissioned her to lead militias in her hometown. As she recalled:

> My brother was the channel [with the FPL]. Immediately they gave me the responsibility to form popular militias in my town. I knew how to do it. We spent the day at the church and at night we engaged in political and military training in the hills. The National Guard started persecuting us but we managed to evade them. We conducted propaganda activities at night. We dressed in black but we lacked weapons. We used harpoons, toy machine guns, and wooden sticks to pretend we were heavily armed. We marched at night. Once a neighbor told me, "Did you happen to notice that last night the boys [*"los muchachos"*–the guerrillas] passed by, some of them were very small, some were chubby,

and all wore black." He did not realize he was describing his own sons. We managed to recruit eighty to ninety militiamen and militiawomen in the town.[82]

Between 1976 and 1980, the militias and the self-defense groups grew exponentially as the counterinsurgent terror devastated rural communities in Chalatenango. "People did not join sparsely, they joined en masse," said Héctor Martínez.[83] However, the militia leaders carefully selected new recruits. After conducting propaganda activities in a certain town or hamlet, they monitored people's reactions to *El Rebelde* and other insurgent publications. Once they had closely scrutinized the backgrounds of those who made favorable commentaries about the insurgency, they approached the prospective new recruits. They used this method to recruit hundreds of combatants. "One by one . . . I alone formed ten platoons," said Martínez.[84] As Martínez explained:

> We analyzed the person's behavior and then talked to them. There was an emphasis on secrecy. We had to be selective because we were building a people's army. . . . We were highly motivated. In the next meeting we assessed the recruit's response. It was a very nice filter. We rarely made a mistake. We knew how to evaluate people. We also wanted to prepare new people to replace us. In case one of us had to go elsewhere the structure could be adjusted. I remember that mystique.[85]

The militias and the self-defense groups operated in both rural and urban areas. Armed with handguns, a few shotguns, and homemade explosives, they conducted attacks against security forces and paramilitaries in towns and hamlets in northeastern Chalatenango. These attacks followed a similar pattern. "Target one: the headquarters of the National Guard; target two: the house of the paramilitary commander; then attacks against people we called henchmen [murderers of peasant activists]," remembered Martínez.[86] The militias and the self-defense groups were often armed with their own personal weapons. Many male peasants in the area possessed their own pistols or revolvers. Martínez owned one. At one time his mother tried to persuade him not to join a demonstration in San Salvador, but when she realized he was determined to go, she handed him a pistol she had bought with money she obtained by selling a cow.[87] Armed with small weapons, the militias often engaged in combat with repressive forces to protect activists who joined demonstrations, strikes, and land occupations, as occurred during the January 22 march in San Salvador.

At times, the insurgents committed atrocities against paramilitaries or civilians they considered collaborators of government forces. According to Guardado, occasionally the peasant militias acted "with a level of irrationality and cruelty in the exercise of violence in places like Quezaltepeque, Aguilares, El Paisnal, and San Vicente." He considered such behavior "[one of] the first expressions of the fanaticism" he attributed to university students who commanded the militias at the national level. Guardado insisted that in contrast to the insurgent students, the peasant leaders in Chalatenango were not "fanatics" but rather mature individuals who engaged in armed violence as the last resort to protect their communities. However, he acknowledged that on occasion the dynamics of local conflicts in Chalatenango exceeded their ability to effectively control the intensity and the scope of insurgent violence.[88] Guardado commented on the personality of Justo Mejía, a former teacher of the radio schools, a leader of the Church-sponsored rural cooperatives in Chalatenango, and one of the first organizers of the self-defense groups, to make the point that peasant leaders were in fact "moderates" and not "fanatics":

> Justo [Mejía] was a tanned, thin man with light-colored eyes. He had eight children. He was very personable, very reasonable. He often smoked a cigar [un pata de cabra] and smiled. One never had an argument with him. He defended his viewpoints in an agreeable manner. He was very dynamic, very active, always willing to help people. He was a moderate, not a fanatic, a person with whom one could reason. The leaders of the UTC were not fanatics due to experience we had working with community groups. Most of us knew each other.[89]

Regardless of the ethos of violence that peasant leaders in Chalatenango might have held at that time, the FPL produced meticulous guidelines on how to fight local repressive forces. For instance, Campo Rebelde (Rebel Countryside), an insurgent publication, explicated the main counterinsurgent functions that ORDEN paramilitaries played among rural communities, namely, surveillance, finger-pointing, capture, and execution of peasant activists (figure 7.4). They urged militants not to fight them in a spontaneous way. Instead, they had to clearly understand why poor individuals like those who made up the peasant movement had joined ORDEN. They must distinguish between leaders of ORDEN and peasants who had joined the organization as a result of coercion or anti-communist propaganda. They should persuade rank-and-file paramilitaries to relinquish their counterrevolutionary activities by contesting key aspects of the indoctrination to which they had been submitted.[90] Most paramilitaries were either coerced or deceived by military officers, local commanders, or affluent individuals to join the organization. They were often told that revolutionaries were unscrupulous and ruthless individuals interested in becoming rich at the expense of others. Communism, on the other hand, was a system based on the expropriation of the rich and the poor that simply did not work. If "communists"

Figure 7.4 Front page of *Campo Rebelde*, the FPL bulletin geared toward rural communities, with the heading "How We Must Fight ORDEN." FPL, *Campo Rebelde*, no. 10, July 1978. Courtesy of CIDAI, Biblioteca "P. Florentino Idoate, S.J." of the Central American University "José Simeón Cañas."

took power, they would take away their houses, small plots of land, and cows. Since they did not respect marriage and often exchanged partners, they were a threat to patriarchal community morale.[91]

The counterinsurgent forces also maligned Cuban socialism to undermine the credibility of the rebels. According to the writers of *Campo Rebelde*: "They tell them a bunch of lies about socialist countries like Cuba ... they tell them 'look how they took everything from them in Cuba'" as if peasants in El Salvador could "see" what actually happened in that country.[92] In contrast, the FPL promoted an idyllic image of the Cuban Revolution and socialism to undo the counterinsurgent narrative. It depicted socialism by using a vague quasi-religious discourse that offered peasants salvation from oppression, repression, and misery. "In Socialism there are no more rich because there are no longer any great exploiters. . . . why is it forbidden to travel to Cuba? Because if workers could see the truth with their own eyes . . . if workers could really see Cuba they will die fighting for SOCIALISM."[93] The organization also articulated a teleological narrative that posited an epochal world transition from capitalism to socialism to make the point that revolutionaries were on the winning side of history. "Socialism is an economic, political, and social system more just and advanced than capitalism. While capitalism decays and finds itself immersed in a tremendous crisis, socialism becomes stronger and develops with splendor. A great segment of humanity lives under the skies of socialism and the other part struggles heroically to achieve socialism, fighting capitalism to death."[94]

Another issue of *Campo Rebelde* with the headline "The Revolution Advances!" advised its readers to secretly share the material with illiterate rural workers (as most of them were at that time). It discussed in detail counterinsurgent operations in San Pedro Perulapán, an area east of San Salvador, to delineate clandestine methods for combating paramilitaries and evading the persecution of state forces.[95] It also counseled its readers to defend the validity of socialism among peasant communities and explicated succinctly the question "What is revolution?":

> Revolution is the destruction of the oppressor state, starting with the reactionary army of the rich that sustained that state through the force of arms; also, it is the destruction of all institutions of the bourgeois state like the ministries, the bourgeois legislative assembly and all the institutions that help to sustain the economic, political, and social injustice of the capitalist regime. Once the state of the enemies of the people has been destroyed, a new state is created over the ashes of the old oppressor state. The revolutionary state is built with its own popular armed forces of liberation and supported by the exploited classes and sectors. Thus the popular revolutionary government with proletarian hegemony and based on the worker-peasant alliance is created.[96]

Counterinsurgency, on the other hand, created or aggravated multiple local conflicts in Chalatenango. Local authorities and elites used their connections with the repressive forces to abuse their neighbors, to settle old scores, to cut deals on remnants of communal lands (*ejidos*), to murder and torture activists, and to commit various crimes from extortion to rape.[97] This state policy confronted neighborhoods, hamlets, and clans depending on their affiliation with either the repressive forces or the insurgency. Generally, those who had been previously affiliated with opposition parties like the Christian Democrats or progressive Catholics leaned toward the insurgency; those with ties to the PCN (the official party), the Caballeros de Cristo Rey (a paramilitary group created by conservative Catholic sectors), or the military leaned toward the repressive forces. But there were exceptions to this rule. Some paramilitary commanders or individuals affiliated with the PCN joined the insurgency for various reasons. Occasionally, they refused to repress their own communities, adhered to a progressive Catholic ethos (i.e., a sense of justice and solidarity), and had kinship ties with clans that joined the rebels. During the furies of state terror in the late 1970s, entire hamlets or clans joined the insurgency as paramilitaries and security forces murdered or tortured their leaders. For instance, Los Dubon, a clan from Los Filos, a hamlet near Arcatao, which comprised some eighty families, joined the insurgency en masse after National Guardsmen killed some of their relatives.[98] In a similar manner, after peasant militias attacked paramilitaries, entire clans or hamlets became sworn enemies of the insurgency. Such were the cases of clans based in Teosinte and La Aserradera, two hamlets near Arcatao. In Ocotal, a hamlet near Dulce Nombre de María, peasant militias "killed fifteen members of ORDEN and the entire hamlet became radicalized against the rebels." They also attacked and "sacked" the town of Ojos de Agua, producing similar results.[99]

As the dialectics between insurgency and counterinsurgency in the countryside intensified, so did the urban confrontation between the Romero government and the social movements. In May 1979, state agents abducted Facundo Guardado along with other top BPR leaders.[100] By that time, the BPR had become a powerful movement able to mount a serious challenge to state power. Guardado was badly beaten by plainclothesmen in downtown San Salvador and taken to a clandestine jail by his captors.[101] The BPR responded to the crackdown on its top leaders in earnest. Activists occupied the embassies of Venezuela, Costa Rica, and France, as well as the Metropolitan Cathedral of San Salvador and six Catholic churches, to demand the release of the kidnapped leaders (figure 7.5). They also built barricades, burned buses and government vehicles, and conducted demonstrations and rallies in San Salvador and other cities. Unions carried out fifty strikes in key industrial and commercial firms. Teachers and students paralyzed schools across the country. On May 8, in broad daylight, policemen massacred scores of activists who occupied the cathedral (journalists actually taped this mass killing). On May 14, state forces killed fourteen activists, including three university students (Mauricio Scaffini, Delfina Góchez Fernández, and Antonio Girón M.), and one teacher (Emma Guadalupe Carpio) outside the Venezuelan embassy.[102] The latter was the daughter of the top FPL commander, Salvador Cayetano Carpio.[103] In response to these massacres, the FPL launched coordinated attacks against state forces, killing scores of "soldiers, national guardsmen,

Figure 7.5 Rally in downtown San Salvador demanding the release of Facundo Guardado, a leader of the UTC in Chalatenango and secretary general of the BPR, May 1979. The headline reads: "The CCS [Coordinating Committee of Trade Unions José Guillermo Rivas, a group affiliated with the BPR] Implements Fifty-Four Work Stoppages in Eight Days." CCS, *Combate Proletario*, Year 1, no. 2, June 1979. Courtesy of CIDAI, Biblioteca "P. Florentino Idoate, S J." of the Central American University "José Simeón Cañas."

policemen, and paramilitaries." The guerrillas also executed the minister of education, Carlos Herrera Rebollo, a Christian Democrat leader who had joined the Romero government.[104] These actions finally prompted President Romero to make an accommodating gesture. After consistently denying any knowledge of the abducted leaders, the government freed Guardado and Ricardo Mena, two key BPR leaders. Security forces apparently executed

Numas Escobar, Marciano Meléndez, and Oscar López, the other three abducted leaders. The BPR read these events, which it labeled "Heroic May," as evidence that "a dual popular power" had in fact emerged in El Salvador:

> [During May 1979,] the BPR constituted a force of dual power in re-
> lation with the tyranny; it managed to rescue two leaders, to put in
> evidence its counterrevolutionary essence, to achieve the massive in-
> corporation of the people to the struggle, to obtain [international] sol-
> idarity, to elevate the levels of revolutionary violence of the masses. It
> was a battle with insurrectionary characteristics.[105]

While the confrontations between state and insurgent forces intensified in Chalatenango, delinquents who had operated in the area tried to position themselves in the fight. A group of moonshiners based near Cerro Eramón, a mountain that divides the departments of Chalatenango and Cabañas, who had repelled National Guard and Treasury Police patrols for many years attempted to join the peasant insurgency.[106] "For them to live in the mountains, to carry a gun, and to shoot at the guardsmen was nothing extraordinary," said Guardado. At the time of the 1979 coup, when many communities affiliated with the insurgency fled to the mountains, this group joined the rebels. However, they hastily deserted the insurgency as soon as they realized that there was no monetary gain involved in this activity. "They were people who were in a business that gave them money and privileges they did not have in the guerrilla thus they left it. They became the first separatist movement," said Guardado wittily. In San José Cancasque they formed a group they called Unión de Pensadores Ellos Solos (Union of Solitary Thinkers), perhaps imagining that such a move would give them some leverage in the insurgency. It clearly did not.[107]

Time and again Archbishop Romero tried to console and support the victims of repression in Chalatenango during this critical period. Irma Serrano, who met the archbishop, depicted him as a jovial man who showed great respect and appreciation for peasants. In one incident, Romero and a group of peasant activists played a collective game in Chalatenango city circa 1978. They asked him to "dance la cucaracha as a penitence" as part of the game. The archbishop rolled up his cassock and happily danced the steps.[108] However, the exchanges between Romero and the peasant militants were not always cordial. On one occasion, he visited Arcatao in 1979 to express moral support to relatives of peasant activists (members of CBCs) who were murdered by National Guardsmen. Romero spoke about the "injustice committed against the peasants." A peasant activist in the audience saluted Romero's presence in Arcatao but also criticized his discourse. He advised Romero to speak about "injustice not in a vague way. . . . it was necessary to denounce the authors of such injustice, those who had committed crimes against peasants, the National Guardsmen." The archbishop was livid after this episode. He told a priest who accompanied him: "Now even a peasant [*un caitudo*; a derogatory term used to describe peasants who at that time wore rudimentary sandals known as *caites*] dares to tell the archbishop what he needs to preach." The priest replied to Romero: "Now the members of the Christian Communities feel entitled to have their say."[109]

In the aftermath of the October 1979 coup, towns and hamlets in north-eastern Chalatenango descended into unabated terror. Paramilitaries and guardsmen sacked hamlets near Arcatao on January 13 and Las Vueltas and Ojos de Agua on January 16, 1980, resulting in scores of civilian victims.[110] In Arcatao, paramilitaries burned an entire neighborhood where families they deemed supporters of the insurgency lived. "They torched 250 houses out of 300 in Barrio San José or El Calvario, they spared some near the town center to give them to ORDEN paramilitaries to inhabit," said Guardado.[111] The majority of dwellers of El Calvario joined the guerrillas after these atrocities.

The insurgency fomented a radical anticapitalist ideology among peasant communities; however, for most peasant activists in Chalatenango their involvement in the rebellion was first and foremost a matter of survival and complementarily an effort to eradicate militarism. "People from the Barrio [El Calvario] . . . became radicalized, they went to the mountains en masse. Nobody was asking if someone had heard about Marx, Lenin or Trotsky," said Guardado. In the end, what they wanted was to "get rid of that lid [*ese tapón*, figuratively, "that obstacle"], the military [dictatorship]," and to engage in an open political process.[112] Soon the guerrillas counterattacked the security forces in Arcatao. On February 5, 1980, they took over the town. They held a rally in the town center and called people to join the movement. They also routed army reinforcements that tried to ambush them. At that time, the peasant militias were becoming potent combat forces. Similar insurgent forces mounted increasingly effective attacks against paramilitaries, security forces, and army units across El Salvador. In one of the copious *partes de guerra* (war reports) distributed by the guerrillas that year, *El Rebelde* claimed that combatants had *ajusticiado* (executed) "53 henchmen [*esbirros*] of the repressive corps and chiefs of the assassin bands of ORDEN stained with the heroic and generous blood of the best sons of our people."[113]

The Start of the Civil War in Chalatenango

In December 1979, top insurgent commanders initiated the unification of the guerrilla organizations and the Communist Party. They formed La Coordinadora Político-Militar, a working group that integrated the FPL, the PCS, and the RN. These rebel leaders produced a succinct analysis on the origins of the insurgency in El Salvador. They maintained that in the past twenty-five years oligarchic elites had "closed a peaceful exit" to the crisis and "imposed violence on people." The insurgent commanders pondered the multiple efforts conducted by opposition parties and social movements to carry out institutional reforms through electoral politics and peaceful demonstrations in the past two decades. They also denounced the persistent massacres of civilians conducted by army and security forces in urban and rural areas in the 1970s to make the case that historically, armed struggle in El Salvador had emerged as a legitimate response of vast segments of the population against tyranny. They labeled elites who demanded "peace" while they sponsored state terror "hypocritical": "They want to impose such peace with massacres, disappearances, jail and exile; it is the peace of cemeteries." They claimed that the country's deep political crisis could not be resolved with *parches y masacre[s]* (roughly "partial solutions and massacres").[114] The sole alternative to it was democratic revolution:

> Nobody should be mistaken: the only true and efficacious solution to the national crisis in benefit of the people is popular armed revolution. . . . this revolution will not be an act of vengeance but of justice and emancipatory transformation; it will ensure democratic rights and freedoms to all the people, it will install a true democracy; it will give land to the great majorities in the countryside . . . it will conquer true national independence . . . it will ensure, with these and other fundamental changes dignified material and cultural living conditions for workers.[115]

In March 1980, La Coordinadora Político-Militar articulated a forceful critique of US counterinsurgency and claimed that revolutionary forces in El Salvador were ready to defeat it. The insurgent leaders depicted the Christian Democrat-Military Junta as a desperate US effort to salvage the oligarchic-military regime. It called the Junta's program "Matanzas y Reformas" (Killings and Reforms). The rebel leaders considered the nationalization of the banking system, the agrarian reform, and the state of siege sanctioned by the Junta that month elements of US counterinsurgency that matched state terror. These efforts sought to destroy the social movements and the left through a combination of military, political, and socioeconomic strategies. Duarte and the conservative Christian Democrats had become instruments of US counterinsurgency in El Salvador. Their alliance with the Salvadoran military sought to legitimize the massive US involvement in the Salvadoran conflict. In this logic, the rebel commanders denounced an alleged US plan to directly intervene in El Salvador with the complicity of the Christian Democrat government of President Luis Herrera Campins of Venezuela. Such a plan ostensibly involved the mobilization of US forces made up of Puerto Rican soldiers and Venezuelan military. The rebel commanders also depicted the US military buildup in El Salvador and Central America, which was aided by Israel and counterinsurgency experts from Uruguay and Argentina, to make this case. They stated that multilateral preparations for a US invasion of El Salvador were underway and claimed to be ready to face it. Evoking the mobilizations of the Central American armies that defeated the filibusterer William Walker in Nicaragua between 1856 and 1857, the resistance against the US Marines led by Augusto César Sandino in Nicaragua between 1927 and 1933, and the "Salvadorans, Central Americans, and Latin Americans" who fought alongside Sandino, they rhetorically declared: "Our soil will become hell for the imperialist invaders!"[116]

In May 1980, the insurgency took new steps in the institutionalization of its political and military power. The ERP joined the second command structure formed by the top insurgent leaders called DRU-PM. They praised the unification of the social movements (i.e., the CRM) and the creation of the Democratic Revolutionary Front (FDR), a broad-based alliance made up of political parties, social movements, churches, universities, and other civil society institutions. They lauded the role that the Catholic Church played during the crisis, particularly the appeal to members of the army and the security forces to disobey orders to murder civilians issued by Archbishop Romero. They also called on "patriotic, sane, and progressive" sectors of the military to "repudiate the genocide" and US intervention in El Salvador and to join the revolutionary-democratic forces. They officially endorsed La Plataforma de Gobierno Democrático Revolucionario (Democratic Revolutionary Government Platform), the left's proposal to form a transitional government to overcome the crisis. Such a move constituted an important departure from the Marxist-Leninist programs formulated by the guerrilla organizations in the 1970s. The Democratic Revolutionary Government Platform advocated ideological pluralism, respect for human rights, democratic freedoms, elections, and major socioeconomic reforms.[117] It was a program that echoed Third World and social democratic politics rather than Cuban socialism.

The creation of the FMLN was a crucial moment in the modern history of El Salvador. The DRU-PM announced its foundation on October 10.[118] The integrated rebel leadership led a twelve-year revolutionary war that undermined US counterinsurgent efforts in El Salvador. The new movement evoked deeply rooted collective imaginaries of indigenous rebellions, labor struggles, anti-oligarchic mobilizations, and internationalism among left intellectuals and activists in El Salvador. It vindicated the legacies of Farabundo Martí, the communist leader who joined Sandino in Nicaragua and was executed by the Salvadoran military in the aftermath of the 1932 uprising. It named the FMLN war fronts after Anastasio Aquino, the leader of the 1832 indigenous rebellion in Los Nonualcos and San Vicente, and Modesto Ramírez, Feliciano Ama, and Francisco Sánchez, three major figures of the 1932 indigenous peasant uprising.[119] In this context, insurgent forces in Chalatenango became part of the FMLN Modesto Ramírez Central Front. In 1980, they waged war on local government forces and prepared to carry out a strategic offensive, which took place in January 1981. The 1981 FMLN offensive known as "the Final Offensive" has been generally considered the start of the civil war proper.

As army, public security, and paramilitary forces implemented scorched-earth campaigns in northeastern Chalatenango, the peasant leaders intensified their war preparations.[120] Thousands of peasants in northeastern Chalatenango were ready to join the insurgency in 1980. Irma Serrano, who witnessed this mobilization, recalled that one Franco, a peasant activist from Potonico, often claimed: "The guava is already mature." He meant that peasants in Chalatenango were eager to fight the forces of repression at that time. Franco used this expression so often during meetings held in Potonico and the nearby hamlets that other activists started calling him "Guayaba Madura" (Mature Guava). But, in retrospect, Serrano deemed that peasant communities in the area were not fully prepared to face the dire consequences of state terror and war in 1980. "Perhaps the Guava was not so mature after all," she said.[121]

Héctor Martínez played a key role in the massive insurgent mobilization in Chalatenango in 1980. He recalled that in early May, one "Chapael," an FPL commander in the area (a former peasant leader from El Tamarindo, a hamlet near San José Las Flores), ordered him to gather hundreds of militiamen and to send them to a guerrilla training camp near Las Aradas de Yurique, a hamlet near the Sumpul River. "I remember it was raining a lot and the rivers were already flooded."[122] Evoking this mobilization, Martínez said emphatically:

> The peasant movement was very audacious. If the revolutionary movement [the FPL] had had the capacity to arm all those thousands of people in 1980, we would have taken care of the government at once [the peasant movement would had ousted the government at once]. I formed no fewer than ten platoons with people from Corral Falso, Potonico, and El Portillo del Norte. These people left everything. Their morale was very high. They left their little cows, tiny plots of land, little horses, families, and little pigs. We all joined in a selfless manner. That was not easy. The peasant is really attached to what he owns, but the organization was capable of persuading them to leave all that.[123]

As part of the mobilization, Chapael ordered Martínez to disarm the forces under his command before they marched to the training camp. He had to collect the militiamen's personal weapons because the FPL allegedly would "give

[them] guns" and train militarily "all those between sixteen and sixty years of age who were able to participate in assaulting military garrisons. Handguns will be given to men older than sixty."[124] Martinez continued:

> I told them: gentlemen please deposit all your pistols and your ammunition here in these little sacks because these are the instructions I have received from the organization. You are heading toward a training camp and you won't need your handguns there. You will receive war weapons there. People did not say "No, I am older than sixty" [to keep their handguns]. They turned in their weapons. The pistols they have bought by selling their little cows and small plots of land. They did not mind joining the movement empty-handed because they trusted the liberation and the equality the movement had promised them.[125]

Urban activists from San Salvador also joined the insurgent mobilization in 1980. For instance, members of CBCs from Santa Lucía, a working-class neighborhood in Ilopango, along with hundreds of urban activists joined the FPL during a public meeting held at a high school in San Salvador circa May 1980. Insurgent recruiters openly collected the activists' personal information during this event in order to assign them to nascent guerrilla army units.[126] In a similar fashion, the insurgency conducted massive recruitment among activists of social movements across the country that year. Other militants like Captain Juan-Juan who had received military training in Cuba and had participated in the 1979 Sandinista campaign that toppled the Somoza dictatorship in Nicaragua returned to the country to join the revolutionary war in 1980.[127]

Héctor Martínez did not join his troops at the training camp in Las Aradas de Yurique because the FPL appointed him commander of guerrilla forces stationed at El Cerro de Guazapa, an insurgent stronghold near San Salvador. "There I joined German Serrano [a peasant leader turned into a guerrilla commander]. We were in charge of a large force," remembered Martínez.[128]

On May 14, the Salvadoran army massacred approximately six hundred civilians at Las Aradas de Yurique, on the banks of El Sumpul River, with the complicity of the Honduran army. Ester Arteaga, a native of Las Aradas who survived the massacre, recalled the formation of the peasant movement in her hometown, the circumstances that preceded the mass killings, and how she and other women managed to escape the ordeal. According to Arteaga, her father, Francisco Arteaga, a small landowner, and Buenaventura Chinchilla, a teacher affiliated with ANDES, were the main leaders of the peasant movement in Las Aradas. Francisco Arteaga, like most peasant leaders in the area, had studied at Chacalcoyo, the Catholic cooperative training center near La Nueva Concepción. He had also attended "analyses of the national reality"—lectures on the country's socioeconomic and political structures—given by Ignacio Ellacuría and Segundo Montes, two Jesuit scholars at Central American University. The elder Arteaga founded a cooperative in Las Aradas circa 1975, which operated until 1979. Ester Arteaga joined the peasant movement in 1977 when she was barely twelve years old. She remembered that Mélida Anaya Montes and other ANDES leaders visited peasant leaders in Las Aradas in the late 1970s. Chinchilla, a local teacher, became the "intellectual ideologue" of the peasant movement in the area. He "started losing credibility" with parents of the schoolchildren as "he talked about the national reality even to fourth-graders." "They [Chinchilla and other peasant leaders] talked as if all the problems could be resolved at once. That wore down their credibility" with peasants in the area. Since 1977, according to Arteaga, "there was an uncontrollable repression" in Las Aradas, and the neighboring towns Ojos de Agua, San José Las Flores, and Las Vueltas. "Members of ORDEN only observed who met with whom and reported it to the National Guard. Then the guardsmen came just to capture people." Before the massacre, guardsmen had committed numerous "acts of terror" in the area. "They hanged peasants from the trees, beheaded them. The soldiers entered the hamlet, they burned cornfields, raped women, and assassinated people." By May 1980, "most people had fled to the hills; only a few women and small children remained in the hamlet."[129]

The Salvadoran troops responsible for the massacre gathered in Las Vueltas, San José Las Flores, and Ojos de Agua and moved toward Las Aradas, forcing thousands of displaced peasants as well as some insurgents (militiamen) in the area to move toward the Sumpul River. They trapped hundreds of men, women, and children on the banks of the river with the "hammer and the anvil," the scorched-earth tactic the army used repeatedly to massacre civilians in this period. Some people attempted to cross the river into Honduran territory, but Honduran army units and paramilitaries turned them back to the Salvadoran army. Many people drowned attempting to swim in the river's turbulent waters. Arteaga and three other women hid near the river. They witnessed how Salvadoran soldiers "killed many people."[130] As Arteaga described it:

Some ran from here to there, others tried crossing the river. They never imagined that the Honduran army would be waiting for them there. The Salvadoran soldiers separated people, two women, two men, and two children. They pulled people by the hair and put them face down over the rocky terrain [*el pedrero*] and shot them. Some drowned and the soldiers shot at those who started swimming.[131]

Arteaga vividly remembered a group of high school students from Chalatenango city who perished in the massacre. They had attended a guerrilla training camp in the area but were apparently unarmed. They gathered at an abandoned house that belonged to Arteaga's grandfather. They calmly smoked in the aisle *esperando lo suyo* (awaiting their fate). When Arteaga asked them why they were just standing there, without attempting to escape, one of them responded: "There is nothing we can do now." But Arteaga and her friends knew the area well. They managed to cross the river but were captured by the Honduran military. Fortunately for them, a Honduran paramilitary commander from Santa Lucía, a hamlet near Guarita, had befriended Arteaga's father, whom he called "Don Panchito."[132] Arteaga recalled having the following conversation with her Honduran captors:

ESTER ARTEAGA: Why are you going to send us back to El Salvador? We are
    Hondurans.
HONDURAN MILITARY OFFICER: Are you Hondurans? What were you doing
    over there [in El Salvador]?
ARTEAGA: My mother sent us to bring food to a Honduran lady, who lives there.
    Then the river was flooded and we could not cross it.
HONDURAN PARAMILITARY COMMANDER: Yes, I know this girl's father [point-
    ing at Arteaga], Don Panchito, he is Honduran.
HONDURAN MILITARY OFFICER: Go away, but you haven't seen anything here
    otherwise we will go get you.[133]

Arteaga called the mass killings at El Sumpul "a massacre without bodies" because most people who perished during this episode disappeared in the river currents. She recalled that a group of "disarmed militias who were [stationed] at El Jícaro and Las Aradas" also died. She alluded to the militias sent by Héctor Martínez and other insurgent commanders to that area a few days before the massacre.[134]

Militiamen who survived the Sumpul massacre blamed Martínez for sending them to what turned out to be a trap. He recalled that upon his return to Chalatenango from his command post in Guazapa, he faced a group of furious combatants.[135] Martínez recalled what a baffled militiaman told him at a meeting held in San Antonio Los Ranchos in May 1980:

You traitor sent us to die. You knew it. You took away our guns and told us that they will give us weapons and the weapons we found there were a military operation and the air force on top of us. Many people have died and you will pay for this.[136]

Martínez responded that he had only followed Chapael's orders, but the militiamen kept calling him "a traitor."

The worst was when I got back to my hometown [Corral Falso]. The mothers, the wives, and the elderly women who had stayed in the hamlet looked at me as if I were the devil. They cursed me and mis-treated me. They shouted at me: You have become Judas Iscariot![137]

Nevertheless, these tensions subsided as most militiamen from Corral Falso sur-vived the massacre largely because they were expert swimmers who managed to brave the Sumpul's turbulent waters and to evade the soldiers' fire. They returned to the hamlet exhausted but unharmed roughly two weeks after the event.[138]

In the aftermath of the Sumpul massacre, many people from Chalatenango became refugees in Mesa Grande, Honduras, while others like Ester Arteaga be-came guerrilla combatants. As Arteaga recalled:

After the army annihilated the civilian population, I felt a great indigna-tion and my reaction was to give a military response. My reaction was not unique or isolated. It was better to become a guerrilla than to let them [the military] kill you defenseless. The only alternative left to pro-mote social change was through the formation of the guerrilla army.[139]

Peasant leaders focused on the creation of guerrilla forces after this episode. Ever Hernández, a peasant leader and a former member of a Catholic community in northeastern Chalatenango, remembered how he joined the guerrilla army in 1980 while his younger brother became a soldier in the Salvadoran army.[140]

We were all accused of being a focal point of communism, which threatened the country's security. Thus they chased us. We played cat and mouse in our own community. We lived in the hills. In 1979 they burned our house. I told my younger brother: you leave with our mother to San Salvador and take care of her. I will stay here. I joined the guerrilla army but I was never part of the militias, per-haps they did not trust me [he laughed]. In January 1981, when we attacked Chalatenango city, I was in charge of tying up the colonel at the Military Detachment 1. We got a block away from the garrison because our planning was too superficial. My brother was forcibly recruited by the paramilitaries and then decided to join the Artillery Brigade because the guerrillas could kill him where he lived [he was stigmatized after joining the paramilitaries]. He then joined the Atlacatl Battalion [a special unit of the Salvadoran army] as a "*chuca*" [Salvadoran military's slang for a veteran trooper in a special army unit during the civil war].[141]

In 1980, the government forces destroyed most peasant communities in northeastern Chalatenango, and the peasant movement morphed into a peasant insurgency, which effectively battled the Salvadoran army until the end of the civil war in 1992. While thousands of peasants fled their communities as a result of the conflict and went to other regions in El Salvador, to neighboring countries, and eventually to the United States, many joined the insurgency. Peasants affiliated with the state and paramilitary forces also fled the area and settled near major army garrisons in Chalatenango city and El Paraíso to escape the guerrillas. This dialectic between state terror and peasant insurgency anticipated the militarization of the conflict in El Salvador in the 1980s.

Conclusion

From Resistance to War

Reforms are worthless if they are tainted with so much blood.
Archbishop Oscar A. Romero, March 23, 1980

They shed their blood for their love of their own people.
Gerardo, FMLN combatant (1986)

Insurgent intellectuals became leaders of the civil war that pitted the FMLN and its allies against US-sponsored Salvadoran governments between 1980 and 1992. They led a transition from politics to war that posed an unprecedented challenge to oligarchic-military rule and US hegemony in El Salvador. This transition involved the massive conscription of social activists into insurgent forces, the creation of a guerrilla army under a centralized command, and the consolidation of the rebels' territorial control over rural areas. These insurgent intellectuals were former students, scholars, laypeople, peasant leaders, teachers, poets, and dissidents of political parties who embodied the movement's social, ideological, and cultural diversity. They crucially shaped the revolutionary power that effectively divided the state's sovereignty during the civil war.[1]

The characteristics of revolutionary power changed dramatically in the early years of the conflict. In the late 1970s, the social movements' capacity to mobilize tens of thousands of activists in cities and rural areas and the public recognition that charismatic figures such as Mélida Anaya Montes, the head of the teachers' union ANDES, and other similar leaders had among vast sectors of the population constituted crucial elements of the rebels' power. The growing repression and the enlistment of thousands of activists into the guerrilla army in 1980 dispersed the potent social movements formed in the previous decade. Simultaneously, the creation of the guerrilla army and the insurgents' efforts to consolidate rearguards in rural areas in Santa Ana, Chalatenango, Cuscatlán, Cabañas, San Salvador, San Vicente, Usulután, San Miguel, and

Morazán transformed the FMLN into a formidable military power. Politically, the revolutionaries also gained enormous strength at that time. The creation of the FDR-FMLN, a broad-based alliance founded by opposition parties, social movements, civil society groups, and the insurgency, greatly increased the movement's national and international legitimacy.

Such an alliance reflected a major political shift among elite intellectuals that occurred at the outset of the civil war. Prominent figures such as Guillermo Manuel Ungo, a social democrat leader, and Rubén Zamora, a Social Christian intellectual, both important figures in the Revolutionary Government Junta formed in October 1979, relinquished institutional politics and joined the FDR. Salvador Samayoa, a lecturer of philosophy at the Central American University who had served as the minister of education in the Junta, publicly joined the insurgency in January 1980. Enrique Álvarez Córdova, a US-educated engineer and member of the country's elite who had served as minister of agriculture in PCN governments in the 1970s, became the first president of the FDR. The defection of Álvarez Córdova and other similar figures to the insurgency infuriated the reactionary military and civilian elites. Clearly, the confluence between these public figures and the urban and peasant intellectuals that made up the rebel leadership constituted a major threat to oligarchic and military power insofar as it endowed the movement with extraordinary legitimacy and a set of theoretical, political, and strategic capacities. On November 27, 1980, a Treasury Police unit that was later identified as a death squad captured top FDR leaders during a meeting they held at the Jesuit high school Externado de San José in San Salvador and summarily executed them. Álvarez Córdova, the social democrat leader Enrique Barrera, and key leaders of the social movements, including Juan Chacón, Manuel Franco, Humberto Mendoza, and Doroteo Hernández, were victims of state terror.[2] It has been stated that Álvarez Córdova "was the first rich man who died . . . for the poor" in El Salvador.[3] But despite the assassination of the FDR leaders, the critical mass of elite and insurgent intellectuals formed in 1980 became another crucial element of the emerging revolutionary power.

These intellectuals became leaders, policymakers, and diplomats of the democratic revolution. They condensed the central demands of political parties, civil society groups, and the insurgency in the FDR-FMLN's Democratic Revolutionary Government platform issued in 1980. This program called for the overthrow of the oligarchic-military dictatorship "imposed against the will of the Salvadoran people for fifty years," the destruction of its political and military apparatus, and the creation of a democratic revolutionary government. It also advocated the elimination of El Salvador's economic, political, and military dependence on the United States. It promised to respect "democratic rights and freedoms" and to conduct a comprehensive state reform. The platform also

featured major socioeconomic reforms, including land reform; the nationalization of foreign trade, banking, and public transportation; and the expropriation
of industrial and commercial monopolies. It included plans for the creation of
a "people's army" that integrated the insurgent forces and those members of
the official armed forces who had a clean service record. It pledged to dismantle all private and state repressive structures, to halt state terror, to clarify the
whereabouts of individuals who had been captured and disappeared by government forces from 1972 onward, and to bring to justice civilians and state
agents accused of committing political crimes. It envisioned a foreign policy
based on "principles of independence and self-determination, solidarity, peaceful coexistence, equal rights, and mutual respect between states." This blueprint
summarized the fundamental tasks and objectives of the democratic revolution
in the early 1980s.[4]

FDR-FMLN leaders also articulated a dialogue and negotiation policy from
the start of the conflict. They appointed a political-diplomatic commission to
carry out the movement's foreign policy and negotiation initiatives. Intellectuals
who had been active in the country's public life for several decades and insurgent
leaders made up this body. These figures gained access to the highest levels of
government in Western Europe, Latin America, Asia, and Africa and established
unofficial relations with members of the US Congress, United Nations institutions, and other international organizations. During the 1980s, they pioneered
an innovative activist diplomacy that became a key component of the political
settlement that put an end to the civil war in 1992.

However, at the outset of the conflict, the intransigence of state elites and
the mounting counterinsurgent terror undermined various peace initiatives and
accelerated the transition from politics to war. Archbishop Romero, President
Omar Torrijos of Panama, and the Socialist International, an organization
formed by major social democratic and socialist parties from Western Europe
and Latin America, among other actors, at one time conducted initiatives to
avoid a protracted armed conflict.[5] For instance, President Torrijos, a graduate
of El Salvador's military academy who had ties with high-ranking Salvadoran
military officers, carried out a failed attempt to mediate between the rebel leaders and the army's high command. On several occasions in 1979 and 1980,
Torrijos gathered top Salvadoran rebel leaders at his residence at El Farrallón
in an attempt to find a political settlement to the looming civil war.[6] The rebels showed their willingness to carry out unofficial talks with top Salvadoran
army commanders, but the latter plainly rejected Torrijos's proposal.[7] This
is one of the least-known peace initiatives that preceded the civil war. At that
time, the army's high command and the Christian Democrat–Military Junta
formed in January 1980 rejected dialogue with the rebels and fully embraced

US counterinsurgency. This lethal policy sought to exterminate, demobilize, and co-opt the actual or alleged social base of the insurgency through a combination of reforms, particularly agrarian reform, and terror.

US counterinsurgency profoundly reshaped state, society, and politics until the end of the conflict and beyond. Behavioral sciences (i.e., "hearts and minds") and rational choice theories informed the implementation of US counterinsurgency in El Salvador.[8] The state terror intrinsic to this strategy devastated the country's entire social fabric, especially religious and academic communities, political parties, and social movements, thus undermining any viable political alternative to the civil war. US Catholic missionaries, diocesan priests, almost the entire FDR leadership, university intellectuals, peasants, workers, students, teachers, poets, professionals, and thousands of common Salvadorans, particularly young men and women, were victims of counterinsurgent terror. Death squads also tried to eliminate army officers they considered potential supporters of a political settlement with the left. For instance, they tried to assassinate Colonel Adolfo A. Majano, a reformist member of the Revolutionary Government Junta.[9] The murder of Archbishop Romero and the subsequent massacre at his funeral in March, in particular, sent a chilling message to most Salvadorans: death squads and government forces acting together or separately were willing and able to murder anyone they labeled "communist." The reactionary military, the oligarchic elites, and the United States plainly rejected dialogue between the Christian Democrat–Military Junta and the FMLN-FDR insofar as counterinsurgency pursued first and foremost the mass extermination of the left's social base.

In 2005, Ernesto A. Alvarez, a former BPR activist, assessed the social and political consequences of counterinsurgent terror in the early 1980s as follows:

> Electoral politics were closed down at the start of the seventies as a real option for [social] change or as a mechanism to access government. Then it lost even more validity when the PCN governments and the military dictatorship and the oligarchs cracked down on any labor protest. . . . they saw behind any socioeconomic demand a vehicle for the development of subversive organizations.
>
> The oligarchy and the dictatorship did not have the ability to open up small [political] spaces. They closed down absolutely all spaces. The consequence was that the massive, broad, and growing social movements became better organized as repression escalated. They had that slogan ["facing more repression with more organized struggle"; *a más represión más lucha organizada*]. After each repressive episode the population increased the protests.
>
> That policy [counterinsurgency] had in my judgment the intention to annihilate [the social movements]. . . . there was political repression

in the 1970s, but it was not as massive or cruel as the one that started in 1980. . . . from the beginning of 1980 to mid-1983 there was a massive extermination. . . . that was the period of more repression and paradoxically it was the period of the Government Junta. Of course the Christian Democrats, the military, and the gringos [the US government] assumed the direction of the Junta. . . . [They] took on the direction of the war. . . . then a strategy of mass annihilation against anyone who was [considered part of the] opposition was implemented. . . . The highest number of massacres in El Salvador occurred in this period. For instance in the case of San Vicente and La Paz there were twenty-eight massacres; of those, only one occurred in 1974 at La Cayetana.[10]

The unabated counterrevolutionary terror sparked the fury that drove Salvadorans from all walks of life to join or support the revolution.[11] It motivated social activists to join en masse the emerging guerrilla army in 1980. Insurgent recruiters attended events organized by social movements at the University of El Salvador, high schools, and other venues across the country to enlist activists who were willing to take up arms against the state.[12]

The state terror also generated widespread moral outrage in the international community. Countless groups, communities, institutions, and individuals in the United States, Canada, Western Europe, and Latin America condemned US intervention and the grotesque human rights violations committed by government forces and death squads in El Salvador. Religious leaders, students, activists, trade unionists, writers, musicians, celebrities, scholars, professionals, politicians, Salvadoran communities living abroad, and refugees of the civil war formed solidarity movements that supported the FDR-FMLN and demanded a political settlement to the Salvadoran conflict for more than a decade.

El Salvador's civil war had considerable international reverberations from the late 1970s onward. The United States became a party to the conflict at the time of the October 1979 coup and the formation of the Revolutionary Government Junta.[13] The Carter administration feared that the Sandinista victory in Nicaragua in July would generate a similar revolutionary uprising in El Salvador. A State Department envoy played a direct role in the formation of the Christian Democrat–Military Junta, the centerpiece of US counterinsurgency in El Salvador in the early 1980s.[14] The Reagan administration overlooked the historical roots of the civil war in El Salvador and simply considered the FMLN as a Soviet, Cuban, and Sandinista proxy that constituted a major threat to US interests in the region. It provided massive military and economic aid to the Christian Democrat–Military Junta and subsequent governments to crush it. Reagan's "rollback" policy in Central America ultimately led to protracted US political, military, and diplomatic involvement in the Salvadoran conflict.

Broadly speaking, the rebels developed significant political and diplomatic ties with the Socialist International; the Socialist Bloc; revolutionary and anti-colonial movements from Latin America, the Middle East, Asia, and Africa; the Non-Aligned Movement; and countries such as Mexico, Venezuela, Panama, Spain, and France. FMLN-FDR representatives cultivated extensive relations with social democratic governments and parties in Latin America and Western Europe. At the same time, some insurgent organizations had long-standing bonds with the socialist world. Cayetano Carpio and Schafik Jorge Hándal, the leaders of the FPL and the PCS, respectively, were communist figures with close ties with Cuba, the Soviet Union, Vietnam, and other socialist nations. Other groups like the RN, the ERP, and the FPL established unofficial relations with social democratic parties and governments in Europe and Latin America. Throughout the conflict, the FMLN's ideology and politics oscillated between Marxist-Leninist and socialist democratic tendencies, with the latter ethos gaining more traction among the top rebel leadership as the civil war unfolded.

In recent years, Schafik Hándal revealed that socialist countries provided military aid to the FMLN at the start of the conflict. Ethiopia, the German Democratic Republic, and Bulgaria provided some military hardware to the Salvadoran rebels at the request of Hándal in 1980.[15] But apparently, Vietnam supplied most of the weaponry that rebel forces used in the early stages of the civil war. Hándal met Le Duan, the secretary general of the Communist Party of Vietnam, in late 1980 to discuss the recent foundation of the FMLN and the rebels' plan to launch a decisive military campaign. According to Hándal, his meeting with Le Duan went beyond mere politics and diplomacy insofar as the Vietnamese leader was genuinely interested in the evolution of the civil war in El Salvador. Hándal commented that Le Duan was *un guerrero hecho y derecho* (well-rounded warrior) for he clearly understood the military challenges that FMLN forces faced on the ground. Le Duan offered Hándal "13 thousand weapons" that included M16 rifles and some four million rounds of ammunition confiscated from US forces in Vietnam, as well as Soviet-made machine guns and antitank weapons. In Moscow, Hándal requested functionaries of the Secretariat of the Central Committee of the Soviet Communist Party to manage the transportation of the arsenal from Vietnam to an unspecified location. They were initially reluctant to approve Hándal's request, but in the end top Soviet officials authorized the operation.[16]

The FMLN's General Command, the top insurgent leadership, announced a major offensive against the state and the elites in January 1981. This declaration mirrored the public indignation generated by counterinsurgent terror. The statement signaled the ongoing transition from politics to war in unequivocal terms. The rebels declared their intention to combine a potent military mobilization, a popular insurrection, and a national strike to oust the Christian Democrat–Military Junta. They also called on military officers and soldiers who rejected the extermination of civilians carried out by government forces to join the rebel forces.

The insurgent leaders issued two general orders to announce the 1981 offensive. Radio Liberación, a fleeting clandestine radio station, broadcast the declarations. Five commanders read the orders, signaling the fact that the movement was a conjunction of five different organizations, not a single unified party. Cayetano Carpio, a senior commander and leader of the FPL, read the whole of General Order No. 1 over the radio. The directive instructed rebel forces and their supporters to initiate "the decisive military and insurrectional battles" to take power and form a democratic revolutionary government. It also made an appeal to all "progressive and patriotic" officers and soldiers to join the revolution and to turn their weapons against the "cruel and bloodthirsty chiefs of the high command and the command of the counterrevolutionary army."[17] Other rebel commanders read portions of General Order No. 2. Fermán Cienfuegos, the leader of the RN, specifically addressed the rebel forces: "We order all chiefs and combatants to be at their combat posts, in their trenches arms in hand . . . and to comply [with] this order number two of the General Military Offensive and the Insurrection."[18] Schafik Jorge Hándal, the secretary general of the PCS, depicted the 1981 offensive as a national effort to defeat the dictatorship and to end state terror:

> This is the most important moment in the History of our Beloved Homeland since the proclamation of its Independence from Spain: this is the hour in which we rise up in the final offensive to put an end to 50 years of bloody Right Wing Military Dictatorship and to one century of merciless and insatiable Domination of the Oligarchy. . . .
>
> Let's put an end to this brutal slaughter. Let's throw into the dustbin of history the Fascist Dictatorship. The main weapon of the Salvadoran people is its heroism, its limitless combativeness, its unbreakable will to defeat the assassins. Any sacrifice is small to achieve Liberation; much more significant and painful is the sacrifice of thousands of lives in this endless slaughter [*matanza*] carried out by the Fascist Assassins.[19]

Roberto Roca, the top commander of the Central American Workers' Revolutionary Party (PRTC), made a direct appeal to civilians or, in his parlance, to "the masses," to carry out an insurrection and a general strike. "Today, the revolutionary combativeness of the Masses shown a thousand times, both in the countryside and the city, must achieve in the General Insurrection its maximum expression, its maximum resolution."[20] Joaquín Villalobos, the leader of the PRS-ERP, addressed FMLN officers and combatants, civilian supporters of the insurgency, and members of the official armed forces. "We are confident, according to what it seems [*según se refleja*], in the willingness of Patriotic soldiers, noncommissioned officers, and officers to point their weapons in the correct direction against the assassins of our people."[21] Villalobos also addressed the military in general: "To the members of the Armed Forces of El Salvador, the People from their trenches risen up in peasant settlements, in popular barrios call on you to rebel in the garrisons all over the country. Our People and the FMLN will. . . . . . judge your participation with the people or against the people."[22] The tone of these war declarations showed the stern combat morale of the rebel forces and their supporters at the outset of the conflict. The slogans inscribed in these statements indicated the rebels' definitive will: "¡Unidos para Combatir Hasta la Victoria Final! ¡Revolución o Muerte, Venceremos!" ("United to Fight Until Final Victory! Revolution or Death, We Will Vanquish!").

The revolutionaries did not take power in January 1981 as they had expected, but the magnitude of the insurgent offensive clearly announced things to come. While this is not the place to offer a thorough analysis of the rebel campaign, it is well worth considering salient features of this event insofar as it marked the start of the civil war proper. FMLN forces launched simultaneous attacks against army, security forces, and paramilitaries in cities, towns, and hamlets in twelve out of the fourteen departments that constitute El Salvador.[23] They laid sieges to army garrisons in Chalatenango, El Paraíso, Suchitoto, Santa Ana, Metapán, Chalchuapa, Acajutla, Sonsonate, Villa Victoria, Cinquera, Jutiapa, Tecoluca, San Vicente, Perquín, Osicala, San Francisco Gotera, and other places. Guerrilla forces also ambushed large army units that included armored vehicles and artillery at sites like Rio Seco (Morazán) and near the Port of La Unión. Rebel units also took control of major highways and roads throughout the country. In the metropolitan area of San Salvador, guerrilla commandos carried out attacks against the air force base in Ilopango and the National Guard and the Treasury Police garrisons. The insurgents also operated in Soyapango, a large industrial city, and cities in the northern periphery of San Salvador, including Mejicanos, Cuscatancingo, Ciudad Delgado, and Tonacatepeque. In Santa Ana, the country's second-largest city, the guerrillas conducted a major attack against the army's Second Infantry Brigade, which was supported by a company of rebel soldiers led by two army captains.[24] The military rebellion in Santa Ana showed that despite the heavy anti-communist indoctrination and control to which army officers were subjected in this period, some of them considered the slaughter of civilians conducted by government forces morally reprehensible to the point that they were willing to collaborate or to join the insurgency.[25] In sum, the 1981 FMLN offensive featured the mobilization of thousands of insurgent combatants under a centralized command who inflicted heavy casualties to army and public security forces throughout the country. In the end, the government forces retook control of cities and towns, and the guerrilla army retreated to rural areas. In the aftermath of this episode, FMLN leaders devised a strategy they called *resistir, desarrollarse y avanzar* (to resist, to develop, and to advance). It consisted in a simultaneous effort to consolidate insurgent rearguards in the countryside and to create military forces able to fight a protracted revolutionary war.

The Salvadoran armed forces endured the 1981 insurgent campaign and were able to defend state power across the national territory without substantial US military aid, which escalated after this episode.[26] However, the rebel offensive decisively altered the dynamics of the conflict. It showed to national and international observers that the FMLN was able to mobilize a major military force and likely to sustain a protracted war effort. Governments and political parties in Western Europe and Latin America soon realized that the sovereignty of El Salvador was, for all intents and purposes, divided between the FMLN and the government after January 1981. Mexico and France recognized the FMLN-FDR as legitimate representatives of the Salvadoran people, and the Socialist International declared its official support for a negotiated settlement to end the conflict at that time. These declarations formulated by major US allies in Western Europe and Latin America gave El Salvador's civil war an extraordinary symbolic meaning insofar as they challenged President Reagan's efforts to portray the conflict as a case of Soviet expansionism in Central America. They also conferred on the FMLN, an organization maligned by the Reagan administration as a terrorist group, remarkable international legitimacy as a party to the Salvadoran conflict.[27] However, at the outset of the civil war, Reagan administration officials rejected talks between the government of El Salvador and the FDR-FMLN insofar as they expected a rapid victory of the Salvadoran army over the rebels. This outcome ostensibly would make known to US "allies and potential foes alike" President Reagan's serious intent to "roll back communism" in Central America and to eradicate the Vietnam Syndrome that had undermined US foreign policy since the fall of Saigon in 1975.[28] These calculations turned out to be inexact. US-sponsored Salvadoran governments conducted major military and political efforts to defeat the FMLN insurgency for nearly twelve years and ultimately failed to do so.

Vietnam was also an important historical reference for the Salvadoran rebels. To a significant extent they drew on Vietnamese war experiences to articulate their own war strategy and tactics. Mélida Anaya Montes (aka Ana Maria), a teacher and scholar who became a FMLN commander, studied the Vietnamese resistance against French colonialism and US forces in Vietnam. In her 1982 book, *Experiencias vietnamitas en su guerra de liberación* (Vietnamese experiences in its war of liberation), Anaya Montes condensed some of the most important lessons she drew from Vietnam, particularly from the Vietnamese resistance against US and local forces in South Vietnam. In the preface to her book Anaya Montes wrote:

> The book is an attempt to analyze systematically and in a simple way that wealth of experience that offers the GREAT VIETNAM; the Heroic Vietnam. We will see in it a reflection of our own reality, the essentials of the aggression of Yankee Imperialism, the behavior of local puppets, the sufferings and heroism of the people to build a Homeland free of exploitation and misery based on the practice of the highest human values.[29]

A comprehensive history of the civil war in El Salvador that incorporates the perspectives of all national and international actors to the conflict has yet to be written. Some experts have suggested that during the civil war the FMLN became one of the most potent insurgencies in the modern history of the Americas.[30] The guerrilla army routed numerous army units, public security forces, and paramilitaries and effectively defended the rebels' rearguards in the early 1980s. A US assessment of the civil war that circulated at that time reads, "The attempted offensive of January 10, 1981, and the armed forces' response resulted in both sides fighting to a draw." The report concluded that "the guerrillas have the initiative on their side—they can attack when and where they want—and the government has the capacity to contain insurgent assaults on a case-by-case basis. Consequently, there is no military end in sight to the war of attrition in El Salvador."[31]

Recent work illustrates the insurgency's growing military power in the early 1980s and reveals the degree to which the Salvadoran rebels assimilated revolutionary experiences from around the globe.[32] On the night of December 30, 1983, FPL-FMLN forces overran the army's Fourth Infantry Brigade at El Paraíso, Chalatenango, one of the largest, most modern, and most heavily fortified military installations in El Salvador, which was designed by US military engineers.[33] This was arguably one of the most complex military operations conducted by an insurgent movement in modern Latin American history. It involved the simultaneous deployment of Special Forces and regular guerrilla battalions in an attack against "a military installation designed ... by US counterinsurgency specialists."[34] Insurgent commandos infiltrated the barracks and conducted a lethal attack against army battalions stationed at El Paraíso. In turn, guerrilla battalions assaulted the place. They captured hundreds of soldiers and several officers and confiscated the entire arsenal at the garrison. Some three decades after this episode, veteran combatants, many of them former peasant and student activists in the 1970s who participated in the attack against

El Paraíso, talked candidly about the planning and execution of the operation. Héctor Martínez, a former peasant leader from Corral Falso, Chalatenango, led guerrilla battalions that assaulted the garrison.[35]

"Gerardo," a rebel combatant who was wounded at El Paraíso, commented on the circumstances that led him to join the rebel forces when he was barely twelve years old. He was born to a landless family near Cantón Platanares, Suchitoto, in the late 1960s. Like most people living in that area, his family rented small plots of land to cultivate subsistence crops. When he was a small child, Gerardo and his mother often joined peasant demonstrations in San Salvador and gatherings of peasant activists near Suchitoto. He enjoyed listening to songs that celebrated peasant leaders killed by government forces that he learned at that time. Recalling his time as a child growing up in the midst of the peasant mobilizations of the 1970s and his trajectory as a seasoned guerrilla fighter despite his young age, Gerardo asserted: "They shed their blood for their love of their own people."[36]

Left intellectuals in Latin America experienced substantial ideological, political, and cultural transformations toward the end of the Cold War. FMLN leaders relinquished the Marxist-Leninist ideology that had characterized the movement prior to and during the civil war and instead embraced democratic socialism in the late 1980s. Exchanges between FMLN and social democratic figures and the evolution of the civil war on the ground informed that mutation. Paradoxically, this process took place at a time when social democratic and socialist parties in Europe were abandoning the welfare state paradigm and embracing neoliberalism. The collapse of the Soviet Union and to lesser extent the 1990 Sandinista electoral defeat also informed the metamorphosis of left intellectuals in El Salvador.[37] Insurgent intellectuals became politicians, pundits, social activists, entrepreneurs, and founders of nongovernmental organizations. This transformation echoed technocratic discourses on development, social violence and crime, and democratic governance formulated by international financial institutions and UN agencies from the early 1990s onward; hence, these refashioned intellectuals ended up articulating a peculiar neoliberal ideology that tempered the grievances and demands of urban and rural workers in postwar El Salvador. However, they also envisioned new political horizons, particularly in the context of the São Paulo Forum, a transnational debate that involved the most influential left parties and movements in the region, including the FMLN. In 1994, the Zapatista National Liberation Army took up arms in Chiapas, posing a major challenge to neoliberalism in Mexico. The uprising in Chiapas also defied predictions about the imminent collapse of left movements in Latin America. The 1998 election of Hugo Chávez as president and the start of the Bolivarian Revolution in Venezuela made democratic revolution, once again, thinkable in Latin America. Left parties and movements in Bolivia, Brazil, Argentina, Uruguay, Ecuador, and elsewhere were also part of that revolutionary impetus. This book has traced imaginaries of democracy and revolution articulated by urban and peasant intellectuals who stood at the forefront of resistance against dictatorship and empire in Latin America for nearly two decades, a movement that heralded the revival of the left in the 1990s.

ACRONYMS

ACUS	Salvadoran University Catholic Action
AGEUS	General Association of Salvadoran University Students
ALPRO	Alliance for Progress
ANDES	National Association of Salvadoran Educators–June 21
ANEP	National Association of Private Enterprise
ANSESAL	Salvadoran National Security Agency
ARENA	Nationalist Republican Alliance
ARS	Salvadoran Revolutionary Action
ATACES	Association of Agrarian Workers and Peasants of El Salvador
BPR	Popular Revolutionary Bloc
BFA	Agricultural Promotion Bank
CACM	Central American Common Market
CBC	Christian Base Communities also known as CEB (Ecclesial Base Communities)
CCS	Coordinating Committee of Trade Unions "José Guillermo Rivas"
CELAM	Conference of Latin American Bishops
CESPROP	Center of Social Studies and Popular Promotion
CGS	General Confederation of Salvadoran Unions
CGTS	General Confederation of Salvadoran Workers
CNI	National Center of Information
CONDECA	Central American Defense Council
CRAC	Committee of Representatives of General Studies
CRM	Revolutionary Coordination of the Masses
DRU-PM	The Unified Revolutionary Directorate of Politico-Military Organizations
ERP	People's Revolutionary Army
FAPU	Unified Front of Popular Action

FARO	Agrarian Front of the Eastern Region
FDR	Democratic Revolutionary Front
FECCAS	Christian Federation of Salvadoran Peasants
FENASTRAS	National Union Federation of Salvadoran Workers
FESTIAVCES	Union Federation of Workers of Food, Clothing, Textile, and similar Industries of El Salvador
FMLN	Farabundo Martí National Liberation Front
FNOC	National Front of Civic Orientation
FPL	Popular Liberation Forces–Farabundo Martí–
FSR	Federation of Revolutionary Unions
FTC	Federation of Rural Workers
FUAR	United Front of Revolutionary Action
FUNPROCOOP	Foundation for the Promotion of Cooperatives
FUSS	Unitary Union Federation of El Salvador
GAR	Revolutionary Action Groups
JAC	Catholic Agrarian Youth
JEC	Catholic Student Youth
JOC	Catholic Worker Youth
LP-28	Popular Leagues February 28
MERS	High School Students Revolutionary Movement
MILGROUP	US Military Group in El Salvador
MIPTES	Independent Movement of Professionals and Technicians of El Salvador
MLP	Popular Liberation Movement
MNR	National Revolutionary Movement
MPSC	Popular Social Christian Movement
OAS	Organization of American States
OCPA	State Department's Office of Central American and Panamanian Affairs
ORDEN	Nationalist Democratic Organization
OLAS	Organization of Latin American Solidarity
ORT	Organization of Revolutionary Workers
PAR	Party of Renovating Action
PCS	Communist Party of El Salvador
PCN	Party of National Conciliation
PDC	Christian Democrat Party
PRAM	Revolutionary Party of April and May
PRTC	Central American Workers' Revolutionary Party
PRS-ERP	Party of the Salvadoran Revolution-People's Revolutionary Army
PRUD	Revolutionary Party of Democratic Unification

RN	National Resistance
STISS	Workers Union of the Salvadoran Social Security Institute
STIUSA	Union of Textile United Industries
UCA	Central American University "José Simeón Cañas"
UDN	Nationalist Democratic Union
UGB	Union of White Warriors
UNO	National Opposition Union
UNOC	National Union of Catholic Workers
UPT	Union of Dwellers of Shantytowns
UR-19	Revolutionary University Students July 19
UTC	Union of Rural Workers

APPENDIX

| Revolutionary Party of April and May (PRAM) |
| National Front of Civic Orientation (FNOC) |
| Party of Renovating Action (PAR) |
| Communist Party of El Salvador (PCS)* |
| Christian Democrat Party (PDC) |

Figure A.1 Opposition parties and movements in El Salvador between 1960 and 1961.
*The PCS operated as a clandestine political organization from 1932 until the end of El Salvador's civil war in 1992. Sources: Valle, *Siembra de vientos El Salvador 1960–69*, pp. 42-47; Dada interview.

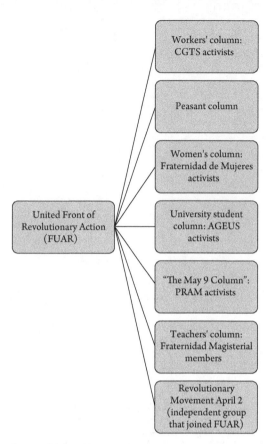

Figure A.2 United Front of Revolutionary Action, 1961 to 1963. Source: Santacruz interview.

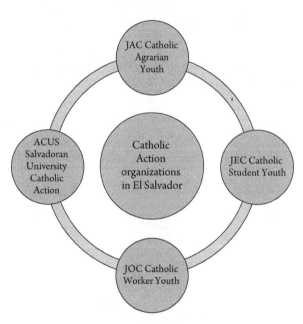

Figure A.3 Catholic Action organizations in El Salvador in the 1960s. Sources: Paniagua interview; Vega, *Las 54 cartas pastorales de Monseñor Chávez*, p. 12.

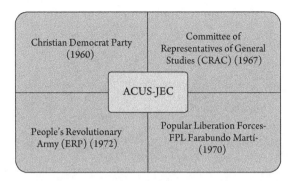

Figure A.4 Organizations cofounded by former members of the Salvadoran University Catholic Action (ACUS) and the Catholic Student Youth (JEC). Sources: Rodríguez interview; Dada interview; Paniagua interview; Peña Mendoza interview; Ramírez interview; Velásquez interview.

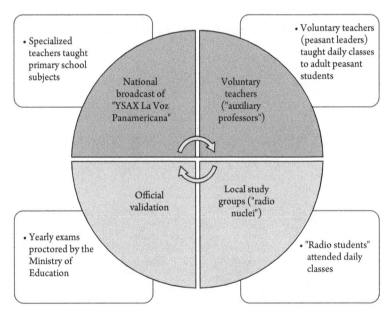

Figure A.5 Functioning of the radio schools sponsored by the Archdiocese of San Salvador in the 1960s and 1970s. Sources: Compiled from "Escuelas Radiófonicas un Medio para Acercarnos a Grupos Marginados," *Orientación*, September 28–October 4, 1970, pp. 1, 6; "Exámenes Finales de Escuelas Radiofónicas," *Orientación*, October 7–13, 1968, p. 4.

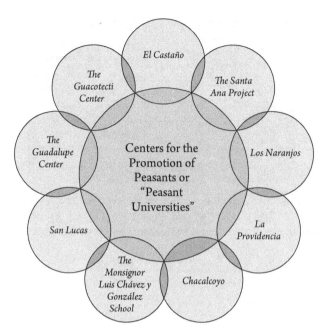

Figure A.6 Centers for the Promotion of Peasants, or "peasant universities," sponsored by the Salvadoran Catholic Church in the 1960s and 1970s. Source: Vega, *Las comunidades Cristianas*, p. 84.

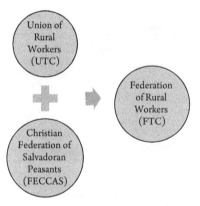

Figure A.7 Major peasant organizations in the 1970s. Source: Guardado interview.

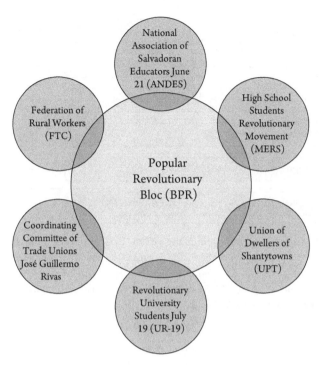

Figure A.8 Popular Revolutionary Bloc, 1975 to 1980. Source: Guardado interview.

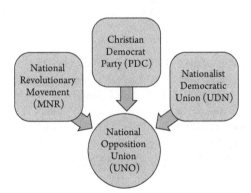

Figure A.9 Legal opposition parties that formed the National Opposition Union (UNO) in 1971. Source: "Bases Programáticas de la UNO," mimeograph 1972.

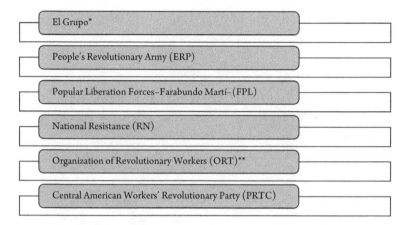

Figure A.10 Guerrilla organizations in the 1970s. *El Grupo merged into the ERP.
**The ORT was a predecessor of the PRTC. Sources: Compiled from Resistencia Nacional, *Por la causa proletaria: Apuntes para el estudio de 13 años de historia de la Resistencia Nacional 2*, pp. 7, 9; Sancho, *Crónicas entre los espejos*, p. 73; Sancho interview; Montalvo interview; Jovel interview; Diaz, "Aproximación a la Historia del PRTC," p. 2.

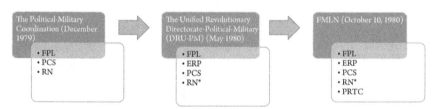

Figure A.11 Foundation of the FMLN from December 1979 to October 1980. Sources: Compiled from Coordinadora Político-Militar, "Se unifica la Izquierda," and Dirección Revolucionaria Unificada (DRU-PM), "Manifiesto de la Dirección Revolucionaria Unificada de las Organizaciones Político-Militares al pueblo salvadoreño, a los pueblos Centroamericanos y del mundo," and "Comunicado de la Dirección Revolucionaria Unificada (DRU-PM) a los pueblos de El Salvador, Centroamerica y el mundo,", *Pensamiento Revolucionario FMLN*, no. 12, pp. 3–6, 10–11, 15–16. *The RN withdrew from the DRU and eventually rejoined the FMLN on November 8, 1980.

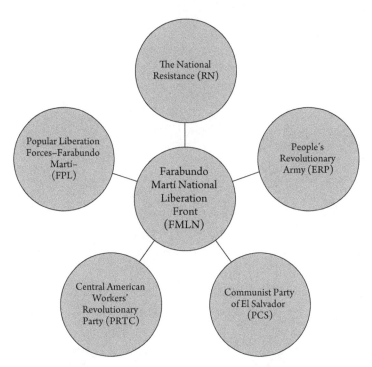

Figure A.12 Founding organizations of the historical FMLN. Source: Compiled from "Comunicado de la Dirección Revolucionaria Unificada (DRU-PM) a los pueblos de El Salvador, Centroamerica y el mundo," October 10, 1980, *Pensamiento Revolucionario FMLN*, no. 12, pp. 15–16.

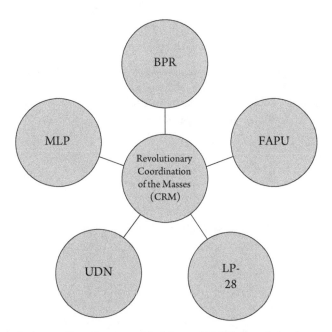

Figure A.13 Revolutionary Coordination of the Masses (CRM), founded in January 1980, the coordinating committee formed by the merger of revolutionary social movements and the UDN, the electoral party influenced by the PCS. Sources: Compiled from Escobar, "En la línea de la muerte," pp. 22–25, 28–30; and FAPU, LP-28, BPR, and UDN, "Nuestras organizaciones populares en marcha hacia la Unidad: Posición del FAPU, LP-28, BPR, UDN," mimeograph, January 11, 1980.

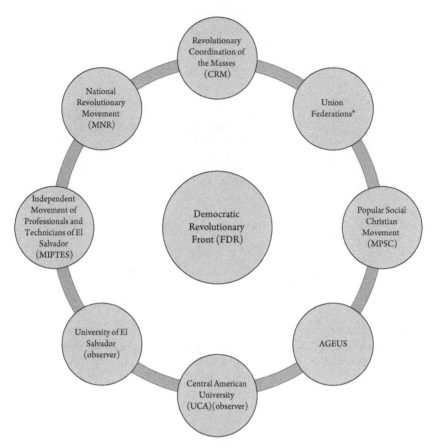

Figure A.14 The Democratic Revolutionary Front, founded in 1980. *FSR, FENASTRAS, FUSS, FESTIAVCES, STISS, and STIUSA. Source: Compiled from Frente Democrático Revolucionario (FDR), "Primera Declaración del Frente Democrático Revolucionario," April 18, 1980. http://www.cedema.org/ver.php?id=3877, accessed September 24, 2016.

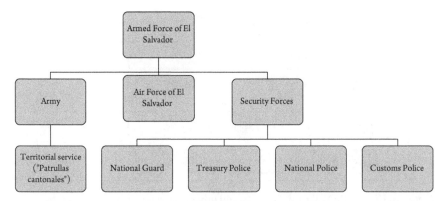

Figure A.15 Main components of the Armed Force of El Salvador between 1960 and 1980. Sources: Compiled from Montgomery, *Revolution in El Salvador*, p. 282n85; McClintock, *The American Connection*, pp. 169, 196–216.

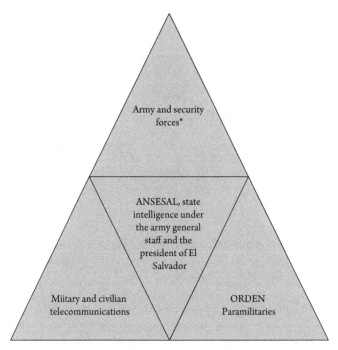

Figure A.16 Functioning of the Salvadoran National Security Agency (ANSESAL), the state intelligence agency, in the 1970s. *FALANGE, a death squad, apparently operated under ANSESAL control. Source: Compiled from McClintock, *The American Connection*, pp. 175, 219–221.

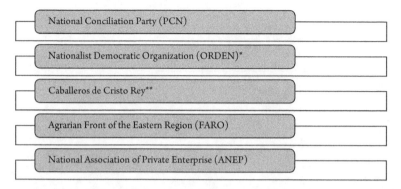

Figure A.17 The PCN, the official party, and other right-wing organizations in the 1970s. *State paramilitary network. **Catholic paramilitary group. Sources: Compiled from National Resistance, "Desenmascarando a los revisionistas de 'Voz Popular,'" in *Por La Causa Proletaria*, Year II, no. 15, February 1975, pp. 1–3; Sancho interview; Flamenco interview.

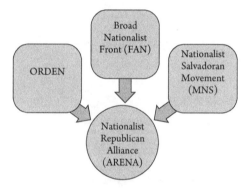

Figure A.18 Groups that constituted ARENA, 1980. Sources: Compiled from Koivumaeki, "El Salvador: Societal Cleavages, Strategic Elites, and the Success of the Right," p. 269; Mejívar Ochoa, *Tiempos de locura El Salvador 1979–1981*, pp. 189, 193.

NOTES

Introduction

1. Julio Cortázar, epilogue, "Una muerte mounstruosa: Roque Dalton," in Roque Dalton, *Pobrecito poeta que era yo* (San José, Costa Rica: EDUCA, 1976), p. 483.
2. Jorge G. Castañeda underlines the role played by the Departamento América, a Cuban state agency, in the origins of the revolutionary movements in El Salvador, Guatemala, and Nicaragua in the 1970s and 1980s. Jorge G. Castañeda, *Utopia Unarmed: The Latin American Left after the Cold War* (New York: Knopf, 1993), pp. 59–67.
3. Guevara penned the document in 1966, and it was published in 1967. Ernesto "Che" Guevara, "Two, Three, Many Vietnams" (1967), excerpt of "Message to the Tricontinental," in *Latin America and the United States: A Documentary History*, 2nd ed., ed. Robert H. Holden and Eric Zolov (New York: Oxford University Press, 2011), pp. 251–253.
4. Roque Dalton, *Revolución en la revolución? Y la crítica de Derecha*, Cuadernos Casa 9 (Havana: Casa de las Américas, 1970), pp. 10–11.
5. PRS-ERP, *Publicación especial octubre 1977: Balance histórico del 1er Congreso del PRS*, in *Prensa Comunista* (mimeograph, October 1977), pp. 37–38. For a thorough discussion of the characteristics of anti-intellectualism in Latin America in the late 1960s and early 1970s, see Claudia Gilman, *Entre la pluma y el fusil: Debates y dilemas del escritor revolucionario en América Latina* (Buenos Aires: Siglo XXI, 2003), pp. 163–167.
6. Miguel Huezo Mixco, "Roque Dalton: Un corazón aventurero," in Roque Dalton, *No pronuncies mi nombre: Poesia completa III* (San Salvador: Dirección de Publicaciones e Impresos CONCULTURA, 2008), p. 15.
7. Manlio Argueta, interview by Joaquín M. Chávez (June 22, 2012).
8. Roque Dalton et al., *El intelectual y la sociedad* (Mexico City: Siglo Veintiuno Editores, [1969] 1981).
9. Michiel Baud and Rosanne Rutten, eds., *Popular Intellectuals and Social Movements: Framing Protest in Asia, Africa, and Latin America* (Cambridge: Press Syndicate of the University of Cambridge, 2004), p. 2.
10. "About one in 56 Salvadorans lost their lives as a result of the conflict"; see Elisabeth Jean Wood, *Insurgent Collective Action and Civil War in El Salvador* (Cambridge: Cambridge University Press, 2003), p. 8.
11. James Dunkerley estimated that in 1987 the total number of internally displaced people and refugees as a result of the civil war reached between 1,176,900 and 1,606,900. There were 500,000 internally displaced people in El Salvador. The breakdown of the Salvadoran refugee population abroad was at follows: 900 in Panama, 6,200 in Costa Rica, 7,600 in Nicaragua, 24,000 in Honduras, 10,000 in Guatemala, between 120,000 and 250,000 in Mexico, between 500,000 and 800,000 in the United States, 4,600 in Canada, 600 in Australia, and 3,000 in Belize; see James Dunkerley, *The Pacification of Central America* (London: Verso, 1994), p. 47.

12. Carlos Rafael Cabarrús, *Génesis de una revolución: Análisis del surgimiento y desarrollo de la organización campesina en El Salvador* (Mexico City: Ediciones de la Casa Chata, 1983); Douglas Kincaid, "Peasants into Rebels: Community and Class in Rural El Salvador," *Comparative Studies in Society and History* 29, no. 3 (1987), pp. 466–494; Jenny Pearce, *Promised Land: Peasant Rebellion in Chalatenango, El Salvador* (London: Zed Books, 1986); Tommie Sue Montgomery, *Revolution in El Salvador: From Civil Strife to Civil Peace* (Boulder, CO: Westview Press, 1995); Wood, *Insurgent Collective Action and Civil War in El Salvador*; Leigh Binford, "Peasants, Catechists, Revolutionaries: Organic Intellectuals in the Salvadoran Revolution, 1980–1992," in *Landscapes of Struggle*, ed. Aldo Lauria-Santiago and Leigh Binford (Pittsburgh: University of Pittsburgh Press, 2004), pp. 105–125.

13. Chalatenango covers an area of approximately two thousand square kilometers. Antonio R. Arocha, *Cartograma histórico-geográfico de El Salvador: Síntesis de la geografía física y humana de la República de El Salvador* (San Salvador: Ediciones Culturales de la Compañía General de Seguros, 1985), p. 99.

14. Arocha, *Cartograma histórico-geográfico de El Salvador*, pp. 17–18.

15. Small landholdings in Chalatenango were legacies of indigo production in the eighteenth and nineteenth centuries; see Aldo A. Lauria-Santiago, *An Agrarian Republic: Commercial Agriculture and the Politics of Peasant Communities in El Salvador, 1823–1914* (Pittsburgh: University of Pittsburgh Press, 1999), pp. 21–22, 75, 200–204. Despite the decline of indigo production in the twentieth century, some *minifundistas* still planted and processed indigo in hamlets near La Nueva Trinidad and Arcatao in 1975. They epitomized the impoverished peasant communities of distinct Spanish origin living in this area; see Concepción Clará de Guevara, "El Añil de Los 'Indios Cheles,'" *America Indígena* 35, no. 4 (1975): 778–794.

16. The anthropologist Carlos Cabarrús labeled "ideological unblocking" the emergence of a progressive religious and political consciousness among peasant communities in Aguilares in the early 1970s. The pastoral work conducted by Jesuits and the pedagogical activities carried out by university students (some of them Jesuit students) with *delegados de la palabra* (lay preachers) created this new social consciousness. Cabarrús, *Génesis de una revolución*, pp. 141–163.

17. For a discussion of the meaning of the term "New Left" in the Latin American context, see Eric Zolov, "Expanding Our Conceptual Horizons: The Shift from an Old to a New Left in Latin America," *A Contracorriente: A Journal on Social History and Literature in Latin America* 5, no. 2 (2008): 48–53.

18. Joaquín M. Chávez, "How Did the Civil War in El Salvador End?," *American Historical Review* 120, no. 5 (2015): 1784–1797.

19. Scholars offer similar readings of the trajectory of Soviet relations with Latin America and the origins of the Latin American New Left between 1959 and 1980. They frame this discussion in the context of major shifts in Soviet foreign policy, from Khrushchev's peaceful coexistence with the West in the 1960s, to Brezhnev's support of revolutionary movements and pro-socialist states in the 1970s, to Gorbachev's emphasis on mutual dependency and cooperation between the Soviet Union and the West in the mid-1980s. Jan S. Adams, *A Foreign Policy in Transition: Moscow's Retreat from Central America and the Caribbean, 1985–1992* (Durham, NC: Duke University Press, 1992), pp. 10–12.

20. That is, "a mixture of libertarian voluntarism and ethical idealism," featured in Marx's earlier writings; see FLACSO El Salvador and Fundación "Dr. Manuel Gallardo," *Prensa clandestina: El Salvador 1970–1975* (San Salvador: FLACSO El Salvador and Fundación "Dr. Manuel Gallardo," 2011), p. 112.

21. Jeremy Varon, *Bringing the War Home: The Weather Underground, the Red Army Faction, and Revolutionary Violence in the Sixties and Seventies* (Berkeley: University of California Press, 2004), p. 1.

22. Atilio Montalvo, interview by Joaquín M. Chávez (November 6, 2006).

23. Varon, *Bringing the War Home*, pp. 2–4.

24. Martin Klimke, *The Other Alliance: Student Protest in West Germany and the United States in the Global Sixties* (Princeton, NJ: Princeton University Press, 2010), pp. 1–9.

25. I list here the best-known guerrilla groups of the early 1970s, although other insurgent groups also emerged in that period. Lesser-known organizations like the "F.C.R., AORI, and FRAP"

had a fleeting existence at that time. Resistencia Nacional, *Por la causa proletaria: Apuntes para el estudio de 13 años de historia de la Resistencia Nacional #2* (mimeograph, June 1983), pp. 7, 9.

26. Domingo Santacruz, interview by Joaquín M. Chávez (April 17, 2007).
27. Resistencia Nacional, *Por la causa proletaria*, pp. 7, 9; Eduardo Sancho, *Crónicas entre los espejos*, 2nd ed. (San Salvador: Editorial Universidad Francisco Gavidia, 2003), p. 73.
28. Eduardo Sancho, interview by Joaquín M. Chávez (June 19, 2012).
29. Marta Harnecker, *Con la mirada en alto: Historia de Las Fuerzas Populares de Liberación Farabundo Martí a través de entrevistas con sus dirigentes* (San Salvador: UCA Editores, 1993), p. 15.
30. Montalvo interview.
31. Resistencia Nacional, *Por la causa proletaria*, p. 10.
32. Francisco Jovel, interview by Joaquín M. Chávez (April 18, 2007). According to Nidia Diaz, a former FMLN commander, the founders of the ORT were "Francisco Jovel, Fabio Castillo Figueroa, Manuel Federico Castillo, Roberto Galeano, Francisco Montes, Alfonso Hernández, Nidia Diaz, Mercedes Turcios, Acosta, Luis Diaz, Mario López, Humberto Mendoza, Joaquín Morales Chávez, Margarita Villa Franco, [and] Ricardo Sol." Nidia Diaz, "Aproximación a la historia del PRTC" (mimeograph, undated), p. 2.
33. Díaz, "Aproximación a la historia del PRTC," p. 3.
34. Resistencia Nacional, *Por la causa proletaria*, pp. 15, 16.
35. Arno J. Mayer, *The Furies: Violence and Terror in the French and Russian Revolutions* (Princeton:, NJ Princeton University Press, 2000), p. 4.
36. A dominant narrative on the origins and social composition of the Salvadoran insurgency has been established during the past two decades. It posits that university students and dissidents of political parties formed the Salvadoran guerrillas. See, for instance, Timothy P. Wickham-Crowley, *Guerrillas and Revolution in Latin America: A Comparative Study of Insurgents and Regimes since 1956* (Princeton, NJ: Princeton University Press, 1992), pp. 30–48, 219–225; Yvon Grenier, *The Emergence of Insurgency in El Salvador: Ideology and Political Will* (Pittsburgh: University of Pittsburgh Press, 1999), pp. 33, 34; and Manuel Montobbio, *La metamorfosis del pulgarcito: Transición política y proceso de paz en El Salvador* (Barcelona: Icaria Antrazyt-FLACSO, 1999), p. 257.
37. Gabriel Zaid, *De los libros al poder* (Mexico City: Grijalbo), pp. 157–213; Wickham-Crowley, *Guerrillas and Revolution in Latin America*, pp. 30–48, 211, 219–225, Grenier, *The Emergence of Insurgency in El Salvador*, pp. 33, 34, 42, 134–135, 67; Montobbio, *La metamorfosis del pulgarcito*, p. 257; Montgomery, *Revolution in El Salvador*, pp. 103–104; Hugh Byrne, *El Salvador's Civil War: A Study of Revolution* (Boulder, CO: Lynne Rienner, 1996), p. 34; Cynthia McClintock, *Revolutionary Movements in Latin America: El Salvador's FMLN and Peru's Shining Path* (Washington, DC: United States Institute of Peace Press, 1998), pp. 49–51; and Wood, *Insurgent Collective Action and Civil War in El Salvador*, p. 11.
38. Fina Rubio and Eduard Balsebre, *Rompiendo silencios: Desobediencia y lucha en Villa El Rosario* (Barcelona: REDSolidaridad and MUPI, 2009), pp. 80, 81, 93.
39. Grenier, *The Emergence of Insurgency in El Salvador*, pp. 2, 33–34.
40. Grenier argued that the rebels were not simply the byproducts of deeply ingrained structural processes (i.e., social exclusion and state repression) but the incarnation of "a distinct and forceful political will"; see Grenier, *The Emergence of Insurgency in El Salvador*, p. 33.
41. Zaid called the Salvadoran insurgency a "university guerrilla [movement]"; see Zaid, *De los libros al poder*, pp. 157–213.
42. Castañeda, *Utopia Unarmed*, pp. 59–67.
43. Carlos Eduardo Rico Mira, one of the first guerrilla operatives in El Salvador in the early 1970s, wrote about his training in Cuba. Rico Mira reported that he and Roque Dalton joined a military school in Cuba circa 1971; see Carlos Eduardo Rico Mira, *En silencio tenía que ser: Testimonio del conflicto armado en El Salvador (1967–2000)* (San Salvador: UFG Editores, 2003), pp. 54–71.
44. The roles that Catholics played in the mobilizations of the 1970s and 1980s in El Salvador have been widely analyzed. But despite the ubiquitous roles that Catholic Action intellectuals played in the formation of the New Left, their contributions to these movements have rarely been considered in the academic literature. Phillip Berryman, *The Religious Roots of Rebellion* (New York: Orbis Books, 1984); Jon Sobrino, Ignacio Martín-Baró, and Rodolfo Cardenal,

eds., *La voz de los sin voz: La palabra viva de Monseñor Romero*, 7th ed. (San Salvador: UCA Editores, [1980] 2007); Anna L. Peterson, *Martyrdom and the Politics of Religion: Progressive Catholicism in El Salvador's Civil War* (Albany: State University of New York Press, 1997); Rodolfo Cardenal, *Historia de una esperanza: Vida de Rutilio Grande* (San Salvador: UCA Editores, 1987); Teresa Whitfield, *Paying the Price: Ignacio Ellacuría and the Murdered Jesuits of El Salvador* (Philadelphia: Temple University Press, 1994); Robert Lassalle-Klein, *Blood and Ink: Ignacio Ellacuría, Jon Sobrino, and the Jesuit Martyrs of the University of Central America* (Maryknoll, NY: Orbis Books, 2014); Binford, "Peasants, Catechists, Revolutionaries," pp. 105–125; Jeffrey Gould and Charles R. Hale, "Utopías menores en América Central en la segunda mitad del siglo XX," Asociación para el Fomento de los Estudios Históricos en Centroamérica, April–June 2012, http://www.afehc-historia-centroamericana.org/. The sociologist Juan Ramón Vega wrote a short text on ACUS; see Vega, *Las comunidades cristianas de base en America Central: Estudio sociológico* (San Salvador: Publicaciones del Arzobispado de San Salvador, 1994), pp. 74–75.

45. Vega, *Las comunidades cristianas*, p. 75.

46. Jorge Vargas Méndez and J. A. Morasan, *Literatura salvadoreña 1960–2000: Homenaje* (San Salvador: Ediciones Venado del Bosque, 2008), pp. 62–71.

47. The scholarship on militarism, elite politics, and authoritarianism in El Salvador is substantial; see Rafael Guidos Véjar, *Ascenso del militarismo en El Salvador* (San José, Costa Rica: Editorial Universitaria Centroamericana, 1982); William Stanley, *The Protection Racket State: Elite Politics, Military Extortion, and Civil War in El Salvador* (Philadelphia: Temple University Press, 1996); Jeffrey M. Paige, *Coffee and Power: Revolution and the Rise of Democracy in Central America* (Cambridge, MA: Harvard University Press, 1997); Jeff Godwin, *No Other Way Out: States and Revolutionary Movements, 1945–1991* (Cambridge: Cambridge University Press, 2001); and Erik Ching, *Authoritarian El Salvador: Politics and the Origins of the Military Regimes, 1880–1940* (Notre Dame, IN: University of Notre Dame Press, 2014).

48. Héctor Lindo-Fuentes and Erik Ching, *Modernizing Minds in El Salvador: Education Reform and the Cold War, 1960–1980* (Albuquerque: University of New Mexico Press, 2012), pp. 19–20.

49. Walter LaFeber famously made this case. Walter LaFeber, *Inevitable Revolutions: The United States in Central America*, 2nd ed. (New York: Norton, 1993).

50. James Dunkerley, *The Long War: Dictatorship and Revolution in El Salvador* (London: Verso, 1985), pp. 75–76; Montgomery, *Revolution in El Salvador*, pp. 54–56; Stephen G. Rabe, *The Killing Zone: The United States Wages Cold War in Latin America* (Oxford: Oxford University Press, 2012), p. 165; LaFeber, *Inevitable Revolutions*, pp. 173–178.

51. "[Presidents] Kennedy and Johnson ensured that it received more Alliance funds ($63 million between 1962 and 1965) than any other Central American country. In 1964 the C.I.A. called it 'one of the hemisphere's most stable, progressive republics.'" LaFeber, *Inevitable Revolutions*, pp. 173–174.

52. Montgomery, *Revolution in El Salvador*, p. 54; Dunkerley, *The Long War*, pp. 76–79.

53. Dunkerley, *The Long War*, p. 53.

54. LaFeber, *Inevitable Revolutions*, pp. 176–177.

55. Montgomery, *Revolution in El Salvador*, pp. 59–67; Dunkerley, *The Long War*, pp. 80–86; Paul D. Almeida, *Waves of Protest: Popular Struggle in El Salvador, 1925–2005* (Minneapolis: University of Minnesota Press, 2008), pp. 70–102.

56. Dunkerley, *The Long War*, pp. 75–76; Montgomery, *Revolution in El Salvador*, pp. 54–56; Rabe, *The Killing Zone*, p. 165; LaFeber, *Inevitable Revolutions*, pp. 173–178.

57. Walter LaFeber wrote a lapidary statement that summarized this view: "The decade of the Alliance ended in El Salvador as the decade of revolution began. The country that Johnson believed to be the 'model' for the Alliance became instead a model for violent Central American revolutions." LaFeber, *Inevitable Revolutions*, p. 178.

58. The Sandinista Revolution had major reverberations in the Americas, but ironically, it caught Soviet specialists by surprise. Still, it informed a crucial reassessment of Soviet foreign policy in the region. Specialists at *Latinskaia Amerika* (the journal of the Latin American Institute of the USSR Academy of Sciences) and the Institute of World Economy and International Relations pondered the strategic implications of the Sandinista Revolution. They revisited

debates considered passé on armed or peaceful paths to revolution, revolutionary vanguards, the reunification of the left, and revolutionary programs in Latin America. Edmé Domínguez, "The Latin American Communist Movement: Realities and Relations with the Soviet Union," in *The USSR and Latin America: A Developing Relationship*, ed. Eusebio Mujal-León (Boston: Unwin Hyman, 1989), pp. 135–136.

59. Captain Juan-Juan, a Salvadoran combatant who fought alongside the Sandinistas in Nicaragua, remembered the fetid smell of that place, which doubled as a torture center. "It smelled to death," he said. La Columna Farabundista was named after Farabundo Martí. Juan-Juan, interview by Joaquín Chávez (January 13, 2015).

60. As in the 1960s, support of revolutionary movements in Central America once again became a centerpiece of Cuba's foreign policy at that time. Over the years, scholars specializing in Soviet and US foreign policy in Central America have claimed that the formation of the FMLN, a theme that will be discussed in this book, was largely the byproduct of a Cuban initiative. They also maintained that starting in 1980, the FMLN insurgency received vast amounts of weapons from Cuba and member states of the Warsaw Pact. In this same vein, they asserted that during El Salvador's civil war, Nicaragua became the main logistical hub and headquarters of the FMLN. Edward A. Lynch, for instance, credits Fidel Castro for the creation of the FMLN. Edward A. Lynch, *The Cold War's Last Battlefield: Reagan, the Soviets and Central America* (Albany: State University of New York Press, 2011), pp. 19, 53. Similarly, Richard H. Shultz wrote that Manuel Piñeiro, the chief of the Americas Department of the Cuban Communist Party, played a major role in the foundation of the FMLN. Furthermore, he claimed that the prolonged people's war strategy conducted by the FMLN in the aftermath of its 1981 offensive was modeled after the war strategy carried out by the Sandinista faction led by Tomás Borge. Contrary to what Schultz wrote, the FPL had conceptualized that strategy since the early 1970s. Richard H. Shultz Jr., *The Soviet Union and Revolutionary Warfare: Principles, Practices, and Regional Comparisons* (Stanford, CA: Hoover Institute Press, 1988), pp. 157–159.

61. The Christian Democrat–military junta (also known as the Second Revolutionary Government Junta) replaced the failed Revolutionary Government Junta created in October 1979 after a group of military officers who called themselves El Movimiento de la Juventud Militar "(the Movement of the Military Youth) ousted General Carlos H. Romero, a de facto president imposed by the PCN and high-ranking military after they rigged the 1977 presidential election.

62. Odd Arne Westad, *The Global Cold War: Third World Intervention and the Making of Our Time* (Cambridge: Cambridge University Press, 2008), pp. 331, 338–339.

63. Lynch, *The Cold War's Last Battlefield*, p. 88; Hal Brands, *Latin America's Cold War* (Cambridge, MA: Harvard University Press, 2010), pp. 193, 198, 202, 217; Shultz, *The Soviet Union and Revolutionary Warfare*, pp. 157–159.

64. "Despite its avowedly reformist character, the human rights situation in El Salvador has steadily worsened since the Revolutionary Governing Junta came to power on October 15, 1979. In fact, not since *la Matanza*, the 1932 massacre of as many as 30,000 peasants, has the human rights situation in El Salvador been as bad as it is now. . . . The U.S. government has increased its diplomatic, economic, and military support for El Salvador precisely during the period when human rights violations there have accelerated. Both the Carter and Reagan administrations have followed this policy." See Americas Watch Committee and the American Civil Liberties Union, *Report on Human Rights in El Salvador* (New York: Vintage Books, 1982), p. xlvii. The Socorro Jurídicio Cristiano, a human rights office sponsored by the archdiocese of San Salvador, estimated that 16,266 civilians were killed by state forces in 1981. The Centro de Documentación e Información, a research and documentation center at the Central American University (UCA), estimated that 11,727 civilians were murdered by state forces that year. Stanley offers a monthly breakdown of the number of victims of state forces in 1981; see Stanley, *The Protection Racket State*, table 4, p. 223.

65. Michael McClintock, *The American Connection* vol. 1, *State Terror and Popular Resistance in El Salvador* (London: Zed Books, 1985), pp. 172–173.

66. Joaquín M. Chávez, "El Salvador—The Creation of the Internal Enemy: Pondering the Legacies of U.S. Anticommunism, Counterinsurgency, and Authoritarianism in El Salvador (1952–1981)," in *Hearts and Minds: A People's History of Counterinsurgency*, ed. Hannah Gurman (New York: New Press, 2013), p. 128.

67. The following were the main archives I used for my research: The National Archives of El Salvador, the Historical Archive of the Archdiocese of San Salvador, the Archive of the University of El Salvador, the Documentation and Information Center (CIDAI) at the Central American University, the Museo de la Palabra y la Imágen (MUPI), and the Archives of the National Anthropology Museum David J. Guzmán. I also worked at the following archives in the United States: the National Archives and Records Administration, the National Security Archives at George Washington University, and Bobst Library at New York University.

68. I conducted the interviews under a research protocol approved by the Committee on Activities Involving Human Subjects of New York University.

69. I was cognizant of studies, testimonies, and literary work about the origins of the peasant movement in that area, which were inspirational for my research. Pearce, *Promised Land*; Fernando Áscoli, "El sugimiento de la conciencia: Memoria de Chalatenango" (mimeograph, 2005); Manlio Argueta, *Un día en la vida* (San Salvador: UCA Editores, [1980] 2008).

70. This is probably what Elizabeth J. Wood termed "pleasure in agency"; see Wood, *Insurgent Collective Action and Civil War in El Salvador*, pp. 234–237.

71. Roque Dalton, *No pronuncies mi nombre: Roque Dalton poesía completa III* (San Salvador: Dirección de Publicaciones e Impresos CONCULTURA, 2008), pp. 633–635.

72. Dalton, *No pronuncies mi nombre*, p. 98.

73. My analysis of interactions between urban and peasant intellectuals in El Salvador is clearly informed by Gramsci's classical discussion on intellectuals. Gramsci considers every human being an intellectual in that every form of labor or social production requires rationalization and certain skills. However, from a social perspective, Gramsci deems intellectuals those individuals who perform leadership, educational, and organizational functions in processes of state formation. Gramsci writes that intellectuals perform two main functions in state formation, namely, the organization of "social hegemony" and "political government." Intellectuals do not represent an autonomous social group in processes of state formation, that is, they do not constitute a hegemonic group in terms of either capital accumulation or political and ideological leadership. Instead, Gramsci posits that each emerging social group (or class) generates one or several strata of intellectuals that he calls "organic intellectuals." that is, technicians, planners, politicians, and professionals directly linked to the economic and political interests of the rising social group. Gramsci also refers to another category of intellectuals that he terms "traditional," that is, those who have played intellectual functions in previous modes of production or political regimes. Antonio Gramsci, *Selections from the Prison Notebooks*, ed. Quintin Hoare and Geoffrey Nowell Smith (New York: International Publishers, 1999), pp. 5–15.

Chapter 1

1. Santacruz interview (April 17, 2007). The Soviet Union generally opposed the existence of armed revolutionary movements in Latin America in the 1960s; see Wayne Smith, "The End of World Revolution in Latin America," in *The Russians Aren't Coming: New Soviet Policy in Latin America*, ed. Wayne Smith (Boulder, CO: Lynne Rienner, 1992), p. 37.

2. Scholars concur that the Lemus regime oscillated between a partial political opening and repression; see Montgomery, *Revolution in El Salvador*, pp. 48–49; Almeida, *Waves of Protest*, pp. 61–63.

3. Members of the Partido Revolucionario Abril y Mayo (PRAM) included social democrats, "radicalized liberals," and communists. Héctor Dada Hirezi, interview by Joaquín Chávez (April 23, 2007). PRAM's name alluded to the civic-military mobilizations against the dictator Maximiliano Hernández Martínez in April and May 1944. The Frente Nacional de Orientación Cívica (FNOC) was a center-left coalition made up of political parties and social movements. The PRAM, the Partido de Acción Renovadora (PAR), the Radical Democratic Party (PRD), the General Association of Salvadoran University Students (AGEUS), and the General Confederation of Salvadoran Workers (CGTS) made up FNOC. Víctor Valle, *Siembra de vientos El Salvador 1960–69* (San Salvador: CINAS, 1993), pp. 42–47.

4. Valle, *Siembra de vientos*, pp. 44–45; "Fidel Castro Planea Más Fusilamientos," *La Prensa Gráfica* January 4, 1960, p. 5; "Castro Militariza al Campesino Cubano," *La Prensa Gráfica*, January 9, 1960, pp. 4, 25.

5. Greg Grandin, *The Last Colonial Massacre: Latin America in the Cold War*, 2nd ed. (Chicago: University of Chicago Press, [2004] 2011), p. 5. The literature on the CIA coup against Arbenz is vast. See, for instance, Nick Cullather, *Secret History: The Cia's Classified Account of Its Operations in Guatemala 1952–1954* (Stanford, CA: Stanford University Press, 1999); Piero Gleijeses, *Shattered Hope: The Guatemalan Revolution and the United States, 1944–1954* (Princeton, NJ: Princeton University Press, 1991).

6. Anonymous informant 1, interview by Joaquín Chávez (March 20, 2007).

7. Correspondence between President José María Lemus and the rector of the University of El Salvador, Dr. Romeo Fortín Magaña: "Exposición de motivos al Presidente de la República," October 1, 1958; "Carta al Presidente Lemus sobre Derechos Legítimos de la Universidad," September 24, 1958; "Carta al Presidente de la Republica sobre Autonomía Universitaria," August 12, 1958; "Contestación del Presidente de la República sobre los problemas de autonomía universitaria," August 28, 1958; and "Carta réplica del rector al Presidente de la República sobre autonomía de la universidad," undated, in *La Universidad*, (July–December 1958): 389–408.

8. For discussions on Osorio's position regarding the CIA coup against Arbenz, see Fabio Castillo, "Episodios desconocidos de la historia Centroamericana," *Cartas Centroamericanas*, July 1986, p. 5; and Cullather, *Secret History*, pp. 48–49, 88. Abraham Rodríguez, a university student leader in the early 1950s, stated that the ousting of Arbenz did not have major repercussions in Salvadoran politics. Abraham Rodríguez, interview by Joaquín Chávez (December 27, 2006).

9. Most analyses of the origins of the Salvadoran civil war focus on the internal causes of the conflict; see, for instance, Cabarrús, *Génesis de una revolución*; Kincaid, "Peasants into Rebels"; Montgomery, *Revolution in El Salvador*; Pearce, *Promised Land*; and Wood, *Insurgent Collective Action and Civil War in El Salvador*.

10. University intellectuals were ubiquitous actors in the formation of the Salvadoran guerrillas in the 1970s. Wickham-Crowley, *Guerrillas and Revolution in Latin America*, p. 30.

11. "This coup was under the total direction of the Central Intelligence Agency (CIA) through the Military Mission of that country. In this way, it modified the character of state power in El Salvador: before January 25, 1961, the governments, even if they served Yankee imperialism, were governments of the oligarchy, which it directed and profited from. Since that date the governments (the directory [*sic*]), Cordón's [the provisional president that followed the Directorate] and the one that Julio Rivera attempt[ed]to lead) are, in contrast, manufactured by US imperialism, are directly in its service and only serve secondarily the interest of the oligarchy. It is precisely this change in the control of state power that proves that we are being victims of an accelerated process of colonization that will transform us, if we don't stop it, into the second 'Free Associate State' of the United States, in the second Puerto Rico." Tercera Plenaria Nacional del FUAR, "Proyecto plataforma programática del FUAR" (mimeograph, May 1962), p. 8.

12. Ernest B. Vaccaro, "U.S. Warned to Guard Hemisphere Interests," *Washington Post*, March 26, 1957, p. A6.

13. Department of State (DOS), Office of Central American and Panamanian Affairs (OCPA), US National Archives and Records Administration (NARA), box 1, years 1958–1960, entry A1 3159: Records Relating to El Salvador (1958–1975), folder: Lemus Visit (1960), "Visit of President Lemus of El Salvador—Memo from Mr. Rubottom to Acting Assistant Secretary of State," September 24, 1958.

14. Five State Department officials identified as Buchanan, Hall, Murphy, Olson, and Lightner signed a "position paper" regarding Lemus's state visit. DOS-OCPA, NARA, box 1, years 1958–1960, entry A1 3159: Records Relating to El Salvador (1958–1975), folder: Lemus Visit Briefing Book (1959) DAP 64D16, E., "State Visit by Salvadoran President Lemus March 10–20 1959, Position Paper Communist Activities in El Salvador," March 10–20, 1959.

15. Almeida, *Waves of Protest*, p. 59.

16. DOS-OCPA, NARA, box 1, years 1958–1960, entry A1 3159: Records Relating to El Salvador (1958–1975), folder: Lemus Visit Briefing Book (1959) DAP 64D16, E., "State Visit by Salvadoran President Lemus March 10–20 1959, Position Paper Communist Activities in El Salvador."

17. DOS-OCPA, NARA, box 1, years 1958–1960, entry A1 3159: Records Relating to El Salvador (1958–1975), folder: Lemus Visit Briefing Book (1959) DAP 64D16, E., "State Visit by Salvadoran President Lemus March 10–20 1959, Position Paper Communist Activities in El Salvador."

18. DOS-OCPA, NARA, box 1, years 1958–1960, entry A1 3159: Records Relating to El Salvador (1958–1975), folder: Lemus Visit Briefing Book (1959) DAP 64D16, F, "State Visit by Salvadoran President Lemus March 10–20 1959, Position Paper."

19. DOS-NARA, box 1, years 1958–1960, entry A1 3159: Records Relating to El Salvador (1958–1975), folder: Labor—El Salvador (1960), "Memorandum of Conversation—Participants: Thorsten V. Kalijarvi, American Ambassador, Serafino Romualdi, Inter American Representative of Orit [Inter-American Regional Organization of Workers], Andrew McClellan, Latin American Representative of the International Federation of Food and Drink Workers, Bruce Green, Labor Advisor USOM, William B. Sowash, Labor Reporting Officer; Subject: Various Labor Matters," March 23, 1960.

20. Dada interview.

21. Almeida, *Waves of Protest*, p. 61.

22. Valle, *Siembra de vientos*, pp. 42–47.

23. DOS-OCPA, NARA, box 1, years 1958–1960, entry A1 3159: Records Relating to El Salvador (1958–1975), folder: Political International—General; El Salvador (1960), "Memorandum of Conversation—Present: Lt. Col. Jose Maria Lemus President of El Salvador, C. Allan Stewart, Director Office of Central American and Panamanian Affairs, State Department, and Donald P. Downs, Chargé d'affairs, U.S. Embassy in El Salvador," June 7, 1960.

24. Almeida, *Waves of Protest*, p. 61.

25. Montgomery, *Revolution in El Salvador*, p. 48; Valle, *Siembra de vientos*, pp. 42–47.

26. Montgomery, *Revolution in El Salvador*, pp. 48–49.

27. Schafik Hándal, a leader of the PCS, became the coordinator of the FUAR. Santacruz interview.

28. Valle, *Siembra de vientos*, pp. 42–47, 50.

29. Consejo Superior Universitario, Archive of the University of El Salvador, "Minutes of the Meeting of the Supreme University Council, August 29, 1960."

30. "Carta del Presidente Lemus al rector de La Universidad de El Salvador," (September 1, 1960), *La Prensa Gráfica*, September 2, 1960, p. 13.

31. "Atropellos crean ambiente de indignación y zozobra," "Muere golpeado," "En el hospital," "Manifestación de duelo," "Solicita exhibición personal," "Estudiantes golpeados reconocidos por el juez," and "Estado de Sitio en todo el país," *La Prensa Gráfica*, September 3, 1960, p. 3.

32. "500 Mil Cols. en daño a La Universidad," *La Prensa Gráfica*, September 7, 1960, pp. 3, 18.

33. Oscar Fernández, interview by Joaquín Chávez (March 21, 2007).

34. Judge Alas personally inspected the campus. He stated that "phones, furniture, academic titles, . . . blackboards, file cabinets, . . . professional documents and didactic material" were destroyed during the raid. Judge Alas reported that the National Police and the National Guard damaged "aisles, rooms, the offices of the Rectory, classrooms, bathrooms, warehouses" as they perforated "big holes" in the walls in order to capture people who took refuge in those places. "Files, money and many other objects of the University and of employees" also disappeared during the charge. Judge Alas and the forensic experts who accompanied him showed particular indignation at the destruction of the portrait of Francisco Gavidia. "500 Mil Cols. En Daño a La Universidad," pp. 3, 18.

35. René Angulo Urbina, an economics student at the National University, suffered cranial fractures, as well as "blows in the face and in other parts of the body." Forensic experts performed "medical-legal" exams on Teodoro Abel Moreno Guillén, Elda Lucila Guirola, Orlando López Peña, Roberto Góchez Hill, Rodolfo Ramírez Amaya, Vicente Argueta Escobar, Lotario Bayardo Gomez, Bonifacio García, and numerous other victims of the raid who received medical treatment "at various medical centers of the capital." "En el hospital" and "Estudiantes golpeados reconocidos por el juez," *La Prensa Gráfica*, September 6, 1960, pp. 3, 38.

36. "Manifestación de duelo," *La Prensa Gráfica*, September 6, 1960, p. 3.

37. "Señora de síndico relata atropello," *La Prensa Gráfica*, September 7, 1960, pp. 3, 15.

38. Adrián Roberto Aldana, *Aventuras y desventuras de un periodista Salvadoreño* (San Salvador, circa 1985), p. 97; "Canessa agradece foto que le salvó la vida," *La Prensa Gráfica*, October 31, 1960, p. 5; "Ex-Canciller detenido," *La Prensa Gráfica*, September 4, 1960, p. 1.

39. José Reales Escobar, Angel Carballo Domínguez, José Snaton Bolaños Iraheta, and José Balbino Rivera Herrera were labeled "Dalton's bodyguards" by Lemus's public relations office. "Severo Mentís a Los Profesionales de La Calumnia y La Mentira: Roque Dalton García Capturado," advertisement published by Relaciones Públicas de Casa Presidencial in *La Prensa Gráfica*, October 13, 1960, p. 31.

40. Salvador Cayetano Carpio, a member of the PCS's political commission in the 1950s, discussed the formation of GAR with Marta Harnecker. Harnecker, *Con la mirada en alto*, p. 24.

41. DOS-OCPA, NARA, box 1, years 1958–1960, entry A1 3159: Records Relating to El Salvador (1958–1975), folder: Junta Memoranda, "Memorandum of Conversation, Participants: Roberto Dutriz, Business Manager, La Prensa Gráfica and Robert F. Delaney, Public Affairs Officer U.S. Embassy in El Salvador," September 13, 1960. The word "Prensa" underlined in the original.

42. DOS-OCPA, NARA, box 1, years 1958–1960, entry A1 3159: Records Relating to El Salvador (1958–1975), folder: Junta Memoranda, "Memorandum of Conversation, Participants: Roberto Dutriz, Business Manager, La Prensa Gráfica and Robert F. Delaney, Public Affairs Officer U.S. Embassy in El Salvador," September 13, 1960.

43. DOS-OCPA, NARA, box 1, years 1958–1960, entry A1 3159: Records Relating to El Salvador (1958–1975), folder: Junta Memoranda, "Memorandum of Conversation between Monsignor Luis Chavez y Gonzalez, Archbishop of San Salvador and Robert F. Delaney Public Affairs Officer, U.S. Embassy in El Salvador," September 12, 1960.

44. DOS-OCPA, NARA, box 1, years 1958–1960, entry A1 3159: Records Relating to El Salvador (1958–1975), folder: Junta Memoranda, "Memorandum of Conversation, Participants: H.E. President José María Lemus and Ambassador Thorsten V. Kalikarji," September 16, 1960.

45. Valle, *Siembra de vientos*, p. 49.

46. DOS-OCPA, NARA, box 1, years 1958–1960, entry A1 3159: Records Relating to El Salvador (1958–1975), folder: Junta Memoranda, "Memorandum of Conversation, Participants: H.E. President José María Lemus and Ambassador Thorsten V. Kalikarji," September 16, 1960.

47. DOS-OCPA, NARA, box 1, years 1958–1960, entry A1 3159: Records Relating to El Salvador (1958–1975), folder: Junta Memoranda, "Memorandum of Conversation, Participants: H.E. President José María Lemus and Ambassador Thorsten V. Kalikarji," September 16, 1960.

48. DOS-OCPA, NARA, box 1, years 1958–1960, entry A1 3159: Records Relating to El Salvador (1958–1975), folder: Junta Memoranda, "Memorandum of Conversation, Participants: H.E. President José María Lemus and Ambassador Thorsten V. Kalikarji," September 16, 1960.

49. "Rectores de Centroamérica Llegan al País," *La Prensa Gráfica*, September 26, 1960, p. 1.

50. Consejo Superior Universitario, Archive of the University of El Salvador, "Minutes of the Meeting of the Supreme University Council, October 17, 1960."

51. The term "economic autonomy" refers to the allocation of an adequate budget for the university in the national budget. *Consejo Superior Universitario*, Archive of the University of El Salvador, "Minutes of the Meeting of the Supreme University Council, October 28, 1960."

52. Consejo Superior Universitario, Archive of the University of El Salvador, "Minutes of the Meeting of the Supreme University Council, November 4, 1960."

53. Consejo Superior Universitario, Archive of the University of El Salvador, "Minutes of the Meeting of the Supreme University Council, November 4, 1960."

54. Abel Salazar Rodezno told the press a similar story to Dalton's: "I have lost 32 pounds as a consequence of all the sufferings I experienced at the National Police [headquarters] and the penitentiary. At the detention center I was subject to constant interrogation. At the penitentiary, along with other political prisoners, I was held at the famous cell number 9 reserved for hardened criminals." "Recobran su libertad los detenidos políticos," *La Prensa Gráfica*, October 27, 1960, p. 21.

55. Two additional brief openings occurred in the aftermath of the 1932 repression, one in 1944 after the ousting of the dictator Hernández Martínez and another at the time of the "1948 Revolution." Almeida, *Waves of Protest*, p. 9; Tula Alvarenga, interview by Joaquín Chávez (February 3, 2014).

56. "Junta de gobierno expone su ideología," *La Prensa Gráfica*, November 1, 1960, pp. 3, 17.

57. "Es arrestado agente acusado de torturas," *La Prensa Gráfica*, November 9, 1960, pp. 3 and 34.

58. "Devuelven ficha policial en Casa Presidencial," *La Prensa Grafica*, November 6, 1960, pp. 3, 20.
59. Castillo Figueroa, "Los problemas de democratización y de educación siempre presentes: Hace 36 años los dos proyectos de la Junta de Gobierno," *Co-Latino*, October 26, 1996, p. 6.
60. Fabio Castillo Figueroa, "Vivencia y trascendencia social de El Salvador," in *La auditoria social*, José Antonio Ventura Sosa ed. (San Salvador: Avanti Gráfica S.A. de C.V., 2002), pp. 30–41.
61. Castillo Figueroa, "Los problemas de democratización y de educación," p. 7; René Fortín Magaña, "Cuarenta años después: Hechos y comentarios," *Co Latino*, January 9, 2001, pp. 14–15.
62. "Boletín del Frente de Orientación Civica," *La Prensa Gráfica*, October 27, 1960, pp. 3, 28.
63. "Boletín de Prensa del PRAM," in "Refiéranse a Atentado contra Fiscal," *La Prensa Gráfica*, December 23, 1960, pp. 2, 39.
64. Rodríguez, the cofounder of ACUS, in 1949 was a reformist Catholic who opposed communist activism at the National University. Lara Velado was the leader of a well-established group of professionals. Rodríguez interview.
65. Dada interview.
66. The Junta's minister of justice was Dr. Arturo Zeledón Castrillo, and the minister of labor was Dr. Angel Góchez Marín. René Fortín Magaña, "Cuarenta años después," pp. 14–15.
67. DOS-OCPA, NARA, box 1, years 1958–1960, entry #A1 3159: Records Relating to El Salvador (1958–1975), folder: Junta Memoranda, "Memorandum Ambassador Thorsten V. Kalijarvi," November 6, 1960.
68. DOS-OCPA, NARA, box 1, years 1958–1960, entry A1 3159: Records Relating to El Salvador (1958–1975), folder: Junta Memoranda, "Memorandum to the Secretary from Mr. Mann—Subject: Recognition of Junta Government in El Salvador," November 13, 1960; "Memorandum to the Secretary from Mr. Mann—Subject: Recognition of El Salvador," November 15, 1960; and "Memorandum to the Secretary from Mr. Mann—Subject: Coup D'etat in El Salvador," October 31, 1960.
69. DOS-OCPA, NARA, box 1, years 1958–1960, entry A1 3159: Records Relating to El Salvador (1958–1975), "Memorandum of Conversation—Participants: Ambassador Kalijarvi, Mr. Donald P. Downs, Dr. Kuri Dean of Medical School, Dr. De Sola Assistant Dean, Dr. Byers," September 29, 1959.
70. DOS-OCPA, NARA, box 1, years 1958–1960, entry A1 3159: Records Relating to El Salvador (1958–1975), folder: Junta Correspondence, "Memo on the New Government in El Salvador Central America" by Blair Birdsall, November 11, 1960.
71. DOS-OCPA, NARA, box 1, years 1958–1960, entry A1 3159: Records Relating to El Salvador (1958–1975), folder: Junta Correspondence, "Memo on the New Government in El Salvador Central America" by Blair Birdsall, November 11, 1960.
72. DOS-OCPA, NARA, box 1, years 1958–1960, entry A1 3159: Records Relating to El Salvador (1958–1975), folder: Junta Memoranda, "Memorandum of Conversation—Subject: Communist Influence in Medical School in El Salvador—Participants: Dr. Jacob Sacks, University of Arkansas, Mrs. Katherine W. Bracken, Director, Office of Central American and Panamanian Affairs; Mr. Maxwell Chaplin, Office in Charge, Honduran Affairs," December 27, 1960.
73. Castillo Figueroa, "Los problemas de democratización y de educación," pp. 6–7.
74. Castillo Figueroa, "Los problemas de democratización y de educación," p. 7.
75. DOS-OCPA, NARA, box 1, years 1958–1960, entry A1 3159: Records Relating to El Salvador (1958–1975), folder: Junta Memoranda, "Memorandum to the Acting Secretary from Mr. Mann—Subject: Recent Development in El Salvador," November 5, 1960.
76. Kalijarvi paraphrased Downs in the letter he addressed to the secretary of state regarding this matter. DOS-OCPA, NARA, box 1, years 1958–1960, entry A1 3159: Records Relating to El Salvador (1958–1975), folder: Junta Memoranda, "Thorsten V. Kalijarvi to the Secretary—Further Delay in U.S. Recognition of Junta Government of El Salvador," November 11, 1960.
77. DOS-OCPA, NARA, box 1, years 1958–1960, entry A1 3159: Records Relating to El Salvador (1958–1975), folder: Junta Memoranda—El Salvador (1960), "Donald P. Downs Letter to Ambassador Thorsten Kalijarvi," November 10, 1960.

78. DOS-OCPA, NARA, box 1, years 1958–1960, entry A1 3159: Records Relating to El Salvador (1958–1975), folder: Junta Memoranda, "From Mr. Mann to the Acting Secretary—Reply to Letter from Secretary Gates on Question of Recognition of New Government of El Salvador," December 28, 1960.
79. "EEUU reconoció a Junta de Gobierno," *La Prensa Gráfica*, December 4, 1960, pp. 3, 14; "Junta de Gobierno es reconocida por Cuba," *La Prensa Gráfica*, December 5, 1960, pp. 3, 30; "Dos paises más reconocen a La Junta Cívico-Militar," *La Prensa Gráfica*, November 10, 1960, p. 2.
80. Castillo Figueroa, "Los problemas de democratización y de educación," p. 7.
81. "La Junta de Gobierno de El Salvador Decreta Remoción de Alcaldes (Decreto No. 44 de la Junta de Gobierno de El Salvador, dado en La Casa Presidencial el 14 de Diciembre de 1960)," *La Prensa Gráfica*, December 16, 1960, pp. 1, 3.
82. "Desmilitarización de la policía está en estudio," *La Prensa Gráfica*, December 16, 1960, pp. 2, 47; "Policía y bomberos se desmilitarizan," *La Prensa Grafica*, December 17, 1960, pp. 2, 51.
83. "Tirotean residencia del Fiscal General," *La Prensa Gráfica*, December 22, 1960, p. 3, 56.
84. "Boletín de Prensa del PRAM" in "Refiérense a atentado contra Fiscal," *La Prensa Gráfica*, December 23, 1960, p. 39.
85. "Elecciones libres promete Directorio," *La Prensa Gráfica*, January 28, 1961, pp. 1, 3, 25.
86. Almeida, *Waves of Protest*, p. 61.
87. "Directorio asume poder en el país—fue establecida La Ley Marcial," *La Prensa Gráfica* January 26, 1960, p. 3, 10; "Osorio, Falla Cáceres y Fortín M. salen del país," *La Prensa Gráfica*, January 27, 2007, 1961, p. 3.
88. Dada interview.
89. "It was evident the pro–North American orientation that the coup leaders [*golpistas*] had. It was evident and it was perceived with certain clarity, how a vehicle of the North American military mission traveled between *El Zapote* and the *San Carlos*, the garrisons at odds, like mediating the situation. It was evident how the *golpistas*, consciously and in terms of vision yield to the North American position of the Alliance for Progress, which then became a program of more or less large scope." Valle, *Siembra de vientos*, pp. 119–120.
90. Montgomery, *Revolution in El Salvador*, pp. 52–53.
91. "Rompen relaciones EEUU con Cuba," *La Prensa Gráfica*, January 4, 1961, pp. 1, 5, 26.
92. Holden and Zolov, *Latin America and the United States*, p. 224.
93. Dada interview.
94. Santacruz interview.
95. "Osorio and those who surrounded him [attempted to create a] reformist government [but] one thing is to want it, declare it and think about it, and another is to do it. They had the intention, but they couldn't do it. They didn't have time to do it and they couldn't do it. Why? Because what they were really doing was holding onto the rock, nothing more. They didn't have the capacity. They didn't accept popular support. We [members of FNOC] marched in the streets. We supported them. We were there at the Presidential House immediately after [the coup]." Santacruz interview.
96. Fabio Castillo Figueroa, "Letter to the Minister of Education of El Salvador" (San Salvador, July 21, 2003).
97. Dada interview; Santacruz interview.
98. Members of the Directorate were Colonel Julio Rivera, Colonel Anibal Portillo, Major Oscar Rodríguez Simó, and two civilians, Dr. Antonio Rodríguez Port and Dr. José Francisco Valiente. "Directorio asume poder en el país—fue establecida la Ley Marcial," *La Prensa Gráfica*, January 26, 1960, pp. 3, 10.
99. Dada interview.
100. "I was the first civilian called when the government was organized at the San Carlos [garrison]," recalled Abraham Rodríguez. "They [military leaders of the coup] asked me to join the Directorate but we [the founders of the PDC] wanted permanent political parties, to break with [the practice] of forming parties after the coups, [to form] parties as institutions of a democratic system. . . . I suggested them [to appoint] Dr. [Antonio] Rodríguez Port and Dr. Valiente but we did not take part [in the Directorate]." The military "asked us [the Christian Democrats] to become the official party . . . for hours we discussed at [José

Napoleón] Duarte's house" and decided that "it was not convenient [to accept the offer]" because the country needed "permanent parties" in order to achieve democratization. But despite the official PDC position to endorse the rightist coup, a conservative faction of the PDC led by Italo Giammatei left the party to form the new official party, the PCN. Giammatei reportedly labeled Rodríguez, Duarte, and other PDC leaders "naive children," for rejecting the military's proposal to become the new official party. Rodríguez interview. Based on interviews she conducted with Rubén Zamora, a leader of the PDC until 1980, and Hugo Carrillo, the secretary general of the PCN in the late 1980s, Montgomery offered a similar version on the foundation of the PDC. Montgomery, *Revolution in El Salvador*, p. 53.

101. UPI, "500,000 Salvadorans Vote for New Congress," *Washington Post*, December 18, 1961, p. A12.
102. Montgomery, *Revolution in El Salvador*, p. 53.
103. Artículo 112 de la Constitución Política de la República de El Salvador 1962 (San Salvador: Ministerio de Educación, Dirección General de Publicaciones, 1962), p. 95.
104. Montgomery, *Revolution in El Salvador*, p. 53.
105. Santacruz interview.
106. Dada interview.
107. Tercera Plenaria Nacional del FUAR, "Proyecto Plataforma Programática del FUAR," p. 8.
108. Tercera Plenaria Nacional del FUAR, "Proyecto Plataforma Programática del FUAR," p. 5.
109. Tercera Plenaria Nacional del FUAR, "Proyecto Plataforma Programática del FUAR," p. 5.
110. Tercera Plenaria Nacional del FUAR, "Proyecto Plataforma Programática del FUAR," p. 8.
111. Tercera Plenaria Nacional del FUAR, "Proyecto Plataforma Programática del FUAR," pp. 13–16.
112. Tercera Plenaria Nacional del FUAR, "Proyecto Plataforma Programática del FUAR," p. 10.
113. "CGTS members constituted FUAR's workers' column; members of Fraternidad Magisterial, the teacher's column; members of PRAM, 'the May 9 Column'; members of AGEUS, the university students' column; members of Fraternidad de Mujeres Salvadoreñas, the women's column; and Miguel Mármol, Daniel Castaneda, Modesto Ramírez, and Segundo Ramírez, all of them survivors of the 1932 massacre, organized the peasants' column. Members of the short-lived 'Revolutionary Movement April 2' known as 'MR 2-4,' led by Domingo Santacruz, which emerged independently from the PCS, also joined the FUAR." Santacruz interview.
114. Santacruz interview.
115. Valle, *Siembra de vientos*, pp. 62–63.
116. Valle, *Siembra de vientos*, pp. 62–63.
117. Valle, *Siembra de vientos*, pp. 60–61.
118. Jorge Arias Gómez, "Anastasio Aquino, recuerdo, valoración y presencia," *La Universidad*, nos. 1–2, (January–June, 1964): pp. 65, 89, 108–109.
119. Tercera Plenaria Nacional del FUAR, "Proyecto Plataforma Programática del FUAR," pp. 1–4.
120. FUAR produced educational materials to distribute among peasant communities. Santacruz, interview.
121. Santacruz interview.
122. Santacruz interview.
123. Santacruz interview.
124. Santacruz interview.
125. Santacruz interview.
126. Santacruz interview.
127. Santacruz interview.
128. This finding fills out Wickham-Crowley's depiction of Latin American universities as "political enclaves" during the 1960s. Wickham-Crowley, *Guerrillas and Revolution in Latin America*, p. 35.
129. Menjívar observed that this debate also impacted union politics in the 1960s. Rafael Menjívar, *Formación y lucha del proletariado industrial Salvadoreño* (San Salvador: UCA Editores, 1979), p. 94.

Chapter 2

1. In 1949, Catholic students founded La Agrupación Cultural Universitaria Salvadoreña (Salvadoran Cultural University Association), which was renamed Salvadoran University Catholic Action (ACUS) in 1954. Letter of the Junta Directiva of ACUS to Monseñor Luis Chávez y González, San Salvador, circa 1954, Archivo Histórico de la Arquidiócesis de San Salvador (AHAS).

2. "Bajo el imperio de la vulgaridad," *ACUS Pax Christi in Regno Christi*, July 23, 1958, AHAS.

3. *ACUS Pax Christi in Regno Christi*, August 31, 1958, AHAS.

4. "Comentando una nota: Carta de Roque Dalton a los editores de ACUS," *ACUS Pax Christi in Regno Christi*, August 31, 1958, AHAS.

5. "Editorial," *ACUS Pax Christi in Regno Christi*, August 31, 1958, AHAS.

6. Christian Smith, *The Emergence of Liberation Theology: Radical Religion and Social Movement Theory* (Chicago: University of Chicago Press, 1991), pp. 72–79.

7. Michael Löwy, *The War of Gods* (London: Verso, 1996), pp. 4–31.

8. *Documentos completos del Vaticano II* 4th ed. (Bilbao: Mensajero, 1966); Juan Ramón Vega, *Las 54 cartas pastorales de Monseñor Chávez* (San Salvador: Ediciones del Arzobispado de San Salvador, 1997); Andrés Opazo,"El movimiento religioso popular en Centroamérica: 1970–1983," in *Movimientos populares en Centroamérica*, ed. Daniel Camacho and Rafael Menjívar (San José, Costa Rica: EDUCA, 1985), pp. 166–167.

9. Smith, *The Emergence of Liberation Theology*, pp. 125, 126, 159. The doctrine of the "just war" generally posits that the objective of such war "should be to vindicate justice and restore peace"; see Roland H. Bainton, *Christian Attitudes toward War and Peace: A Historical Survey and Critical Re-evaluation*, 14th ed. (Nashville, TN: Abingdon Press, [1960] 1985), pp. 14, 15, 37, 44.

10. Löwy, *The War of Gods*, pp. 4–31.

11. Kathleen Sprows Cummings, "Teaching about Women, Gender, and American Catholicism," in *The Catholic Studies Reader*, ed. James T. Fisher and Margaret M. McGuinness (New York: Fordham University Press, 2011), p. 226.

12. Vega, *Las comunidades cristianas*, pp. 71–74; Whitfield, *Paying the Price*, pp. 29, 30; Peterson, *Martyrdom and the Politics of Religion*, pp. 48–53.

13. Vega, *Las 54 cartas pastorales*, p. 3; Vega, *Las comunidades cristianas*, p. 72.

14. Vega, *Las comunidades cristianas*, p. 75.

15. Rodríguez interview.

16. Drawing on Mexico's PRI, Osorio promoted the modernization of El Salvador in the context of US Cold War anti-communism.

17. "Carta del Padre Isidro Iriarte a Monseñor Luis Chávez y González" (San Salvador, August 18, 1950), AHAS.

18. Opazo, "El movimiento religioso popular en Centroamérica," p. 165.

19. Smith, *The Emergence of Liberation Theology*, pp. 77, 80.

20. Smith, *The Emergence of Liberation Theology*, p. 81.

21. Deborah Levenson-Estrada, *Trade Unionist against Terror: Guatemala City, 1954–1985* (Chapel Hill: University of North Carolina Press, 1994), pp. 80–104.

22. In 1953, the University of El Salvador served 1,704 students; see Juan Mario Castellanos, *El Salvador 1930–1960: Antecedentes históricos de la guerra civil* (San Salvador: DPI, 2002), table 69, p. 279.

23. "Cómo nació la ACUS," *Boletín de la ACUS* (May 1950), AHAS.

24. Letter from the Junta Directiva of ACUS to Monseñor Luis Chávez y González, San Salvador, circa 1954, AHAS.

25. "Materialismo he ahí el enemigo," *ACUS Pax Christi in Regno Christi*, circa January 1961, AHAS.

26. Editorial in *ACUS Pax Christi in Regno Christi*, July 23, 1958, AHAS.

27. Stefan Wilkanowicz and Zophia Wlodek, "Algunos aspectos sobre los problemas educativos actuales en Polonia," *ACUS Pax Christi in Regno Christi*, July 23, 1958, AHAS.

28. "Guerra y Paz," *ACUS Pax Christi in Regno Christi*, August 31, 1958, AHAS.

29. Grandin, *The Last Colonial Massacre*, p. 5.

30. Grandin, *The Last Colonial Massacre*, p. 5.
31. Valle, *Siembra de vientos*, pp. 42–47.
32. Dada interview.
33. "Ante un nuevo peligro," *ACUS Pax Christi in Regni Christi*, circa March 1961, AHAS.
34. "Revolución o evolución," ACUS (mimeograph, circa March 1961), AHAS.
35. Mario Efraín Callejas, interview by Joaquín Chávez (October 10, 2007).
36. "Apóstoles Universitarios en Semana Santa," *ACUS Boletín Mensual Número 1*, March 1963, AHAS.
37. Callejas interview.
38. José Inocencio Alas, *Iglesia, tierra y lucha campesina: Suchitoto, El Salvador, 1968–1977* (San Salvador: Asociación Equipo Maíz, 2003), pp. 41–45.
39. Peterson, *Martyrdom and the Politics of Religion*, p. 48.
40. Tomás Castillo, "Iglesia, renovación, concilio," *Orientación*, October 23–29, 1967, pp. 4, 7.
41. Castillo, "Iglesia, renovación, concilio."
42. Ignacio Paniagua, interview by Joaquín Chávez (July 20, 2007).
43. "Informe de la Delegación de ACUS Asistente al Segundo Seminario Latinoamericano de Pax Romana MIEC celebrado en Lima del 14 al 28 de Abril de 1963, Tema: Reforma Universitaria en América Latina" (mimeograph, San Salvador, May 1963), AHAS.
44. "Reunión para preparar Día de Acción Católica," *Orientación*, June 26–July 1, 1967, p. 4.
45. "Fray Fuentes Castellanos es inexacto en sus críticas a Monseñor McGrath: Carta de Monseñor McGrath a Monseñor Luis Chávez y González," *Orientación*, May 19–26, 1968, pp. 1, 8.
46. "Camilo Torres Restrepo: Quinto aniversario de su muerte (febrero 1929–15 de febrero de 1966, asesinado brutalmente)," *Orientación*, February 7–13, 1971, p. 5.
47. "El progreso de los pueblos y la universidad," *Orientación*, October 23–29, 1967, pp. 5, 7.
48. Paniagua interview.
49. Although Latin American bishops were not central figures in the council, they witnessed the theological transformations of the Church animated by European bishops and theologians. The council was also a space of encounter for Latin American bishops, which set the conditions for the organization of the CELAM Conference in 1968, a watershed in the history of Latin American Catholicism; see Smith, *The Emergence of Liberation Theology*, pp. 97–100.
50. "Carta de Juan Ramón Vega a Monseñor Luis Chávez y González" (San Salvador, November 10, 1965); "Carta de José Romeo Maeda a Monseñor Luis Chávez y González" (San Salvador, November 16, 1965), AHAS.
51. Paniagua interview.
52. "Una nueva tarea para la juventud universitaria," *Orientación*, May 22–28, 1967, pp. 5, 7.
53. Paniagua interview.
54. Paniagua interview.
55. Paniagua interview.
56. Vega, *Las comunidades cristianas*, p. 102.
57. Paulo Freire, *Pedagogy of the Oppressed* (New York: Continuum, 2006), pp. 71–86.
58. Freire, *Pedagogy of the Oppressed*, pp. 67–69.
59. Lorena Peña Mendoza, interview by Joaquín Chávez (October 10, 2006); Rafael Velásquez, interview by Joaquín Chávez (March 22, 2007); Paniagua interview.
60. Velásquez interview.
61. Miguel Huezo Mixco, interview by Joaquín Chávez (December 21, 2006).
62. Rubén Zamora, interview by Joaquín Chávez (August 15, 2005).
63. Rutilio Sánchez, interview by Joaquín Chávez (October 1, 2007).
64. Vega, *Las comunidades cristianas*, p. 103.
65. Paniagua interview.
66. Paniagua interview.
67. Paniagua interview.
68. Castellanos, *El Salvador 1930–1960*, pp. 201–202.
69. FLACSO El Salvador and Fundación "Dr. Manuel Gallardo," *Prensa clandestina*, p. 109.
70. In 1962, the University of El Salvador served 3,236 students; see Castellanos, *El Salvador 1930–1960*, table 69, p. 279.

71. Manuel Luis Escamilla, "La reforma universitaria de El Salvador: Breve discusión doctrinaria" (San Salvador: Universidad de El Salvador, 1967), p. 37.
72. Victoria Ramírez, interview by Joaquín Chávez (October 10, 2006).
73. Velásquez interview.
74. *Diagnóstico global de la universidad*, vol. 1 (San Salvador: Secretaría de Planificación,, 1972), pp. 119, 120, 125.
75. Velásquez interview; Ramírez interview.
76. Francisco Jovel, interview by Joaquín Chávez (April 18, 2007).
77. Jovel interview.
78. Probably Luis Felipe Quezada. Jovel interview.
79. *Opinión Estudiantil*, Special Issue, November 1968, front page, University of El Salvador Library, Special Collections.
80. Jovel interview.
81. Manuel Sorto, "El planeta de los cerdos," *ContraPunto: Noticias de El Salvador*, October 31, 2009, http://www.archivocp.contrapunto.com.sv//la-anecdota/el-planeta-de-los-cerdos, accessed October 30, 2013.
82. Sorto, "El planeta de los cerdos."
83. Sorto, "El planeta de los cerdos."
84. Rodríguez interview.
85. Sonia Aguiñada Carranza, interview by Joaquín Chávez (November 24, 2006); Ana Sonia Medina, interview by Joaquín Chávez (November 24, 2006).
86. Aguiñada Carranza interview; Medina interview.
87. *Diagnóstico global de la universidad*, vol. 1, pp. 119–120, 125.
88. Velásquez interview; Aguiñada Carranza interview.
89. FLACSO El Salvador and Fundación "Dr. Manuel Gallardo," *Prensa clandestina*, pp. 19–45.
90. Montalvo interview; ACISAM, *Movimientos estudiantiles de secundaria en los años 70 en El Salvador* (San Salvador: ACISAM, 2012), pp. 6–7; Harnecker, *Con la mirada en alto*, p. 15.
91. The anthropologist Carlos R. Cabarrús argued that urban intellectuals, mostly Jesuits, played a major role in the "unblocking of the peasants' consciousness," that is, in the formation of social awareness of peasant communities in Aguilares, a town north of San Salvador, in the 1970s. Cabarrús, *Génesis de una revolución*, pp. 141–163.
92. Popular Liberation Forces—FPL Farabundo Martí, *Estrella Roja 2* (February 11, 1975), pp. 21–30, CIDAI-UCA.
93. FPL, *Estrella Roja 2*, p. 1.
94. FPL, *Estrella Roja 2*, pp. 9–12.
95. FPL, *Estrella Roja 2*, p. 11.
96. Joaquín Villalobos, "Homenaje a Rafael Antonio Arce Zablah," *El Diario de Hoy*, September 28, 2005.
97. Jeffrey L. Gould, "Solidarity under Siege: The Latin American Left, 1968," *American Historical Review* 114, no. 2 (April 2009): 348–375.
98. Gould, "Solidarity under Siege," p. 374.
99. According to Grenier, the New Left insurgency provoked the escalation of state terror in El Salvador; see Grenier, *The Emergence of Insurgency in El Salvador*, pp. 2, 35–66, 160–161.
100. Chávez, "The Creation of the Internal Enemy," pp. 116–123.

Chapter 3

1. José Santos Martínez, interview by Joaquín Chávez (December 25, 2007).
2. Hilda Mejía, interview by Joaquín Chávez (October 10, 2008).
3. "Resumen Estadístico de las Escuelas Radiofónicas de El Salvador (1964)," Archbishopric of San Salvador (San Salvador, 1964), p. 1, AHAS.
4. Some twenty-five thousand adult peasants graduated from this program between 1964 and 1970. "Resumen Estadístico de las Escuelas Radiofónicas de El Salvador (1964)"; "La mayor riqueza de los pueblos es el elemento humano capacitado," *Orientación*, November 23–29, 1970, pp. 1, 7.

5. Opazo, "El movimiento religioso popular en Centroamérica," pp. 179–180; Vega, *Las comunidades cristianas*, p. 84; Pearce, *Promised Land*, p. 113.
6. Cabarrús, *Génesis de una revolución*, pp. 141–163; Pearce, *Promised Land*, pp. 107–139.
7. I draw on Steven Feierman's notions of peasant intellectuals to discuss the emergence of a new stratum of peasant leaders in Chalatenango in the early 1970s; see my discussion of this topic in the introduction. Also see Steven Feierman, *Peasant Intellectuals: Anthropology and History in Tanzania* (Madison: University of Wisconsin Press, 1990), pp. 18–19.
8. Baud and Rutten, *Popular Intellectuals and Social Movements*, p. 2.
9. What anthropologist Carlos R. Cabarrús called the *apremio campesino* (peasant's predicament), namely, the extreme social exclusion and exploitation workers at sugar cane haciendas and minifundistas in the Aguilares region endured in the early 1970s; see Cabarrús, *Génesis de una revolución*, p. 54.
10. Carlos Pérez Pineda, "La patria unida para ir a la guerra: Cien horas de 1969," *El Faro Académico*, July 12, 2015, http://www.elfaro.net/es/201507/academico/17180/La-patria-unida-para-ir-a-la-guerra-cien-horas-de-1969.htm, accessed February 21, 2016.
11. Facundo Guardado, interview by Joaquín Chávez (August 31, 2005).
12. "Herman," a peasant interviewed by Pearce, reported that in the early 1970s, the cost of renting one *manzana* (1 *manzana* = 0.7 hectare) of land in Chalatenango rose to 100 *colones*; see Pearce, *Promised Land*, pp. 69–70.
13. The Salvadoran economist Rafael Menjívar wrote about the rapid pace of industrialization in El Salvador in the heyday of the Central American Common Market (CACM). The industrial sector "grew almost two and a half times" from US$74.8 million to US$186.48 million between 1959 and 1969. At the end of the 1960s, the industrial sector constituted 19.6 percent of the country's economy, which grew at annual rates of 13.2 percent between 1962 and 1966. It nosedived to a 5.5 percent annual growth rate in the aftermath of the 1969 war between El Salvador and Honduras, which shattered the CACM; see Menjívar, *Formación y lucha del proletariado industrial Salvadoreño*, pp. 94–95.
14. Pearce, *Promised Land*, p. 53.
15. Pearce, *Promised Land*, p. 53.
16. Pearce, *Promised Land*, pp. 53, 55.
17. Pearce, *Promised Land*, p. 55.
18. Pearce, *Promised Land*, p. 55.
19. Guardado interview.
20. Lauria-Santiago, *An Agrarian Republic*, pp. 21–22, 75, 200–204.
21. Héctor Lindo-Fuentes, *La economía de El Salvador en el siglo XIX* (San Salvador: CONCULTURA, 2002), pp. 191–206; Clará de Guevara, "El Añil de Los 'Indios Cheles,'" pp. 778–794.
22. Chalatenango had one of the highest rates of internal migration in the 1960s; see Pearce, *Promised Land*, pp. 49–50.
23. Guadalupe Mejía, interview by Joaquín Chávez (October 2, 2008); FECCAS UTC, "Temporada 78–79 una Jornada más de Explotación, Maltrato, Hambre y Miseria para los Trabajadores del Campo" (San Salvador, mimeograph, 1978).
24. Juan Ramón Vega, interview by Joaquín Chávez (December 3, 2007).
25. Pearce, *Promised Land*, p. 31.
26. Curia Metropolitana, "Acerca de la injusticia de la actual forma de tenencia de la tierra," *La Universidad* no.1, (January–February 1970): pp. 18–19, 23–24.
27. Alas, *Iglesia, tierra y lucha campesina*, pp. 112–128.
28. Sara Gordon, *Crisis política y guerra en El Salvador* (Mexico City: Siglo XXI, 1989), p. 164; anonymous informant 2, interview by Joaquín Chávez (November 6, 2007).
29. Gordon, *Crisis política y guerra en El Salvador*, p. 178.
30. José Inocencio Alas and Rutilio Sánchez, two priests working in Suchitoto, and Miguel Argueta, a priest working in Chalatenango, joined this movement. The communities affected by the flooding in Chalatenango were San José, San Francisco Lempa, San Luis del Carmen, Potonico, Santa Teresa, and San Juan La Reina. Anonymous informant 2; see also Gordon, *Crisis política y guerra en El Salvador*, p. 178.
31. Ismael Merlos, interview by Joaquín Chávez (December 6, 2007); Pearce, *Promised Land*, p. 93.
32. José Romeo Maeda, interview by Joaquín Chávez (November 30, 2007).

33. Maeda interview.
34. Guadalupe Mejía interview.
35. Gumercinda "Chinda" Zamora, interview by Joaquín Chávez (October 10, 2008); Guadalupe Mejía interview.
36. Maeda interview; Merlos interview.
37. Merlos interview.
38. Vega, *Las comunidades cristianas*, p. 84.
39. Merlos interview.
40. Merlos interview; Guardado interview; Martínez interview.
41. State agents killed Morales and Zamora in the 1970s. Merlos interview.
42. Merlos interview.
43. Merlos interview.
44. Guardado interview; Alberto Enríquez, interview by Joaquín Chávez (March 16, 2007).
45. Guadalupe Mejía interview.
46. Maeda interview.
47. Martín Barahona, "Escuela de Capacitación Cooperativa Agropecuaria en Chalatenango," *Orientación*, November 9–15, 1970, p. 2.
48. Nicolás González, "San José Ojos de Agua un bello rincón," *Orientación*, January 17–23, 1971, p. 7.
49. González, "San José Ojos de Agua un bello rincón."
50. "Decreto sobre los medios de comunicación social," in *Documentos completos del Vaticano II*, p. 404.
51. Benjamín Rodríguez Najarro, "El Encuentro Campesino con el Papa," *Orientación*, August 26–September 1, 1968, p. 4; "El Papa recomienda las Escuelas Radiofónicas," *Orientación*, September 9–15, 1968, p. 4.
52. The radio schools in Colombia originated in Radio Sutatentzas; see "Escuelas Radiofónicas un medio para acercarnos a grupos marginados," *Orientación*, September 28–October 4, 1970, pp. 1, 6.
53. "Las Escuelas Radiofónicas y el Párroco," *Orientación*, July 28–August 4, 1968, p. 2; "Escuelas Radiofónicas," *Orientación*, June 10–16, 1968, p. 4; "Escuelas Radiofónicas un medio para acercarnos a grupos marginados," pp. 1, 6.
54. Miguel Angel Araujo, Carlos Alberto Rodríguez, and Ricardo Ayala Kreus, "Situación agraria en El Salvador: Ponencia presentada por la Universidad de El Salvador," in *La Universidad*, no.1 (January–February 1970): pp. 8–15.
55. "Escuelas Radiofónicas," *Orientación*, June 10–16, 1968, p. 4.
56. "Muere Presidente del Comité Administrativo de Escuelas Radiofónicas," *Orientación*, June 17–23, 1968, p. 5.
57. In 1968, the Ministry of Education proctored final exams for radio students in the following places: "San Pedro Perulapán, Candelaria, Tonacatepeque, San José Guayabal, Suchitoto, Opico, Tacachico, Quezaltepeque, . . . Nejapa, . . . San Juan de Cojutepeque, Ciudad Arce, Ilobasco, Victoria, San Sebastián, Coatepeque, Chalatenango, Guazapa, Agua Caliente, La Palma, Nueva Concepción, Tejutla y [*sic*] Iglesia de la Rábida en San Salvador." "Exámenes finales de Escuelas Radiofónicas," *Orientación*, October 7–13, 1968, p. 4.
58. "Escuelas Radiófonicas un medio para acercarnos a grupos marginados," pp. 1, 6.
59. "Las Escuelas Radiofónicas y el Párroco," p. 2.
60. "Qué son las Escuelas Radiofónicas," *Orientación*, June 24–30, 1968, p. 2; "Observaciones en la Elaboración de la Estadística de las Escuelas Radiofónicas de El Salvador, Año 1964," AHAS.
61. "Estadística General de Escuelas Radiofónicas de El Salvador 1967," AHAS.
62. In 1967, there were radio schools in the towns of Agua Caliente, La Palma, Nueva Concepción, San Juan Chalatenango, and Tejutla. There were six radio schools functioning at El Jícaro and one in Talchaluya, two neighbouring hamlets of La Ceiba. "Estadística General de Escuelas Radiofónicas de El Salvador 1967," AHAS.
63. Hilda Mejía interview.
64. Martínez interview; Guadalupe Mejía interview; Hilda Mejía interview.
65. Guadalupe Mejía interview.
66. "El Señor Arzobispo visita Escuelas Radiofónicas," *Orientación*, June 10–16, 1968, p. 7.

67. Hilda Mejía interview.
68. "Observaciones en la Elaboración de la Estadística de las Escuelas Radiofónicas de El Salvador, Año 1964," AHAS.
69. Hilda Mejía interview.
70. Manuel Aguirre, "Carta de un Cooperativista," *Orientación*, September 30–October 6, 1968, p. 4; Ricardo Acosta Rivera, "Promoción Humana a través de Escuelas Radiofónicas," *Orientación*, September 23–29, 1968, pp. 4, 7.
71. Guardado interview; Martínez interview; Guadalupe Mejía interview; Hilda Mejía interview.
72. Rubio and Balsebre, *Rompiendo silencios*, pp. 99–100.
73. Gumercinda Zamora interview.
74. Gumercinda Zamora interview.
75. Vega, *Las comunidades cristianas*, pp. 98–99.
76. Guardado interview; Maeda interview.
77. Gumercinda Zamora interview.
78. Gumercinda Zamora interview.
79. Guadalupe Mejía interview.
80. Guadalupe Mejía interview.
81. Guardado interview.
82. Cabarrús, *Génesis de una revolución*, pp. 197–234.
83. Guardado interview.
84. Leigh Binford, *The El Mozote Massacre* (Tucson: University of Arizona Press, 1996), p. 45.
85. Gumercinda Zamora interview.
86. Guadalupe Mejía interview.
87. Hilda Mejía interview.
88. Guardado interview; Martínez interview.
89. Patricia Alvarenga, *Cultura y ética de la violencia, El Salvador, 1880–1932* (San José, Costa Rica: EDUCA, 1996), pp. 9–30.
90. This committee was initially named Coordinadora Nacional de Comunidades (National Coordination of Communities) and later renamed Coordinadora Nacional de la Iglesia Popular (CONIP). Trinidad de Jesús Nieto, interview by Joaquín Chávez (October 1, 2006).
91. Nieto interview.
92. Vega, *Las comunidades cristianas*, pp. 81–84.
93. Walter Guerra et al., *Testigos de la fe en El Salvador: Nuestros sacerdotes y seminaristas diocesanos mártires 1977–1993* (San Salvador: Walter Guerra et al., 2007), pp. 40–43.
94. Guerra et al., *Testigos de la fe en El Salvador*, pp. 75–77.
95. Nieto interview.
96. Anonymous informant 2 interview.
97. Anonymous informant 2 interview.
98. Anonymous informant 2 interview.
99. Anonymous informant 2 interview.
100. Anonymous informant 2 interview.
101. For a comprehensive sociological analysis of the Catholic pedagogies in El Salvador in the 1960s and 1970s, see Vega, *Las comunidades cristianas*, pp. 101–115.
102. Irma Serrano, interview by Joaquín Chávez (April 18, 2007).
103. Anonymous informant 2 interview.
104. Anonymous informant 2, interview.
105. Pearce, *Promised Land*, pp. 113–114.
106. Benito Tovar cited in Áscoli, "El surgimiento de la conciencia," p. 21.
107. A former member of the UTC cited as an anonymous informant ("Q8") in Áscoli, "El surgimiento de la conciencia," 20.
108. In San Vicente, the conservative bishop Arnulfo Aparicio created the Caballeros de Cristo Rey a right-wing Catholic militant group, as a response to the emergence of CBCs in the area. Anonymous informant 2 interview.
109. "Evaristo" interview by Joaquín Chávez (August 6, 2007).
110. Gumercinda Zamora interview; Martínez interview.
111. Áscoli, "El surgimiento de la conciencia," p. 19.

112. Tovar cited in Áscoli, "El surgimiento de la conciencia," p. 19.
113. Victoria Ramírez, interview by Joaquín Chávez (December 8, 2006).
114. Enríquez interview.
115. Enríquez interview.
116. Pearce, *Promised Land*, p. 156.
117. Martínez interview.
118. Guardado interview.
119. Tovar cited in Áscoli, "El surgimiento de la conciencia," p. 19.
120. Anonymous informant 2 interview.
121. FPL, *Estrella Roja 2*, pp. 1–8.
122. For a thorough discussion of Christian ideas about the just war, see Bainton, *Christian Attitudes toward War and Peace*, pp. 14, 15, 37, 44.
123. The FPL ethos comprised, according to the document, the following principles: "collective revolutionary spirit, subordination of individual interests to the fundamental interests of the proletariat and the people, conscious disposition to sacrifice personal interest—even life itself—to promote the revolutionary cause; conscious and strict discipline, spirit of planning [sic]; unlimited love for people, camaraderie, high level of responsibility, modesty, and constant effort to develop personal qualities to be more useful to the Popular Revolution"; see FPL, *Estrella Roja 2*, p. 12.
124. FPL, *Estrella Roja 2*, p. 26.
125. FPL, *Estrella Roja 2*, p. 25.
126. Tovar cited in Áscoli, "El surgimiento de la conciencia," p. 22.
127. Tovar cited in Áscoli, "El surgimiento de la conciencia," p. 22.
128. FECCAS-UTC, "Boletín Informativo No 3: Se agudiza criminal represión contra familias campesinas en Chalatenango, San Vicente, Cinquera y demás regiones del campo Salvadoreño" in *La Prensa Gráfica*, 27 January 1980, pp. 13–14.
129. Gumercinda Zamora interview.
130. José Alejandro Duarte Fuentes, *Borbollones Padre Nicolás Rodríguez: Mártir* (San Salvador: Editorial e Imprenta Universitaria, 1999), pp. 9–10
131. "Sacerdote Asesinado," *El Diario de Hoy*, December 1, 1970, front page, p. 3; Duarte Fuentes, *Borbollones*, p. 9.
132. For a compilation of documents and interviews on Nicolás Rodríguez's murder, see Duarte Fuentes, *Borbollones*.
133. Anonymous informant 2 interview.
134. Anonymous informant 2 interview.
135. Binford, *The El Mozote Massacre*, p. 39.
136. Guardado interview; Martínez interview.
137. Dirección Ejecutiva Nacional (DEN) FECCAS-UTC, "Ante la demagogia de los planes reformistas del enemigo FECCAS-UTC a todos los organismos y bases de nuestras organizaciones" (mimeograph, August 1978).
138. Guardado interview; Enriquez interview.
139. FECCAS-UTC, "UTC-FECCAS informa a los trabajadores del campo y pueblo en general" (mimeograph, November 1977).
140. FECCAS-UTC, "FECCAS-UTC la tiranía militar invade zonas" (mimeograph, December 18 1977).
141. FECCAS-UTC, "UTC-FECCAS a la clase trabajadora y pueblo en general" (mimeograph, October 1977).
142. FECCAS-UTC, "FECCAS-UTC plataforma reivindicativa de los campesinos pobres y medios respecto a los insumos agrícolas y los intereses de los créditos para la temporada 1979–80" (mimeograph, circa October 1979).
143. Guardado interview.
144. FECCAS-UTC was made up of departmental, municipal, and local committees and other specialized structures (i.e., finance, propaganda, security, public relations, conflicts, and organization commissions).
145. Dirección Ejecutiva Nacional (DEN) of FECCAS-UTC, "Ante la demagogia de los planes reformistas del enemigo" (mimeograph, August 1978).

146. FECCAS-UTC, "UTC FECCAS a los Cristianos de El Salvador y Centroamérica" (mimeograph, circa 1978).
147. "UTC FECCAS a los Cristianos."
148. "UTC FECCAS a los Cristianos."
149. "UTC FECCAS a los Cristianos."
150. "UTC FECCAS a los Cristianos."
151. "UTC FECCAS a los Cristianos."
152. Jose Santos Martínez and Facundo Guardado, who were among the first peasant leaders in the area to join the FPL, had similar recollections about this matter. Martínez interview; Guardado interview.
153. Montalvo interview.
154. Martínez interview.
155. Martínez interview.
156. Martínez interview.
157. Martínez interview.
158. Martínez interview.
159. Martínez interview.
160. Martínez interview.
161. Martínez interview.
162. Martínez interview.
163. Martínez interview.
164. Martínez interview.
165. Martínez interview.
166. Guardado interview.
167. Martínez interview.
168. Martínez interview.

Chapter 4

1. Sancho interview.
2. According to Vargas Méndez and Morasan, the group was formed circa 1967. However, Sancho recalled that he started his weekly meetings with the poets from San Vicente in 1966. Vargas Méndez and Morasan, *Literatura salvadoreña 1960–2000*, p. 63; Sancho, *Crónicas entre los espejos*, p. 60.
3. Sancho interview.
4. Scholars writing on this topic generally attribute the formation of the insurgency to communist and Christian Democrat dissidents, university students, and radicalized sectors of the Catholic Church, which took up arms against the state as a result of the growing repression, economic oppression, and recurrent electoral frauds in the late 1960s and 1970s. Dunkerley, *The Long War*, p. 87; Montgomery, *Revolution in El Salvador*, pp. 102–104; Grenier, *The Emergence of Insurgency in El Salvador*, pp. 42, 67; Wickham-Crowley, *Guerrillas and Revolution in Latin America*, pp. 211, 219–221, 224–225; Byrne, *El Salvador's Civil War*, p. 34; McClintock, *Revolutionary Movements in Latin America*, pp. 49–51.
5. In El Salvador, as in other Latin American countries, *rockeros* (youth influenced by rock culture), countercultural movements, students, and Catholic university intellectuals played key roles in the formation of New Left movements. Zolov, "Expanding Our Conceptual Horizons," pp. 47–73; Eric Zolov, *Refried Elvis: The Rise of the Mexican Counterculture* (Berkeley: University of California Press, 1999); Special Issue: Latin America in the Global Sixties, *The Americas* 70, no. 3 (January 2014): 349–601; Victoria Langland, *Speaking of Flowers: Student Movements and the Making and Remembering of 1968 in Military Brazil* (Durham, NC: Duke University Press, 2013); Jaime Pensado, *Rebel Mexico: Student Unrest and Authoritarian Political Culture during the Long Sixties* (Stanford, CA: Stanford University Press, 2013).
6. For a nuanced discussion of this topic, see Luis Alvarenga, *Roque Dalton: La radicalización de las vanguardias* (San Salvador: Editorial Universidad Don Bosco, 2011), pp. 33–45.
7. Sancho interview.
8. Emiliano Androski Flamenco, interview by Joaquín Chávez (January 30, 2014).

9. Manuel Sorto, interview by Joaquín Chávez (July 22, 2014).
10. Luisfelipe Minhero, written interview by Joaquín Chávez (February 12, 2015).
11. Flamenco interview.
12. Vargas Méndez and Morasan, *Literatura salvadoreña*, p. 63. The Salvadoran poet Alfonso Quijadurias, who befriended Alfonso Hernández in the 1960s and remained his friend until Hernández's death in 1988, pondered Hernández's keen interest in the poetry of Dylan Thomas; see Alfonso Quijada Urías, "Imagen de Alfonso Hernández: O una temporada en el ingenio," in Alfonso Hernández, *Esta es la hora: Antologia*, Alfonso Quijada Urías and Alfonso Velis ed. (San Salvador: Ediciones Plural, 1989), p. 12.
13. Sancho, *Crónicas entre los espejos*, p. 62.
14. Alvarenga, *Roque Dalton*, p. 29.
15. Flamenco interview.
16. Flamenco interview.
17. Sorto interview. Walter Béneke was the architect of an educational television program that made up the core of the reform, which generated the strong opposition of ANDES, the main teachers' union in El Salvador. Lindo-Fuentes and Ching, *Modernizing Minds in El Salvador*, pp. 145–154.
18. Vargas Méndez and Morasan, *Literatura salvadoreña*, p. 63; Sorto interview; Minhero interview; Sancho interview; Flamenco interview.
19. Minhero interview.
20. Sancho, *Crónicas entre los espejos*, p. 63.
21. Flamenco interview.
22. Minhero interview.
23. Lauria-Santiago, *An Agrarian Republic*, pp. 99–101.
24. Mariano Prado, the second president of El Salvador, for instance, was Vicentino; see Academia Salvadoreña de la Historia, *Biografías de Vicentinos ilustres* (San Salvador: Ministerio de Educación Dirección General de Publicaciones, 1962), pp. 31–37.
25. Academia Salvadoreña de la Historia, *Biografías de Vicentinos ilustres*, p. 8.
26. Vargas Méndez and Morasan, *Literatura salvadorena*, p. 78; Flamenco interview.
27. Luis Gallegos Valdés, *Panorama de la literatura salvadoreña del período precolombino a 1980* (San Salvador: UCA Editores, 1981), pp. 46, 48, 158.
28. Flamenco interview; Minhero interview.
29. Vargas Méndez and Morasan, *Literatura salvadoreña*, p. 63.
30. Dylan Thomas, *Quite Early in the Morning* (New York: New Directions, [1960] 1968), p. 3; Quijada Urías, "Imagen de Alfonso Hernández," p. 12.
31. Vargas Méndez and Morasan, *Literatura salvadoreña*, pp. 64–65 (capitalization as in the original).
32. Hernández, *Esta es la hora*, p. 93.
33. For instance, Arias Gómez, "Anastasio Aquino, recuerdo, valoración y presencia," pp. 61–112; Matilde Elena López, *La balada de Anastasio Aquino*, 3rd ed. (San Salvador: Editorial Universitaria [1978], 1996).
34. Julio Alberto Domínguez Sosa challenged the veracity of the tale of Aquino's coronation. He attributed this story to the nineteenth-century historian Antonio Cevallos. Julio Alberto Domínguez Sosa, *Anastasio Aquino: Caudillo de las Tribus Nonualcas* (San Salvador: Ediciones Venado del Bosque, [1962] 2007), pp. 129–130.
35. Flamenco interview.
36. Flamenco interview.
37. Flamenco rarely dated his poems. "Anastasio amigo" is part of *Al filo del silencio*, a volume that features poems Flamenco wrote in the 1960s, the 1970s, and during El Salvador's civil war (1980–1992). Emiliano Androski Flamenco, *Al filo del silencio* (San Vicente, mimeograph, 2011), pp. 30–31.
38. Flamenco interview.
39. Flamenco interview.
40. Flamenco interview.
41. Vargas Méndez and Morasan, *Literatura salvadoreña*, p. 66.
42. Sancho interview.

43. Flamenco interview.
44. Minhero interview.
45. Flamenco interview.
46. Flamenco interview.
47. Minhero interview; Vargas Méndez and Morasan, *Literatura salvadoreña*, p. 66.
48. Sancho interview.
49. Vargas Méndez and Morasan, *Literatura salvadoreña*, p. 67.
50. Vargas Méndez and Morasan, *Literatura salvadoreña*, p. 68.
51. Minhero recalled that he, Hernández, Sancho, and Monterrosa hitchhiked to Managua "two months before the [July 1969] Soccer War." Minhero interview. Sancho and Flamenco did not mention Hernández as part of the group that went to Nicaragua. Sancho interview; Flamenco interview.
52. Flamenco interview.
53. Flamenco interview.
54. Sancho interview.
55. Flamenco interview.
56. Sancho interview.
57. Minhero interview.
58. Sancho interview.
59. Flamenco interview.
60. Flamenco interview.
61. According to Sancho, military officers used expressions such as the following to refer to La Masacuata in the 1960s: "These crazy intellectuals just talk BS, they don't know what to do"; "They are a bunch of bums"; and "They are poets; they speak stuff." Sancho interview.
62. Minhero interview.
63. Flamenco interview.
64. Flamenco interview.
65. Schafik Hándal, *Legado de un revolucionario: Del rescate de la historia a la construcción del futuro* (San Salvador: Ediciones Instituto Schafik Hándal, 2011), p. 157.
66. Flamenco interview.
67. Sancho interview.
68. Flamenco interview.
69. Sancho interview.
70. Sancho interview; Flamenco interview; Minhero interview.
71. *Brigada La Masacuata* (San Vicente: Editorial Ramírez, 1970), n.p.
72. Sancho interview.
73. Alberto Masferrer, *El dinero maldito* (San Salvador: Editorial Jurídica Salvadoreña, 2013); Masferrer, *Leer y escribir/Cartas a un obrero* (San Salvador: Editorial Jurídica Salvadoreña, 2011); Masferrer, *Leer y escribir/El minimun vital* (San Salvador: Dirección de Publicaciones e Impresos de CONCULTURA, [1929] 2000); Masferrer, *Una vida en el cine* (San Salvador: Editorial Jurídica Salvadoreña, 2007).
74. Sancho interview.
75. Sancho interview.
76. *Brigada La Masacuata*.
77. Sancho interview.
78. Sancho interview.
79. Sancho interview.
80. Sancho interview.
81. Schafik Jorge Hándal, "Reflexiones sobre los problemas de la revolución Latinoamericana" (mimeograph, 1968), pp. 11–17.
82. Sancho interview.
83. Sancho interview.
84. The other initiators of El Grupo were one Melesia, Alejandro Rivas Mira, Ricardo Sol, Carlos Menjívar, and Salvador Montoya. Fabio Castillo—the former rector of the University of El Salvador—supported El Grupo; see Sancho, *Crónicas entre los espejos*, p. 73.
85. Sancho interview.

86. For a journalistic account of the origins of El Grupo, the ERP, and the FPL, see Giovani Galeas, *Héroes bajo sospecha* (San Salvador: Athena, 2013).
87. Alejandro Rivas Mira has often been considered the instigator of Roque Dalton's execution in 1975. He later left the ERP, allegedly taking with him the organization's war fund. Since that time, the whereabouts of Rivas Mira are unknown. The journalist Juan J. Dalton speculated about the death of Rivas Mira circa 2009 but did not offer conclusive evidence to make his case. Juan J. Dalton, "La Muerte del Instigador del Asesinato de Roque Dalton," *Contrapunto*, June 28, 2013, http://www.contrapunto.com.sv/literatura/la-muerte-del-instigador-del-asesinato-de-roque-dalton, accessed February 26, 2014.
88. Rico Mira, *En silencio tenía que ser*, p. 65.
89. Rodríguez interview.
90. Sancho interview.
91. Sancho interview.
92. Rico Mira, *En silencio tenía que ser*, pp. 74–83.
93. Sancho interview.
94. Sancho interview.
95. Sancho interview.
96. Sancho interview.
97. Flamenco interview.
98. *Brigada La Masacuata.*
99. *Brigada La Masacuata.*
100. Roberto Roca, Armando Sibrián, Carlos Menjívar, one Manuel, Julia Rodríguez, and Leonel Lemus Arévalo (aka "Luis"); see Rico Mira, *En silencio tenía que ser*, pp. 31–32. "In March 1972, the People's Revolutionary Army (ERP) was constituted with surviving members of the 'GRUPO;' two military units that conducted the first military confiscation (*recuperación militar*) were formed. These were structured as follows: Military Unit 1: Chief Leonel Lemus, Pancho (RN militant) [Rico Mira], Armando Sibrián (fallen), Manuel Angulo, Roberto Roca (Secretary General of the PRTC); Military Unit 2: Chief Carlos Menjívar (fallen in 1972 in an accidental explosion. Died at the Military Hospital), Gilberto Orellana, Gonzalo (RN militant) [Alfonso Hernández], Julia Rodríguez (conspirator expelled from the RN)." Resistencia Nacional, *Por la causa proletaria*, p. 10.
101. Rico Mira, *En silencio tenía que ser*, pp. 31–32; Resistencia Nacional, *Por la causa proletaria*, p. 10.
102. For instance, he described in agonizing detail the attack against a paramilitary garrison commanded by the death squad leader Fabián Ventura carried out by RN combatants in Guazapa on August 14, 1980. Rico Mira did not mince words in his depiction of the awful combat between the RN and the paramilitaries and the killing of Ventura, a figure who had terrorized peasant communities in the area for several years. The RN displayed Ventura's corpse for weeks among peasant communities in Guazapa to destroy the purported myth of the invincibility of Ventura's death squads. Rico Mira, *En silencio tenía que ser*, pp. 269–281.
103. Rico Mira, *En silencio tenía que ser*, pp. 38–39.
104. Comando Armado "José Feliciano Ama," E.R.P., "Comunicado Numero 1 del Ejercito Revolucionario del Pueblo–ERP–." MUPI sv/mupi/cf002/002/F180.01.
105. Binford, *The El Mozote Massacre*, pp. 27–48; Flamenco interview.
106. Flamenco interview.
107. Flamenco interview.
108. Flamenco interview.
109. Minhero interview.
110. Sorto interview.

Chapter 5

1. "Miss Universo inició enorme plan turístico," *La Prensa Gráfica*, July 30, 1975, pp. 2, 42; "Heridos al disolver ayer manifestación," *La Prensa Gráfica*, July 31, 1975, pp. 3, 70.
2. Roberto Antonio Miranda and Ibalmore Cortez Vásquez, two students wounded by state agents during these incidents, died at a nearby hospital. An incomplete list of the

students who disappeared during the crackdown includes José Domingo Aldana, Ebert Gómez Mendoza, Carlos Humberto Hernández, Napoleón Orlando Calderón Grande, Luis Armando Villalobos, Ana Cecilia Mercedes Milla, Carlos Alberto Fonseca, Reynaldo Enrique Hasbún Jiménez, and Sergio Antonio Cabrera. More than fifty people received medical treatment at various hospitals as a result of the gunshots, stabbings, and contusions they suffered during the incidents. "Exigen formación de comisión investigadora," *Opinión Estudiantil*, August 14, 1975, p. 2.

3. "Bellezas Mundiales," *La Prensa Gráfica*, July 13, 1975, p. 1.
4. Consejo Ejecutivo ANDES 21 de Junio, "ANDES 21 de Junio frente a Miss Universo," in ANDES, *Resoluciones de congresos y posiciones de ANDES 21 de Junio en la lucha ideológica que se lleva a cabo en el país, periodo 1974–1977* (San Salvador, 1977), pp. 17–18.
5. Gordon, *Crisis política y guerra en El Salvador*, pp. 180–181.
6. For a comprehensive study of this event, see Jeffrey L. Gould and Aldo A. Lauria-Santiago, *To Rise in Darkness: Revolution, Repression, and Memory in El Salvador, 1920–1932* (Durham, NC: Duke University Press, 2008).
7. Richard Lee Turits, *Foundations of Despotism: Peasants, the Trujillo Regime, and Modernity in Dominican History* (Stanford, CA: Stanford University Press, 2003), pp. 80–114. For a cultural history of the Trujillo regime, see Lauren Derby, *The Dictator's Seduction: Politics and the Popular Imagination in the Era of Trujillo* (Durham, NC: Duke University Press, 2009).
8. For a study on paramilitary structures prior to the 1932 indigenous uprising, see Alvarenga, *Cultura y ética de la violencia, El Salvador*.
9. Gordon, *Crisis política y guerra en El Salvador*, pp. 181–182.
10. Pierre Bourdieu cited in Michel-Rolph Trouillot, *Silencing the Past: Power and the Production of History* (Boston: Beacon Press, 1995), pp. 82–83.
11. To this day, Salvadoran elites as well as retired and active Salvadoran military officers subscribe to this explanation of the origins of the Salvadoran civil war; see, for instance, Juan Orlando Zepeda Herrera, *Perfiles de la guerra en El Salvador* (San Salvador: New Graphics, 2008).
12. The reflections on the impact of public discourses that silence, justify, promote, or attenuate the seriousness of state-sponsored human rights violations against groups or individuals, conducted respectively by Theodor W. Adorno and Henry A. Giroux, informed my analysis of the reverberations of media coverage and state propaganda as discourses that matched the mounting state terror against intellectuals; see Theodor W. Adorno, "Education after Auschwitz," in *Critical Models: Interventions and Catch Words* (New York: Columbia University Press, 1998), pp. 191–204.; and Henry A. Giroux, "Education after Abu Ghraib: Revisiting Adorno's Politics of Education," *Cultural Studies* 18, no. 6 (November 2004): 779–815.
13. "When I got off the bus around 4 p.m. [in Potonico circa January 1965], I faced a dramatic situation," said López. Carlos López, interview by Joaquín Chávez (April 9, 2007).
14. López interview.
15. Salvador Sánchez Cerén, interview by Joaquín Chávez (April 9, 2007).
16. In 1971, the average salary for high school teachers ranged between 350 *colones* (US$140) and 450 *colones* (US$180). That year, ANDES demanded that salaries be increased to amounts ranging between 425 *colones* (US$170) and 650 *colones* (US$260). Mélida Anaya Montes, *La segunda gran batalla de ANDES* (San Salvador: Editorial Universitaria de El Salvador, 1972), pp. 9, 13.
17. Anaya Montes, *La segunda gran batalla de ANDES*, p. 9.
18. López interview; Sánchez Cerén interview; Anaya Montes, *La segunda gran batalla de ANDES*, p. 39.
19. López interview.
20. López interview.
21. López interview.
22. Anaya Montes, *La segunda gran batalla de ANDES*, p. 40.
23. López interview.
24. Anaya Montes, *La segunda gran batalla de ANDES*, pp. 7–8.
25. Sánchez Cerén interview; López interview; Anaya Montes, *La segunda gran batalla de ANDES*, pp. 8–12.
26. Lindo-Fuentes and Ching, *Modernizing Minds in El Salvador*, pp. 120–136.

27. Lindo-Fuentes and Ching, *Modernizing Minds in El Salvador*, pp. 160–161.
28. Lindo-Fuentes and Ching, *Modernizing Minds in El Salvador*, pp. 187–191.
29. "Declaraciones del X Congreso de ANDES 21 de Junio," in ANDES, *Resoluciones de Congresos y Posiciones de ANDES 21 de Junio*, p. 26.
30. ANDES, "Declaraciones del X Congreso de ANDES 21 de Junio," pp. 22–23.
31. ANDES, "Declaraciones del X Congreso de ANDES 21 de Junio," pp. 22–25.
32. "Inevitable la huelga general mañana de maestros de ANDES [sic]," *La Prensa Gráfica*, July 7, 1971, pp. 3, 58.
33. "234 Escuelas laboran cuando comienzan a aplicar descuentos," *La Prensa Gráfica*, July 16, 1971, pp. 3, 49.
34. Anaya Montes, *La segunda gran batalla de ANDES*, p. 40.
35. The PCN-dominated National Assembly sanctioned *La Ley de Asistencia al Magisterio* (Law of Assistance to Teachers) *and La Ley General de Educación* (General Law of Education), which provided legal bases for the government's educational reform, but it rejected ANDES's petition for a salary increase for teachers. Anaya Montes, *La segunda gran batalla de ANDES*, p. 41. José Mario López argued in favor of the creation of the Consejo Nacional de Escalafón at the National Assembly on July 16, 1971; see "Violentos debates por Ley de Escalafón Ayer," *La Prensa Gráfica*, July 17, 1971, pp. 5, 13.
36. Anaya Montes, *La segunda gran batalla de ANDES*, pp. 42–45.
37. "Violencia asesina del Gobierno de Sánchez Hernandez," *Opinión Estudiantil*, Epoca 23, No. 10 Edición Extraordinaria, 1 de Julio de 1971, p. 2.
38. ANDES and AGEUS published lists of numerous victims of the repression. "Gobierno Ametralla Maestros y Estudiantes," *Opinión Estudiantil*, Epoca 23, No. 10 Edición Extraordinaria, 1 de Julio de 1971, front page; "Últimos datos de golpeados y desaparecidos," *Opinión Estudiantil*, Epoca 23, No. 10 Edición Extraordinaria, 1 de Julio de 1971, p. 3; "Atropellos del gobierno," *Opinión Estudiantil*, Epoca 23, No. 10 Edición Extraordinaria, 1 de Julio de 1971, p. 2; "Indignación en Todo el País 84 Mitines en Dos Días," *Opinión Estudiantil*, Epoca 23, No. 11 Tercera Semana de Julio de 1971, front page.
39. The victims of the repression included the following persons: José Balmore Saca García, a university student, Dr. Alberto Vásquez, a professor at the University of El Salvador, Luis Felipe Quezada, a Mexican professor who survived the Tlatelolco massacre who taught at the University of El Salvador, and Mario Rosales Araujo, an agricultural engineer. "Violencia asesina del gobierno de Sánchez Hernandez," *Opinión Estudiantil*, Epoca 23, No. 10 Edición Extraordinaria, 1 de Julio de 1971, p. 2.
40. Anaya Montes, *La segunda gran batalla de ANDES*, pp. 54–55.
41. Anaya Montes, *La segunda gran batalla de ANDES*, pp. 58–60.
42. Paramilitaries and state agents attacked the homes of ANDES leaders Anaya Montes, José Mario López, Arnoldo Vaquerano, Carmen Cañas de Lazo, and Norma de Sotelo. Anaya Montes, *La segunda gran batalla de ANDES*, p. 52.
43. Anaya Montes, *La segunda gran batalla de ANDES*, p. 104.
44. Carlos López commented that two fellow teachers who worked in Chalatenango in 1971 whom he identified as "Toqui Toqui" and Olmedo were also gunned down by state agents in Chalatenango. López interview.
45. López interview.
46. "Querido maestro, porqué abandonas a tus alumnos y a tus propias responsabilidades?," *La Prensa Gráfica*, July 8, 1971, p. 24.
47. "Lo que piensan los niños de sus maestros," *La Prensa Gráfica*, July 10, 1971, p. 34.
48. "Lo que piensan los niños de sus maestros," p. 34.
49. La Niña Menchita, a teacher at Escuela República del Paraguay in San Salvador, supported the teachers' strike from "the beginning to the end." Anaya Montes, *La segunda gran batalla de ANDES*, pp. 141–142.
50. Alfredo Chávez Saravia, Julia Yolanda Durán Castro, and Oscar Armando Avendaño, "Manifiesto a la Conciencia del Magisterio Salvadoreño," *La Prensa Gráfica*, July 7, 1971, p. 47.
51. "Repudio de padres de familia a la huelga de maestros," *La Prensa Gráfica*, July 9, 1971, p. 32.
52. "No declarará Cáceres P. al ser enviado al juez," *La Prensa Gráfica*, July 6, 1971, pp. 3, 27.

53. "Cáceres Prendes niega su declaración extrajudicial," *La Prensa Gráfica*, July 8, 1971, pp. 3, 9; "Citan al Dr. Fabio Castillo a declarar en caso de secuestro," *La Prensa Gráfica*, July 16, 1971, pp. 2, 41 La Prensa published pictures of the alleged members of El Grupo; see *La Prensa Grafica*, July 7, 1971, pp. 2, 46.
54. "Literatura subversiva se le decomisa a maestro de ANDES," *La Prensa Gráfica*, July 14, 1971, p. 3.
55. "La verdad de dos líderes," *La Prensa Gráfica*, July 14, 1971, p. 42.
56. "Torres ve mano roja en movimiento de ANDES," *La Prensa Gráfica*, July 17, 1971; "Comunistas buscan violencia," *La Prensa Gráfica*, July 20, 1971, pp. 3, 37.
57. "Violentos debates por Ley de Escalafón Ayer," pp. 5, 13.
58. "Carta abierta de Fabio Castillo," *Opinión Estudiantil*, Epoca 23, No. 11, Tercera Semana de Julio 1971, p. 2.
59. "Con gusto declarará sobre el secuestro dijo Fabio Castillo," *La Prensa Gráfica*, November 17, 1971, p. 4; "Carta abierta de Fabio Castillo," *Opinión Estudiantil*, Epoca 23, No. 11, Tercera Semana de Julio 1971, p. 2.
60. "Fabio C.: Farsa judicial caso Prendes," *El Tiempo*, Tercera Semana de Julio de 1971, p. 3.
61. "Violentos debates por Ley de Escalafón Ayer," pp. 5, 13.
62. Anaya Montes, *La segunda gran batalla de ANDES*, p. 87.
63. Anaya Montes, *La segunda gran batalla de ANDES*, p. 49.
64. Anaya Montes, *La segunda gran batalla de ANDES*, pp. 119, 182, 183.
65. Anaya Montes, *La segunda gran batalla de ANDES*, pp. 118–119.
66. López interview.
67. "Los catedráticos de Ciudad Normal 'Alberto Masferrer' y maestros de Televisión Educativa ante el pueblo," *La Prensa Gráfica*, July 12, 1971, p. 30.
68. "Violencia asesina del Gobierno de Sánchez Hernández," *Opinión Estudiantil*, Epoca 23, No. 10 Edición Extraordinaria, 1 de Julio de 1971, p. 2.
69. In the 1970s, intellectuals and activists also founded the Popular Leagues February 28 (LP-28), the Leagues for Liberation (LL), and other similar movements.
70. Montalvo interview.
71. Carlos Evaristo Hernández, "Notas para un testimonio. Ciudad Universitaria, San Salvador 30 de Julio de 1975" (San Salvador, 2001), http://www.monografias.com/trabajos15/masacre-san-salvador/masacre-san-salvador.shtml, accessed October 4, 2014.
72. Rico Mira, "La Masacre del 30 de Julio de 1975: Testimonio Mirna Antonieta Perla," in *En silencio tenía que ser*, pp. 120–122.
73. Fernández interview.
74. Hernández, "Notas para un testimonio. Ciudad Universitaria, San Salvador 30 de Julio de 1975."
75. Montalvo interview.
76. Oscar Miranda, interview by Joaquín Chávez (April 11, 2007).
77. "Ibalmore Cortez Vásquez otra víctima del 30 de Julio," *Opinión Estudiantil*, Epoca 25, No. 2, 14 de Agosto de 1975, p. 2.
78. "Exigen formación de Comisión Investigadora," *Opinión Estudiantil*, Epoca 25, No. 2, 14 de Agosto de 1975, p. 2.
79. Rico Mira, "La Masacre del 30 de Julio de 1975," p. 123.
80. The official communiqué claimed that the demonstrators threw "phosphorus grenades, Molotov cocktails, and fired automatic and semiautomatic weapons" at the state agents. "Ministerio de Defensa da a conocer sucesos de ayer," *La Prensa Gráfica*, July 31, 1975, p. 63.
81. "Cuál debe ser la respuesta ante la escalada represiva?," *Opinión Estudiantil*, Epoca 25 No. 2, 14 de Agosto 1975, p. 3.
82. "Cuál debe ser la respuesta ante la escalada represiva?," *Opinión Estudiantil*, Epoca 25 No. 2, 14 de Agosto 1975, p. 3.
83. "Retiro de la UNO: Caducidad de la Vía Electoral," *Opinión Estudiantil*, Epoca 26 No. 5, Primera Quincena de Marzo 1976, front page; "Sobre las formas de lucha," *Opinión Estudiantil*, Epoca 26 No. 5, Primera Quincena de Marzo 1976, p. 3.
84. "Carlos Alfaro Castillo ¡Renuncie!," *Opinión Estudiantil*, Epoca 25 No. 2, 14 de Agosto de 1975, p. 4.

85. FPL, "Comunicado de las Fuerzas Populares de Liberación -FPL- Farabundo Martí sobre la Operación Héroes Revolucionarios de Agosto: Carlos Fonseca, Juan Sebastián y Alberto, Ignacio, Úrsula y Arnoldo," *El Rebelde* 5, no. 58 (August 1977), pp. 3–5.
86. Enríquez interview.
87. "Grupo que tomaron [sic] Catedral externan [sic] motivo de desalojo," *La Prensa Gráfica*, August 7, 1975, pp. 2, 42.
88. "Comunicado al Pueblo Salvadoreño del Grupo de Cristianos que se Tomó la Catedral," *La Prensa Gráfica*, August 8, 1975, p. 25.
89. Secretaría de Información de la Presidencia de la República, "Aclaración al Pueblo Salvadoreño," *La Prensa Gráfica*, August 11, 1975, p. 23.
90. The Movimiento de Estudiantes Revolucionarios de Secundaria (High School Students Revolutionary Movement [MERS]), the Universitarios Revolucionarios 19 de Julio (Revolutionary University Students July 19 [UR-19]), the Unión de Pobladores de Tugurios (Union of Dwellers of Shantytowns [UPT]), and the Comité Coordinador de Sindicatos José Guillermo Rivas (Coordinating Committee of Unions José Guillermo Rivas) were also founding organizations of the BPR.
91. Facundo Guardado, interview by Joaquín Chávez (November 12, 2007).
92. FECCAS-UTC, "FECCAS-UTC la tiranía militar invade zonas.".
93. FECCAS-UTC, "UTC-FECCAS informa a los trabajadores del campo y pueblo en general.".
94. FECCAS-UTC, "UTC-FECCAS denunciamos" (mimeograph, February 1978).
95. Guardado interview; Enríquez interview.
96. The National Resistance (RN), an insurgent group, criticized the PCS stance vis-à-vis Molina. Citing *Voz Popular*, a PCS newspaper, the RN rejected the PCS's policy of "critical support" to the reformist agrarian policies conducted by the Molina government in the early 1970s. National Resistance, "Desenmascarando a los Revisionistas de 'Voz Popular,'" in *Por La Causa Proletaria*, year II, no. 15 (February 1975), pp. 1–3.
97. Ignacio Ellacuría, "A sus órdenes mi capital," in *Veinte años de historia en El Salvador (1969–1989): Escritos políticos*, ed. Ignacio Ellacuría, 649–656 (San Salvador: UCA Editores, 1993), pp. 650–651.
98. Merlos interview.
99. Guardado interview.
100. Cardenal, *Historia de una esperanza*, pp. 570–577.
101. According to FECCAS-UTC, the landowners "Kurt Nottebom [sic], Francisco H. [sic] de Sola, Francisco Orellana, Gustavo Contreras, Solina Escobar, Carlos York [sic] [Carlos Llort]" were involved in the killing of Rutilio Grande and the repression against the peasant movement in Aguilares. FECCAS-UTC, "La tiranía criminal ataca bestialmente la heróica toma de tierra 'Nelson, Manuel y Rutilio' y a toda la zona de Aguilares" (mimeograph, May 17, 1977).
102. FECCAS-UTC, "Combatamos sin descanso a la pandía [sic] de criminales de ORDEN que opera en la zona de Aguilares" (mimeograph, August 1977).
103. FECCAS-UTC, "La tiranía criminal ataca bestialmente la heróica toma de tierra 'Nelson, Manuel y Rutilio' y a toda la zona de Aguilares."
104. FECCAS-UTC, "La tiranía criminal ataca bestialmente la heróica toma de tierra 'Nelson, Manuel y Rutilio' y a toda la zona de Aguilares."
105. FECCAS-UTC, "Combatamos sin descanso a la pandía [sic] de criminales de ORDEN que opera en la zona de Aguilares."
106. Consejo Ejecutivo ANDES 21 de Junio, "ANDES 21 de Junio solidaria con el pueblo de Aguilares," ANDES, *Resoluciones de congresos y posiciones de ANDES 21 de Junio en la lucha ideológica que se lleva a cabo en el país, Periodo 1974–1977* (San Salvador, 1977), pp. 96–99.
107. FECCAS-UTC, "Con la lucha organizada y combativa obtienen triunfos los campesinos pobres y medios" (mimeograph, May 1, 1979).
108. Carl von Clausewitz, a nineteenth-century theorist of war, pondered the role of subjectivity in the outbreak of war. His ideas on the role of emotions (i.e., "hostile intent") in the origin of war suggest that in fact conflicts manifest in the intensification of animosity toward the "enemy" forces. Carl von Clausewitz, *On War*, ed. Michael Howard and Peter Paret; trans. Michael Howard and Peter Paret (Princeton, NJ: Princeton University Press, 1984), p. 76.

109. Martínez interview.
110. FECCAS-UTC, "Viva la lucha reivindicativa de los jornaleros," *FECCAS-UTC Informa* (mimeograph, undated).
111. UTC-FECCAS, "UTC-FECCAS a la clase obrera y pueblo en general."
112. UTC-FECCAS, "UTC-FECCAS a los campesinos pobres" (mimeograph, undated).
113. "Por primera vez se toman ministerio en el país," *El Mundo*, November 11, 1977, p. 2.
114. "Por primera vez se toman ministerio en el país," p. 2; "Con violencia entró BPR al despacho del Ministro de Trabajo," *El Mundo*, November 12, 1977, p. 21.
115. Letra de "Lucha Reivindicativa":

> Acérquese compañero
> a reclamar su salario (bis)
> Porque es lo que exigimos
> Todos los revolucionarios (bis)
>
> ¡Guerra! A la tiranía
> ¡Tiembla¡ Ante la guerrilla (bis)
>
> Nosotros lo que pedimos
> Es salario de once colones (bis)
> Y también lo que exigimos
> Arroz, tortilla y frijoles (bis)
>
> ¡Guerra! A la tiranía
> ¡Tiembla¡ Ante la guerrilla (bis)
>
> Los señores de allá arriba
> Están con culillera (bis)
> Porque aquí está todo el Bloque
> Dispuestos a hacer la huelga (bis)
>
> ¡Guerra! A la tiranía
> ¡Tiembla¡ Ante la guerrilla (bis)
>
> Los señores de las fincas
> Están llamando hasta la guardia (bis)
> Para que no reclamemos
> Nuestro aumento de salario (bis)
>
> ¡Guerra! A la tiranía
> ¡Tiembla¡ Ante la guerrilla (bis)

Tambor boletín informativo del Departamento de Promoción Artística, Bando No. 2, Universidad de El Salvador, June 9, 1980, p. 4.
116. Iraheta rhetorically asked, "How is it possible that a teacher leader . . . can lead a group like this?" "Ocupantes del ministerio violan los derechos humanos," *El Diario de Hoy*, November 12, 1977, pp. 5, 11; "Gobierno no negocia con ocupantes de ministerio," *El Diario de Hoy*, November 12, 1977, pp. 5, 27.
117. "Desocupan ministerio tras 50 horas de sitio," *El Diario de Hoy*, November 14, 1977, pp. 9, 89.
118. Guardado interview.
119. Guardado interview.
120. Zamora interview; Hilda Mejía interview; Guadalupe Mejía interview.
121. Zamora interview; Hilda Mejía interview; Guadalupe Mejía interview.
122. Zamora interview.

Chapter 6

1. The safe house was the headquarters of the FPL committee in charge of relations with social movements, known as the National Commission of Masses (CONAMAS). Montalvo interview; Atilio Montalvo, "Clarita, Alejandro y Andrés," in Victoria Eugenia Ramírez Acosta, *Eva, Chico y Toño* (San Salvador: Fundabril, 2010), p. 37.

2. They wrote, with their own blood, the letters "FPL" on a wall. Ramirez Acosta, *Eva, Chico y Toño*, p. 9.

3. The reporter who covered this episode for *El Diario de Hoy* wondered: "How many 'Chicos,' 'Marcos' [*sic*] and 'Evas' are waiting for their turn? . . . There is expectation to know the identities of the dead"; see Francisco Romero Cerna, "Suicídanse tres terroristas después de 8 hrs. de fuego," *El Diario de Hoy*, October 12, 1976, p. 2.

4. Montalvo interview; Victoria Ramírez, interview by Joaquín Chávez (October 10, 2006); Ramírez Acosta, *Eva, Chico y Tono*, pp. 11–13.

5. I use the term "insurgent intellectuals" to mean university students, dissidents of political parties, peasant leaders, and teachers who articulated the ideology and politics of the guerrilla movement in El Salvador in the 1970s and 1980s.

6. FPL, *Estrella Roja No 3*, p. 1.

7. Héctor Martínez, interview by Joaquín Chávez (April 18, 2007). The Andrés Torres Sánchez Battalion, or SS-20, was part of the FPL's Felipe Peña Mendoza Brigade. It operated in the department of San Vicente. Armando Salazar, *Los secretos de El Paraíso* (San Salvador: UCA Editores, 2016), table 2, p. 211.

8. Ramírez interview.

9. Ramírez interview.

10. Gilman, *Entre la pluma y el fusil*, pp. 57–66.

11. Gilman, *Entre la pluma y el fusil*, pp. 97–120.

12. Gilman, *Entre la pluma y el fusil*, pp. 113–120.

13. Gilman, *Entre la pluma y el fusil*, pp. 81–82, 113.

14. Gilman, *Entre la pluma y el fusil*, p. 113.

15. Dalton, *Revolución en la revolución?*; Dalton et al., *El intelectual y la sociedad*.

16. Dalton, *No pronuncies mi nombre*, pp. 415–433.

17. Gilman, *Entre la pluma y el fusil*, pp. 164, 169–175.

18. Gilman, *Entre la pluma y el fusil*, p. 168.

19. Gilman, *Entre la pluma y el fusil*, pp. 178, 181.

20. Gilman, *Entre la pluma y el fusil*, pp. 158–187.

21. Donald C. Hodges, ed., *Legacy of Che Guevara: A Documentary Study* (London: Thames and Hudson, 1977), p. 101.

22. Hodges, *Legacy of Che Guevara*, pp. 100–101.

23. Santacruz interview (April 17, 2007).

24. Jorge I. Domínguez, *To Make the World Safe for Revolution: Cuba's Foreign Policy* (Cambridge, MA: Harvard University Press, 1989), p. 125.

25. Pearce, *Promised Land*, pp. 126–127.

26. Harnecker, *Con la mirada en alto*, p. 16.

27. Hándal, "Reflexiones," p. 1.

28. Hándal, "Reflexiones," p. 1.

29. Hándal, "Reflexiones," pp. 1–2.

30. Hándal, "Reflexiones," p. 3.

31. Hándal, "Reflexiones," pp. 1–4.

32. Hándal wrote: "Dozens of guerrilla experiences have failed or face a chronic situation of stagnation and weakness. But this truth cannot serve to hide this other: during the last thirty years *all* the experiences that sought a peaceful transit to revolution have failed. . . . All these attempts have been defeated through a mercenary invasion as in Guatemala [in 1954], through a coup like in Brazil [in 1964], through a counterrevolutionary civil war like in Costa Rica [in 1948], [or] through the betrayal [of the communists] by the bourgeois allies that led the government [of President Gabriel González Videla] in Chile [between 1946 and 1948] and [the subsequent] cruel repressive violence against the revolutionaries." Hándal, "Reflexiones," pp. 6–7 (emphasis in original).

33. Hándal, "Reflexiones," pp. 11–17.

34. Underscore in the original. In "Reflexiones" Hándal also wrote: "In general terms in the case of the Latin American revolutions, taking into account all that has been said about the counterrevolutionary strategy of [US] Imperialism, the armed struggle will be central to take over power. . . . it will be a means to complete the accumulation of forces and it will lead to taking over power after a prolonged revolutionary war. Armed struggle is a general rule to take

over power, but [it] is not a general rule in the accumulation of [political] forces. Hándal, "Reflexiones," pp. 52–53.

35. Santacruz interview.
36. Organization of Latin American Solidarity, "OLAS General Declaration," *International Socialist Review* 28, no. 6 (November–December 1967): 50–55, Marxist Internet Archive, http://www.marxists.org/history/etol/newspape/isr/vol28/no06/olas.htm, accessed February 28, 2014.
37. Hándal, "Reflexiones," p. 11.
38. Santacruz interview.
39. Dalton, *Revolución en la revolución?*; Régis Debray, *Revolution dans la revolution? Lutte armée et lutte politique en Amérique Latine* (Paris: Maspero, 1967).
40. Santacruz interview.
41. FLACSO El Salvador and Fundación "Dr. Manuel Gallardo," "Treinta y cinco años después . . . ," in *Prensa clandestina*, pp. 111–113.
42. FLACSO El Salvador and Fundación "Dr. Manuel Gallardo," "Treinta y cinco años después . . . ," in *Prensa clandestina*, p. 114; Marta Harnecker, *Los conceptos elementales del materialismo histórico*, sexta edición (Buenos Aires: Siglo Veintiuno Editores, 1971).
43. FLACSO El Salvador and Fundación "Dr. Manuel Gallardo" "Treinta y cinco años después . . . ," in *Prensa clandestina*, p. 114.
44. Debray, *Revolution dans la revolution?*, pp. 23–44.
45. "La guérilla est le Parti en gestation," famously wrote Debray; see *Revolution dans la revolution?*, p. 114.
46. Debray, see *Revolution dans la revolution?*, pp. 107–108.
47. Pompeyo Márquez cited in Dalton, *Revolución en la revolución?*, p. 69.
48. Márquez cited in Dalton, *Revolución en la revolución?* pp. 70–71.
49. Dalton rhetorically asked: Is it possible to "take power . . . without militarily defeating the oligarchies and in case of [US] direct intervention imperialism itself [?]" Was it viable to achieve those objectives "without building a force capable of defeating . . . the armed forces of such enemy[?]" Was it plausible to build such force without first conducting "guerrilla warfare in the countryside"[?]; see Dalton, *Revolución en la revolución?*, p. 72.
50. FLACSO El Salvador and Fundación "Dr. Manuel Gallardo," "Treinta y cinco años después . . . ," in *Prensa clandestina*, p. 116.
51. The PCS leadership called on its militants to join the Salvadoran military's war effort against Honduras. Jovel interview.
52. Santacruz interview.
53. Harnecker, *Con la mirada en alto*, p. 15.
54. Harnecker, *Con la mirada en alto*, pp. 31–32, 42–44.
55. Harnecker, *Con la mirada en alto*, pp. 57–58.
56. Hodges, *Legacy of Che Guevara*, pp. 100–102.
57. Sancho interview.
58. Sancho interview. Ernesto Guevara, *Bolivian Diary [of] Ernesto 'Che' Guevara*, introduction by Fidel Castro, translated by Carlos P. Hansen and Andrew Sinclair (London: Lorrimer Publishing, 1968).
59. Hodges, *Legacy of Che Guevara*, p. 102.
60. Sancho interview.
61. Alvarenga, *Roque Dalton*, pp. 102–106.
62. Jovel interview.
63. Sancho interview.
64. Sancho interview.
65. Hándal, *Legado de un revolucionario*, pp. 197–199.
66. In 1982, Carpio wrote about his interactions with El Grupo; see "Cuaderno No. 2 nuestros esfuerzos por compartir nuestras obligaciones con otros sectores que se califican de Marxistas (estrictamente interno)," (mimeograh, 1982). Also see Salvador Cayetano Carpio, *Nuestras montañas son las masas* (San Salvador: Carpio-Alvarenga Editores, 2011), pp. 148–149.
67. Sancho interview.
68. Most members of El Grupo were former members of the Revolutionary Federation of Social Christian University Students (FRUSC), a student organization at the National University.

69. Ernesto Regalado Dueñas was the grandson of the former presidents Tomás Regalado and Francisco Dueñas. "Ernesto Regalado Dueñas secuestrado," *El Independiente*, February 13, 1971, p. 4. Michael McClintock, a scholar who studied the history of US counterinsurgency in El Salvador in the 1980s, raised the possibility that the real culprits of Regalado's abduction and murder were in fact state agents. In his view, this crime served to create a "red scare" and to justify a major crackdown on the left and legal opposition parties in 1971. McClintock, *The American Connection*, p. 168. In 2002, Eduardo Sancho, a founder of the Salvadoran guerrillas, publicly acknowledged that El Grupo in fact kidnapped and assassinated Regalado. Sancho, *Crónicas entre los espejos*, pp. 74–75.

70. Sancho interview.

71. Montalvo interview.

72. Aguiñada Carranza interview.

73. Medina interview.

74. Montalvo interview.

75. Sancho, *Crónicas entre los espejos*, pp. 73–87, 120–122.

76. Sancho, *Crónicas entre los espejos*, pp. 96–97.

77. Lil Milagro Ramírez, letter addressed to her mother (San Salvador, March 1972).

78. Montalvo interview.

79. Velásquez interview. ERP, "Es tu arma, el voto?" (mimeograph, December 1971).

80. Velásquez interview.

81. Montalvo interview.

82. FPL, *Estrella Roja 2*, pp. 21–30.

83. Resistencia Nacional, *Por la causa proletaria*, p. 16.

84. Sancho, *Crónicas entre los espejos*, p. 90.

85. Rico Mira, *En silencio tenía que ser*, pp. 30–47, 116–128. Rico Mira's account is consistent with the RN's version of this episode. Resistencia Nacional, *Por la causa proletaria*, p. 10, Carlos Marighella, *Minimanual of the Urban Guerrilla* (1969), Marxist Archive, https://www.marxists.org/archive/marighella-carlos/1969/06/minimanual-urban-guerrilla/index.htm accessed September 4, 2016.

86. Rafael Velásquez, a leader of the ERP in the 1970s, claimed that Schafik Hándal blasted the guerrillas at a public assembly at the University of El Salvador that took place a few days after the ERP first military operation in 1972. Velásquez interview.

87. Organización Revolucionaria de los Trabajadores (ORT), "Manifiesto de la Organización Revolucionaria de los Trabajadores (O.R.T.) en el Dia Internacional del Trabajo" (mimeograph, May 1, 1974).

88. Rico Mira, *En silencio tenía que ser*, p. 40.

89. Resistencia Nacional, *Por la causa proletaria*, p. 10; Fermán Cienfuegos, *Veredas de la audacia: Historia del FMLN* (San Salvador: Editorial Arcoiris, 1993), p. 23.

90. Salvador Cayetano Carpio, "Cuaderno No 1 sobre algunos problemas de organización que consideró el Comando Central" (mimeograph, 1982), pp. 4–6.

91. Partido de la Revolución Salvadoreña–Ejercito Revolucionario del Pueblo (PRS-ERP), "Nuestro partido abre relaciones con el Partido Comunista Chino," *Prensa Comunista* (1975), p. 12.

92. PRS-ERP, "Sólo con la Lucha Armada de Masas Podremos Derrotar al Fascismo," *Prensa Comunista*, no. 4 (mimeograph, 1975).

93. Resistencia Nacional, *Por la causa proletaria*, p. 10.

94. Montalvo interview.

95. Juan Ramón Medrano, *Memorias de un guerrillero: Comandante Balta* 3ʳᵈ. ed. (San Salvador: New Graphics S.A. de C.V., 2007), pp. 13–27.

96. ACUS, Pax Christi in Regno Christi, August 31, 1958.

97. Relaciones Públicas de Casa Presidencial, "Severo Mentís a Los Profesionales de La Calumnia y La Mentira: Roque Dalton García Capturado," *La Prensa Gráfica*, October 13, 1960, p. 31.

98. In 2005, a group of self-identified former ERP combatants still asked Joaquín Villalobos to reveal the whereabouts of Dalton's remains. Reagrupamiento Político del Ejército Revolucionario del Pueblo, "Coyuntura Política ERP" (mimeograph, May 2005).

99. For instance, Juan Ramón Medrano (aka "Balta"), a top ERP commander during the civil war, offered a detailed account of the circumstances of Dalton's murder. According to Medrano, Alejandro Rivas Mira, Joaquín Villalobos, and Vladimir Rogel, "supported by Rafael Arce Zablah ("Amílcar") and Jorge Meléndez ("Jonás"), conducted a summary trial against Dalton and Arteaga in which they served as "accusers." Eduardo Sancho ("Fermán Cienfuegos") served as Dalton's sole "defender." Dalton's executioners also faulted him for his decision to circulate some of his poems at the University of El Salvador. These poems were later published under the title "Clandestine Poems." Medrano, *Memorias de un guerrillero*, pp. 13, 16.

100. For a detailed account of the circumstances that led to Dalton's murder, see Sancho, *Crónicas entre los espejos*, pp. 100–111, 124.

101. In the early 1970s, Dalton's works circulated at the University of El Salvador. For instance, Francisco Jovel remembered that Dalton's *Miguel Mármol*, the testimony of a founder of the PCS and survivor of the 1932 massacre, edited by Dalton, circulated widely at the university. Jovel interview.

102. Roque Dalton, *El intelectual y la sociedad* (San Salvador: Estudios Centroamericanos, June–July 1976), pp. 233–339; originally published as Dalton et al., *El intelectual y la sociedad*, p. 14.

103. Dalton engaged a detailed discussion on this matter; see Dalton et al., *El intelectual y la sociedad*, pp. 15–28.

104. Dalton admired Castillo's participation in revolutionary mobilizations in Central America in the 1950s and 1960s. Castillo joined the Partido Guatemalteco del Trabajo (Guatemalan Communist Party [PGT]) at the time of the Arbenz government (1950–1954). In the aftermath of the 1954 CIA coup against Arbenz, he lived in exile in El Salvador and conducted clandestine activities in Guatemala. Castillo also studied German, literature, and film in the German Democratic Republic and joined the "Joris Ivens Brigade," a group of filmmakers who produced documentaries on guerrilla movements in Latin America. Roque Dalton, "Otto René Castillo: Su ejemplo y nuestra responsabilidad," in *Informe de una injusticia* (Guatemala City: FC Editorial Cultura, 1993), pp. xix–xxx.

105. Dalton, "Otto René Castillo," pp. xxxiii, xxxiv.

106. Dalton, "Otto René Castillo," p. xxxiii.

107. PRS-ERP, *Publicación Especial Octubre 1977: Balance Histórico del 1er Congreso del PRS*, pp. 37–38.

108. PRS-ERP, *Publicación Especial Octubre 1977: Balance Histórico del 1er Congreso del PRS*, p. 37.

109. PRS-ERP, *Publicación Especial Octubre 1977: Balance Histórico del 1er Congreso del PRS*, pp. 35–36.

110. PRS-ERP, *Publicación Especial Octubre 1977: Balance Histórico del 1er Congreso del PRS*, p. 31.

111. According to the PRS-ERP, Dalton wrote the following documents during his fleeting participation in the ERP: "Realidad Nacional y Dictadura Fascista," "El Combatiente No. 6," "El Ejército Nacional y Contrarevolución en El Salvador," "una publicación sobre ORDEN," and military analyses, which purportedly revealed "Dalton's militaristic tendencies." PRS-ERP, *Publicación Especial Octubre 1977: Balance Histórico del 1er Congreso del PRS*, pp. 38–39.

112. PRS-ERP, *Publicación Especial Octubre 1977: Balance Histórico del 1er Congreso del PRS*, pp. 27–28.

113. "Dalton arrived in the country in December 1973 after living eleven years abroad where he had the life of a poet and writer in Cuba, Czechoslovakia and other countries, moving among the revisionist bureaucracies [communist bureaucracies] and circles of inconsequential and parasitic leftist petit bourgeois intellectuals. . . . Dalton is not a founder of the [ERP]. . . . Dalton did not come by his own will, he came as a result of commitments that were never clearly known (at least by the membership and current leadership of the [PRS-ERP]) between Sebastián Urquilla [Alejandro Rivas Mira] and the Communist Party of Cuba. . . . Dalton was not a military chief and only participated in one military operation as a combatant (the occupation of Radio Station YSKL in March 1974). . . . The political participation of Dalton in this period does not have much significance, his contributions are few and without much significance, although some of his works have certain political value, these are linked to his capacity as a writer and historicist [*sic*]. . . . [He] was a cadre with many problems of indiscipline and liberalism, the product of his low ideological quality and his bourgeois pragmatic tendencies. . . . Dalton was an intellectual adventurer . . . interested

in his individual promotion. . . . To this end he had started works to heighten his figure internally and externally . . . through a subtle line of publication of poems and personal writings using the organization's publications, gradually transforming the organization's political and ideological instruments into tribunes of his writings, which will transform him in time into a 'revolutionary caudillo.'" PRS-ERP, *Publicación Especial Octubre 1977: Balance Histórico del 1er Congreso del PRS*, pp. 38–39.

114. According to the ERP, working-class Salvadoran revolutionaries who died fighting the dictatorship were not "poets and writers and did not spend ten years doing revolutionary tourism, serving among the bureaucracies of international revisionism or attending congresses or participating in contests to show their leftist idiomatic abilities. Some of our comrades who died in heroic combats could not even read and write. In our homeland had fallen many whose weight and worth was 100 times more than Dalton's worth, the difference is that Dalton the poet and writer made his life where publicity and the cult to individualism is the norm and now that he is dead, many have condemned the 'assassins' of such an eminent poet, writer, sympathetic and cordial friend. It does not matter to these gentlemen that Dalton was responsible for a fratricidal struggle and they convert him into the hero writer and poet, the banner of petit bourgeois thinkers, 'revolutionary of revolutionaries.'" PRS-ERP, *Publicación Especial Octubre 1977: Balance Histórico del 1er Congreso del PRS*, p. 37.

115. PRS-ERP, *Publicación Especial Octubre 1977: Balance Histórico del 1er Congreso del PRS*, p. 34.

116. PRS-ERP, *Publicación Especial Octubre 1977: Balance Histórico del 1er Congreso del PRS*, p. 34.

117. Cortázar, "Una muerte monstruosa: Roque Dalton," pp. 477–478.

118. PRS-ERP, *Publicación Especial Octubre 1977: Balance Histórico del 1er Congreso del PRS*, p. 37.

119. Medina interview.

120. Sancho, *Crónicas entre los espejos*, p. 120.

121. Sancho, *Crónicas entre los espejos*, pp. 109, 111–120.

122. The RN analysis of this matter illustrates this view; see Resistencia Nacional, "Desenmascarando a los revisionistas de 'Voz Popular,'" pp. 4–5.

123. Schafik Hándal, "Interrelación indisoluble," in *Fundamentos y Perspectivas Revista Teórica del Partido Comunista de El Salvador*, Comisión Nacional de Propaganda, June 1981, no. 4, pp. 9–10. To the best of my knowledge, the New Left insurgencies never advocated the occupation of houses as Hándal claimed.

124. Hándal, "Interrelación indisoluble," p. 13.

125. FPL, *Estrella Roja 3, Órgano Ideológico* (mimeograph, January 1977), p. 1.

126. FPL, *Estrella Roja 3*, p. 2.

127. FPL, *Estrella Roja 3*, pp. 5–6.

128. FPL, *Estrella Roja 3*, p. 9.

129. FPL, *Estrella Roja 3*, p. 10.

130. FPL, *Estrella Roja 3*, p. 12.

131. FPL, *Estrella Roja 3*, p. 14.

132. These were bodies of knowledge produced by Latin American sociologists and economists working at the Latin American Institute of Economic and Social Planning (ILPES) affiliated with the UN Economic Commission on Latin America (CEPAL) and the Center of Socioeconomic Studies (CESO) of the University of Chile in the late 1960s and early 1970s. FLACSO El Salvador and Fundación "Dr. Manuel Gallardo" "Treinta y cinco años después . . . ," in *Prensa clandestina*, p. 118.

133. FLACSO El Salvador and Fundación "Dr. Manuel Gallardo," "Treinta y cinco años después . . . ," in *Prensa clandestina*, p. 119.

134. For an example of how dependency theory informed the formulation of the New Left revolutionary strategies, see Resistencia Nacional, *Por la Causa Proletaria Publicación Clandestina de la Resistencia Nacional (R.N.) y de su brazo armado, las Fuerzas Armadas de la Resistencia Nacional, No. 26*, pp. 3–6.

135. Partido de la Revolución Salvadoreña (PRS), *Grano de Oro*, in *Prensa clandestina*, p. 70.

136. PRS, *Grano de Oro*, in *Prensa clandestina*, pp. 72, and 81–83.

137. PRS, *Grano de Oro*, in *Prensa clandestina*, pp. 64, 81, 89-90.

138. Partido Comunista de El Salvador, "45 Años de Sacrificada Lucha Revolucionaria," in *Prensa clandestina*, p. 15.

Chapter 7

1. Francisco Andrés Escobar, "En la línea de la muerte: Manifestación del 22 de Enero de 1980," *Estudios Centroamericanos ECA* 375–376, no. 35 (January–February 1980): pp. 22 and 25.
2. For instance, General Jaime Abdul Gutiérrez, a member of the Junta who witnessed the demonstration from a hospital room, was alarmed by the magnitude of the demonstration; see Rafael Mejívar Ochoa, *Tiempos de locura El Salvador 1979–1981*, 2nd ed. (San Salvador: FLACSO El Salvador, 2006), p. 244.
3. Between one hundred thousand and three hundred thousand persons joined the march. McClintock estimated that "between 200[,000] and 300, 000 marchers" joined the demonstration; see McClintock, *The American Connection*, p. 262. Escobar calculated that 136,000 people joined the march. The following social movements and political parties joined the demonstration: the BPR, the LP-28, the FAPU, the UDN, the MLP, which made up the CRM, and other smaller organizations like the Socialist Organization of Workers (OST), the Socialist Party of Workers (PST), and the Socialist Internationalist Organization (OSI). Escobar, "En la línea de la muerte," pp. 22–25, 28–30.
4. Roberto D'Aubuisson, an army major, and leaders of the Broad Nationalist Front denounced the march as a "communist conspiracy" and called on "patriots" to impede it. Escobar, "En la línea de la muerte," p. 22.
5. The mass killings they carried out in downtown San Salvador in the 1970s, such as the July 30, 1975, massacre against university students discussed in chapter 5, involved careful planning.
6. The sharpshooters occupied the top floors of the following buildings: ANTEL (The National Administration of Telecommunications), Palacio Nacional, Banco Hipotecario, Banco Agrícola Comercial, Teatro Nacional, Librería Hispanoamérica, Corte de Cuentas, Ministerio de Trabajo, Compañía Salvadoreña de Café, La Prensa Gráfica, El Diario de Hoy, Biblioteca Nacional, several buildings at the Centro de Gobierno, and others; see Escobar, "En la línea de la muerte," pp. 30–31.
7. Escobar, "En la línea de la muerte," pp. 23–32.
8. Tunes by " Cri-Cri El Grillito Cantor" (Cri-Cri the Little Cricket Singer), Francisco Gabilondo Soler—a Mexican composer and performer of children's songs; see Escobar, "En la línea de la muerte," pp. 34–35.
9. Escobar, "En la línea de la muerte," pp. 34–35.
10. Insurgent movements in El Salvador and the FSLN established close ties in the 1970s. Salvadoran combatants joined the FSLN's 1978–1979 offensive against the Somoza dictatorship in Nicaragua. For instance, the FPL posthumously acknowledged militants who perished in Nicaragua at that time: "Comrades Luis, Neto, Pablo, Moris [and] Quique . . . . were FPL internationalist fighters who gave their lives for the liberation of Nicaraguan people." FPL, "Noticia: En fecha reciente, en un lugar del país, se celebró la Sexta Reunión Ordinaria del Consejo Revolucionario de las FPL," *El Rebelde*, nos. 86–87 (February 1980), p. 11.
11. Fearful of being accused of "losing" El Salvador to the rebels, Carter issued a presidential order on January 16, 1980, for $5 million in emergency military aid and advisers for El Salvador. President Reagan substantially increased military and economic aid to the Christian Democrat–Military Junta. In March 1981, the United States provided an allocation of $20 million in military aid (weapons, training, and US military advisers) and an additional $18 million in June as "emergency 'Economic Support Funds.'" McClintock, *The American Connection*, pp. 286, 288.
12. Benjamin Schwarz, "Dirty Hands: The Success of U.S. Policy in El Salvador—Preventing a Guerrilla Victory—Was Based on 40,000 Political Murders," *Atlantic Monthly*, December 1998.
13. Greg Grandin, *Empire's Workshop: Latin America, the United States, and the Rise of New Imperialism* (New York: Holt Paperback, 2006), pp. 105–110.
14. For an insightful analysis of this process, see Mejívar Ochoa, *Tiempos de locura El Salvador 1979–1981*, pp. 195–211.
15. For an excellent study of this period, see Mejívar Ochoa, *Tiempos de locura El Salvador 1979–1981*.
16. Luis de Sebastián, "La memoria histórica: Un instrumento para la paz," in Rubio and Balsebre, *Rompiendo silencios*, pp. 8–9. In 2005, Colonel Adolfo A. Majano stated that the leaders of the

coup discussed three drafts of their program called "La Proclama de la Fuerza Armada de El Salvador del 15 de Octubre de 1979," one written by Ignacio Ellacuría, a Jesuit scholar, one by Francisco Roberto Lima, a lawyer, and one by Ulises Flores and retired lieutenant colonel Mariano Castro Morán. They chose Ellacuría's draft as the basis of the *proclama*. Mejívar Ochoa, *Tiempos de locura El Salvador 1979–1981*, p. 157.

17. Figures of this movement included Lieutenant Colonel René Guerra y Guerra, his brother Rodrigo Guerra y Guerra (a civilian), Major Alvaro Salazar Brenes, and Captains Román Barrera, Francisco Mena Sandoval, Leonel Alfaro, and two captains identified as Velasco Alvarado and Samayoa; see Mejívar Ochoa, *Tiempos de locura El Salvador 1979–1981*, p. 139.

18. Majano penned a memoir about the 1979 coup. Adolfo A. Majano, *Una oportunidad perdida: 15 de Octubre de 1979* (San Salvador: Índole Editores, 2009).

19. *Proclama de la Fuerza Armada de El Salvador 15 de Octubre de 1979*, in Mejívar Ochoa, *Tiempos de locura El Salvador 1979–1981*, pp. 338–340.

20. Roberto Turcios, *Guillermo Manuel Ungo: Una vida por la democracia y la paz* (San Salvador: FUNDAUNGO, 2012), pp. 146–151.

21. For detailed discussions of the origins and authorship of the coup, see Mejívar Ochoa, *Tiempos de locura El Salvador 1979–1981*, pp. 121–134; Rubio and Balsebre, *Rompiendo silencios*, pp. 120–132; and Turcios, *Guillermo Manuel Ungo*, pp. 142–165.

22. According to Román Mayorga Quiroz, a member of the Junta, Colonels Eugenio Vides Casanova and Guillermo Garcia announced to members of the cabinet their intention to slaughter "tens of thousands of 'subversives'" (civilians) to contain the social movements. Mejívar Ochoa, *Tiempos de locura El Salvador 1979–1981*, p. 206.

23. Rubén Zamora interview.

24. Zamora interview.

25. Zamora interview.

26. Mejívar Ochoa, *Tiempos de locura El Salvador 1979–1981*, pp. 244–245.

27. Zamora interview. Mejívar Ochoa, *Tiempos de locura El Salvador 1979–1981*, p. 246. Schafik Hándal accused Rubén Zamora of conducting negotiations with the reactionary military on behalf of Duarte after the progressive members of first Junta's cabinet resigned their posts in January 1980. He wrote: "At that moment Rubén was the leader of the left within the PDC and had a majority; he negotiated with the new military chiefs, with the assassins who were leading the government into a crisis. He is fully responsible for the shift [*viraje*] that broke the alliances within UNO. And that was led [*jalonado*] by Duarte." Hándal, *Legado de un revolucionario*, p. 230. Whatever the case, Zamora eventually resigned from the Second Junta, broke with Duarte and the right-wing Christian Democrats, and joined the Democratic Revolutionary Front.

28. FPL, "Editorial Sangre y Represión: El Sello de la Nueva Junta," *El Rebelde* Nos. 86–87 (February 1980), pp. 1, 3–5; "The People's Revolutionary Army (ERP) of El Salvador to All Nations of the World," advertisement published in the *New York Times* under the subheading "This publication with humanitarian means is to complete with the demands of the group E.R.P. in El Salvador in order to gain the release of one of its hostages," *New York Times*, March 12, 1980, p. A21.

29. On the El Mozote massacre, see Mark Danner, *The Massacre at El Mozote: A Parable of the Cold War* (New York: Vintage Books, 1994); and Binford, *The El Mozote Massacre*. To date there is no comprehensive study on the El Sumpul massacre. See references to this event in McClintock, *The American Connection*, p. 306.

30. McClintock writes about the "quantum leap" in "summary executions of non-combatants" perpetrated by state forces from "1,030 in 1979 to 8,062 in 1980" to 2,644 "in the single month of January 1981." McClintock, *The American Connection*, p. 303. The US State Department estimated that there were 9,000 victims of political violence in 1980. The Socorro Jurídico, the legal aid office of the Archdiocese of San Salvador, estimated that there were 10,000 victims of political violence that year; of this number, state forces murdered 8,000 people. The victims included more than 3,700 peasants, 400 industrial workers, 100 teachers, and 10 priests. Americas Watch and the American Civil Liberties Union, *Report on Human Rights in El Salvador*, p. xxvi–xxvii.

31. For a detailed analysis of this process, see Mejívar Ochoa, *Tiempos de Locura El Salvador 1979–1981* pp. 162–179.

32. Mejívar Ochoa, *Tiempos de locura El Salvador 1979–198*, p. 174.

33. "The People's Revolutionary Army (ERP) of El Salvador to All Nations of the World"; FPL, "La Crisis del Régimen y el Auge de la Revolución," *El Rebelde*, nos. 84–85 (January 1980), front page.

34. Zamora argued that the BPR, the coalition of social movements influenced by the FPL, agreed, upon the Junta's request, to put an end to the occupation of the Ministry of Labor and the Ministry of Foreign Trade. He personally negotiated this deal with Juan Chacón, the secretary general of the BPR at that time. Zamora interview.

35. Sancho referenced this shift; see Mejívar Ochoa, *Tiempos de locura El Salvador 1979–1981*, p. 177.

36. FPL, "La Crisis del Régimen y el Auge de la Revolución," front page.

37. Domingo Santacruz Castro, "Antecedentes del movimiento de masas de 1970," in *Para que no olvidemos: Una recopilación de testimonios sobre el surgimiento de organizaciones populares salvadoreñas y sus luchas durante los años 1970 y 1980*, ed. Jorge Palencia (Madrid: Castilla La Mancha, Yolocamba Solidaridad and Procomes, 2008), p. 37.

38. Coordinadora Político-Militar, "Se unifica La Izquierda," undated, *Pensamiento Revolucionario FMLN*, no. 12 (Centro de Documentación e Información del FMLN, mimeograph, 1981), pp. 3–6.

39. DRU-PM, "Manifiesto de la Dirección Revolucionaria Unificada de las Organizaciones Político-Militares, al pueblo salvadoreño, a los pueblos Centroamericanos y del mundo," May 1980, *Pensamiento Revolucionario FMLN*, no. 12 (Centro de Documentación e Información del FMLN, July 1981), pp. 10–11.

40. DRU-PM, "Comunicado de la Dirección Revolucionaria Unificada (DRU-P.M.) a los pueblos de El Salvador, Centroamérica y el mundo," October 10, 1980, *Pensamiento Revolucionario FMLN*, no. 12 (Centro de Documentación e Información del FMLN, mimeograph, 1981), pp. 15–16.

41. Riita-Ilona Koivumaeki, "El Salvador: Societal Cleavages, Strategic Elites, and the Success of the Right," in *The Resilience of the Latin American Right*, Juan Pablo Luna and Cristóbal Rovira Kaltwasser ed. (Baltimore: Johns Hopkins University Press, 2014), p. 269; Mejívar Ochoa, *Tiempos de locura El Salvador 1979–1981*, p. 193.

42. Giovani Galeas, "El día del golpe," *La Prensa Gráfica*, suplemento *Enfoques*, August 22, 2004, cited in Mejívar Ochoa, *Tiempos de locura El Salvador 1979–1981*, p. 189.

43. Mejívar Ochoa, *Tiempos de locura El Salvador 1979–1981*, p. 193.

44. Mejívar Ochoa, *Tiempos de locura El Salvador 1979–1981*, pp. 186–189.

45. Galeas "El día del golpe," p. 190.

46. Jesús Delgado, *Oscar A. Romero biografía* (San Salvador: UCA Editores, [1990] 2008), p. 95.

47. Delgado, *Oscar A. Romero biografía*, p. 99.

48. Guerra et al., *Testigos de la fe en El Salvador*, p. 30.

49. Guerra et al., *Testigos de la fe en El Salvador*, pp. 113–114.

50. P. A. Aparicio et al., "Declaración de cuatro obispos de la Conferencia Episcopal de El Salvador," *Estudios Centroamericanos* 359, no. 33 (September 1978): 774–775; FECCAS-UTC, "FECCAS-UTC a los Cristianos de El Salvador y Centroamérica" (mimeograph, September 29, 1978).

51. O. A. Romero and A. Rivera y Damas, "La iglesia y las organizaciones políticas populares," *Estudios Centroamericanos ECA* 359, no. 33 (August 1978): 760–773.

52. Romero and Rivera y Damas, "La iglesia y las organizaciones políticas populares," pp. 770–771.

53. "Homilía del Quinto Domingo de Cuaresma (23.3.1980) La Iglesia. Un Servicio de Liberación Personal, Comunitaria, Transcendente," in *La voz de los sin voz: La palabra viva de Monseñor Romero*, ed. Jon Sobrino, Ignacio Martín-Baró, and Rodolfo Cardenal (San Salvador: UCA Editores, 2007), pp. 270, 284, 291.

54. Binford, *The El Mozote Massacre*, pp. 104–105.

55. Rubio and Balsebre, *Rompiendo silencios*, pp. 158–191.

56. "Forman comité hijos reos políticos," *La Crónica del Pueblo*, December 27, 1978, front page.

57. Examples of these are the following: "Represión en Cinquera recrudece afirma Monseñor," *La Crónica del Pueblo*, November 6, 1978, front page; "El comité pro-libertad de los presos

políticos de El Salvador a un año de la captura del profesor Efraín Arevalo Ibarra," *La Crónica del Pueblo*, November 7, 1978, p. 4; "El Pueblo se incorpora a la lucha por la libertad de los presos políticos," *La Crónica del Pueblo*, November 8, 1978, p. 15; "El Bloque Popular Revolucionario condena el criminal ataque a los trabajadores de las rutas 5 y 28," *La Crónica del Pueblo*, February 6, 1979, p. 14; and "ARDES repudia y condena la represion en las huelgas de la Constancia S.A. y Tropical," *La Crónica del Pueblo*, March 12, 1979, p. 15.

58. Martínez interview (April 18, 2007).
59. José Audulio Tobar, "Me libré de la masacre del Sumpul," in *La Lucha así es: Memoria Oral en Chalatenango*, Carlos Henríquez Consalvi "Santiago" ed. (San Salvador: MUPI, 2012), pp. 41–42.
60. Martínez interview.
61. Irma Serrano interview (April 18, 2007).
62. Martínez interview.
63. FECCAS-UTC, "Viva nuestro primer consejo departamental! 'Héroes y Mártires de Chalatenango'" (mimeograph, 1978).
64. FECCAS-UTC, "Viva nuestro primer consejo departamental!," p. 1.
65. FECCAS-UTC, "Viva nuestro primer consejo departamental!," p. 8.
66. FECCAS-UTC, "Viva nuestro primer consejo departamental!," p. 1.
67. *Jornalero Revolucionario Periódico de la Federación de Trabajadores del Campo F.T.C. Numero 1, Año 1978, Mes: Julio–Agosto* (mimeograph, 1978), p. 3.
68. Martínez interview.
69. Martínez interview.
70. José Santos Martínez interview.
71. Guadalupe Mejía interview.
72. Guardado interview (November 12, 2007).
73. Martínez interview.
74. Martínez interview.
75. Guardado interview.
76. Martínez interview.
77. Guardado interview.
78. Martínez interview.
79. Martínez interview.
80. Martínez interview.
81. Serrano interview.
82. Serrano interview.
83. Martínez interview.
84. Martínez interview.
85. Martínez interview.
86. Martínez interview.
87. Martínez interview.
88. Guardado interview.
89. Guardado interview.
90. FPL, "Cómo debemos combatir a ORDEN," *Campo Rebelde Periodico Revolucionario Dedicado a los Trabajadores del Campo*, no. 10 (El Salvador, July 1978), pp. 1–2.
91. "Cómo engaña el enemigo a los trabajadores que están en ORDEN?," *Campo Rebelde Periodico Revolucionario Dedicado a los Trabajadores del Campo*, no. 10 (El Salvador, July 1978), pp. 2–3.
92. "Cómo engaña el enemigo a los trabajadores que están en ORDEN?," pp. 2–3.
93. "Cual es ésa verdad?," *Campo Rebelde Periodico Revolucionario Dedicado a los Trabajadores del Campo*, no. 10 (El Salvador, July 1978), pp. 3–4.
94. "Por la Revolución Popular hacia el Socialismo," *Campo Rebelde Periodico Revolucionario Dedicado a los Trabajadores del Campo*, no. 10 (El Salvador, July 1978), pp. 5–7.
95. FPL, "La revolución avanza! El pueblo responde valientemente frente a los crímenes de la tiranía," *Campo Rebelde Periodico Revolucionario Clandestino Dedicado a los Trabajadores del Campo*, no. 8 (El Salvador, May 1978), pp. 2–4.
96. FPL, "La revolución avanza!," p. 6.

97. Guardado interview.
98. Guardado interview.
99. Guardado interview.
100. BPR leaders Numas Escobar, Marciano Meléndez, Oscar López, and Ricardo Mena were also disappeared by state agents at that time. Bloque Popular Revolucionario (BPR), "Julio 75–79 la alternativa del pueblo se fortalece," *Combate Popular*, 1979, p. 7.
101. Guardado interview.
102. BPR, "Julio 75–79 la alternativa del pueblo se fortalece," pp. 7–8; BPR, "El pueblo exige: Libertad para sus dirigentes!!," *Combate Popular*, no. 9, (second week in May 1979), front page; BPR, "Nueva masacre al pueblo," *Combate Popular*, no. 12 (fourth week in May 1979), front page; Mejívar Ochoa, *Tiempos de locura El Salvador 1979–1981*, p. 26.
103. BPR, "Honor eterno a la Compañera Enma Guadalupe Carpio," *Combate Popular* (fourth week in May 1979).
104. Mejívar Ochoa, *Tiempos de locura El Salvador 1979–1981*, p. 38.
105. BPR, "Julio 75–79 la alternativa del pueblo se fortalece," p. 2.
106. They operated in a region that comprised Cancasque, Nueva Trinidad, Nombre de Jesús, San Antonio La Cruz, Arcatao, and Cerro Eramón. Guardado interview.
107. Guardado interview.
108. Serrano interview.
109. "Evaristo" interview; Nieto interview (October 1, 2006).
110. FECCAS-UTC, "Boletín Informativo Número 3 de FECCAS-UTC: Se agudiza criminal represión contra familias campesinas en Chalatenango, San Vicente, Cinquera y demás regiones del campo salvadoreño" in *La Prensa Gráfica*, 27 January, 1980.
111. Guardado interview.
112. Guardado interview.
113. FPL, "Más de 50 verdugos de nuestro pueblo fueron ajusticiados—tomas a poblaciones," *El Rebelde*, nos. 86–87 (February 1980), p. 8.
114. Coordinadora Politico-Militar, "Se unifica La Izquierda," pp. 3–6.
115. Coordinadora Politico-Militar, "Se unifica La Izquierda," p. 6.
116. Coordinadora Político-Militar, "Segundo Manifiesto de la Coordinadora Politico-Militar, Salvadoreña a los Pueblos Centroamericanos y del Mundo," *Matanzas y reformas fórmula siniestra del imperialismo yanqui y de la Junta Militar Democristiana, Pensamiento Revolucionario FMLN*, no. 12 (Centro de Documentación e Información del FMLN, July 1981), pp. 7–9.
117. DRU-PM, "Manifiesto de la Dirección Revolucionaria Unificada de las Organizaciones Politico-Militares, al pueblo salvadoreño, a los pueblos Centroamericanos y del mundo," pp. 10–11.
118. DRU-PM, "Comunicado de la Direccion Revolucionaria Unificada (DRU-P.M.) a los pueblos de El Salvador, Centroamérica y el mundo," pp. 15–16.
119. DRU-PM, "Comunicado de la Direccion Revolucionaria Unificada (DRU-P.M.) a los pueblos de El Salvador, Centroamérica y el mundo," pp. 15–16.
120. FECCAS-UTC reported that National Guard troops and ORDEN paramilitaries conducted military operations in rural areas across El Salvador. FECCAS-UTC, "Boletín Informativo Número 3 de FECCAS-UTC: Se agudiza criminal represión contra familias campesinas en Chalatenango, San Vicente, Cinquera y demás regiones del campo salvadoreño."
121. Serrano interview.
122. Martínez interview.
123. Martínez interview.
124. Martínez interview.
125. Martínez interview.
126. Luisa Tolentino, interview by Joaquín Chávez (September 27, 2007).
127. Juan-Juan, interview by Joaquín Chávez (January 13, 2015)
128. Martínez interview.
129. Ester Arteaga, interview by Joaquín Chávez (September 10, 2008).
130. Arteaga interview.
131. Arteaga interview.
132. Arteaga interview.

133. Arteaga interview.
134. Arteaga interview.
135. Martínez interview.
136. Martínez interview.
137. Martínez interview.
138. Martínez interview.
139. Arteaga interview.
140. Ever Hernández, interview by Joaquín Chávez (April 18, 2007).
141. Hernández interview.

Conclusion

1. Joaquín M. Chávez, "Revolutionary Power, Divided State," in *Mapping Latin America: Space and Society, 1492–2000*, ed. Karl Offen and Jordana Dym (Chicago: University of Chicago Press, 2011), pp. 250–253.
2. Menjívar Ochoa, *Tiempos de locura El Salvador 1979–1981*, p. 25.
3. Bishop Ricardo Urioste cited in John Lamperti, *Enrique Alvarez Presente!*, November 19, 2003, https://math.dartmouth.edu/~lamperti/centralamerica_presente.html, accessed May 10, 2016.
4. "Democratic Revolutionary Platform (1980)," in *The Central American Crisis Reader*, ed. Robert S. Leiken and Barry Rubin (New York: Summit Books, 1987), pp. 395–400.
5. "Socialist International: Communiqué on El Salvador (March 1981)," in Leiken and Rubin, *The Central American Crisis Reader*, pp. 627–628; and "La Primera Junta de Gobierno (15 de Octubre 1979–5 de Enero 1980)," in Sobrino, Martín-Baró, and Cardenal, eds., *La voz de los sin voz: La palabra viva de Monseñor Romero*, pp. 379–384.
6. Sancho, *Crónicas entre los espejos*, pp. 131–132; Hándal, *Legado de un revolucionario*, pp. 228–229; Montalvo interview.
7. Montalvo interview.
8. Chávez, "The Creation of the Internal Enemy," pp. 128–134.
9. "Comunicado del FMLN en relación al atentado al coronel Majano," *Pensamiento Revolucionario FMLN*, no. 12 (Centro de Documentación e Información del FMLN, July 1981), pp. 19–20.
10. Ernesto A. Álvarez, interview by Joaquín Chávez (August 11, 2005).
11. Mayer, *The Furies*, pp. 4–7; Menjívar Ochoa, *Tiempos de locura El Salvador 1979–1981*, p. 25.
12. María Marta Valladares, "Una experiencia y aporte personal en la construcción del movimiento de masas," in Palencia, *Para que no Olvidemos*, p. 95; Tolentino interview.
13. Menjívar Ochoa, *Tiempos de locura El Salvador 1979–1981*, p. 39; Dunkerley, *The Long War*, pp. 128–131.
14. Zamora interview.
15. Hándal, *Legado de un revolucionario*, pp. 257–260.
16. Hándal, *Legado de un revolucionario*, pp. 259–260.
17. "Orden General No. 1," *Pensamiento Revolucionario FMLN*, no. 12, July 1981, p. 24.
18. "Orden General No. 2," *Pensamiento Revolucionario FMLN*, no. 12, July 1981, p. 25.
19. "Orden General No. 2," p. 25.
20. "Orden General No. 2," p. 26.
21. "Orden General No. 2," p. 26.
22. "Orden General No. 2," p. 26.
23. The rebels attacked government forces in Chalatenango, San Salvador, Cuscatlán, Santa Ana, Sonsonate, Cabañas, San Vicente, La Paz, Usulután, San Miguel, Morazán, and La Unión. "Informe de la Comandancia General del Frente Farabundo Martí para la Liberación Nacional, January 22, 1981," *Pensamiento Revolucionario FMLN*, no. 12 July 1981, p. 30.
24. "Informe de la Comandancia General del Frente Farabundo Martí para la Liberación Nacional, January 22, 1981," p. 30.
25. Captain Francisco Mena Sandoval cited in Rubio and Balsebre, *Rompiendo silencios*, pp. 206–212.
26. Brian J. Bosch, *The Salvadoran Officer Corps and the Final Offensive of 1981* (Jefferson, NC: McFarland, 2013), pp. 106, 108.

27. Gerardo Rénique, "Latin America: The New Neoliberalism and Popular Mobilization," *Socialism and Democracy* 23, no. 3 (November 2009): 1–26.

28. Rabe, *The Killing Zone*, p. 158.

29. Mélida Anaya Montes, [aka] Comandante Ana María, *Experiencias vietnamitas en su guerra de liberación* (Ediciones Enero 32, 1982), p. i "Dedicatoria."

30. Captain Herard von Santos, a Salvadoran military historian and veteran of the Atlacatl Battalion, wrote: "Here with total objectivity I can affirm that [the Salvadoran insurgency] constituted the most combative and audacious irregular military force in the recent history of the continent." Herard von Santos, "La Ofensiva Hasta el Tope desde el Punto de Vista de la Academia" (talk presented at the Department of History, University of El Salvador, November 29, 2009).

31. "Colonel Bosch: Guerrilla Strength (February 1981)," in Leiken and Rubin, *The Central American Crisis Reader*, p. 423.

32. Salazar, *Los secretos de El Paraíso*.

33. Salazar, *Los secretos de El Paraíso*, p. 117.

34. Salazar, *Los secretos de El Paraíso*, p. 227.

35. Salazar, *Los secretos de El Paraíso*, pp. 225–227.

36. Gerardo interview by Joaquín M. Chávez and Rebecca T., circa 1986.

37. Chávez, "How Did the Civil War in El Salvador End?," pp. 1784–1797.

BIBLIOGRAPHY

Archives

Archivo de la Universidad de El Salvador, San Salvador, El Salvador.

Archivo del Museo Nacional de Antropología David J. Guzmán, San Salvador, El Salvador.

Archivo Histórico de la Arquidiócesis de San Salvador, San Salvador, El Salvador.

Bobst Library, New York University, New York City.

Centro de Documentación e Información (CIDAI) de la Universidad Centroamericana José Simeón Cañas, San Salvador, El Salvador.

Museo de la Palabra y la Imagen (MUPI), San Salvador, El Salvador.

National Security Archives, George Washington University, Washington, DC

US National Archives and Records Administration (NARA), College Park, Maryland.

Secondary Sources

Academia Salvadoreña de la Historia. *Biografías de vicentinos ilustres.* San Salvador: Ministerio de Educación Dirección General de Publicaciones, 1962.

Adams, Jan S. A. *Foreign Policy in Transition: Moscow's Retreat from Central America and the Caribbean, 1985–1992.* Durham, NC: Duke University Press, 1992.

Adorno, Theodor W. "Education after Auschwitz." In *Critical Models: Interventions and Catch Words,* 191–204. New York: Columbia University Press, 1998.

Almeida, Paul D. *Waves of Protest: Popular Struggle in El Salvador, 1925–2005.* Minneapolis: University of Minnesota Press, 2008.

Alvarenga, Luis. *Roque Dalton: La radicalización de las vanguardias.* San Salvador: Editorial Universidad Don Bosco, 2011.

Alvarenga, Patricia. *Cultura y ética de la violencia, El Salvador, 1880–1932.* San José, Costa Rica: EDUCA, 1996.

Anzaldúa, Gloria E. *The Gloria Anzaldúa Reader.* Ed. Ana Louise Keating. Durham, NC: Duke University Press, 2009.

Argueta, Manlio. *Un día en la vida.* San Salvador: UCA Editores, [1980] 2008.

Arias Gómez, Jorge. "Anastasio Aquino, recuerdo, valoración y presencia," *La Universidad,* nos. 1–2 (January-June, 1964): 61–112.

Arocha, Antonio R. *Cartograma histórico-geográfico de El Salvador: Síntesis de la geografía física y humana de la República de El Salvador.* San Salvador: Ediciones Culturales de la Compañía General de Seguros, 1985.

Bainton, Roland H. *Christian Attitudes toward War and Peace: A Historical Survey and Critical Re-evaluation.* 14th ed. Nashville, TN: Abingdon Press, [1960] 1985.

Baud, Michiel, and Rosanne Rutten, eds. *Popular Intellectuals and Social Movements: Framing Protest in Asia, Africa, and Latin America.* Cambridge: Press Syndicate of the University of Cambridge, 2004.

Berryman, Phillip. *The Religious Root of Rebellion.* New York: Orbis Books, 1984.

Binford, Leigh. *The El Mozote Massacre.* Tucson: University of Arizona Press, 1996.

Binford, Leigh. "Peasants, Catechists, Revolutionaries: Organic Intellectuals in the Salvadoran Revolution, 1980–1992," In *Landscapes of Struggle,* edited by Aldo Lauria-Santiago and Leigh Binford, 105–125. Pittsburgh: University of Pittsburgh Press, 2004.

Bosch, Brian J. *The Salvadoran Officer Corps and the Final Offensive of 1981.* Jefferson, NC: McFarland, 2013.

Brands, Hal. *Latin America's Cold War.* Cambridge, MA: Harvard University Press, 2010.

Byrne, Hugh. *El Salvador's Civil War: A Study of Revolution.* Boulder, CO: Lynne Rienner, 1996.

Cabarrús, Carlos R. *Génesis de una revolución: Análisis del surgimiento y desarrollo de la organización campesina en El Salvador.* Mexico City: Ediciones de la Casa Chata, 1983.

Cardenal, Rodolfo. *Historia de una esperanza: Vida de Rutilio Grande.* San Salvador: UCA Editores, 1987.

Castañeda, Jorge G. *Utopia Unarmed: The Latin American Left after the Cold War.* New York: Knopf, 1993.

Castellanos, Juan Mario. *El Salvador 1930–1960: Antecedentes históricos de la guerra civil.* San Salvador: DPI, 2002.

Chakrabarty, Dipesh. *Provincializing Europe Postcolonial Thought and Historical Difference.* Princeton, NC: Princeton University Press, 2000.

Chávez, Joaquín M. "The Creation of the Internal Enemy: Pondering the Legacies of U.S. Anticommunism, Counterinsurgency, and Authoritarianism in El Salvador, 1952–1981." In *Hearts and Minds: A People's History of Counterinsurgency,* edited by Hannah Gurman, 104–134. New York: New Press, 2013.

Chávez, Joaquín M. "How Did the Civil War in El Salvador End?" *American Historical Review* 120, no. 5 (2015): 1784–1797.

Chávez, Joaquín M. "Revolutionary Power, Divided State." In *Mapping Latin America: Space and Society, 1492–2000,* edited by Karl Offen and Jordana Dym, 250–253. Chicago: University of Chicago Press, 2011.

Ching, Erik. *Authoritarian El Salvador: Politics and the Origins of the Military Regimes, 1880–1940.* Notre Dame, IN: University of Notre Dame Press, 2014.

Clará de Guevara, Concepción. "El añil de los 'Indios Cheles.'" *América Indígena* 35, no. 4 (1975): 778–794.

Clausewitz, Carl von. *On War.* Ed. Michael Howard and Peter Paret; trans. Michael Howard and Peter Paret. Princeton, NJ: Princeton University Press, 1984.

Crais, Clifton, and Pamela Scully. *Sara Baartman and the Hottentot Venus: A Ghost Story and a Biography.* Princeton, NJ: Princeton University Press, 2009.

Cullather, Nick. *Secret History: The Cia's Classified Account of Its Operations in Guatemala 1952–1954.* Stanford, CA: Stanford University Press, 1999.

Dalton, Roque. *No pronuncies mi nombre: Roque Dalton poesia completa III.* San Salvador: Dirección de Publicaciones e Impresos CONCULTURA, 2008.

Dalton, Roque. "Otto René Castillo: Su ejemplo y nuestra responsabilidad." In Otto René Castillo, *Informe de una injusticia,* xix-xxxiv. Guatemala City: FC Editorial Cultura, 1993.

Dalton, Roque. *Pobrecito poeta que era yo.* San José, Costa Rica: EDUCA, 1976.

Dalton, Roque. *Revolución en la revolución? Y la crítica de Derecha.* Havana: Casa de las Américas, 1970.

Dalton, Roque, René Depestre, Edmundo Desnoes, Roberto Fernández Retamar, Ambrosio Fornet, and Carlos María Gutiérrez. *El intelectual y la sociedad.* Mexico City: Siglo Veintiuno Editores, [1969] 1981.

Danner, Mark. *The Massacre at El Mozote: A Parable of the Cold War.* New York: Vintage Books, 1994.

Debray, Régis. *Revolution dans la Revolution? Lutte armée et lutte politique en Amérique Latine.* Paris: Maspero, 1967.

Delgado, Jesús. *Oscar A. Romero biografía.* San Salvador: UCA Editores, [1990] 2008.

Derby, Lauren. *The Dictator's Seduction: Politics and the Popular Imagination in the Era of Trujillo.* Durham, NC: Duke University Press, 2009.

Domínguez, Jorge I. *To Make the World Safe for Revolution: Cuba's Foreign Policy.* Cambridge, MA: Harvard University Press, 1989.

Domínguez Sosa, Julio Alberto. *Anastasio Aquino: Caudillo de las Tribus Nonualcas.* San Salvador: Ediciones Venado del Bosque, [1962] 2007.

Dunkerley, James. *The Long War: Dictatorship and Revolution in El Salvador.* London: Verso, 1985.

Dunkerley, James. *The Pacification of Central America.* London: Verso, 1994.

Feierman, Steven. *Peasant Intellectuals: Anthropology and History in Tanzania.* Madison: University of Wisconsin Press, 1990.

Freire, Paulo. *Pedagogy of the Oppressed.* New York: Continuum, 2006.

Furet, François. *The Passing of an Illusion: The Idea of Communism in the Twentieth Century.* Chicago: University of Chicago Press, 1999.

Galeas, Giovani. *Héroes bajo sospecha.* San Salvador: Athena, 2013.

Gallegos Valdés, Luis. *Panorama de la literatura Salvadoreña del período precolombino a 1980.* San Salvador: UCA Editores, 1981.

Gilman, Claudia. *Entre la pluma y el fusil: Debates y dilemas del escritor revolucionario en América Latina.* Buenos Aires: Siglo XXI, 2003.

Giroux, Henry A. "Education after Abu Ghraib: Revisiting Adorno's Politics of Education." *Cultural Studies* 18, no. 6 (November 2004): 779–815.

Gleijeses, Piero. *Shattered Hope: The Guatemalan Revolution and the United States, 1944–1954.* Princeton, NJ: Princeton University Press, 1991.

Godwin, Jeff. *No Other Way Out: States and Revolutionary Movements, 1945–1991.* Cambridge: Cambridge University Press, 2001.

Gordon, Sara. *Crisis política y guerra en El Salvador.* Mexico City: Siglo XXI, 1989.

Gould, Jeffrey L. *To Lead as Equals: Rural Protest and Political Consciousness in Chinandega, Nicaragua 1912–1979.* Chapel Hill: University of North Carolina Press, 1990.

Gould, Jeffrey L. "Solidarity under Siege: The Latin American Left, 1968." *American Historical Review* 114, no. 2 (April 2009): 348–375.

Gould, Jeffrey L., and Aldo A. Lauria-Santiago. *To Rise in Darkness: Revolution, Repression, and Memory in El Salvador, 1920–1932.* Durham, NC: Duke University Press, 2008.

Gramsci, Antonio. *Selections from the Prison Notebooks.* Ed. Quintin Hoare and Geoffrey Nowell Smith. New York: International Publishers, 1999.

Grandin, Greg. *Empire's Workshop: Latin America, the United States, and the Rise of New Imperialism.* New York: Holt Paperbacks, 2006.

Grandin, Greg. *The Last Colonial Massacre: Latin America in the Cold War.* 2nd ed. Chicago: University of Chicago Press, [2004] 2011.

Grenier, Yvon. *The Emergence of Insurgency in El Salvador: Ideology and Political Will.* Pittsburgh: University of Pittsburgh Press, 1999.

Guardino, Peter. *Peasant, Politics, and the Formation of Mexico's National State: Guerrero 1800–1857.* Stanford, CA: Stanford University Press, 1996.

Guidos Véjar, Rafael. *Ascenso del militarismo en El Salvador.* San José, Costa Rica: Editorial Universitaria Centroamericana, 1982.

Gurman, Hannah, ed. *Hearts and Minds. A People's History of Counterinsurgency.* New York: New Press, 2013.

Harnecker, Marta. *Con la mirada en alto: Historia de Las Fuerzas Populares de Liberación Farabundo Martí a través de entrevistas con sus dirigentes.* San Salvador: UCA Editores, 1993.

Harnecker, Marta. *Los conceptos elementales del materialismo histórico,* sexta edición. Buenos Aires: Siglo Veintiuno Editores, 1971.

Hodges, Donald C., ed. *Legacy of Che Guevara: A Documentary Study*. London: Thames and Hudson, 1977.

Holden, Robert H. and Eric Zolov, eds. *Latin America and the United States: A Documentary History*. 2nd ed. New York: Oxford University Press, 2011.

Huezo Mixco, Miguel. "Roque Dalton: Un corazón aventurero." In Roque Dalton, *No pronuncies mi nombre: Poesia completa III*, 133–1. San Salvador: Dirección de Publicaciones e Impresos CONCULTURA, 2008.

James, Daniel. *Doña María Story*. Durham, NC: Duke University Press, 2000.

Jelin, Elizabeth. *State Repression and the Labors of Memory*. Trans. Judy Rein and Marcial Godoy-Anativia. Minneapolis: University of Minnesota Press, 2003.

Kincaid, Douglas. "Peasants into Rebels: Community and Class in Rural El Salvador." *Comparative Studies in Society and History* 29, no. 3 (1987): 466–494.

Klimke, Martin. *The Other Alliance: Student Protest in West Germany and the United States in the Global Sixties*. Princeton, NJ: Princeton University Press, 2010.

Koivumaeki, Riita-Ilona. "El Salvador: Societal Cleavages, Strategic Elites, and the Success of the Right." In *The Resilience of the Latin American Right*, edited by Juan Pablo Luna and Cristóbal Rovira Kaltwasser, 268–293. Baltimore: Johns Hopkins University Press, 2014.

LaFeber, Walter. *Inevitable Revolutions: The United States in Central America*. 2nd ed. New York: Norton, 1993.

Langland, Victoria. *Speaking of Flowers: Student Movements and the Making and Remembering of 1968 in Military Brazil*. Durham, NC: Duke University Press, 2013.

Lassalle-Klein, Robert. *Blood and Ink: Ignacio Ellacuría, Jon Sobrino, and the Jesuit Martyrs of the University of Central America*. Maryknoll, NY: Orbis Books, 2014.

Lauria-Santiago, Aldo A. *An Agrarian Republic: Commercial Agriculture and the Politics of Peasant Communities in El Salvador, 1823–1914*. Pittsburgh: University of Pittsburgh Press, 1999.

Lauria-Santiago, Aldo A., and Leigh Binford, eds. *Landscapes of Struggle*. Pittsburgh: University of Pittsburgh Press, 2004.

Leiken, Robert S., and Barry Rubin, eds. *The Central American Crisis Reader*. New York: Summit Books, 1987.

Levenson-Estrada, Deborah. *Trade Unionists against Terror: Guatemala City, 1954–1985*. Chapel Hill: University of North Carolina Press, 1994.

Lindo-Fuentes, Héctor. *La economía de El Salvador en el siglo XIX*. San Salvador: CONCULTURA, 2002.

Lindo-Fuentes, Héctor, and Erik Ching. *Modernizing Minds in El Salvador: Education Reform and the Cold War, 1960–1980*. Albuquerque: University of New Mexico Press, 2012.

López, Matilde Elena. *La balada de Anastasio Aquino*. 3rd ed. San Salvador: Editorial Universitaria [1978], 1996.

Löwy, Michael. *The War of Gods*. London: Verso, 1996.

Lynch, Edward A. *The Cold War's Last Battlefield: Reagan, the Soviets and Central America*. Albany: State University of New York Press, 2011.

Mallon, Florencia. *Peasant and Nation: The Making of Postcolonial Peru and Mexico*. Berkeley: University of California Press, 1995.

Martín-Baró, Ignacio. "The Psychological Value of Violent Political Repression." In *Writings for a Liberation Psychology*, edited by Adrianne Aron and Shawn Corne, 151–167. Cambridge, MA: Harvard University Press, 1994.

Masferrer, Alberto. *El dinero maldito*. San Salvador: Editorial Jurídica Salvadoreña, 2013.

Masferrer, Alberto. *Leer y escribir/Cartas a un obrero*. San Salvador: Editorial Jurídica Salvadoreña, 2011.

Masferrer, Alberto. *Leer y escribir/El minimun vital*. San Salvador: Dirección de Publicaciones e Impresos de CONCULTURA, [1929] 2000.

Masferrer, Alberto. *Una vida en el cine*. San Salvador: Editorial Jurídica Salvadoreña, 2007.

Mayer, Arno J. *Dynamics of Counterrevolution in Europe, 1870–1956: An Analytical Framework*. New York: Harper and Row, 1971.

Mayer, Arno J. *The Furies: Violence and Terror in the French and Russian Revolutions*. Princeton, NJ: Princeton University Press, 2000.

Mayer, Arno J. *The Persistence of the Old Regime: Europe to the Great War*. New York: Pantheon Books, 1981.

McClintock, Cynthia. *Revolutionary Movements in Latin America: El Salvador's FMLN and Peru's Shining Path*. Washington, DC: United States Institute of Peace Press, 1998.

McClintock, Michael. *The American Connection*. Vol. 1, *State Terror and Popular Resistance in El Salvador*. London: Zed Books, 1985.

Menjívar, Rafael. *Formación y lucha del proletariado industrial Salvadoreño*. San Salvador: UCA Editores, 1979.

Mejívar Ochoa, Rafael. *Tiempos de locura El Salvador 1979–1981*. 2nd ed. San Salvador: FLACSO El Salvador, 2006.

Montgomery, Tommie Sue. *Revolution in El Salvador: From Civil Strife to Civil Peace*. Boulder, CO: Westview Press, 1995.

Montobbio, Manuel. *La metamorfosis del pulgarcito: Transición política y proceso de paz en El Salvador*. Barcelona: Icaria Antrazyt-FLACSO, 1999.

Mujal-León, Eusebio, ed. *The USSR and Latin America: A Developing Relationship*. Boston: Unwin Hyman, 1989.

Opazo, Andrés. "El movimiento religioso popular en Centroamérica: 1970–1983." In *Movimientos populares en Centroamérica*, edited by Daniel Camacho and Rafael Menjívar, 143–199. San José, Costa Rica: EDUCA, 1985.

Paige, Jeffrey M. *Coffee and Power: Revolution and the Rise of Democracy in Central America*. Cambridge, MA: Harvard University Press, 1997.

Pearce, Jenny. *Promised Land: Peasant Rebellion in Chalatenango, El Salvador*. London: Zed Books, 1986.

Pensado, Jaime. *Rebel Mexico: Student Unrest and Authoritarian Political Culture during the Long Sixties*. Stanford, CA: Stanford University Press, 2013.

Perks, Robert, and Alistair Thomson. *The Oral History Reader*. London: Routledge, [1998] 2005.

Peterson, Anna L. *Martyrdom and the Politics of Religion: Progressive Catholicism in El Salvador's Civil War*. Albany: State University of New York Press, 1997.

Portelli, Alessandro. *The Death of Luigi Trastulli and Other Stories: Form and Meaning in Oral History*. Albany: State University of New York Press, 1991.

Portelli, Alessandro. *The Order Has Been Carried Out: History, Memory, and Meaning of a Nazi Massacre in Rome*. New York: Palgrave Macmillan, 2003.

Rabe, Stephen G. *The Killing Zone: The United States Wages Cold War in Latin America*. Oxford: Oxford University Press, 2012.

Ramírez, Alfredo. "El discurso anticomunista de las derechas y el estado como antecedente de la Guerra Civil en El Salvador (1967–1972)." Tesis de licenciatura, Universidad de El Salvador, Facultad de Ciencias y Humanidades, Escuela de Ciencias Sociales "Lic. Gerardo Iraheta Rosales," August 11, 2008.

Rénique, Gerardo. "Latin America: The New Neoliberalism and Popular Mobilization." *Socialism and Democracy* 23, no. 3 (November 2009): 1–26.

Roldán, Mary. *Blood and Fire: La Violencia in Antioquia, Colombia, 1946–1953*. Durham, NC: Duke University Press, 2002.

Salazar, Armando. *Los secretos de El Paraíso*. San Salvador: UCA Editores, 2016.

Schwarz, Benjamin. "Dirty Hands: The Success of U.S. Policy in El Salvador—Preventing a Guerrilla Victory—Was Based on 40,000 Political Murders." *Atlantic Monthly*, December 1998.

Sewell, William H. "Historical Events as Transformations of Structures: Inventing Revolution at the Bastille." *Theory and Society* 25, no. 6 (December 1996): 841–881.

Shultz, Richard H., Jr. *The Soviet Union and Revolutionary Warfare: Principles, Practices, and Regional Comparisons*. Stanford, CA: Hoover Institute Press, 1988.

Smith, Christian. *The Emergence of Liberation Theology: Radical Religion and Social Movement Theory*. Chicago: University of Chicago Press, 1991.

Smith, Wayne. "The End of World Revolution in Latin America." In *The Russians Aren't Coming: New Soviet Policy in Latin America*, edited by Wayne Smith, 37–53. Boulder, CO: Lynne Rienner, 1992.

Sobrino, Jon, Ignacio Martín-Baró, and Rodolfo Cardenal, eds. *La voz de los sin voz: La palabra viva de Monseñor Romero*. 7th ed. San Salvador: UCA Editores, [1980] 2007.

Special Issue: Latin America in the Global Sixties. *The Americas* 70, no. 3 (January 2014): 349–601.

Sprows Cummings, Kathleen. "Teaching about Women, Gender, and American Catholicism." In *The Catholic Studies Reader*, edited by James T. Fisher and Margaret M. McGuinness. 211–234. New York: Fordham University Press, 2011.

Stanley, William. *The Protection Racket State: Elite Politics, Military Extortion, and Civil War in El Salvador*. Philadelphia: Temple University Press, 1996.

Thomas, Dylan. *Quite Early in the Morning*. New York: New Directions, [1960] 1968.

Thompson, Paul. *The Voice of the Past*. 3rd ed. Oxford: Oxford University Press, [1978] 2000.

Trouillot, Michel-Rolph. *Silencing the Past: Power and the Production of History*. Boston: Beacon Press, 1995.

Turcios, Roberto. *Guillermo Manuel Ungo: Una vida por la democracia y la paz*. San Salvador: FUNDAUNGO, 2012.

Turits, Richard Lee. *Foundations of Despotism: Peasants, the Trujillo Regime, and Modernity in Dominican History*. Stanford, CA: Stanford University Press, 2003.

Vargas Méndez, Jorge, and J. A. Morasan. *Literatura salvadoreña 1960–2000: Homenaje*. San Salvador: Ediciones Venado del Bosque, 2008.

Varon, Jeremy. *Bringing the War Home: The Weather Underground, the Red Army Faction, and Revolutionary Violence in the Sixties and Seventies*. Berkeley: University of California Press, 2004.

Vaughan, Mary Kay. *Cultural Politics in Revolution: Teachers, Peasants, and Schools in Mexico 1930–1940*. Tucson: University of Arizona Press, 1997.

Vaughan, Mary Kay. *Portrait of a Young Painter: Pepe Zúñiga and Mexico City's Rebel Generation*. Durham, NC: Duke University Press, 2015.

Westad, Odd Arne. *The Global Cold War: Third World Intervention and the Making of Our Time*. Cambridge: Cambridge University Press, 2008.

Whitfield, Teresa. *Paying the Price: Ignacio Ellacuría and the Murdered Jesuits of El Salvador*. Philadelphia: Temple University Press, 1994.

Wickham-Crowley, Timothy P. *Guerrillas and Revolution in Latin America: A Comparative Study of Insurgents and Regimes since 1956*. Princeton, NJ: Princeton University Press, 1992.

Wolf, Eric. *Peasant Wars of the Twentieth Century*. 2nd ed. Norman: University of Oklahoma Press, [1963] 1999.

Wood, Elisabeth Jean. *Insurgent Collective Action and Civil War in El Salvador*. Cambridge: Cambridge University Press, 2003.

Zaid, Gabriel. *De los libros al poder*. Mexico City: Grijalbo, 1988.

Zolov, Eric. "Expanding Our Conceptual Horizons: The Shift from an Old to a New Left in Latin America." *A Contracorriente: A Journal on Social History and Literature in Latin America* 5, no. 2 (Winter 2008): 48–53.

Zolov, Eric. *Refried Elvis: The Rise of the Mexican Counterculture*. Berkeley: University of California Press, 1999.

Memoirs and Primary Sources

ACISAM. *Movimientos estudiantiles de secundaria en los años 70 en El Salvador*. San Salvador: ACISAM, 2012.

Alas, José Inocencio. *Iglesia, tierra y lucha campesina: Suchitoto, El Salvador, 1968–1977*. San Salvador: Asociación Equipo Maíz, 2003.

Aldana, Adrián Roberto. *Aventuras y desventuras de un periodista Salvadoreño*. San Salvador, circa 1985.

Americas Watch Committee and the American Civil Liberties Union. *Report on Human Rights in El Salvador*. New York: Vintage Books, 1982.

Anaya Montes, Mélida. *La segunda gran batalla de ANDES*. San Salvador: Editorial Universitaria de El Salvador, 1972.

Anaya Montes, Mélida. *Experiencias vietnamitas en su guerra de liberación*. Ediciones Enero 32, 1982.

ANDES. *Resoluciones de congresos y posiciones de ANDES 21 de Junio en la lucha ideológica que se lleva a cabo en el país, periodo 1974–1977*. San Salvador, 1977.

Aparicio, P. A., B. Barrera y Reyes, J. E. Alvarez, M. R. Revelo, and F. Delgado. "Declaración de cuatro obispos de la Conferencia Episcopal de El Salvador." *Estudios Centroamericanos 359*, no. 33 (September 1978): 774–775.

Araujo, Miguel Angel, Carlos Alberto Rodríguez, and Ricardo Ayala Kreus. "Situación agraria en El Salvador: Ponencia presentada por la Universidad de El Salvador," *La Universidad*, no.1, (January–February 1970): 8–15.

Arce Zablah, Rafael. *Grano de oro*. San Salvador: Partido de la Revolución Salvadoreña P.R.S. San Salvador, 1974.

Áscoli, Fernando. "El surgimiento de la conciencia: Memoria de Chalatenango." Mimeograph, 2005.

Bloque Popular Revolucionario (BPR). "Julio 75–79 la alternativa del pueblo se fortalece." In *Combate Popular*. 1979.

Bloque Popular Revolucionario (BPR). "Nueva masacre al pueblo." In *Combate Popular*. Fourth week in May 1979.

Bloque Popular Revolucionario (BPR). "Honor eterno a la Compañera Enma Guadalupe Carpio." In *Combate Popular*. Fourth week in May 1979.

Bloque Popular Revolucionario (BPR). "El pueblo exige: Libertad para sus dirigentes!!." In *Combate Popular*. Second week in May 1979.

Bloque Popular Revolucionario (BPR). "Lucha reivindicativa" (song). In Tambor boletín informativo del Departamento de Promoción Artística, Bando No. 2. Universidad de El Salvador, June 9, 1980.

Brigada La Masacuata. San Vicente: Editorial Ramírez, 1970.

Carpio, Salvador Cayetano. "Cuaderno No 1 sobre algunos problemas de organización que consideró el Comando Central." Mimeograph, 1982.

Carpio, Salvador Cayetano."Cuaderno No. 2 nuestros esfuerzos por compartir nuestras obligaciones con otros sectores que se califican de Marxistas (estrictamente interno)." Mimeograh, 1982.

Carpio, Salvador Cayetano. *Nuestras montañas son las masas*. San Salvador: Carpio-Alvarenga Editores, 2011.

Castillo, Fabio. "Episodios desconocidos de la historia Centroamericana." *Cartas Centroamericanas*. Mimeograph, July 1986.

Castillo, Fabio. "Los problemas de democratización y de educación siempre presentes: Hace 36 años los dos proyectos de la Junta de Gobierno." *Co Latino*, October 26, 1996.

Castillo, Fabio. "Vivencia y trascendencia social de El Salvador." In *La auditoria social*, edited by José Antonio Ventura Sosa, 30–41. San Salvador: Avanti Gráfica S.A. de C.V, 2002.

Cienfuegos, Fermán. *Veredas de la audacia: Historia del FMLN*. San Salvador: Editorial Arcoiris, 1993.

Coordinadora Político-Militar. "Se unifica La Izquierda," undated, *Pensamiento Revolucionario FMLN*, no. 12. Centro de Documentación e Información del FMLN. Mimeograph, 1981.

Coordinadora Político-Militar. "Segundo Manifiesto de la Coordinadora Politico Militar, Salvadoreña a los Pueblos Centroamericanos y del Mundo," *Matanzas y Reformas Formula siniestra del imperialismo yanqui y de la Junta Militar Democristiana, Pensamiento Revolucionario FMLN*, no. 12. Centro de Documentación e Información del FMLN. Mimeograph, July 1981.

Correspondence between President José María Lemus and the rector of the University of El Salvador, Dr. Romeo Fortín Magaña: "Exposición de motivos al Presidente de la República, " October 1, 1958; "Carta al Presidente Lemus sobre Derechos Legítimos de la Universidad," September 24, 1958; "Carta al Presidente de la República sobre Autonomía Universitaria," August 12, 1958; "Contestación del Presidente de la Republica sobre los problemas de autonomía universitaria," August 28, 1958; "Carta réplica del rector al Presidente de la Republica sobre autonomía de la universidad," undated, in *La Universidad*, (July–December 1958): 389–408.

Curia Metropolitana. "Acerca de la injusticia de la actual forma de tenencia de la tierra." In *La Universidad* no.1 (January–February 1970): 17–26.

Diagnóstico global de la universidad. Vol. 1. San Salvador: Secretaría de Planificación, 1972.

Diario Oficial de la República de El Salvador. Vol. 257. San Salvador, November 25, 1977.

Diaz, Nidia. "Aproximación a la historia del PRTC." Mimeograph, undated.

Documentos completos del Vaticano II 4th ed. Bilbao: Mensajero, 1966.

Duarte Fuentes, José Alejandro. *Borbollones Padre Nicolás Rodríguez: Mártir.* San Salvador: Editorial e Imprenta Universitaria, 1999.

DRU-PM. "Comunicado de la Dirección Revolucionaria Unificada (DRU-P.M.) a los pueblos de El Salvador, Centroamérica y el mundo." October 10, 1980. *Pensamiento Revolucionario FMLN*, no. 12. Centro de Documentación e Información del FMLN. Mimeograph, July 1981.

DRU-PM. "Manifiesto de la Dirección Revolucionaria Unificada de las Organizaciones Político-Militares, al pueblo salvadoreño, a los pueblos Centroamericanos y del mundo." May 1980. *Pensamiento Revolucionario FMLN*, no. 12. Centro de Documentación e Información del FMLN. Mimeograph, July 1981.

Ellacuría, Ignacio. "A sus órdenes mi capital." In *Veinte años de historia en El Salvador (1969–1989): Escritos políticos*, 649–656. San Salvador: UCA Editores, 1993.

"Encíclica 'Quadragesimo Anno' de S.S. Pio XI con ocasión de los cuarenta años de la Rerum Novarum." San Salvador: Arzobispado de San Salvador, undated.

Escamilla, Manuel Luis. "La reforma universitaria de El Salvador: Breve discusión doctrinaria" (San Salvador: University of El Salvador, 1967).

Escobar, Francisco Andrés. "En la línea de la muerte: Manifestación del 22 de Enero de 1980." *Estudios Centroamericanos ECA* 375–376, no. 35 (January–February 1980): 22–35.

FAPU, LP-28, BPR, and UDN, "Nuestras organizaciones populares en marcha hacia la Unidad: Posición del FAPU, LP-28, BPR, UDN." Mimeograph, January 11, 1980.

FECCAS-UTC. "Boletín informativo No 3: Se agudiza criminal represión contra familias campesinas en Chalatenango, San Vicente, Cinquera y demás regiones del campo Salvadoreño." *La Prensa Gráfica*, 27 January 1980: 13–14.

FECCAS-UTC. "Combatamos sin descanso a la pandía (sic) de criminales de ORDEN que opera en la zona de Aguilares." Mimeograph, August 1977.

FECCAS-UTC. "Con la lucha organizada y combativa obtienen triunfos loscampesinos pobres y medios." Mimeograph, 1 May 1979.

FECCAS-UTC."UTC-FECCAS a los Cristianos de El Salvador y Centroamérica." Mimeograph, circa 1978.

FECCAS-UTC. "Temporada 78–79 una jornada más de explotación, maltrato, hambre y miseria para los trabajadores del campo." Mimeograph, 1978.

FECCAS-UTC. Direccción Ejecutiva Nacional (DEN) FECCAS-UTC, "Ante la demagogia de los planes reformistas del enemigo FECCAS-UTC a todos los organismos y bases de nuestras organizaciones." Mimeograph, August 1978.

FECCAS-UTC."Viva nuestro primer consejo departamental! 'Héroes y Mártires de Chalatenango.'" Mimeograph, 1978.

FECCAS-UTC. *Jornalero Revolucionario Periódico de la Federación de Trabajadores del Campo F.T.C. Numero 1, Año 1978, Mes: Julio–Agosto.* Mimeograph, 1978.

FECCAS-UTC. "La tiranía criminal ataca bestialmente la heróica toma de tierra 'Nelson, Manuel y Rutilio' y a toda la zona de Aguilares." Mimeograph, May 17, 1977.

FECCAS-UTC. "FECCAS-UTC la tiranía militar invade zonas." Mimeograph, December 18, 1977.

FECCAS-UTC. "UTC-FECCAS denunciamos." Mimeograph, February 1978.

FECCAS-UTC. "UTC-FECCAS informa a los trabajadores del campo y pueblo en general." Mimeograph, November 1977.

FECCAS-UTC. "Viva la lucha reivindicativa de los jornaleros." *FECCAS-UTC Informa.* Mimeograph, undated.

FECCAS-UTC."UTC-FECCAS a la clase obrera y pueblo en general." Mimeograph, October 1977.

FECCAS-UTC. "UTC-FECCAS a los campesinos pobres." Mimeograph, undated.

FLACSO El Salvador and Fundación "Dr. Manuel Gallardo." *Prensa clandestina: El Salvador 1970–1975.* San Salvador: FLACSO El Salvador and Fundación "Dr. Manuel Gallardo," 2011.

Flamenco, Emiliano Androski. *Al filo del silencio.* San Vicente, mimeograph, 2011.

Fortín Magaña, René. "Cuarenta años después: Hechos y comentarios." *Co Latino,* January 9, 2001.

FPL. *Estrella Roja 2.*

FPL. *Estrella Roja 3.*

FPL."Comunicado de las Fuerzas Populares de Liberación—FPL—Farabundo Martí sobre la operación héroes revolucionarios de Agosto: Carlos Fonseca, Juan Sebastián y Alberto, Ignacio, Úrsula y Arnoldo." *El Rebelde* Año 5, no. 58 (August 1977): 3–4.

FPL. "Comunicado No 1 de las FPL sobre la operación 'héroes revolucionarios del 11 de Octubre Eva-Francisco-Antonio.'" *El Rebelde* Año 5, no. 55 (May 1977): 2–5.

FPL."Cómo debemos combatir a ORDEN." *Campo Rebelde Periodico Revolucionario Dedicado a los Trabajadores del Campo,* no. 10. El Salvador, July 1978.

FPL. "Cómo engaña el enemigo a los trabajadores que están en ORDEN?" *Campo Rebelde Periodico Revolucionario Dedicado a los Trabajadores del Campo,* no. 10. El Salvador, July 1978.

FPL. "Cual es ésa verdad?" *Campo Rebelde Periodico Revolucionario Dedicado a los Trabajadores del Campo,* no. 10. El Salvador, July 1978.

FPL. "Por la revolución popular hacia el Socialismo." *Campo Rebelde Periodico Revolucionario Dedicado a los Trabajadores del Campo,* no. 10. El Salvador, July 1978.

FPL. "La revolución avanza! El pueblo responde valientemente frente a los crímenes de la tiranía" *Campo Rebelde Periodico Revolucionario Clandestino Dedicado a los Trabajadores del Campo,* no. 8. El Salvador, May 1978.

FPL."La Crisis del Régimen y el Auge de la Revolución," *El Rebelde,* nos. 84–85. El Salvador, January 1980.

FPL. "Más de 50 verdugos de nuestro pueblo fueron ajusticiados—tomas a poblaciones," *El Rebelde,* nos. 86–87. El Salvador, February 1980.

FPL. "Editorial sangre y represión: El Sello de la nueva Junta." *El Rebelde* nos. 86–87 (February 1980): 1–7.

FPL. "Noticia: En fecha reciente, en un lugar del país, se celebró la Sexta Reunión Ordinaria del Consejo Revolucionario de las FPL." *El Rebelde,* no. 86–87 (February 1980): 11.

Frente Democrático Revolucionario (FDR), "Primera Declaración del Frente Democrático Revolucionario," April 18, 1980. http://www.cedema.org/ver.php?id=3877, accessed September 24, 2016.

FUAR. Tercera Plenaria Nacional del FUAR. "Proyecto plataforma programática del FUAR." Mimeograph, May 1962.

FUAR. Columna Campesina del FUAR. "Trinchera." Mimeograph, November 18, 1961.

Guerra, Walter, Benito Tobar, Reino Morán, and Efraín Villalobos. *Testigos de la fe en El Salvador: Nuestros sacerdotes y seminaristas diocesanos mártires 1977-1993.* San Salvador: Walter Guerra et al., 2007.

Guevara, Ernesto. *Bolivian Diary [of] Ernesto 'Che' Guevara,* introduction by Fidel Castro, translated by Carlos P. Hansen and Andrew Sinclair. London: Lorrimer Publishing, 1968.

Hándal, Schafik Jorge. *Legado de un revolucionario: Del rescate de la historia a la construcción del futuro.* San Salvador: Ediciones Instituto Schafik Hándal, 2011.

Hándal, Schafik Jorge. "Reflexiones sobre los problemas de la revolución latinoamericana." Mimeograph 1968.

Hándal, Schafik Jorge. "Interrelación indisoluble," in *Fundamentos y Perspectivas Revista Teórica del Partido Comunista de El Salvador*, Comisión Nacional de Propaganda, June 1981, no. 4.

Henríquez Consalvi, Carlos "Santiago" ed. *La Lucha así es: Memoria Oral en Chalatenango*. San Salvador: MUPI, 2012.

Hernández, Alfonso. Alfonso Quijada Urías and Alfonso Velis Tovar, eds. *Esta es la hora:Antologia*. San Salvador: Ediciones Plural, 1989.

Hernández, Carlos Evaristo. "Notas para un testimonio. Ciudad Universitaria, San Salvador 30 de Julio de 1975." San Salvador, 2001. http://www.monografias.com/trabajos15/masacre-san-salvador/masacre-san-salvador.shtml, accessed October 4, 2014.

Majano, Adolfo A. *Una oportunidad perdida: 15 de Octubre de 1979*. San Salvador: Índole Editores, 2009.

Marighella, Carlos. *Minimanual of the Urban Guerrilla* (1969). Marxist Archive. https://www.marxists.org/archive/marighella-carlos/1969/06/minimanual-urban-guerrilla/index.htm accessed September 4, 2016.

Medrano, Miriam. "Lil Milagro, recuperación de una memoria [1]." *Contrapunto*, November 25, 2009.

Medrano, Juan Ramón. *Memorias de un guerrillero: Comandante Balta*. 3rd ed. San Salvador: New Graphics S.A. de C.V., 2007.

Organización Revolucionaria de los Trabajadores (ORT). "Manifiesto de la Organización Revolucionaria de los Trabajadores (O.R.T.) en el Dia Internacional del Trabajo." Mimeograph, May 1, 1974.

Palencia, Jorge, ed. *Para que no olvidemos: Una recopilación de testimonios sobre el surgimiento de orga-nizaciones populares salvadoreñas y sus luchas durante los años 1970 y 1980*. Madrid: Castilla La Mancha, Yolocamba Solidaridad and Procomes, 2008.

Partido Comunista de El Salvador. "45 Años de sacrificada lucha revolucionaria." In *Prensa clan-destina: El Salvador 1970–1975*, 79–105. San Salvador: FLACSO El Salvador and Fundación Dr. Manuel Gallardo, 2011.

Perla, Mirna Antonieta. "La masacre del 30 de Julio de 1975: Testimonio Mirna Antonieta Perla." In Carlos Eduardo Rico Mira, *En silencio tenía que ser: Testimonio del conflicto armado en El Salvador (1967-2000)*, 116–128. San Salvador: UFG Editores, 2003.

PRS-ERP. "Es tu arma, el voto?" Mimeograph, December 1971.

PRS-ERP. Comando Armado "José Feliciano Ama," E.R.P., "Comunicado Número 1 del Ejército Revolucionario del Pueblo–ERP–."

PRS-ERP. *Prensa Comunista*, no. 4. Mimeograph, 1975.

PRS-ERP. "Sólo con la Lucha Armada de Masas Podremos Derrotar al Fascismo," *Prensa Comunista*, no. 4. Mimeograph, 1975.

PRS-ERP.*Publicación especial octubre 1977: Balance histórico del 1er Congreso del PRS*. In *Prensa Comunista*. El Salvador, October 1977.

PRS-ERP. *Grano de Oro* in FLACSO El Salvador and Fundación "Dr. Manuel Gallardo," *Prensa clandestina: El Salvador 1970–1975*, 19-46. San Salvador: FLACSO El Salvador and Fundación "Dr. Manuel Gallardo," 2011.

PRS-ERP."The People's Revolutionary Army (ERP) of El Salvador to All Nations of the World." *New York Times*, March 12, 1980, p. A21.

Ramirez Acosta, Victoria Eugenia. *Eva, Chico y Toño*. San Salvador: Fundabril, 2010.

"Rerum Novarum Encíclica de S.S. León XIII sobre la Cuestión Obrera." Guatemala City: Ediciones San Pablo, undated.

Resistencia Nacional (RN). *Por la causa proletaria: Apuntes para el estudio de 13 años de historia de la Resistencia Nacional 2*. Mimeograph, June 1983.

Rico Mira, Carlos Eduardo. *En silencio tenía que ser: Testimonio del conflicto armado en El Salvador (1967-2000)*. San Salvador: UFG Editores, 2003.

Romero, O. A., and A. Rivera y Damas. "La iglesia y las organizaciones políticas populares." *Estudios Centroamericanos ECA* 359, no. 33 (August 1978): 760–773.
Rubio, Fina, and Eduard Balsebre. *Rompiendo silencios: Desobediencia y lucha en Villa El Rosario.* Barcelona: REDSolidaridad and MUPI, 2009.
Sancho, Eduardo. *Crónicas entre los espejos.* 2nd ed. San Salvador: Editorial Universidad Francisco Gavidia, 2003.
Unión Nacional Opositora (UNO), "Bases Programáticas de la UNO." Mimeograph 1972.
Valle, Víctor. *Siembra de vientos El Salvador 1960–69.* San Salvador: CINAS, 1993.
Vega, Juan Ramón. *Las 54 cartas pastorales de Monseñor Chávez.* San Salvador: Ediciones del Arzobispado de San Salvador, 1997.
Vega, Juan Ramón. Las comunidades cristianas de base en América Central: Estudio sociológico. San Salvador: Publicaciones del Arzobispado de San Salvador, 1994.
Zepeda Herrera, Juan Orlando. *Perfiles de la guerra en El Salvador.* San Salvador: New Graphics, 2008.

Newspapers and Bulletins

Co-Latino
El Diario de Hoy
El Independiente
El Mundo
Opinión Estudiantil
Orientación
La Crónica del Pueblo
La Prensa Gráfica
La Universidad
La Verdad
Washington Post

Interviews conducted by Joaquín M. Chávez

Anonymous informant 1, San Salvador, March 20, 2007.
Anonymous informant 2, San Salvador, November 6, 2007.
Anonymous informant 3, Guatemala, December 14, 2006.
Anonymous informant 4, New York, June 1, 2006.
Anonymous informant 5, New York, June 15, 2006.
Anonymous informant 6, New York, June 15, 2006.
Sonia Aguiñada Carranza, San Salvador, November 24, 2006.
Tula Alvarenga, San Salvador, February 3, 2014.
Ernesto A. Álvarez, San Salvador, August 11, 2005.
Manlio Argueta, San Salvador, June 22, 2012.
Ester Arteaga, San Salvador, September 10, 2008.
Rafael Benavides, San Salvador, April 25, 2007.
Mario Efraín Callejas, San Salvador, October 10, 2007.
Jesús Cartagena, San Salvador, April 25, 2007.
José Roberto Cea, San Salvador, June 21, 2012.
Héctor Dada, San Salvador, April 23, 2007.
Alberto Enríquez, San Salvador, March 16, 2007.
Eduardo Espinoza, San Salvador, December 5, 2006.
Oscar Fernández, San Salvador, March 21, 2007.
Emiliano Androski Flamenco, San Vicente, January 30, 2014.
Gerardo, interview by Joaquín M. Chávez and Rebecca T., Managua, circa 1986.
Facundo Guardado, San Salvador, August 31, 2005 and November 12, 2007.

Evaristo, Chalatenango, August 6, 2007.
Ever Hernández, San Salvador April 18, 2007.
Miguel Huezo Mixco, San Salvador, December 21, 2006.
Francisco Jovel, San Salvador, April 18, 2007.
Juan-Juan, San Salvador, January 13, 2015.
Carlos López, San Salvador, April 9, 2007.
Paolo Luers, San Salvador, March 26, 2007.
José Romeo Maeda, San Salvador, November 30, 2007.
Héctor Martínez, San Salvador, April 18, 2007.
José Santos Martínez, Guarjila, Chalatenango, December 25, 2007.
Ana Sonia Medina, San Salvador, November 24, 2006.
Guadalupe Mejía, San Salvador, October 2, 2008.
Hilda Mejía, Quezaltepeque, October 10, 2008.
Ismael Merlos, San Salvador, December 6, 2007.
Luisfelipe Minhero, written interview, February 12, 2015.
Oscar Miranda, San Salvador, April 11, 2007.
Atilio Montalvo, San Salvador, November 6, 2006.
Rafael Moreno, Mexico City, July 2, 2005.
Trinidad de Jesús Nieto, Santa Tecla, November 6, 2006.
Ignacio Paniagua, San Salvador, July 20, 2007.
Lorena Peña Mendoza, San Salvador, October 10, 2006; November 8, 2007.
Victoria Ramírez, San Salvador, October 10, 2006, December 8, 2006.
Julio Reyes, San Salvador, October 10, 2006.
Abraham Rodríguez, San Salvador, December 27, 2006.
Rutilio Sánchez, San Salvador, October 1, 2008.
Salvador Sánchez Cerén, San Salvador, April 9, 2007.
Eduardo Sancho, San Salvador, June 19, 2012.
Domingo Santacruz, San Salvador, April 17, 2007; April 27, 2007.
Irma Serrano, San Salvador, April 18, 2007; Chalatenango, May 23, 2007.
María Serrano, Arcatao, Chalatenango, August 13, 2005.
Manuel Sorto, Skype interview, July 22, 2014.
Luisa Tolentino, Santa Tecla, September 27, 2007.
Ricardo Urioste, San Salvador, December 26, 2006.
Juan Ramón Vega, San Salvador, December 3, 2007.
Rafael Velásquez, San Salvador, March 22, 2007.
Gumercinda "Chinda" Zamora, Quezaltepeque, October 10, 2008.
Rubén Zamora, San Salvador, August 15, 2005.

INDEX